National Tax Policy in Europe

Krister Andersson · Eva Eberhartinger
Lars Oxelheim (Eds.)

National Tax Policy in Europe

To Be or Not to Be?

With 15 Figures and 13 Tables

Springer

Krister Andersson
Confederation of Swedish Enterprises
Storgatan 19
114 82 Stockholm
Sweden
krister.andersson@svensktnaringsliv.se

Eva Eberhartinger, LL.M
Vienna University of Economics
and Business Administration
Department of Finance and Accounting
Tax Management Group
Althanstraße 39-45
1090 Vienna
Austria
eva.eberhartinger@wu-wien.ac.at

Lars Oxelheim
Lund Institute of Economic Research
P.O. Box 7080
220 07 Lund
Sweden
lars.oxelheim@telia.com
and
The Research Institute of Industrial Economics
P.O. Box 55665
102 15 Stockholm
Sweden
lars.oxelheim@ifn.se

Library of Congress Control Number: 2007928496

ISBN 978-3-540-70709-7 Springer Berlin Heidelberg New York

Springer is a part of Springer Science+Business Media
springer.com

Typesetting: Integra Software Services Pvt. Ltd., Puducherry, India
Cover design: WMX Design, Heidelberg

Printed on acid-free paper SPIN: 11982685 5 4 3 2 1 0

Preface

European taxes have long been debated for their potential role as barriers to increased investment and welfare. The discussion has often circulated around the size of the tax bases and the magnitude of the tax rate. In this book we argue that in the taxation context the European Union (EU) is at a cross-road facing strong forces pushing it into two polar positions. One of these is the scenario with all welfare provided by the national regime and financed by taxes collected entirely by national authorities. The other extreme is the situation where all welfare is offered at an EU level financed entirely by taxes collected at that level. The two forces pressing the tax situation into one of these two poles are spelt *tax competition* and *welfare arbitrage*. The research question addressed in this book covers the existence of a potential steady state in between these to poles. Our basic hypothesis is that their might be such a steady state due to the immobility of some tax bases and where the taxation of these bases have no externalities affecting investment. We argue that the very complex tax structures of Europe and the tax uncertainty facing investors in Europe need to be addressed in a comprehensive way. A crucial part of such an analysis is the need for the issues to be discussed in an interdisciplinary way – containing aspects – in terms of traditional academic principles – from Economics to the Political and Legal sciences.

The interdisciplinary approach required for a proper analysis of the multidimensional tax concept and its application makes most traditional scientific journals less well fitted as outlet for the result of such an analysis. This motivates why the results are here presented in the form of a book. The process behind the book was similar to that behind refereed journals. Following presentation of the main ideas of the project along the lines now appearing in Chapter 1, a number of researcher teams were invited to contribute and to address different parts of the research question while maintaining a European perspective. First drafts were discussed at a workshop held at the Trolleholm Castle in the south of Sweden in January 2006. Each contribution was refereed by two of the participating contributors to the book in addition to the editors and then discussed at a seminar during the three day meeting where the appointed referees acted as discussant. A second draft of each chapter was discussed at the annual European Integration conference of the Swedish Network for European Studies in Economics and Business (SNEE) in Mölle in May, 2006. Also on this case, each contribution had two appointed discussants. The final manuscript was then delivered to us at the end of February 2007.

Our greatest gratitude now goes to all those who have contributed different chapters and participated in the Trolleholm workshop and the Mölle conference. We are grateful for their efforts and constructive attitudes in working with their own chapters, but also in reading and commenting on the other contributions. We would also like to thank colleagues at our home universities and at places where we are affiliated for their contribution in one way or the other.

We are most thankful to the SNEE for providing necessary support, particularly for the three-day workshop at Trolleholm. SNEE's support made it possible to bring together scholars from many countries and to develop this network of colleagues doing research on European taxation issues.

Stockholm, Vienna and Lund in March 2007

Krister Andersson Eva Eberhartinger Lars Oxelheim

Table of Contents

List of Contributors

Krister Andersson is Head of the Tax Policy Department, Confederation of Swedish Enterprise. Since 2005, he has been Chairman of the Fiscal Affairs Group of BUSINESSEEUROPE (formerly the UNICE), Brussels. He served as an expert to the European Commission on its Corporate Tax Study (published in 2001). He is assistant professor (Docent) in Economics at Lund University and he has worked for the International Monetary Fund and as Chief economist of the Swedish Central Bank. He is a board member of the Swedish National Tax Authority, the Swedish IFA branch, and the Association of Industry Treasurers. He is also a member of the BIAC Taxation and Fiscal Policy Committee and the International Chamber of Commerce Tax Commission, in Paris.

Christian Bellak is associate professor at the Vienna University of Economics and Business Administration in Vienna. His research interests are centered around foreign direct investment, industrial and tax policy, internationalization, international business and multinational enterprises. Dr. Bellak's research within these areas has appeared in numerous books, and in journals such as *Oxford Bulletin of Economics and Statistics, Journal of International Money and Finance, Transnational Corporations,* and *Applied Economics.* He has also acted as advisor on industrial policy to UNCTAD, The World Economic Forum and to various committees and working groups within the Austrian federal administration.

Mattias Dahlberg is professor of finance law at Uppsala University in Uppsala, Sweden. His main research area is European tax law, and recent publications include the book *Direct Taxation in Relation to the Freedom of Establishment and the Free Movement of Capital* (Kluwer Law International, 2005). His previous articles and notes have appeared in major tax law outlets, such as *European Taxation, Cahier de Droit Fiscal International, Scandinavian Studies in Law,* and *Intertax.* Professor Dahlberg is the editor of the Swedish tax law journal *Skattenytt,* and has previously held positions at the Stockholm School of Economics.

Eva Eberhartinger is professor and Head of the Tax Management Department at the Vienna University of Economics and Business Administration. Her research focuses on international taxation, finance and taxation, tax management, and international and European financial reporting. Her research within these areas is published in numerous articles and shorter commentaries in Austrian and international professional and academic journals, and as chapters in books, and she is the author or (co)editor of over a dozen books. Professor Eberhartinger has spent time as a visiting researcher at the University of Illinois at Urbana-Champaign (USA), the University of Exeter (GB), the Ecole des Hautes Etudes Commerciales (HEC) in Paris, and at McGill University in Montreal. Before assuming her present position in Vienna, she was professor at the University of Münster, Germany.

Åsa Hansson is assistant professor in economics at the Department of Economics at Lund University, fellow researcher at the RATIO institute, and currently visiting the Department of Economics at Copenhagen University. Åsa's main research interest is in economics of taxation. She has written and published on topics ranging from the effects of taxes on the macro economy (e.g., growth and employment) to how taxation affect individuals' and firms' behavior, as well as several papers studying the effect of globalization on taxes and public spending.

Michael Lang is professor and Head of the Department of Austrian and International Tax Law at the Vienna University of Economics and Business Administration. He is the author of more than 300 journal articles, book contributions, and commentaries, and author or (co)editor of numerous research monographs. He is also editor of a number of professional journals and book series on Austrian and international tax law. Other professional activities include the presidency of the Austrian branch of the International Fiscal Association, and membership of the Academic Committee of the European Association of Tax Law Professors. Between 2000 and 2004, he was a partner with Deloitte Austria. Professor Lang has won several awards for teaching excellence and for academic achievements, and has held visiting positions at Université de Paris I (Sorbonne), and the New York University School of Law.

Markus Leibrecht is assistant professor at the Vienna University of Economics and Business Administration in Vienna, Austria. He specializes in the areas of public finance and applied econometrics. Dr. Leibrecht's research has appeared in books as well as in journals such as *Applied Economics, Open Economies Review, Structural Change and Economic Dynamics, Applied Economics Letters* and *Austrian Journal of Statistics*.

August Österle is associate professor at the Vienna University of Economics and Business Administration in Vienna. His research interests include the economics of ageing, health economics, economic and social policy, and European integration, and he is the author of a half-dozen books and numerous journal articles and book chapters within these areas. Dr. Österle has previously held visiting positions at the University of Bath and the London School of Economics and Political Science, UK, and a Jean Monnet Fellowship at the European University Institute in Florence, Italy. He is the recipient of several awards both for his teaching and for his research.

Lars Oxelheim holds a chair in International Business and Finance at Lund University, Lund, and is an affiliate of the Research Institute of Industrial Economics, Stockholm and of the Fudan University, Shanghai. His current research focuses on the implications of macroeconomic disturbances for corporate performance and issues related to economic and financial integration. He has published some 25 books and numerous articles in the areas of international business and finance, corporate finance and corporate governance. Among his recent monographs in English are *European Union and the Race for Foreign Direct Investment in Europe* (Elsevier, 2004; co-edited/authored with Pervez Ghauri), *Corporate and Institutional Transparency for Economic Growth in Europe* (Elsevier, 2006; edited/co-authored), and *Corporate Performance and the Exposure to Macroeconomic Fluctuations* (Oxford University Press, 2007; with Clas Wihlborg).

Ulrike Schneider is professor of Economic Theory and Economic Policy at the Vienna University of Economics and Business Administration, where she also acts as Director of the research institute for the Economics of Ageing. Her areas of expertise include the economics of ageing, social policy, health economics, and nonprofit organizations, and she has published widely within these areas. An award-winning teacher, Professor Schneider has held numerous visiting positions, including the University of California at Berkeley, Johns Hopkins University, and the University of Maryland.

Martin Six is a researcher at the Vienna University of Economics and Business Administration, specializing in industrial tax management, finance and taxation, reorganization tax law, and balance sheet analysis. He currently participates in the research projects 'International taxation of hybrid finance' and 'International Tax Co-ordination', and his recent publications have concerned company valuation and cross-border financing.

Franz Sutter holds a doctorate of law from the University of Vienna, Austria, and currently works as a lawyer with the Austrian Federal Ministry of Finance, and as adjunct lecturer at the Vienna University of Economics and Business Administration. As an expert on European state aid law and on Austrian, international and European tax law, Dr. Sutter has represented the Republic of Austria in procedures before the Austrian Constitutional Court and the European Court of Justice in tax matters. He is the author of numerous articles and notes on tax law. He is also the Austrian correspondent of *European Taxation*.

Chapter 1
The Role of National Tax Policies in the European Union

Krister Andersson, Eva Eberhartinger and Lars Oxelheim

1.1 Introduction

Taxes are used not only to collect revenues for public programs but also to try to improve the functioning of the market economy. At the same time, in a world where in most cases, taxes – and not only those used for internalizing social costs in private behaviour – are not neutral, they result in changed behaviour by households and corporations. Policymakers have therefore for decades tried to strike a balance between different objectives. The economy must function well and the tax burden must be shared in an equitable way. The level of sophistication of policy makers varies over time and from country to country. Some politicians emphasize the increase in net income over time resulting from faster growth while others emphasize the allocation of tax payments in a given year.

Despite the already complex situation, policymakers now face an even more intricate problem – the division of national tax policy and supranational tax policies in an economic union like the European Union (EU). For those countries participating in the European Economic and Monetary Union (EMU) as well, an evaluation of the role of national tax policies may seem even more important. The efficiency arguments now extend to the allocation of resources, production and investment, throughout the Union. At the same time, taxes are collected at the national level and revenues are to a very large extent used in the domestic economy.

Governments are faced with a policy dilemma. An efficient and prosperous economic union, which governments have endorsed in the Lisbon accord, seems to call for the elimination of tax obstacles. At the same time, elections are national and to ensure re-election of governments, the domestic economy must be a winner in the global competitive race between countries. Furthermore, an ageing population may call for further public programs and a demand for revenues. Hence, national tax policy is restricted by the need to safeguard sufficient tax revenue and social security revenue to finance the welfare state. To ensure such revenues, the national economy must be in good shape. Externalities may have to be handled by using the tax instrument, while incentives to work, save and invest must be maintained or enhanced further.

From a legal point of view, taxation to a large extent (with the major exception of VAT) still falls within the competence of the Member State. This is particularly true for direct taxation, for personal and corporate income tax. Within the European Union national tax policy is frequently driven by tax competition, as can easily be seen by the considerable decline in statutory tax rates among Member States during the last decades and by the efforts to achieve fairness in tax competition. The Member States however, even though being in principle autonomous in their tax policy, face considerable restrictions that result from the Treaty of Rome and political aim to eliminate tax obstacles to make the EU an efficient economic union. Those restrictions are mirrored in primary and secondary EU Law, in jurisdiction by the European Court of Justice (ECJ) and also, with a longer tradition, in bilateral double tax conventions. Additionally, national tax policy is restricted by the need to safeguard sufficient tax and social security revenues to finance government spending.

1.2 Taxation and the Changing Economic and Legal Environment

Will it then be possible for national governments to pursue adequate national tax policies while at the same time eliminating tax obstacles to make the EU an efficient economic union? Which are the economic incentives for governments to continue to strive for national tax policies and what legal room do they have to pursue them in a globally competitive environment, being members of an economic union – the EU? To what degree does the EU restrict Member States' discretionary freedom to pursue national tax polices? These questions arise from several economic and legal developments in the European Union. In particular at a union level:

- the setting of an open economy
- the use of taxes to internalize costs
- the lack of democratic legitimacy in the European Union for taxation
- different views on the role of the government
- the degree of (de-)centralization of tax legislation
- the degree of (de-)centralization of social security

Tax Policy in a Closed Economy Versus in an Open Economy

In a closed economy the design of tax policy is to some extent easier to handle and leaves more leeway. Whether a tax is levied on investments or savings may yield the same net result. Certainly, high levels of taxation will still impact incentives to work, save and invest, and the tax bases may therefore be eroded by excessive levels of taxation, but the tax base will not migrate out of the country. Only if people leave the country, are they able to fully circumvent taxation.

In an open economy, high levels of taxation may lead to capital outflow. There will now generally be a difference between levying taxes on savings and investments, in terms of the impact on the investment level. For large corporations, investment capital may be found on the international capital market. If a country levies high taxes on resident capital owners, less heavily taxed foreigners can provide financing and the investment level in multinational corporations will therefore not be significantly impacted by high taxes on savings. However, investments in domestic small and medium sized businesses will suffer since they cannot readily finance themselves abroad.

The ownership structure in the corporate sector will be influenced, with a larger share of foreign ownership than if national taxes on savings were lower. This will in turn impact income levels since a larger share of return on capital will be allocated to foreign residents. Since national taxes usually are not applied to dividends and capital gains paid to foreigners, national tax revenues will also be reduced.

But the effects of taxes in an open economy as compared to taxes in a closed economy are also different in many other respects than impacting the ownership structure and tax revenues. It can be generally observed that relocation of production will be larger if economies are open and integrated. Just as trade can allow countries to benefit from their comparative advantages, opening up economies can allow for relocation of production according to comparative advantages.

During World War II, or in the decades following it, most countries adopted some kind of capital and exchange controls. In the 1970s and 1980s, a general wave of deregulation followed propelled by a variety of forces, of which improvements in information technology played a prominent role. The deregulation was to some extent also an acknowledgement (*de jure*) by the authorities that existing regulations had eroded and had (*de facto*) become inefficient. To some extent this was also an expression of a change in the philosophy underlying national economic policy in the 1980s, reflecting a growing recognition that excessive controls are not compatible with efficient resource allocation and solid and balanced growth. In the 1980s it became increasingly evident that controls discourage financial savings, distort investment decisions and render the intermediation between savers and investors ineffective. In the early 2000s taxes are debated for creating some of the dysfunctions previously seen as typical for controls. Hence, there is a delicate balance between taxes needed to pay for public expenditure programs in a country and the cost of these taxes in an open economy in terms of inefficient resource allocation and thereby a lower level of welfare than would otherwise obtain.

What can be achieved by national tax policy as production factors move across borders? To slowdown the process, many countries have imposed so called exit taxes on individuals, corporations or objects leaving a country. The proliferation of CFC regimes (Controlled Foreign Companies) is another example of tax rules imposed to limit relocation of resources across borders.[1] Increased economic integration and the introduction of the euro have meant increased price and tax transparency. This in turn has forced European countries into a process of reviewing their national tax options to reap the benefits of an efficient allocation of production resources across countries, while at the same time protecting their revenue bases. Too high taxes will lead to even more rapid reallocation of resources and erosion of tax bases, while a rapid restructuring of the tax system may have large revenue and income distributional consequences.

The Need to Use Taxes to Internalize Costs

It is well known from economic theory that the social cost may deviate substantially from the private cost of an activity. Externalities need to be considered and corrected if an efficient allocation of resources is to be achieved. Governments use rules, regulations, auctions, taxes etc to rectify negative externalities. An obvious example is taxes on polluting activities. However, since some of the pollution problems are regional or even global, there is a need to cooperate across national borders.

The imposition of green or environmental taxes are primarily intended to reduce pollution and therefore not to collect revenues. However, in many countries these taxes are used for revenue purposes and there are even schemes of how to receive a "double dip" by imposing these taxes and at the same time reducing taxes on labour.

Almost everyone agrees that taxes are needed to pay for pure public goods, like defence, a legal system, etc. The willingness of each individual to pay for pure public goods is low, or zero, and therefore collective decisions and financing are required.

Governments tend however to go further in the direction of correction than alleviating pure market failures. They typically also have social objectives, such as income redistribution between social groups or across geographical regions. The resulting policies try to compensate for lack of income generating capabilities, transport costs or low population density, etc.

Here, the European Union has developed a special set of rules. Lower taxes or direct subsidies may be considered as illegal state aid. In this respect, the European Union is much more restrictive than the 'American Union', the United States, where it is up to each state to decide on programs promoting investment or support.

The limits on national tax policies in the EU decrease the possibilities to alleviate externalities and internalize costs. It also limits the possibilities for governments to go beyond rectifying externalities by adopting distortive tax measures. It is an empirical question whether the limitations on national tax policies are welfare enhancing or actually decreasing the national welfare of a country.

Different Views on the Role of Government

The 27 Member States have rather different views on the role of government in their economies. Also opinions on how to achieve common goals differ across countries. Some Member States are favouring extensive welfare systems with a large role for the government in supplying public goods and redistributing income while others promote private market solutions. The need to collect taxes is far greater in these countries than in countries where the market outcome is broadly accepted.

Even if there were (or are) similar views on the need for government intervention, the views on the way to use tax policy instruments vary across countries. In particular the 12 new Member States have primarily relied on applying more or less proportional taxes on broad bases. Some of these countries have been successful in collecting tax revenues, sometimes twice as high in relation to the size of their economy, as old member states have been with high tax rates and narrow bases.

It is nothing new that countries have embarked on different avenues in their endeavour to collect taxes. The additional interesting element now is the opening up of markets and therefore the increased mobility of tax bases. Will the EC Treaty provide Member States with sufficient flexibility in their national tax policies? Or is the mobility of tax bases the constraining factor and a better functioning European economy a necessary requirement for securing sufficient tax revenues for the expenditure programs?

Centralization Versus Decentralization of Tax Policy and Social Security/ Welfare

There are no federal taxes levied centrally in the EU. Indirectly, however, the VAT is used to finance common expenditures and the base for VAT has also been highly streamlined. The role of the European Union fiscal federalism is not well developed in the European fiscal context. Tax policy is not one of the areas of competence for the European Commission. However, the Commission should safeguard the Treaty and bring breaches of the Treaty to the attention of the European Court of Justice.

Since the Treaty provides for free movement of capital, goods and people and since corporations are free to establish themselves and work throughout the union, there clearly are limitations on national tax policies resulting from the fundamental freedoms. Furthermore, since discrimination is not allowed and state aid may be illegal, the room for manoeuvre is limited. As a matter of fact, the Treaty provides for the basic elements for an efficient allocation of capital, but it does not address how to cope with externalities or deviating national preferences.

There is no federal representation that could make assessment to trade offs between equal treatment and specific national preferences. The role of the European Parliament is however gradually increasing but it has no right to impose taxes.

In theory, an optimal tax structure could be centrally designed and implemented in each Member State according to the decisions made at the federal level. The present Treaty does not provide for such centralised decision-making in the EU. Instead, all Member States seem to prefer decisions to be made according to the subsidiarity principle. According to the Treaty, the Union may intervene in areas which do not fall within its exclusive competence only insofar as the objectives of the intended action cannot be sufficiently achieved by the Member States but can rather, by reason of the scale or effects of the proposed action, be better achieved at Union level. But it is not straightforward to know at what level decisions have to be made in order to achieve maximum efficiency in decision-making and implementation.

Table 1.1. Collecting taxes and financing public expenditure programs in an integrated area

	Public Expenditure Programs financed by national authorities	Public Expenditure Programs financed by the EU
Taxes collected by national authorities	X	
Taxes collected at the EU-level		X

There are strong arguments in favour of decentralised decision-making in order to internalize external effects. At the same time, there are compelling arguments in favour of pan-European decisions to eliminate tax induced investment decisions. The present Treaty of the European Union goes far in removing barriers to free movement and securing non-discrimination. It is not the purpose of this book to express views on the optimal structure of decision-making in tax policy. Instead, we assess the scope for national tax policies, given the existing Treaty, directives adopted and economic pressures on tax bases and tax rates in an ever-increasing competitive environment.

The relation between national versus European taxation and national versus European public expenditure as paradigms can be described as in Table 1.1. Hence, in one extreme, to the top left, we see the taxes entirely collected at the national level and all citizens' public welfare financed domestically. In the other extreme, to the bottom right, we see all people of Europe having access to the European welfare financed centrally by the EU by taxes collected from the member countries or directly from citizens of these countries. The situation in the beginning of the 2000s is far from these two extremes though closer to the first one. It can be assumed that forces such as tax competition and welfare arbitrage will push the development towards one of these two extremes.

A new economic map with perfect price transparency and a considerable tax transparency (especially for the Members of the EMU) will make Member States face very small opportunities to stand out with the help of macroeconomic factors to look attractive for inward foreign direct investment. In this setting, in particular countries in the periphery of the region will try to boost their attractiveness by the use of a battery of economic equivalents of anabolic steroids (see Oxelheim and Ghauri, 2004). Tax exemptions and tailor-made tax solutions – mostly non-transparent – will be part of that menu. In this context, the tension between the 12 new members and the 15 old members in the area of taxes and competition also needs to be addressed.

1.3 Research on National Tax Policy

The previous section illustrated that the ongoing integration of the European Union, the increased mobility of capital and labour, and the increasing challenges for social security and welfare have created an environment which not only challenges much of the conventional wisdom of economic policy, but also creates the need for changes in economic policies. These changes in economic policy may refer to aims, measures, institutions and the vertical shift of responsibilities. This again may lead to limitations for national policies.

Tax policy is no exception. Inter alia constraints in the economic and the legal fields have to be considered: First, the mobility of production factors restrains the possibility to levy taxes at the national level. Second, from a legal perspective, supra-national law may limit the scope for tax policy at the national level. These restrictions on national tax policy may be in sharp contrast with the need to levy taxes in order to finance, among other, social security and/or a welfare state, both of which are still established, to varying degrees, on a national level.

This book discusses views on the future scope of National Tax Policies in an enlarged European Union. From an economic perspective the book tries to answer the question whether there should be scope for national tax policy. Possible negative distributional (e.g. shift of tax burden on the immobile factors) and allocative (e.g. under-supply of public goods) consequences of tax competition have to be weighed against the corresponding gains from coordination. From a legal point of view the question of the impact of primary and secondary EU law as well as of double tax conventions on national tax sovereignty arises. The book concentrates on national scope in various areas of direct taxation, which have been in the centre of the policy discussions in the EU, because the scope of national tax policy with respect to indirect taxation is already quite limited due to a high degree of harmonization. For example, in the legal sphere, a discussion about the increasing limitation of national legislation and jurisdiction through the ECJ has emerged; the budget constraints deriving from tax competition for mobile capital and the consequences for the reform of the welfare states are increasingly discussed from an economic point of view.

The spectrum of taxes is very broad and it is beyond the scope of this book to cover all of them. In the book we have a strong focus on corporate taxes though they just contribute a tiny fraction of most EU-countries' budgets. We motivate our choice of focus by the fact that these taxes will have long-term effects for the level of welfare via their impact on decision-making regarding cross-border investments and efficient resource allocation.

1.4 Content and Structure of the Book

The remainder of the book contains 9 chapters. Each chapter tackles the role of national tax policy within the EU from a different perspective. This is done from an economic (Chaps. 2–5) as well as from a legal (Chaps. 6–9) viewpoint. Chapter 10 concludes. By studying a number of topical issues that illustrate limitations as well as opportunities, the aim is to provide for a comprehensive picture of the scope for domestic tax policy within the Union. To reach this objective, the book is structured in the following way:

In *Chap. 2* Christian Bellak and Marcus Leibrecht raise the question to what extent tax competition for mobile firms is likely in an enlarged Europe. Given that tax competition is a likely scenario the economic desirability of tax coordination is analysed and the position of the European Commission towards coordinating corporate income taxation is discussed.

Restrictions on national tax policy as imposed by the need to finance the welfare state are discussed in Chaps. 3 and 4. In *Chap. 3* Åsa Hansson takes a broad stance, analysing the economic pressures on tax bases and the need to review national tax policies. The chapter focuses on the consequences of EU integration on the ability of Member States to conduct an independent fiscal policy from an economic perspective. The impacts of tax competition and possible countervailing factors on domestic tax policy are dealt with.

Chapter 4 by Ulrike Schneider and August Österle elaborates on the coordination and competition of the welfare state within the EU. The purpose of their chapter is to assess the implication for the welfare state of economic pressures and the desirability of being able to have varying ambitions in the role of the government.

The remaining five chapters focus on the limitations of national tax policy by primary or secondary EC-Law, namely the possible introduction of a Common Consolidated Corporate Tax Base (CCCTB), state aid rules, fundamental freedoms and the respective legal implications of ECJ rulings and directives.

The existence of 27 different, complex and often overlapping national tax systems constitutes a considerable obstacle to reach an efficient and competitive internal market. The Member States have therefore initiated the process of developing a CCCTB. Following the introduction of a CCCTB, participating Member States would face competition from uniform tax systems applicable to activities in participating Member States. In *Chap. 5* Krister Andersson reviews the benefits of a CCCTB in relation to the need and desirability of national tax policies and tax competition within the European Union.

Chapter 6 by Franz Sutter deals with the influence of the EC state aid rules on national tax policy. In general, the EU-state aid legislation (art. 87 EC) restricts any form of aid that threatens to distort competition within the EU. The legislation consequently imposes a very broad restriction on the Member States' scope to use fiscal policy to e.g. stimulate certain activities. The chapter elaborates on different impacts of the state aid rules.

In the absence of a common legislation in the field of direct taxation, the impact of the fundamental freedoms on national tax systems largely follows from the case law of the European Court of Justice (ECJ). In *Chap. 7,* Mattias Dahlberg examines possible changes in the case law of the ECJ, and, to the extent that they have occurred, in what sense they affect the fiscal policy of the Member States.

The concept of national tax policy also encompasses the policy a Member State pursues with regard to its double tax treaties. In *Chap. 8* the limitation of double tax treaties by EC-law, in particular by ECJ jurisdiction, is explored by Michael Lang. He also addresses the application of freedom of capital and payment to third countries.

In *Chap. 9* Eva Eberhartinger and Martin Six deal with the room for national tax policy under the influence of the directives. The topic is approached by analyzing the treatment of hybrid financial instruments in the Parent-Subsidiary Directive and the Interest and Royalties Directive. The chapter concentrates on the options remaining for policy makers in the Member States with respect to the taxation of dividends and on hybrid instruments in the light of these directives.

Finally, in *Chap. 10,* Krister Andersson, Eva Eberhartinger and Lars Oxelheim provide a comprehensive summary and analysis of the findings of the study as presented in the preceding chapters. In this context, the relations from the EU and its Member States to third countries are also taken into account.

1.5 Preview of Conclusions

The book concludes that there should and there will be scope for national tax policies. From an economic point of view, several chapters conclude that coordination of policies may be desirable only to a certain extent. The common conclusion from the discussion of the legal aspects is that there is considerable scope for national tax policy even in areas where directives or bilateral measures of tax coordination exist. For example, with the introduction of a CCCTB a more transparent form of tax competition and a reduction of compliance costs can be achieved while the responsibility to decide on the actual levels of the effective tax burden remains under the control of the national governments. Another example is the Interest and Royalties Directive, which leaves considerable leeway for tax policy, enabling the Member State to levy a withholding tax on certain types of hybrid finance. The flip side of the coin of this observation is that there are still tax planning opportunities and competitive pressure on national tax policies, not only within Europe but also in relation to third countries, like the US and the Americas, India, Japan and China.

There are no plans at present for using the corporate tax system for financing federal expenses, but maybe increased transparency in the future will propel the development versus a federative system. Still, the role and the accountability of the European Parliament in tax matters are not on the agenda. Cultural differences and different strategies for how to secure financing of public expenditure will therefore continue. In any case, we can expect tax competition to continue, in particular in the area of corporate tax rates.

Endnote

1. These measures have often been described as means of protecting the revenue base. An additional objective may have been to extend the taxing rights of a country beyond its national borders. CFC regimes typically tax foreign source income at a rate close to or equal to the equivalent domestic tax rate.

Reference

Oxelheim, L. and P. Ghauri (2004) The Race for FDI in the European Union, in: Oxelheim, L. and P. Ghauri (eds). *European Union and the Race for Foreign Direct Investments in Europe.* Oxford: Elsevier

Chapter 2
Corporate Income Tax Competition and the Scope for National Tax Policy in the Enlarged Europe

Christian Bellak and Markus Leibrecht[1]

2.1 Introduction

Tax competition for mobile capital has recently emerged in the political debate of several European Union (EU) Member States against the background of the enlargement of the EU. Governments in Central and East European Countries (CEECs) have frequently been accused of engaging in tax competition for mobile capital in general and Foreign Direct Investment (FDI) in particular at the cost of the "old" EU member countries. A number of empirical studies have attempted to analyse the existence of tax competition for mobile capital (e.g. Devereux et al. 2004, Slemrod 2004). These studies mainly deal with tax competition between highly developed OECD countries and do not have a focus upon CEECs. These studies use different indicators of the corporate income tax burden, e.g. corporate income tax revenues as percentage of total tax revenues, effective tax rates or statutory tax rates (STRs) as the dependent variable in an econometric model to check for the presence of tax competition. Several studies find that tax rates indeed fall with an increased openness of economies (e.g. Rodrik 1997; Slemrod 2004) or that there is strategic interaction in the tax setting of governments (Devereux et al. 2004).

But these results do not establish the existence of tax competition *per se* as falling tax rates and interdependencies in tax rates may be due to driving forces other than tax competition (e.g. Brueckner 2003, Slemrod 2004; Griffith and Klemm 2005; Nicodème 2006). For example, reductions in corporate income tax rates may not be triggered by the aim to attract mobile capital but may be motivated by the need to reduce "national distortions" of corporate taxes. One example in this respect is the attempt to reduce the deadweight loss of taxation via tax-cut-cum-base-broadening (Griffith and Klemm 2005). Moreover, tax rates may fall in case of joining an economic union, which has a tax law in force that disallows various types of taxes. An example in this respect is the EU parent subsidiary directive. Furthermore tax rates may fall due to yardstick competition or a shift in the political stance towards less government influence (e.g. Griffith and Klemm 2005, Musgrave 1990).

This chapter has two main goals, first to examine if corporate income tax competition for FDI is a likely scenario in the enlarged Europe and second to discuss the implications of corporate income tax competition for the scope of national tax policy in Europe.

To answer the question whether tax competition is likely in the enlarged Europe we do not follow the approaches outlined above. Rather we proceed by giving a definition of tax competition and by deriving preconditions for the existence of tax competition from this definition. The fulfilment of these preconditions is analysed empirically. The four preconditions for tax competition analysed are (i) FDI is technically possible and Multinational Enterprises (MNEs) use this possibility; (ii) governments use the tax instrument actively; (iii) using the tax instrument is explicitly motivated by attracting FDI or not to loose it to competitors; and (iv) taxes are a significant determinant of FDI. Using this approach it is possible to deal more directly with the aim of tax rate cuts (precondition three) than the econometric approaches outlined can do. The first part of this chapter concludes that since all four preconditions are fulfilled, corporate income tax competition for FDI is indeed a likely scenario in an enlarged Europe.

In the second part of the chapter we answer the questions whether there *should* be scope for national tax policy from an economic point of view and whether it *will* be likely, given the political position towards tax competition in the EU. The answer to the first question is derived on the basis of the theoretically predicted and empirically simulated economic effects (esp. efficiency and tax revenue effects) of corporate income tax competition and tax coordination, respectively. To this end we summarise some main results of various theories of tax competition and results from simulation models. The second question is answered based on the Commission's position towards corporate income tax coordination as shown in official EU documents. We conclude that there should and will be sufficient scope for national tax policy in the future.

The chapter starts with a section on definitions of tax competition and its preconditions (Sect. 2.2). Measures of corporate income tax burden are discussed in Sect. 2.3. Section 2.4 reviews the major changes in corporate tax law in selected CEECs during the last decade. Empirical results on the significance of taxes as a determinant of FDI in CEECs are reported in Sect. 2.5. Section 2.6 discusses whether there should and will be scope for national tax policy within an enlarged Europe.

2.2 Definitions and Preconditions of Tax Competition

Until recently, the literature on tax competition devoted little attention to providing a clear definition of tax competition. This gap was filled by Wilson and Wildasin in 2004. They define tax competition in a broad sense as "any form of non-cooperative tax setting by independent governments." (Wilson and Wildasin, 2004, p. 1066) This definition includes other forms of competition where taxes play a role, notably yardstick competition between independent jurisdictions. Yardstick competition is based upon the "voice" option in Hirschman's (1970) terminology and not on the "exit" option (also see Wildasin 2005, Brueckner 2003). It is thus not directly concerned with shifts of tax bases from one jurisdiction to another. Moreover it even may exist in fully closed economies whereas tax competition is an "open economies phenomenon" (Devereux et al. 2004).

Tax competition in a *narrow* sense relies upon the exit option and is defined by Wilson and Wildasin as "non-cooperative tax setting by independent governments under which each government's policy choices influence the allocation of mobile tax base among 'regions' represented by these governments" (Wilson and Wildasin, 2004 p. 1067). In this definition the independent nations are linked via tax revenue effects due to the increase or decrease in mobile tax bases. It is important to note that this definition implies "horizontal" tax competition between governments of the same level (e.g. local governments, states or nations). This definition, therefore, excludes the concept of "vertical" tax competition, which means that governments of different levels (i.e. federal, state, local) are competing in levying taxes upon a given, immobile tax base (Wilson and Wildasin, 2004; Keen 1998).

Non-cooperatively in this definition means that a government does not take into account the impact of its decisions upon other governments. This term thus also captures the aim of tax setting, namely to attract mobile resources at the cost of competitors. One can define tax setting as changing different tax parameters with the aim of varying the tax burden levied upon a specific tax base. Among the main tax parameters which can be varied are the STR, the tax base and the way taxes are collected by public authorities (e.g. delays in collection of taxes; effective control of tax statements of tax payers). Furthermore, the entire tax system, the types and the number of different taxes levied may be changed. In policy discussions about horizontal tax competition the STR on corporate income is the most debated tax parameter. The term "independence" here means that governments have sufficient fiscal sovereignty to be able to use taxes actively as a policy instrument. Of course, government policies in open economies are dependent via trade flows, capital flows etc.

Apart from defining various types of tax competition, some attempts have been made to define "tax coordination" and "tax harmonisation". For example Zodrow (2003, p. 666, footnote 1) defines "harmonisation" as the full equalisation of tax rates and "coordination" as encompassing harmonisation as well as other measures like minimum tax rates or unified tax bases. Genschel (2002 p. 251) defines EU tax-harmonisation in a wider sense as the sum of all tax related measures taken by the EU. In a narrow sense harmonisation is defined as the sum of all measures with the aim of abolishing differences in relevant tax parameters between the EU member states. According to Randzio-Plath (2000, p. 4) tax harmonisation can be seen as the full equalisation of tax bases and tax rates, whereas tax coordination can be seen as the sum of all measures that balance tax policies of independent governments.

Following these authors we here see tax coordination as a generic term which includes all measures that balance tax policies of independent jurisdictions. Tax coordination may exist in *loose* and in *legally binding* forms.

For example the EU's Code of Conduct in business taxation, which can essentially be regarded as a "gentlemens' agreement" is a loose form of delegated tax coordination. Minimum STRs and other types of minimum standards are forms of legally-binding tax coordination, which do not lead to an equalisation of tax codes. Finally, tax harmonisation is a legally binding form of tax coordination which leads to an *equalisation* of tax codes across jurisdictions. "Thereby full tax harmonisation" requires the equalisation of *all* relevant tax parameters and "partial tax harmonisation" the equalisation of a selection of relevant tax parameters (for example, harmonisation of tax bases only). Table 2.1 summarizes the different definitions.

Finally, it should be mentioned that attempts are made by the OECD (1998) and the European Commission (1997) to define "harmful" or unfair tax competition and that "Enhanced Cooperation Agreements" are gaining importance in the EU (see Treaty of Amsterdam, 1997 and Treaty of Nice, 2002). The EU definition and the OECD guidelines of "harmful tax competition" have many similarities (see Weiner and Ault 1998 for details). The EU defines unfair (or harmful) tax competition within its "Code of Conduct" of business taxation as the presence of a – relative to the general level of corporate tax burden in the country – low effective corporate tax burden paired with at least one additional fact. Among the latter are tax preferences granted to non-residents only (ring fencing), tax preferences granted despite the absence of any real firm activity in a

Table 2.1. Definition of tax competition and tax coordination

I. Tax competition = non-cooperation of independent jurisdictions in taxation with an impact on the allocation of tax bases between jurisdictions
a) Horizontal tax competition: non-cooperative tax setting of independent jurisdictions at the same level with the aim of attracting mobile tax bases
b) Vertical tax competition: non-cooperative tax setting of independent jurisdictions at different levels with the aim of taxing a given tax base
II. Tax coordination = cooperation between jurisdictions in the form of loose (i.e. non legally binding) or legally binding measures that balance tax policies of governments
a) Loose forms of tax coordination (e.g. Code of Conduct in business taxation)
b) Legally binding forms of tax coordination **without equalisation** of tax codes (e.g. minimum statutory tax rates)
c) Tax harmonisation: Legally binding forms with equalisation of tax codes
Full tax harmonisation: legally binding form of tax coordination between independent jurisdictions in the form of *equalization* of *all* relevant tax parameters
Partial tax harmonisation: legally binding form of tax coordination between independent jurisdictions in the form of equalization of some but not all relevant tax parameters (e.g. mandatory common consolidated corporate tax base)

country (tax haven), non-traditional rules of taxation and lack of transparency in tax enforcement (European Commission 1998). Hence, one aim of the mentioned Code of Conduct is to ban discriminatory corporate income tax policies by preventing member states to grant preferential tax treatment to non-residents in order to level the playing field.[2] This separation of tax competition in "unfair" and "fair" tax competition also shows that the European Commission's position is in favour of (fair) tax competition, a point which is further elaborated in Sect. 2.6.

Enhanced Cooperation Agreements (ECA) mean that at least 8 member states (since the Treaty of Nice) of the EU can form a "sub-union" with the aim to make it easier to speed up integration by circumventing the general unanimity principle in tax policy (Bordignon and Brusco 2006). For, example ECAs make it easier for a sub-group of EU member countries to harmonize their tax systems as single members no longer have a veto over the establishment of an ECA (except in the field of foreign policy) (see European Commission, www).

Turning back to tax competition, in this paper we focus on horizontal corporate income tax competition between independent jurisdictions for mobile capital, FDI in particular.[3] The definition of horizontal tax competition stated above can be used to derive preconditions of corporate income tax competition. Based on Krogstrup (2004b, pp. 5), Feld (2005, pp. 127) and Griffith and Klemm (2005, pp. 25) we isolate the following preconditions:

1. FDI is technically possible and MNEs use this possibility.
2. Governments use the tax instrument actively.
3. One explicit motivation of tax rate cuts is to attract FDI or to react to downward revisions of other countries' tax rates to avoid loosing investment.
4. Taxes are a significant determinant of FDI.

Each of these preconditions is a necessary condition for corporate income tax competition for FDI to exist. While the first precondition can safely be assumed, the second and third preconditions are discussed briefly in a descriptive way. The fourth precondition is analysed as an econometric study. To this end the choice of a suitable measure of the tax burden levied upon FDI is discussed in the following subsection.

2.3. Measures of the Tax Burden on Corporate Income

Apart from STRs and tax quotas (corporate tax revenue in relation to Gross Domestic Product or total tax revenue), measures of the corporate income tax burden may be split into backward-looking and forward-looking effective tax rates (cf. Fig. 2.1). While each measure has its advantages and disadvantages, the choice of the most appropriate measure of the tax burden should be guided by the underlying research question. In our case, this is the selection of an optimal location of FDI by an MNE.

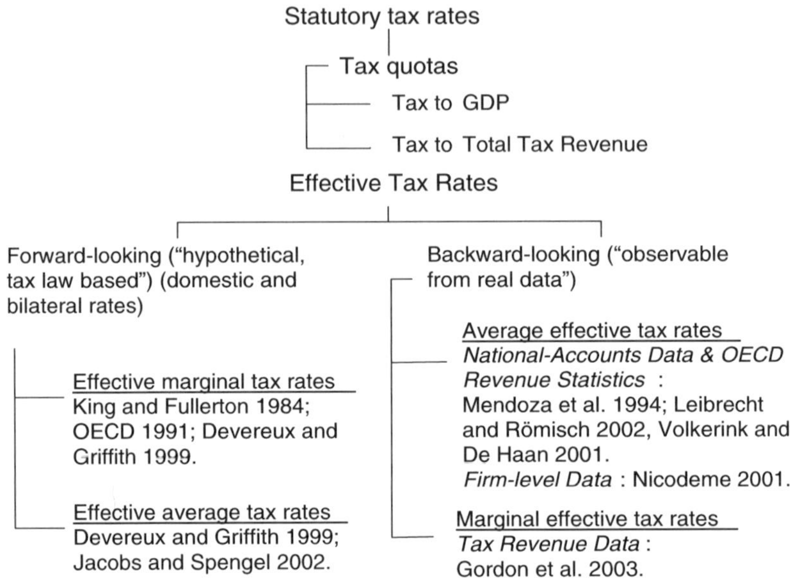

Fig. 2.1. Measures of tax burden

STR and tax quotas data are readily available. STRs are most useful in studying profit shifting behaviour of MNEs and international portfolio investment decisions and tax quotas are useful in analysing changes in the tax structure. But their main drawback is that they do not take account of the tax base at all (STRs) or do so in an improper way only (quotas). Hence, both are not the first choice for analysing FDI decisions of MNEs. Backward-looking tax rates, which are based on taxes paid by firms in the past, are inappropriate, as profits from national and international activities cannot be disentangled. Furthermore, backward-looking rates can be seriously flawed due to data problems.[4] The main advantage of backward-looking tax rates is that they are easily calculated from real data and include tax planning activities of MNEs. Moreover, they may be used as basis when concerned with the formal incidence of taxation.

Forward-looking effective tax rates (FETRs) focus on hypothetical ("future") investments and have, *inter alia,* three conceptual advantages which are of relevance when analysing investment decisions. (i) They distinguish between domestic and international investments (domestic vs. bilateral rates). (ii) They are calculated either as effective average tax rates (EATRs), measuring the tax burden of an infra-marginal (i.e. profitable) investment, or as effective marginal tax rates (EMTRs), measuring the tax burden of an investment which just earns the cost of capital. (iii) They correspond to the investment decision of an MNE which also is "forward-looking". Disadvantages include the relatively high degree of complexity in the calculation of these rates – the net present value of a hypothetical investment has to be calculated with and without taxation – and the fact that tax planning activities of MNEs cannot be addressed.

Which Measures of Corporate Tax Burden are Appropriate if FDI Decisions are to Be Explained?

In order to answer this question, we start from a description of the investment decision by an MNE, as outlined in Devereux and Griffith (2002) and in Devereux (2006a). According to these authors the investment decision should be split into four levels:

- "Level 1" is concerned with discriminating between different types of market servicing, most importantly whether to produce at home or abroad.
- "Level 2" includes the decision where to invest, given that level 1 has resulted in a decision to invest abroad. Levels 1 and 2 comprise discrete and infra-marginal (i.e. profitable) investment decisions.
- "Level 3" governs adjustments to scale, i.e. expansion or downscaling of an *existing* investment abroad. It is concerned with marginal investment decisions.
- "Level 4" is concerned with the place of declaration of the profit earned given the decision to invest a particular amount in a particular location.

The two FETR mentioned above, EATR and EMTR, are now directly related to the first three level decisions in the following way: EATRs are directly related to the decision to produce abroad or at home (level 1) and where to invest (level 2), ranking the investment opportunities according to their net of tax profitability. EMTRs directly impact on the optimal scale of an investment (level 3) conditional upon the choice of the investment location (Devereux and Griffith, 2003).[5] Moreover bilateral rates (BEATRs and BEMTRs) are especially relevant for FDI as all relevant tax laws (home country, host country, international and supranational) are captured. Finally, level 4 decisions should not be addressed with effective tax rates but with the STRs as MNEs have already taken advantage of all possible tax allowances at this stage of decision making (Devereux 2006a).

FDI decisions often are infra-marginal (e.g. Devereux and Hubbard, 2004; Devereux and Griffith, 2002; Markusen, 2002) and therefore should be primarily driven by the EATR. Using EATRs seems to be particularly important for the CEECs as these are young market economies where FDI is a relatively recent phenomenon. It thus is particularly plausible that FDI consists of new and infra-marginal investments. Moreover, it is particularly important to use average tax rates on a bilateral level (i.e. BEATR) as some of the CEECs only recently signed double taxation agreements (e.g. Slovenia with Austria and the USA; or Hungary with several home countries of FDI) or have changed withholding taxes on repatriated profits during the last years (e.g. the New EU Member states due to the adoption of the EU-parent-subsidiary directive). Finally, substantial differences in the overall withholding tax rates on repatriated dividends and interests exist between the various home and host countries of FDI. These changes and differences are well captured by BEATRs, which thus is the tax variable of main interest when dealing with FDI in CEECs.

Bilateral Effective Average Tax Rates

Basically, the BEATR developed by Devereux and Griffith (1999) refers to the scaled difference between the positive pre-tax and the positive post-tax economic rent of an FDI with a given pre-tax financial rate of return. The post-tax economic rent is, *inter alia,* a function of different tax laws (for details see Devereux and Griffith 1999). Some of them are:

- *Host country tax law*: rules for tax allowances and stock valuation, corporate income tax rates on retained earnings as well as on distributed profits (i.e. host country split rate), withholding taxes on repatriated profits and taxes on interests paid to the parent company.
- *Home country tax law*: corporate income tax rates on retained earnings as well as on distributed profits.
- *International, tax law*: double taxation agreements (exemption, credit or deduction systems for dividends and interest payments to the parent company).
- *Supranational tax law*: parent-subsidiary directive, special rules of EC-Court of Justice (e.g. Bosal Holdings case).

More precisely the BEATR is a function of various economic and tax related parameters:

$$BEATR = BEATR\,(\mathrm{r}, \pi, \rho, \delta, \mathrm{p}, \mathrm{E}; \varphi, \tau_j, \tau_n, \sigma, \omega; \mathrm{Inv}, \mathrm{Dep}, \mathrm{S}) \tag{2.1}$$

with: r = real interest rate; π = inflation rate; ρ = discount factor; δ = economic rate of depreciation; p = real pre-tax financial rate of return; E = exchange rate; φ = rate at which capital expenditures can be offset against tax, τ_j and τ = corporate income tax rates of home and host country including local business taxes, σ = overall tax rate on dividend payments from the subsidiary to the parent, ω = overall tax rate on interest payments from the subsidiary to the parent (depending on double taxation agreement); Inv = valuation method for inventories (LIFO, FIFO, average costs), Dep = method of depreciation (linear, declining balance), S = special tax provisions (e.g. non deductibility of interests paid on loans used for FDI).

Due to variations in the tax related parameters shown in (2.1) the BEATR is different for different investment goods considered (here: buildings, machinery, inventories) and it varies between the various ways of financing a FDI by the parent or by the subsidiary (retained earnings, debt, new equity).

2.4 Changes in the CEECs' Corporate Income Taxation Between 1995 and 2005

This section summarises the development of the STRs as well as of the BEATRs for eight CEECs[6] and their seven most important home countries[7] of FDI for the period 1995 to 2005.[8]

The CEECs have undergone a considerable tax-reform process during the past decade, corporate income taxation being no exception. While the tax-reform process "was not uniform across countries" (e.g. Grabowski 2005, p. 294), at least two clear trends are discernible with respect to corporate income taxation (see Table 2.2 for details):

1. STRs have been reduced considerably during the past decade along with changes in allowances. In general, these changes have lowered the overall effective tax burden of foreign investors significantly (cf. Fig. 2.3).
2. The downward movement of various tax parameters gained momentum especially starting with the year 2000. Moreover, Table 2.2 suggests that these steps have not been taken independently by the respective governments.

BEATRs are affected by the development of the *overall* tax rate on dividends (σ) and interests paid (ω) to the parent. These, in turn, depend on the home country's treatment of foreign-source dividends and interest, respectively. This treatment implies specific formulae for the calculation of ω and σ shown in (2.2) and (2.3) (see Devereux and Griffith 1999).

$$\sigma = \begin{cases} c_n & \text{exemption system} \\ \max\left(\dfrac{\tau_j - \tau_n}{1-\tau_n}, c_n\right) & \text{credit system} \\ \tau_j(1-c_n)+c_n & \text{deduction system} \end{cases} \tag{2.2}$$

$$\omega = \begin{cases} w_n - \tau_n & \text{exemption system} \\ \max\left(\tau_j, w_n\right) - \tau_n & \text{credit system} \\ \tau_j(1-w_n)+w_n-\tau_n & \text{deduction system} \end{cases} \tag{2.3}$$

with: c_n = withholding tax rate on gross dividends paid by the subsidiary, w_n = withholding tax rate on interest payments from the subsidiary to the parent.

All home countries considered in this study apply the credit system for interest payments. All home countries except the UK and the US apply the exemption system for dividend payments. The UK and the US apply the credit system.

As the effect of the rules concerning interest and dividends differs across the 56 bilateral relationships, and in view of space limitations, we have chosen to limit our demonstration of the effects of (2.2) and (2.3) to one particular sub-sample, Italy (high tax country) – Hungary (low tax country). Both, Italy and (Hungary), have lowered their STRs between 1995 and 2005 from 52% (18.6%) to 37.25% (17.73%). According to (2.2) [(2.3), respectively] the *overall* dividend [interest] tax changes with changes in the withholding tax rate on dividends [interest], the existence of double taxation agreements or the STR of home and host countries (Citrate in Fig 2.2). Figure 2.2, which is largely self-explanatory, shows the downward trend in interest and dividend taxes. The marked drop of the overall tax-rate on dividend payments in 2004 is due to the adoption of the parent-subsidiary directive in the New Member States.[9] This drop also is one particular example for falling tax rates not caused by tax competition forces.[10]

While we do not argue that this relationship is representative of all of the 56 bilateral tax burdens we analyse in this paper, it nevertheless reflects a main driver

Table 2.2 Host country tax parameters: Initial parameters in 1995 and changes in the non-fixed parameters of the Devereux-Griffith model 1) 2):

1995	Corporate Income Tax (statutory)	Depreciation Method: Machinery	Depreciation Rate: Machinery	Depreciation Method: Buildings	Depreciation Rate: Buildings	Inventory valuation
Hungary (HU)	18.60	straight line (SL)	14.30	straight line	2.00	Average Cost
Czech Republic (CZ)	41.00	declining balance (DB)	12.50	declining balance	2.22	Average Cost
Poland (PL)	40.00	straight line	10.00	straight line	2.50	LIFO
Slovak Republic (SK)	40.00	declining balance	12.50	declining balance	2.00	Average Cost
Slovenia (SI)	30.00	straight line	33.30	straight line	10.00	LIFO
Non-members (2004)						
Bulgaria (BG)	40.00	declining balance	16.30	declining balance	4.00	LIFO
Croatia (CR)	25.00	straight line	4.00	straight line	3.30	LIFO
Romania (RO)	38.00	straight line	15.70	straight line	2.00	FIFO
Changes in						
1996	HU: 19 CZ: 39 SI: 25					
1997	CZ: 35 PL. 36 BG: 36 CR: 35					
1998	HU: 19.14 BG: 30	BG: SL	BG: 20	BG: SL	SK: 2.5	
1999	HU: 19.4 PL: 34 BG: 27		CZ: 16.7		CZ: 3.3	

2000	HU: 19.62	BG: DB	BG: 30	
	CZ: 31			
	PL: 30			
	RO: 25			
	SK: 29			
	BG: 25			
2001	HU: 19.64			
	PL: 28			
	CR: 20*			
	BG: 20			
2002	SK: 25			HU: 4
	BG: 15			CR: 2.5
2003	PL: 27	BG: SL	SK: 16.7	SK: 3.3
	BG: 23.5		SI: 25	SI: 5
				CR: 10
2004	BG: 19.5			SK: 5
	CZ: 28			
	HU: 17.8			
	PL: 19			
	SK: 19			
2005	BG: 15.0			CR: 5
	CZ: 26			
	HU: 17.7			
	RO: 16			

Notes:
1) Inventory valuation: no changes during 1995–2005. If the law grants a choice, the most favourable choice has been selected.
2) Changes in interest and dividend taxation are not shown here, see example below.
* Allowance for Corporate Equity cancelled and reduction of STR for compensation

of the overall downward trend in BEATRs shown by Fig. 2.3 namely changes in dividend and interest taxation. This figure also demonstrates the diminishing variance of the BEATRs into a comparatively small range up to 2005. Hence, CEEC governments use the tax rates actively and in a way that tax rates are converging. Precondition two for tax competition can therefore be safely considered to be fulfilled.

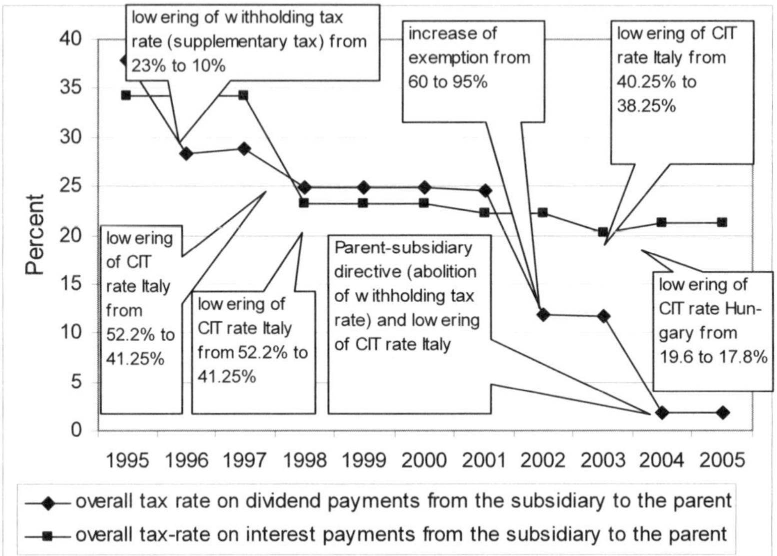

Fig. 2.2 Italy (home country) – Hungary (host country): Development of overall dividend and interest tax (only major changes indicated)

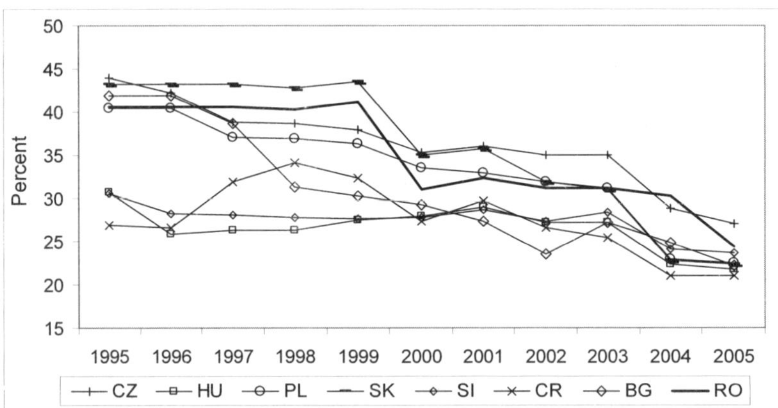

Fig. 2.3 Bilateral effective average tax rates of eight CEECs: Average across seven home countries of FDI 1995–2005

Tax Setting as an Instrument of CEEC Governments to Attract FDI

The descriptive evidence of frequent changes in tax parameters suggests that CEECs actively use tax instruments as an economic policy device. But this use of the tax instrument may be motivated not only by tax competition. Hence, the motive of tax rate cuts has to be analysed separately (precondition three).

As it is difficult to provide quantitative evidence for this precondition we first outline briefly a theoretical rationale for the use of tax policy by governments in order to stimulate inward FDI namely the FDI-growth nexus. Second, we present some descriptive evidence in favour of the "tax competition motive."

The literature on spillovers of foreign technology and skills to local industry (see Blomström and Kokko 2003) describes the FDI-growth nexus in the following way: On the one hand, neo-classical models of growth postulate long-run growth as a consequence of technological progress, captured by the residual actually left unexplained, after the effect of population growth has been accounted for. Subject to the standard assumption of constant-returns-to-scale, technology embodied in FDI would affect growth only in the short-run (transition phase), while it is viewed as an additional (exogenous) input factor which contributes to the capital stock in the long-run. If on the other hand FDI is defined as a bundle of technology, capital and know-how, endogenous growth models assign to FDI the role of increasing the marginal productivity of capital, thus leading to a permanent effect on growth. These latter models thus provide a justification for government support of inward FDI, not least by tax incentives. Empirical macro-economic studies generally suggest a positive role for FDI in generating economic growth (for a recent review, see Carkovic and Levine, 2005).[11]

Countries like the CEECs, which lack domestic savings and investment, are reliant on FDI as an important substitute and we should expect CEEC governments to promote inward FDI actively. The following quotations demonstrate that this is actually the case in the field of tax policy.

A look at the webpages of various investment promotion agencies (IPAs),[12] which are government funded, yield the following examples:[13] The Bulgarian IPA states that "Bulgaria's current income and corporate tax rates continue to be the most competitive in Central and Eastern Europe." The Romanian IPA explains why foreign investors should choose their country as follows: "Competitive Tax Policy: 16% Flat Tax. The cuts affect income tax and corporate profit tax, as well as the levy on dividends, within a reduced and simplified tax regime. The aim of the 9 points cut is to encourage growth and foreign investment." The Hungarian IPA promotes FDI by a "rate of corporate tax: 16% in general, and tax payable may be reduced by the different tax incentives."

In addition, the motives and aims of policies lowering corporate income tax rates can be deduced from the various stability and convergence programmes of New Member States.[14] The goal of attracting FDI can be found most explicitly in the programmes of Slovakia 2003/04, Poland 2003/04 and Hungary 2003/04 and 2004. Examples are: "Tax rates reduction in direct taxes should be considered as the most important. These changes were oriented towards improving the situation of enterprises and attracting direct investments". (PL 2003/2004, p. 36) "Favourable environment is created for foreign investments through the introduction of [...] the low corporate income tax rate [...]." (HU 2003/2004, p. 9) "The introduction of a flat tax [...] (*is*) most likely to attract more foreign investment into Slovakia". (SK 2003/2004, p. 10). Hence, preconditions three for the existence of tax competition seems to be satisfied as well.

2.5 Empirical Results on Tax-Rate Elasticities of FDI in the CEEC-8[15]

A range of studies provide a growing body of evidence on the magnitude of tax-rate elasticities of FDI in general, and in Europe in particular (see DeMooij and Ederveen, 2005; Gorter and Parikh, 2003). The meta-analysis by DeMooij and Ederveen shows that the derived elasticities are very sensitive to the empirical specifications utilised in the studies: whether FDI flows or stocks are used; which indicator of tax burden is used; which (panel) estimator is used; whether aggregate or bilateral data are used; and the time period and the countries considered, to name but a few. Although the survey reveals a broad range of tax-rate elasticities, DeMooij and Ederveen conclude on a median tax-rate elasticity of –3.3.

Yet, some studies included in these surveys are based on STRs and, most importantly, do not include CEECs as host countries. Bellak et al. (2005) surveyed eight studies on FDI to the CEECs which also used STRs as a measure of the tax burden. They found a median tax-rate elasticity of –1.45. As all of these studies are based on STRs, which are flawed measures of the corporate income tax burden (see Sect. 2.3. above), the existence of the fourth precondition is now analysed econometrically using the superior BEATRs shown above.

Dependent Variable

We operationalise the location decisions of MNEs in the CEEC-8 for the years 1995 to 2003 (t) via the net-bilateral-FDI-outflows ($fdimn_{ijt}$) from home country (i) to host country (j).[16] FDI data are taken mainly from the "OECD International Direct Investment Statistics Yearbook 1991–2002" and database as well as the New Cronos database and information provided by national authorities.

Independent Variables

Our independent variables have to be valid proxies for host-country related location advantages (L-factors). Based upon earlier studies (Clausing and Dorubantu 2005; Bevan and Estrin 2004) we use the following variables in addition to BEATRs:

- host-market size, distance between home and host country, unit labour costs, inflation, privatisation revenues and political risk, common border dummy and
- home-country size as we base our analysis on a gravity-setting.

Home-country size (*gdphome*$_{it}$) and host-market size (*gdphost*$_{jt}$), both measured by the corresponding Gross Domestic Product in € million (from New Cronos database), are expected to impact positively upon FDI (Navaretti and Venables 2004). Distance between capital cities (*dist*$_{ij}$), measured in kilometres,[17] is an important determinant of FDI (Brainard 1997). The expected sign of the estimated coefficient is ambiguous *a priori*. While large distance may encourage FDI due to an internalisation advantage (Dunning 1988) it also may discourage FDI due to the lack of market know-how, higher communication and information costs and differences in culture and institutions (Buch and Lipponer 2004). These three variables, *gdphome* and *gdphost* as well as *dist*, are "gravity-specific".

In contrast to other studies, which use STRs as measures of the corporate tax burden (see Bellak et al. 2005 for details) we use the conceptually and empirically superior *BEATR (BEATR*$_{ijt}$*)* described in Sect. 2.3. As corporate income taxes can be considered a cost factor we expect a negative sign on the estimated coefficient.

In the realm of public debate, low labour costs are among the most important determinants of FDI in the CEECs. High unit labour costs (*ulc*$_{jt}$) in the host country should exert a negative impact upon FDI. *Ulc* reflects real unit labour costs in a common currency, based on the formula given in van Ark and Monnikhof (2000) and on data from the AMECO and the New Cronos databases. We expect a negative sign on the coefficient. Note, that *BEATR* and *ulc* are "efficiency-oriented" variables.

Privatisation revenues (*prev*$_{jt}$) on an annual basis are used to reflect progress in privatisation. Data are in € million and are taken from various editions of the EBRD's Transition Report. We expect a positive sign on this coefficient as larger privatisation revenues imply greater opportunities to invest in a host country. In transition countries, property rights may be insecure and political stability may be low. Hence, political risk (*risk*$_{jt}$) may play a role as a determinant of FDI (Navaretti and Venables 2004). We expect a negative relationship (a *positive* coefficient due to the measurement of our risk variable) between political risk and FDI. The expected sign on the coefficient of the inflation variable (*infl*$_{jt}$), measured as the change in producer prices according to EBRD's Transition Reports, is negative. High inflation rates may have a negative impact upon FDI due to the macroeconomic instabilities they imply (Buch and Lipponer 2004). These three variables are "transition-specific".

Finally, we include a dummy variable which takes the value 1 if home and host country share a common border (*combord*$_{ij}$). *Combord* reflects the possibility of intensified trade and capital flows between adjacent home and host countries and, therefore, we expect a positive sign. This variable has often been used in gravity-models, as center-to-center distance may overstate the effective distance between two countries (Head 2003). Table 2.3 provides a summary of the discussion on individual L-factors above.

Empirical Specification and Methodology

In the specification we base our analysis upon a gravity setting as models of that type seem to be successful in explaining bilateral trade flows and, more recently,

Table 2.3. Country-level location factors and their expected signs

Variable	Description	Expected sign
gdphome	GDP home country	+
gdphost	GDP host country	+
dist	Distance	?
BEATR	Bilateral effective average tax rate	-
ulc	Real unit labour costs in common currency	-
prev	Annual privatisation revenues	+
risk	Political Risk	+
infl	Inflation	-
combord	Common border dummy	+

bilateral FDI-flows as well (e.g. Frenkel et al. 2004). More specifically, we use the triple-indexed-Gravity-model proposed by Mátyás (1997). The basic triple-indexed-Gravity-model is specified as follows:

$$\log(fdimn_{ijt}) = b_1 \log(gdphome_{it}) + b_2 \log(gdphost_{jt}) + b_3 \log(dist_{ij}) + \gamma_t + \alpha_i + \beta_j + e_{ijt} \quad (2.4)$$

with: α_i, β_j, γ_t = home, host and time specific effects, e_{ijt} = the remainder error term.

Equation (2.4) is augmented by the various location factors described above, which yields the "generalized" triple-indexed-Gravity-model. From an econometric point of view α_i, β_j and γ_t can be treated either as random, or fixed, effects. For our study, a fixed-effects approach is the appropriate choice because we are interested in the specific effects *per se*: for example home-country fixed effects can be interpreted as an indicator of the propensity of the home countries to undertake FDI in the CEECs (see Mátyás et al. 2001 and Egger 2000 for trade studies). Time effects are treated as fixed as well. They account *inter alia* for the business cycle and for common shocks (Egger and Pfaffermayr 2003).

Our original data set constitutes a balanced panel of bilateral net-FDI-flows for seven home countries, eight host countries and nine years (1995 to 2003), resulting in a total of 504 observations. However, since the logarithm of FDI-flows is used, we have to drop 46 negative observations (about 9 percent of our data set). Table 2.4 shows the descriptive statistics for our data set. In particular, the average bilateral net-FDI flow across countries and time was €205m annually. It becomes clear that the between variability is higher than the within variability in our data.

As a first step in our methodology we estimate Equation 2.4 with all of the location factors described above (in levels[18]). In a next step we test for the significance of the host country dummies. As they are not significant (see Table 2.5) we drop them. Next, we "test down", that is, we stepwise exclude insignificant location

Table 2.4. Descriptive statistics

Variable		Mean	Std. Dev.	Min	Max	Observations
fdimn	overall	205.55	400.20	0.11	4625.00	N = 458
	between		279.81	8.14	1407.89	n = 56
	within		295.75	–863.98	3561.62	T-bar = 8.18
lnfdimn	overall	4.01	1.83	–2.21	8.44	N = 458
	between		1.44	1.67	7.11	n = 56
	within		1.16	–0.71	7.94	T-bar = 8.18
lngdphome	overall	13.90	1.11	12.12	16.24	N = 458
	between		1.13	12.21	16.10	n = 56
	within		0.15	13.44	14.22	T-bar = 8.18
lngdphost	overall	10.41	0.79	8.96	12.24	N = 458
	between		0.77	9.39	11.96	n = 56
	within		0.21	9.96	10.91	T-bar = 8.18
lndist	overall	7.00	0.98	4.04	9.15	N = 458
	between		1.00	4.04	9.15	n = 56
	within		0.00	7.00	7.00	T-bar = 8.18
BEATR	overall	34.77	7.39	16.11	55.92	N = 458
	between		5.39	24.08	48.08	n = 56
	within		5.05	17.50	47.04	T-bar = 8.18
ulc	overall	24.62	9.11	11.00	50.00	N = 458
	between		8.78	15.43	46.14	n = 56
	within		2.87	15.62	32.42	T-bar = 8.18
prev	overall	1338.50	1488.06	61.27	8939.76	N = 458
	between		1067.76	93.03	3519.36	n = 56
	within		1050.13	–767.16	7148.15	T-bar = 8.18
infl	overall	27.66	111.74	-1.20	901.80	N = 458
	between		43.96	1.92	154.04	n = 56
	within		103.08	–122.98	803.24	T-bar = 8.18
risk	overall	13.86	3.36	5.32	19.82	N = 458
	between		2.934297	9.597143	17.48333	n = 56
	within		1.69	7.99	17.52	T-bar = 8.18
combord	overall	0.13	0.34	0.00	1.00	N = 458
	between		0.33	0.00	1.00	n = 56
	within		0.00	0.13	0.13	T-bar = 8.18

factors while considering possible multi-collinearity problems, until the preferred specification is reached. Finally, we reintroduce the host country dummies in the preferred specification and test for their significance. This procedure reduces the probability of an omitted variable bias and it provides information about the robustness of our regression results. Estimation is done via Pooled OLS with cluster-robust standard-errors.[19]

Empirical Results

Table 2.5 shows the results of the estimated model. Model 1 is the most general specification. It shows that host country dummies are jointly not significant at the

Table 2.5. Empirical results

	Model 1	Model 2	Model 3	Model 4	Model 5
lngdphost	−2.55714*	1.07935***	1.16724***	1.66884**	1.18200***
	(−1.89)	(8.85)	(10.77)	(2.61)	(11.60)
lngdphome	−0.27038	−0.27491	−0.24869	1.03610	1.15160**
	(−0.31)	(−0.31)	(−0.28)	(1.41)	(2.14)
lndist	−0.78315**	−0.72324***	−0.88686***	−0.83495***	−0.88489***
	(−2.27)	(−2.87)	(−5.13)	(−3.91)	(−5.21)
combord	0.12769	0.09228		dropped	dropped
	(0.30)	(0.26)			
BEATR	−0.02821*	−0.04015***	−0.04158***	−0.02988*	−0.04501***
	(−1.95)	(−3.07)	(−3.20)	(−1.93)	(−3.67)
prev	0.00015**	0.00016***	0.00016***	0.00015***	0.00016***
	(2.52)	(2.76)	(2.72)	(2.76)	(2.94)
infl	−0.00137**	−0.00088	dropped	dropped	dropped
	(−2.32)	(−1.57)			
ulc	0.03106	−0.03854***	−0.03294***	−0.04659*	−0.03350***
	(0.84)	(−3.63)	(−2.91)	(−1.71)	(−3.11)

risk	0.12863*		0.03032	dropped		dropped		dropped	
	(1.77)		(0.82)						
cons	35.28381**		2.45608		2.64036		−21.20461**	cons	−17.01333**
	(2.08)		(0.19)		(0.20)		(−2.53)		(−2.19)
Host: $X^2(7) = 12.39$		dropped		Dropped		Host: $X^2(7) = 6.02$		Dropped	
Home: $X^2(6) = 74.52$***		Home: $X^2(6) = 75.48$***		Home: $X^2(6) = 85.56$***		Home: $X^2(6) = 81.24$***		Home: $X^2(6) = 87.30$***	
Time: $X^2(8) = 26.00$***		Time: $X^2(8) = 18.16$**		Time: $X^2(8) = 16.56$**		dropped		dropped	
								AT	2.57235**
								FR	0.81602***
								UK	0.36514
								NL	2.28746***
								DE	1.12217***
								US	0.34413
R2_adj	0.62	R2_adj	0.61	R2_adj	0.61	R2_adj	0.60	R2_adj	0.60
N	457	N	457	N	457	N	457	N	457

t-values in parentheses; coefficients and t-values for dummy variables not shown except for Model 5 (coefficients); *** $p < 0.01$, ** $p < 0.05$, * $p < 0.1$

10 percent significance level. Model 2 excludes host country dummies, and Models 4 and 5 show our preferred specification with and without host dummies. The various steps of our "testing down" strategy leading to Models 4 and 5 are not shown, but they reveal that home-country dummy variables are jointly significant in every specification. Time dummies are excluded in Models 4 and 5, as they are not significant individually, and not highly significant jointly, in Model 3. Furthermore they impact heavily on the coefficient of *gdphome*, probably due to multi-collinearity as both may capture business-cycle effects. Host dummies are included again in Model 4, but they are jointly not significant. Hence, our preferred specification is Model 5 with only home country dummy variables included. Significant location factors in Model 5 are the BEATR, the privatisation process, unit labour costs as well as the gravity-specific variables.[20] Moreover these results are rather robust to the inclusion and exclusion of other control variables and countries, respectively as both the "testing-down" strategy and a jackknife analysis show (see Bellak and Leibrecht 2005 for details).

The signs of the coefficients in Model 5 are as expected. Moreover, the magnitudes of the coefficients of the gravity-specific variables are in line with theoretical predictions and empirical evidence. Specifically, the coefficients of *gdphome* and *gdphost* are close to 1, which is the theoretically predicted value. The coefficient for *dist* is –0.88, which is in line with values reported on the average distance effect of –0.94 for models explaining international trade flows (see e.g. Head 2003). The coefficient of *ulc* implies a semi-elasticity of FDI with respect to unit labour costs of –3.4, which seems to be economically meaningful. The coefficient on *prev* implies a relatively small response of FDI. Yet, given that we cover a time period with privatisation programmes already far advanced, the share of FDI unrelated to the privatisation process *per se* should have been large, which is indicated by our results.

Note that the coefficients of the home dummies, which indicate the propensity to invest in the CEEC-8, imply that AT, NL and DE have the largest propensity. This result is in line with descriptive empirical evidence.

Model 5 implies a tax-rate elasticity of about –4.5. A one percentage point reduction of the effective tax rate would increase FDI inflows by 4.5 percent at most, which evaluated at the mean FDI flow of €205.6m amounts to €9.3m, on average. How does this measure compare with results of earlier studies? First of all, the derived semi-elasticity is substantially greater than the median value of –1.45 reported in Bellak et al. (2005). Hence, using the superior BEATRs, results in a greater responsiveness of FDI with respect to taxation. Secondly, the estimated semi-elasticity is similar to that reported by DeMooij and Ederveen (2005) for FDI mainly between more advanced and homogenous countries (semi-elasticity of about –5.8 if average effective tax rates are used. Hence, the response of FDI in the CEECs to changes in taxation is relatively pronounced, and precondition four for tax competition in an enlarged Europe is thus fulfilled.

As all preconditions for corporate income tax competition are fulfilled in an enlarged Europe, corporate income tax competition is a very likely scenario in the EU. In Sect. 2.6 we therefore discuss the implications of corporate income tax competition for FDI for the scope of national tax policies in an enlarged Europe.

2.6 Should and Will There Be Scope for National Tax Policy Within the EU in the Future?

The previous sections have shown that tax competition is, indeed, a likely scenario for the enlarged Europe. In the light of this evidence *should* national tax sovereignty be constrained? Given the stance of the European Commission towards tax coordination *will* there be national tax sovereignty in the future?

In general, the economic implications for national tax policy depend *inter alia* on the welfare effects, including economic efficiency and distributional effects as well as the tax revenue effects of tax competition and tax coordination. These, in turn, are encapsulated in various theories. The modern theories of tax competition may be divided atleast into three different strands, each of which contains certain implications for the desirability of tax competition mostly from an efficiency perspective and each of which is the basis for numerous extensions. [21] The first strand is based on Brennan and Buchanan (BB, 1980) and argues that the selfish behaviour of governments ("Leviathan view") leads to an inefficiently large size of the public sector. Hence, tax competition leads to "taming of the Leviathan". The second strand, which is based on Zodrow and Mieszkowski (ZM, 1986) predicts that tax competition leads to an inefficient and inadequate provision of public goods (inefficient size of the public sector) due to the imposition of distorting non-equivalent taxes on mobile tax bases.[22] The third strand is based on the new economic geography literature (e.g. Baldwin and Krugman, BK, 2004), where tax competition is one-sided due to agglomeration forces. Several partly contradictory policy conclusions on the desirability of tax competition in an enlarged Europe may be deduced from the various theories:

1. BB: If one subscribes to the Leviathan view of governments, our findings imply that intensified tax competition may be a useful device to restrain the size of EU Member state governments and reduce them to a more efficient scale. Hence, tax harmonisation is not desirable, as this leads to a "taxation cartel" and policy failures (e.g. Cnossen 2001 and Breuss 2002). Indeed, little can be said in favour of even the looser forms of tax coordination (cf. Table 2.1). Consequently, measures aimed at avoiding harmful tax competition and levelling the playing field (see Sect. 2.1) would thus be the sole policy recommendation.
2. ZM: If one believes in the negative implications of tax competition, our findings suggest that increased efforts have to be made to co-ordinate corporate tax policies at the supranational level. This would then lead to a reduction in the underprovision of public goods in the separate jurisdictions, and hence to efficiency gains.
3. BK: The New Economic Geography argues that high-income countries ("the core") can levy higher effective tax rates than low-income countries ("the periphery") due to location specific agglomeration rents, which accrue to firms in the core only (BK, p. 12). Tax rates will therefore differ in a systematic way between the core and the periphery ("bell-shaped equilibrium tax gap" depending on trade costs, BK, pp. 17). As the core can react to tax rate cuts in the periphery by lowering their tax rates tax

competition for mobile capital is one sided: the periphery will not try to attract FDI by lowering tax rates, it will set tax rates based on "purely domestic concerns" (BK, p. 21). Moreover, tax harmonisation would maintain the core-periphery divide. BK show that full tax harmonisation may be harmful to both the core and the periphery country-type, as it would lead to further deviation from the Pareto optimum. In particular, they show that harmonising tax rates at any given single level makes one or both country-types worse off. The most the Baldwin and Krugman recommend is a minimum tax rate set just below the lowest (the periphery) equilibrium tax rate. This makes the core better off as tax rate cuts of the periphery are no longer possible, hence relaxing a binding constraint on the core's choice of tax rates, without harming the periphery (BK, p. 21). Moreover, tax harmonisation rules out that the periphery attracts efficiency-oriented FDI which does not profit from agglomeration forces in the core by lowering effective corporate income tax rates and it may result in inefficient levels and / or qualities of public goods and services provided by the core country government (Zodrow 2003).

Given these competing theoretical views on tax competition, the question arises whether empirical evidence may point towards a preferred policy option. One strand of literature uses simulation models to evaluate various scenarios of tax competition and tax harmonisation (Sørensen 2001, 2004, Parry 2003, Mendoza and Tesar 2003, DG-TCU 2004, Brøchner et al. 2006). Although the simulation models tend to differ in various ways, e.g. different aims; different definitions of harmonisation, different types of simulation models etc. some tentative conclusions are still possible on the effects of tax competition and tax coordination, respectively.

1. DG-TCU (2004) arrives at a substantial loss of total tax revenue (approximately a 0.6 percentage change for the EU as a whole) in the full harmonisation scenario, though this result is very sensitive to the assumptions made. They conclude that the "economic gains from tax cooperation cannot be taken for granted … (and that the) … details of policy reform matter." (DG-TCU 2004, p. 18)
2. Parry "calculates the magnitude of the welfare costs of capital tax competition among regional governments in a model that allows for welfare-maximising and Leviathan behaviour by governments, an upward sloping capital supply curve, and non-competitive government behaviour. The welfare costs from the fiscal externalities due to tax competition are modest under many scenarios (Parry 2003, p. 54f.). Moreover the losses may quickly turn into gains if Leviathan behaviour by governments is allowed (Parry 2003).
3. The simulations, based on a two country model, undertaken by Mendoza and Tesar (2003) show that both countries (UK and C3, consisting of IT, DE and FR) may gain from tax competition (compared to a pre-tax competition equilibrium representing tax structures in the early 1980ies), especially if governments adjust to decreasing tax rates on capital by increasing

consumption taxes. In all cases considered they find the gains from tax coordination to be very modest.

4. Sørensen (2004), who compares the welfare gains from regional capital income tax coordination (e.g. coordination in the EU) to welfare gains from global tax coordination finds that the welfare gains from the former are relatively small compared to those of the latter. Moreover, the gains will accrue to countries with relatively high pre-coordination capital income tax rates.
5. DG-TCU (2004) shows that in a scenario without harmonisation and applying at the time of conducting the analysis existing tax rates the New Member States will loose tax revenue compared to the harmonisation scenario. In terms of the central issue of tax competition, the size of the public sector would have to shrink in the New Member States, *ceteris paribus*. As mentioned above, whether this is seen as an advantage or as a disadvantage depends on the view taken: While the ZM model would imply *inter alia* lower expenditure on infrastructure, the Leviathan view would argue that the possible overspending would be reduced to efficient levels. A further conclusion is that these countries would need greater transfer payments from EU structural funds. These transfers are necessary to compensate for tax-revenue losses and to avoid a deterioration of the quality and quantity of public infrastructure provided and/or a shifting of the tax burden to other (more immobile) tax bases, like labour (see point 7 below) and consumption.
6. Brøchner et al. (2006), which is an extension of DG-TCU (2004), similarly conclude that corporate tax coordination would lead to modest aggregate welfare gains only. This is especially the case if only corporate income tax bases are harmonised (Brøchner et al. 2006, p. 24). Moreover this simulation exercise once more shows that there will be loser and winner countries, which makes agreements on harmonisation measures, given the unanimity principle in the EU, unlikely without a suitable clearing mechanism. They also show that outcomes are determined by the details of the coordination policies and hence that the simulated welfare gains of harmonisation cannot be taken for granted.
7. Apart from efficiency effects, one has to consider distributional effects of tax competition. Simulations conducted by Sørensen show that the gains of tax harmonisation, although in total rather low, are highest for the "poorest" quintile of the income distribution (Nicodème 2006). Furthermore, concerning the distribution of the tax burden between capital and labour Winner (2005) finds evidence for a shift of tax burden to labour due to increasing capital mobility; i.e. increasing backward-looking tax rates on labour and decreasing backward-looking tax rates on capital with increasing capital mobility during the period 1965 to 2000. However, for more recent years there is some indication that this shift of tax burden to labour indicated by backward-looking rates has been reversed (see Sørensen 2003).[23]

In summary, like the theoretical models, the economic effects observed in the simulation exercises do not give a clearcut picture whether the EU should proceed with corporate tax coordination. The possible positive welfare effects can be considered as low[24] and – even more importantly – they are also highly uncertain. As models have to be simplifications of reality many important tax related features (e.g. transfer pricing and thin capitalisation issues as well as gains from a reduction in compliance costs[25]) have not been fully incorporated so far (Nicodème 2006). Ex ante, modelling these issues may alter simulation results in either direction – higher welfare gains due to harmonisation or even welfare losses. Furthermore, as the BK model, described above, can be thought of as reflecting more accurately the actual situation of Old (core) versus New Member States (periphery) in the EU. It underpins the view that full tax harmonisation at an intermediate level, which is the most likely outcome of tax harmonisation, might lead to welfare losses of the core and the periphery-countries. In particular, the New Member States would loose an instrument to attract FDI in fields, which do not benefit from agglomeration rents in core countries and core countries would loose tax revenues.

Hence, given the existing theoretical and empirical results as well as the high uncertainty surrounding the simulation results, full tax harmonisation in the EU cannot be recommended. To our opinion a partial tax harmonisation in the form of a (relatively low)[26] minimum statutory tax rate on corporate income combined with a strict enforcement of state aid rules and the Code of Conduct of Business Taxation to tackle harmful tax competition as well as the adoption of much less far reaching tax related measures than full harmonisation, which reduce the tax sensitivity of FDI, notably the introduction of a full cross-border loss offset (see Gèrard and Weiner 2003) is justified both from an efficiency (esp. BK model) as well as distributive point of view (simulation results).

Thereby a minimum tax rate is also capable to reduce profit shifting for which differences in the STRs are relevant (see above). Transfer pricing leads to violation of "inter-nation" or "interjurisdictional equity" (e.g. Musgrave 2000), as tax revenues do not accrue to the countries where public goods and services are used. Hence a reduction of profit shifting via transfer pricing is highly desirable. Moreover, as stressed by DeMooij (2004), a minimum tax rate on corporate income may reconcile the opposing views on tax competition: by establishing a floor on the tax rate it avoids a race to the bottom but it does not prevent strategic interactions in tax setting with efficiency-enhancing effects. Finally, for this type of coordination the likelihood of an agreement at the political level may be much higher than for other, more far reaching proposals.

Yet, in any case one has to bear in mind that in each harmonisation scenario competition with other parts of the tax system (including tax enforcement) is likely to result. Only if the economic impacts of this competition are less severe and more clear-cut than those without harmonisation the latter is justified.[27]

Finally, we turn to the question whether national tax policy *will* be a realistic scenario in Europe. The stance of the EU, the European Commission (EC) in particular, on corporate income tax competition and tax coordination is expressed in official documents. Various reports of the EU (e.g., European Commission 1997, 1998, 2001, 2003) imply first of all, that taxation is a means to reach the common objectives of the EU and secondly, that while the EU does not deny potentially harmful effects of tax competition there is no strong stance on tax coordination either.[28] The first point is expressed in a speech of the European Commissioner for Taxation and Customs: "(T)he question is not of having either tax competition or tax harmonisation. The real issue is the right mix of policies needed to reach our common objectives in the EU."[29]

The second attitude is reflected in the fact that EU measures to coordinate corporate income taxation to date are mainly aimed at levelling the playing field: "A large part of our tax policies in the direct tax field are not aimed at harmonising Member States' tax rules. Rather, we [...] want to ensure that the Member States' tax systems are mutually compatible and that they respect the European Treaties."[30] This view is also expressed in a speech by the European Commissioner for the Internal Market and Services: "Tax harmonisation is not on the agenda, nor will it be. ... Tax competition is a healthy spur to governments across Europe to manage their public finances carefully...".[31] Thus, the EU seems to promote a policy of regulation (regulatory policy) in the field of corporate income taxation with tax competition exerting efficiency-enhancing effects. The various measures to coordinate corporate income taxation within the EU, recently published in the "Bolkestein Report" (especially, optional common consolidated tax base and home state taxation),[32] despite bearing features of partial tax harmonisation, are no exception from this general picture. The aim of this report was to identify the main tax related provisions which distort cross-border economic activities in the EU. The proposed measures in the report therefore do not focus on issues of tax competition and tax coordination *per se*. They have a clear focus upon "more structural issues in corporate taxation" (Devereux 2004). The European Commission itself views these measures as the "only means by which true Internal Market conditions can be established in the corporate tax field" (European Commission 2003).

So it seems that there should and there will be scope for national tax policy for some time to come. Whether this room for discretion will be limited by the workings of tax competition itself will be decided *in praxi*. Finally, putting our results in perspective to Table 1.1 of Chap. 1 the EU will be closer to a position in the upper left hand cell (north-east). However from our analysis we cannot derive any corresponding conclusion about national sovereignty in public expenditure programmes. Yet, as taxes and expenditures are closely linked, it is very likely that there will be scope for national expenditure policy for some time to come, too.

Endnotes

1. This research has been carried out under research grant F-2008 of the FWF project on International Tax Coordination. Comments by Philipp Genschel are highly appreciated.
2. Levelling the playing field may be defined as treating all firms in equal circumstances the same with regard to legislation, taxes or subsidies (Appelman et al. 2003).
3. Note, that this assumption of independent jurisdictions is plausible in Europe. Apart from various measures to level the playing field, fiscal sovereignty in the field of corporate income taxation is in the hand of the member states (see Sect. 2.6 below).

4. Notably, National Accounts Data do not provide reliable data on corporate profits.
5. Note, that location decisions are also *indirectly* determined by EMTRs as these rates determine the optimal output level of an investment. But the *after-tax* profit of an investment is *directly* determined by the EATR (see Devereux and Griffith 1998).
6. BG, CR, CZ, HU, PL, RO, SK, SI.
7. AT, FR, DE, IT, NL, UK, US.
8. Note, that we consider neither the sphere of the shareholder nor net wealth taxes or real estate taxes, because we are concerned with corporate income taxation and because net wealth and real estate taxes do not play a significant role in the CEECs considered here (also see Finkenzeller and Spengel 2004, p. 19).
9. Due to the 95% exemption system in Italy, the rate does not drop to zero.
10. Also, one may argue that the fall in STRs from 2000 onwards may be caused by EU-legislation. In particular state aid rules disallow several tax related incentives. Hence, the drops in the STRs may be considered as a compensation for the abolishing of such tax incentives (see Devereux 2006b). But the crucial point is that the reduction in STRs is not mandatory whereas abolishing withholding tax rates on dividends is.
11. For further empirical evidence, see also Borensztein et al. 1998; Chakraborty and Basu 2004; Choe 2003; Liu et al. 2002; and Nair-Reichert and Weinhold 2001. For surveys, see Chowdhury and Mavrotas 2005; DeMello 1997; Hansen and Rand 2005; Lim 2001; and UNECE 2001.
12. www.waipa.org
13. downloaded 06-01-2006
14. http://europa.eu.int/comm/economy_finance/about/activities/sgp/scplist_en.htm
15. This subsection is based on Bellak and Leibrecht (2005).
16. Net-FDI-flows are a second best measure of location decisions of MNEs. The more suitable "property, plant and equipment" data are currently not available for most of the CEECs.
17. Data are taken from http://www.wcrl.ars.usda.gov/cec/java/lat-long.htm
18. The location factors are included in levels, because data inspection does not show the presence of severe outliers and since level variables imply that we are directly estimating semi-elasticities.
19. According to the Breusch-Pagan test for heteroscedasticity and the Arellano-Bond test for serial correlation the models estimated are confronted with non-spherical errors.
20. A regression-based Hausman-test for the endogeneity of *gdphome* and *gdphost* in Model 5 using home and host country population as instruments (e.g. Swenson 2004) does not reject the null hypothesis of exogeneity (1st stage regression F-values: 445.92 (gdphome) and 320.1 (gdphost), respectively; 2nd stage regression p-value of F-test on 1st stage residuals: 33.51). Furthermore the R^2 of Shea (Baum et al. 2003) is large. Hence the instruments used can be considered sufficient.
21. Models based on the Tiebout-model, which show that tax competition for mobile firms is efficient (see Oates 2001) and "theories of tax exporting" (tax competition may limit tendencies for overprovision of public services (see Zodrow 2003)) or "theories of preferential tax regimes" (preferential tax regimes can make tax competition less harmful (Keen 2001)) may be considered as further theoretical strands. Moreover, the increased likelihood of policy innovations due to fiscal competition as well as the "selection principle" (Sinn 1997) have to be mentioned, when analysing the effects of tax competition. Details on the various strands can be taken from e.g. Krogstrup (2004a), Wilson (1999) and Wilson and Wildasin (2004).
22. Results are valid for marginal investments as well as for investments with a positive economic rent due to firm-specific advantages (see Zodrow 2006).

23. A shift of tax burden from capital to labour, i.e. an increasing effective tax rate on labour and a decreasing tax rate on capital, is also not discernible from the backward-looking (implicit) tax rates as calculated by the European Commission (2005). In 2004 the implicit tax rate (ITR) on labour is slightly lower than in 1995 (for the EU-25, the EU-15 and the New Member States-10 (NMS-10)). The ITR on capital is higher for the EU-25 and EU-15 but lower for the NMS-10 in 2003 than in 1995. Moreover, the ITRs on labour and on capital are lower in 2004 and 2003, respectively, than in 2000 for all country-groups. However, these data show that labour is structurally (much) heavier taxed than capital. For the EU-25, the GDP weighted average ITR was 29.7 for capital vs. 36.6 for labour in 2003 (difference of 6.9 percentage points). The gap was 19 percentage points in 1995 when the ITR of capital is replaced by the ITR on corporate income and 15.8 percentage points in 2003.
24. Here one should ask "low compared to what?" Nicodème (2006) includes an interesting discussion. For example, he argues that the simulated welfare gains of a full tax harmonisation might be as large as those estimated for the adoption of the service directive.
25. These aspects are among the main drivers behind the Common Consolidated Corporate Tax Base (CCTB) proposal (see Andersson, Chap. 5).
26. As capital income is a more mobile tax base than labour income, tax rates on capital income should be lower than that on labour income. Moreover, as some EU-Member States already have rather low statutory tax rates on corporate income, a minimum tax rate of about 20 to 25 percent may be politically feasible only with a clearing mechanism. Moreover the level should be set in accordance with tax rates on interest income to reduce the possibility of a "lock-in effect" of a low corporate income tax rate (backstop-function).
27. An important example in this respect is the CCCTB proposal paired with formulary apportionment (FA) of the "Bolkestein Report" (see Andersson, Chap. 5). The economic effects of FA are unclear. For example, the corporate income tax may degenerate to a tax on the components included in the formula (usually labour, capital and sales; "Massachusetts-formula") (see Feld 2005). Hence, supply and demand distortions may arise with severer economic consequences than faced with the current system based on separate accounting.
28. The position of the EU towards tax coordination has changed over the years. In earlier reports the EU was in favour of harmonization of corporate income tax *systems* (Neumark Committee and van den Tempel Committee) or in favour of a minimum corporate tax rate of 30% (Ruding Committee).
29. Kovacs, p. 8; http://europa.eu.int/rapid/pressReleasesAction.do?reference=SPEECH/05/624&format=PDF&aged=1&language=EN&guiLanguage=en; download 1.2.2006
30. Kovacs, p. 5; http://europa.eu.int/rapid/pressReleasesAction.do?reference=SPEECH/05/624&format=PDF&aged=1&language=EN&guiLanguage=en; download 1.2.2006
31. http://europa.eu.int/rapid/pressReleasesAction.do?reference=SPEECH/05/679&format=PDF&aged=0&language=EN&guiLanguage=en; download 1.2.2006
32. See EC 2001 for details.

References

Appelman, M., Gorter, J., Lijesen, M., Onderstal, S. and R. Venniker (2003) Equal Rules or Equal Opportunities? Demystifying Level Playing Field, CPB Document, No 34.

Bach, S., Seidel, B. and W. Scheremet (2002) Internationale Entwicklungstendenzen nationaler Steuersysteme - von der direkten zur indirekten Besteuerung?, DIW-Sonderhefte 172, Berlin.

Balasubramanyam, V.N., Salisu, M. and D. Sapsford (1996) Foreign Direct Investment and Growth in EP and IS Countries, *The Economic Journal*, 106, pp. 92-105.

Baldwin, R. E. and P. Krugman (2004) Agglomeration, Integration and Tax Harmonisation, *European Economic Review*, 48, pp. 1–23.

Barba Navaretti, G. and A.J. Venables (2004) *Multinational firms in the world economy*, Princeton, N.J.: Princeton University Press.

Baum, C.F., Schaffer, M.E. and S. Stillman (2003) Instrumental Variables and GMM: Estimation and Testing, *Boston College, Department of Economics, Working paper* No. 545.

Bellak, C., Leibrecht, M. and R. Römisch (2005) A note on the appropriate measure of tax burden on Foreign Direct Investment to the CEECs, *HWWA Discussion Paper*, No. 336.

Bellak, C. and M. Leibrecht (2005) Foreign Direct Investment in Central- and East European Countries: A Panel Study, The Leverhulme Centre for Research on Globalisation and Economic Policy (GEP), Conference on "Foreign Direct Investment and Taxation", *Conference Paper*, downloadable at: http://www.nottingham.ac.uk/economics/leverhulme/conferences/Oct_2005_Conf/bellak_leibrecht_nottingham.pdf

Bellak, C. and M. Leibrecht (2006) Taxation of Foreign Direct Investment in Central- and East European Countries: Comparing Alternative Measures of Corporate Tax Burden, Proceedings of European Network on Industrial Policy, International Conference 2006.

Bevan, A., Estrin S., and K. Meyer (2004) Foreign investment location and institutional development in transition economies, *International Business Review*, 13, pp. 43–64.

Blomström, M. and A. Kokko (2003) The Economics of Foreign Direct Investment Incentives, *NBER Working Paper* 9489.

Bordignon, M. and S. Brusco (2006) On enhanced cooperation, *Journal of Public Economics*, vol. 90, pp 2063–2090.

Borenzstein, E., De Gregorio, J. and J.W. Lee (1998) How does Foreign Direct Investment affect Economic Growth? *Journal of International Economics*, 45, pp. 115–135.

Brainard, S. L. (1997) An empirical assessment of the proximity-concentration trade-off between multinational sales and trade, *The American Economic Review*, 87, pp. 520–44.

Brennan, G. and J. Buchanan (1980) *The Power to Tax*, Cambridge University Press.

Breuss, F. (2002) Die wirtschaftspolitische Architektur der WWU, *WIFO-Monatsberichte*, 9, pp. 581–607.

Brøchner, J., J. Jensen, P. Svensson and P.B. Sørensen (2006) The Dilemmas of Tax Coordination in the Enlarged European Union, CESIFO Working Paper No. 1859, Category 1: Public Finance, November.

Brueckner, J.K. (2003) Strategic Interaction among Governments: An Overview of Empirical Studies, *International Regional Science Review*, 26, 2, pp. 175–188.

Buch, C., and A. Lipponer (2004) Clustering or competition? The foreign investment behaviour of German banks, *Deutsche Bundesbank Discussion Paper Series* 1: Studies of the Economic Research Centre No. 06.

Carkovic, M. and R. Levine (2005) Does foreign direct investment accelerate economic growth? In: T. Moran, E. Graham and M. Blomstrom, eds., *Does foreign direct investment promote development?* Institute for International Economics Publication, Washington, DC, pp. 195-220.

Chakraborty, C. and P. Basu (2002) Foreign Direct Investment and Growth in India: a Cointegration Approach, *Applied Economics*, 34, pp. 1061-1073.

Choe, J.I. (2003) Do foreign direct investment and gross domestic investment promote economic growth? *Review of Development Economics*, 7, pp. 44-57.

Chowdhury, A., and G. Mavrotas. (2005) FDI and Growth: A Causal Relationship, *UNU-Wider Research Paper* No. 2005/25.

Clausing, K.A. and C.L. Dorobantu (2005) Re-entering Europe: Does European Union candidacy boost foreign direct investment? *Economics of Transition*, 13, pp. 77-103.

Cnossen, S. (2001) Tax Policy in the European Union: A Review of Issues and Options, *FinanzArchiv*, 58, pp. 1-93.

DeMello, L.R. (1997) Foreign Direct Investment in Developing Countries and Growth: A Selective Survey, *The Journal of Development Studies*, 34, pp. 1-34.

DeMooij, R. (2004) Does the enlarged European Union need a minimum corporate tax rate? *Intereconomics*, 39, pp. 180-182.

DeMooij, R. A. and S. Ederveen (2005) Update von: Taxation and Foreign Direct Investment: A Synthesis of Empirical Research, The Leverhulme Centre for Research on Globalisation and Economic Policy (GEP), Conference on "Foreign Direct Investment and Taxation", *Conference Paper*, downloadable at: http://www.nottingham.ac.uk/economics/leverhulme/conferences/Oct_2005_Conf/ruud_de_mooij_paper.pdf

DeMooij, R. A. and S. Ederveen (2003) Taxation and foreign direct investment: a synthesis of empirical research, *International Tax and Public Finance* 10, pp. 673-693.

Devereux, M.P. and R. Griffith (1998) Taxes and the location of production: evidence from a panel of US multinational, *Journal of Public Economics*, 68, 1998, pp. 335-367.

Devereux, M.P. and R. Griffith (1999) The taxation of discrete investment choices, *IFS Working Paper Series* No. W98/16.

Devereux, M.P. and R. Griffith (2002) The impact of corporate taxation on the location of capital: a review, *Swedish Economic Policy Review*, 9, pp. 79-102.

Devereux, M.P. and R. Griffith (2003) Evaluating tax policy for location decisions. *International Tax and Public Finance*, 10, pp. 107-126.

Devereux, M.P., Lockwood, B. and M. Redoano (2004) Do Countries Compete over Corporate Tax Rates? mimeo, University of Warwick.

Devereux, M. P. and G. R. Hubbard (2004) Taxing Multinationals, *International Tax and Public Finance*, 10, 2004, pp. 469 – 487.

Devereux, M. P. (2004) Debating Proposed Reforms of the Taxation of Corporate Income in the European Union. *International Tax and Public Finance*, 11, pp. 71-89.

Devereux, M. P (2006a) The Impact of taxation on the Location of Capital, Firms and Profit: A Survey of Empirical Evidence, University of Warwick, mimeo, April 2006.

Devereux, M. P (2006b) Taxes in the EU New Member States and the Location of Capital and Profit, University of Warwick, mimeo, January 2006.

DG-TCU (2004) *Economic effects of tax cooperation in an enlarged European Union: Simulations of corporate tax harmonization and savings tax coordination*, Final report, October, DG Taxation and Customs Union, published by Copenhagen Economics.

Dunning, J. H. (1988) *Explaining International Production* (London: Unwin Hyman).

Egger, P. (2000) A note on the proper specification of the gravity equation, *Economics Letters* 66, pp. 25–31.

Egger, P. and M. Pfaffermayr (2003) The proper panel econometric specification of the gravity equation: A three-way model with bilateral interaction effects, *Empirical Economics*, 28, pp. 571–580.

European Bank for Reconstruction and Development (various years), *Transition Report*, London.

European Commission (1997) *Towards Tax Co-ordination in the European Union: A Package to Tackle Harmful Tax Competition*, COM(97) 495 Final, Brussels.

European Commission (1998) Conclusions of the ECOFIN Council Meeting on 1 December 1997 Concerning Taxation Policy, *Official Journal of the European Communities* C2(6/1/98).

European Commission (2001) *Company taxation in the internal market*, COM (2001) 582 final (Bolkestein Report).

European Commission (2003) *An Internal Market without company tax obstacles: achievements, ongoing initiatives and remaining challenges*, Communication from the Commission to the Council, the European Parliament and the European Economic and Social Committee (COM (2003) 726).

European Commission (2005) Structures of the Taxation Systems in the European Union 1995 – 2004, Brussels.

European Commission (www) http://europa.eu/scadplus/nice_treaty/cooperations_en.htm (download: December 2006).

Eurostat (2002) *European Union Foreign Direct Investment Yearbook 2001*, Luxembourg.

Feld, L. P. (2005) Capital Taxation in an Enlarged EU: The Case for Tax Competition, OeNB Workshops, Proceedings of OeNB Workshops, Capital Taxation after EU Enlargement, January, pp. 118 – 150.

Finkenzeller, M. and Ch. Spengel (2004) *Measuring the Effective Levels of Company Taxation in the New Member States: A Quantitative Analysis*, European Commission Taxation Papers, Working Paper 7, Paris.

Frenkel, M., Funke, K. and G. Stadtmann (2004) A panel analysis of bilateral FDI flows to emerging economies, *Economic Systems* 28, pp. 281–300.

Fuest, C. and W. Fuest (2004) A minimum corporate tax rate would be harmful for both high and low tax countries, *Intereconomics*, 39, pp. 183–186.

Fuest, C. and B. Huber (2003) Zur Koordinierung der Unternehmensbesteuerung in Europa, *Vierteljahrshefte zur Wirtschaftsforschung*, 72, pp. 378–390.

Genschel, P. (2002) *Steuerharmonisierung und Steuerwettbewerb in der Europäischen Union*, Campus Verlag, Frankfurt/New York.

Gèrard, M. and J.M. Weiner (2003) Cross-Border Loss Offset and Formulary Apportionment: How Do They Affect Multijurisdictional Firm Investment Spending and Interjursidictional Tax Competition? *CESifo Working Paper*, No. 1004.

Gordon, R., Kalambokidis, L. and J. Slemrod (2003) Do we now collect any tax revenue from taxing capital income? *Journal of Public Economics*, 88, pp. 981–1009.

Gorter, J. and A. Parikh (2003) How sensitive is FDI to differences in corporate income taxation within the EU? *DeEconomist*, 151, pp. 193–204.

Grabowski, M.H. (2005) Reforms of Tax Sytems in Transition Countries, *Transition Studies Review*, 12, pp. 293–312.

Griffith, R. and A. Klemm (2005) What has been the tax competition experience of the last 20 years? *The Institute of Fiscal Studies, Working Paper* 04/05.

Hansen, H. and J. Rand (2005) On the Causal Links between FDI and Growth in Developing Countries, *UNU-Wider Research Paper* No. 2005/31.

Hansson, Å. and K. Olofsdotter (2004) Integration and tax competition: An empirical study for OECD countries, *Department of Economics, Lund University*, mimeo.

Haufler, A. (2001) *Taxation in a Global Economy*, Cambridge University Press.

Head, K. (2003) *Gravity for beginners*, Web Download.

Hellerstein, W. and C. McLure (2004) The European Commission's Report on Company Income Taxation: What the EU Can Learn from the Experience of the US States, *International Tax and Public Finance*, 11, pp. 199–220.

Hirschman, A.O. (1970) *Exit, Voice, and Loyalty: Responses to Decline in Firms, Organizations, and States*, Cambridge: Harvard University Press.

Jacobs, O. H. and C. Spengel (2002) *Effective Tax Burden in Europe*, ZEW Economic Studies, Vol. 15, Heidelberg / New York.

Keen, M. (1996) The welfare economics of tax coordination in the European Community, in: M.P. Devereux (ed.) *The economics of tax policy*, Oxford University Press., pp. 189–214.

Keen, M. (1998) Vertical Tax Externalities in the Theory of Fiscal Federalism, *IMF Staff Papers*, 45, September.

King, M. A. and D. Fullerton (1984) *The Taxation of Income from Capital*, The University of Chicago Press, Chicago and London.

Klemm, A. (2004) A minimum rate without a common base? *Intereconomics*, 39, pp. 186–189.

Krogstrup, S. (2004a) A Synthesis of Recent Developments in the Theory of Capital Tax Competition, *EPRU Working Paper*, 02/2004, Copenhagen.

Krogstrup, S. (2004b) Are Corporate Tax Burdens Racing to the Bottom in the European Union? *EPRU Working Paper*, 04/2004, Copenhagen.

Leibrecht, M. and R. Römisch (2002) Comparison of tax burden, *WIIW Research Report* No. 292, Vienna.

Lim, E.-G. (2001) Determinants of, and the Relation Between, Foreign Direct Investment and Growth: A Summary of the Recent Literature, *IMF Working Paper*, WP/01/175.

Liu, X., Burridge, P. and P.J.N. Sinclair (2002) Relationships between Economic Growth, Foreign Direct Investment and Trade: Evidence from China. *Applied Economics*, 34, pp. 1433–1440.

Maher, M. and H. Christiansen (2001) *Growth, Technology Transfer and Foreign Direct Investment*, OECD Paper presented at the OECD Global Forum on International Investment, Mexico City, November.

Markusen, J. R. (2002) Multinational Firms and the Theory of International Trade, MIT Press, Cambridge, MA.

Mátyás, L. (1997) Proper Specification of the Gravity Model, *The World Economy*, 20, pp. 363–368.

Mátyás, L., Kónya N. and M.N. Harris (2001) Modelling Export Activity of Eleven APEC Countries, *Melbourne Institute Working Paper*, No. 5/00.

Mendoza, E.G., Razin, A. and L.L. Tesar (1994) Effective tax rates in macro-economics, Cross-country estimates of tax rates on factor incomes and consumption, *Journal of Monetary Economics*, 34, pp. 297–323.

Mendoza, E.G, and L.L. Tesar (2003) Winners and Losers of Tax Competition in the European Union, *NBER Working Paper,* No. 10051.

Musgrave, P. B (2000) Interjurisdictional Equity in Company Taxation: Principles and Applications to the European Union, in: Cnossen, S. (ed.) Taxing Capital in the European Union, Oxford University Press, Oxford.

Musgrave, R. A. (1990) Comment on Whalley, J. Foreign responses to US tax reform, in: Slemrod, J. (ed.) Do Taxes Matter? The Impact of the Tax Reform Act of 1986, The MIT Press, Cambridge and London, pp. 315 – 318.

Mutti, J. and H. Grubert (2004) Empirical Asymmetries in Foreign Direct Investment and Taxation, *Journal of International Economics*, 62, pp. 337–358.

Nair-Reichert, U. and D. Weinhold (2001) Causality tests for cross-country panels: a new look at FDI and economic growth in developing countries, *Oxford Bulletin of Economics and Statistics*, 63, pp. 153–171.

Nicodème, G. (2001) Computing effective corporate tax rates: comparisons and results, *Directorate General for Economic and Financial Affairs, Economic Paper* No. 153.

Nicodème, G. (2006) Corporate tax Competition and Coordination in the European Union: what do we know? Where do we stand?, Directorate-General for Economic and Financial Affairs, European Economy, *European Commission, Economic Papers*, no. 250.

Oates, W.E. (2001) Fiscal competition or harmonisation? Some reflections, *National Tax Journal,* LIV, pp. 507–512.

OECD (1991) *Taxing Profits in a Global Economy: Domestic and International Issues*, Paris.

OECD (1998) *Harmful Tax Competition: An Emerging Global Issue*, Paris.

OECD (2004) *International Direct Investment Statistics Yearbook 1991 –2002*, Paris.

Parry, I.W.H. (2003) How large are the Welfare Costs of Tax Competition? *Journal of Urban Economics*, 54, pp. 39–60.

Pinto, C. (2003) *Tax Competition and EU Law*, EUCOTAX Series on European Taxation, Kluwer Law International: The Hague.

Randzio-Plath, C. (2000) Entwurf eines Berichtes über die Fortschritte bei der Steuerkoordinierung in der Europäischen Union*, (2000/2040(INI) Par 2, Ausschuß für Wirtschaft und Währung.*

Rodrik, D. (1997) Has Globalization Gone Too Far, Institute for International Economics, Washington D.C.

Sinn, H.W (1997) The Selection Principle and Market Failure in Systems Competition, *Journal of Public Economics*, 66, pp. 247–274.

Slemrod, J. (2004) Are corporate tax rates, or countries, converging?, *Journal of Public Economics*, vol. 88, pp. 1169–1186.

Sørensen, P.B. (2001) Tax coordination in the European Union: What are the issues? *Swedish Economic Policy Review*, 8, pp. 143–195.

Sørensen, P.B. (2003) International Tax Competition: A New Framework for Analysis, *Economic Analysis & Policy*, 33, pp. 179–192.

Sørensen, P.B. (2004) International Tax Coordination: Regionalism versus Globalism, *Journal of Public Economics*, 88, pp. 1187–1214.

Swenson, D.L. (2004) Foreign Investment and the Mediation of Trade Flows, *Review of International Economics*, 12, pp. 609–629.

Treaty of Nice (2002) http://www.eurotreaties.com/nice.html (download: December 2006).

Treaty of Amsterdam (1997) http://www.eurotreaties.com/amsterdamtext.html (download: December 2006).

UNECE (2001) *Survey of Europe 2001*: Ch. 5: Economic Growth and Foreign Direct Investment in the Transition Economies, Luxembourg.

Van Ark, B. and E. Monnikhof (2000) *Productivity and Unit Labour Cost Comparisons: A Database*, Employment Paper, No. 5, International Labour Organisation, Geneva.

Volkerink, B. and J. DeHaan (2002) Tax ratios in macroeconomics: Do taxes really matter?, *Empirica*, 29, pp. 209–224.

Weiner, J. M and H.J. Ault (1998) The OECD's Report on harmful Tax Competition, *National Tax Journal*, 51, 3, pp. 601–608.

Wildasin, D. E. (2002) Tax coordination: The importance of institutions, *Swedish Economic Policy Review*, 9, pp. 171–194.

Wildasin, D. E. (2005) Fiscal Competition, *IFIR Working Paper* No. 2005–05.

Wilson, J. D. (1999) Theories of Tax Competition, *National Tax Journal*, 52, pp. 269–304.

Wilson, J. D. and D. E. Wildasin (2004) Capital Tax Competition: Bane or Boon? *Journal of Public Economics*, 88, pp. 1065–1091.

Winner, H. (2005) Has Tax Competition Emerged in OECD Countries? Evidence from Panel Data, *International Tax and Public Finance*, 12, pp. 667–687.

Wooldridge, J. M. (2002) *Econometric Analysis of Cross Section and Panel Data* (Cambridge: MIT-Press).
Zodrow, G. R. (2003) Tax Competition and Tax Coordination in the European Union, *International Tax and Public Finance*, 10, pp. 651–671.
Zodrow, G.R. (2006) Capital Mobility and Source-Based Taxation of Capital Income in Small Open Economies, *International Tax and Public Finance*, 13, pp. 269–294.
Zodrow, G. R. and P. Mieskowski (1986) Pigout, Tiebout, Property Taxation and the Underprovision of Local Public Goods, *Journal of Urban Economics*, 19, pp. 356–370.

Chapter 3
Free Factor Mobility and Fiscal Competition: Can the National Welfare State Survive in a "United Europe"?

Åsa Hansson

3.1 Introduction

Providing social protection is an important task and ambition for many European governments. In 2003, for example, the 15 old member states spent on average over 28 percent of their GDP on social protection (Eurostat, 2006). Even though the variation within member states is wide, the government's role as a provider of social protection is generally greater than in other parts of the world. In the US and Japan, for instance, the governments spend about half as much (as a share of GDP) and in Korea only a fifth (OECD, 2001a). That the government should provide generous social protection is well rooted among the European citizens, who in general are positive to current levels of welfare spending and negative to cutbacks (Boeri et al., 2001).

Another important goal in Europe, integration, has been a priority dating back at least to the end of the Second World War. While the motivation for European integration was initially primarily political, including the desire to avoid future warfare in Europe, contemporary discussion often centres on the economic benefits of free factor mobility. Indeed, the Lisbon Strategy aims to make Europe the most competitive and dynamic knowledge-based economy in the world by 2010. To meet the challenges of the Lisbon Strategy, however, many believe that the mobility within EU must increase considerably, and 2006 was, in fact, designated the "European year of workers' mobility". Unfettered mobility has been credited, for instance, with increasing efficiency (lowering costs) by removing barriers to the realisation of scale economics and with increasing competition, thus increasing the range of products offered to consumers while lowering prices (Emerson et al., 1988).

It has become increasingly apparent that these two goals–generous social protection and free mobility–may be hard to combine. Free factor mobility permits economic actors, both labour and capital, to locate where their economic welfare is maximised and, consequently, member states may find it increasingly difficult to levy taxes exceeding those of other Member States without losing capital and the most productive workers or to offer generous transfers without attracting less productive individuals. Over time, the competition for mobile production factors threatens to lead toward a downward spiral in tax rates (Zodrow and Mieszkowski, 1986). In short, not only may generous welfare states struggle to survive as net contributors leave and net beneficiaries enter, but the provision of public services may decline generally across even the initially low-tax countries. As a consequence, many argue for the need to harmonise or coordinate tax and transfer policies within the EU in order to maintain acceptable levels of social protection (Sinn, 2002, and Tanzi, 2002).[1]

It is not obvious that coordination within EU is feasible or even desirable, however. First of all, regional coordination may be fruitless in a world where capital is globally mobile and labour increasingly so. A large threat to the national welfare states in Europe is competition from outside the EU, for instance, firms outsourcing to Asia. Second, there are important efficiency arguments favouring competition (Wilson, 2005). Coordination may also require that nations give up yet another tool available for guiding their economies. Clearly, any gains from coordination must outweigh the gains from competition to justify coordination. As the globalisation process increases the cost of the welfare state the benefits from the welfare state must increase accordingly.

This chapter discusses the consequences of increased integration on the ability of Member States to conduct independent fiscal policy with a focus on redistribution and the survival of the national welfare state. The chapter begins with a short description of the "welfare state" in Europe. The next section discusses how free factor mobility may threaten the national welfare state both by providing downward pressure on tax rates and, thus, the means to finance social spending and by forcing governments to spend strategically in ways attractive to desirable production factors. The chapter then moves on to examine possible countervailing factors which may ensure at least some ability for conducting independent fiscal policies. For instance, labour mobility is so far limited enabling member countries to still conduct some independent fiscal policy. In addition, the need for a welfare state may be reduced as the benefits from integration in terms of increasing market size and efficiency gains are utilised, which may compensate for some of the lost fiscal autonomy. Finally, the chapter discusses the trade-off between coordination and competition where the positive effects of competition are set against the negative externalities of fiscal competition.

3.2 The Welfare State in Europe

Europeans generally agree on the value of extensive social protection. Indeed, relative to other continents, welfare transfers are considerably larger in Europe. In 1998, for example, public expenditures on social protection constituted almost 25 percent of GDP in EU15 compared to less than 21 percent for the whole OECD and on average 17 percent for the US, Canada, Australia, New Zealand, and Japan (OECD, 2001a). In Korea and Mexico, corresponding numbers were only 5.9 and

8.2 percent, respectively. The wide range in public social protection suggests that social protection in other continents is to a larger extent provided by the family or the market.

There are several economic arguments for providing this social protection collectively rather than through private markets. First, moral hazard is a critical problem for insurance against such risks as becoming poor, and private markets are unlikely to operate at efficient levels or to arise altogether. Similarly, adverse selection may also discourage the creation of private social protection markets. Finally, the problem of free riders may limit voluntary redistribution even when most people care about the welfare of others (at least to some extent). Compulsory redistribution may, indeed, result in Pareto improvements.

At the same time, publicly financed social protection has an economic cost. One obvious cost of social protection is that associated with collecting the revenues required to finance social protection. To a large extent this is done through taxes on labour (see Chap. 4). Obtaining the required revenues involves not only redistribution from those working to those receiving the benefit but also a welfare cost (excess burden) due to taxes' distortionary effects. In addition to tax-related distortions, transfer recipients may also change their behaviour creating an additional distortion. The optimal level of social protection is thus when the marginal benefit of social protection equals the marginal cost. To determine this level, however, requires information on both the marginal benefit and the marginal cost of social protection, something that is not easily done in reality.

Though there is no universally accepted definition, the term "welfare state" has loosely come to mean a regime where the state accepts responsibility for the provision of social protection for its citizens in the form of risk insurance and equality. This risk insurance involves public transfers designed to protect against income uncertainty (e.g., due to unemployment or sickness) and to assist the elderly and the poor (e.g., via intergenerational and inter-class transfers).

Even within Europe, however, there is great variation in the ambition, preferences and means for achieving equality and reducing risk and hence in the provision of social protection. In Chap. 4, for instance, numbers are presented showing that expenditures on social protection as a share of GDP range from 14.3 percent in Latvia to 32.5 percent in Sweden. Even within "old Europe", the range is wide: 16 percent in Ireland compared to 32.5 percent in Sweden. Esping-Andersen (1990) identified three different distinct styles of welfare states in Europe: the universal welfare regime predominant in northern Europe, the corporate welfare regime in, for instance, Germany and Austria and the liberal welfare regime in Ireland and the UK (see Chap. 4 for a further description of these welfare regimes).

More recently, Ferrera (1998) and Bertola et al. (2001) suggested a new dichotomy that includes four different categories of welfare states in "old Europe" distinguished by level of social protection provided and target beneficiaries. The wage structure also varies considerably between these welfare states affecting the income distribution. The four models are Nordic, Continental, Mediterranean, and Anglo-Saxon. The welfare state in the Nordic countries, including Denmark, Finland, Sweden, and the Netherlands, is characterised by a high level of social protection, universal welfare benefits based on the citizenship principle, relatively extensive interventions in labour markets and strong labour unions that ensure a relatively compressed wage structure.

In contrast, the Anglo-Saxon countries, including Ireland and the UK, have a less extensive welfare state where social assistance is seen as a last resort and primarily oriented to people in working-age. Weak unions and comparatively wide and increasing wage dispersion and a high incidence of low-pay employment characterise the labour market.

The Continental countries, including Austria, Belgium, Germany, France, and Luxembourg, employ extensive insurance-based non-employment benefits and old-age pensions that rely on contributions on employment income, and while labour unions are on decline they still exercise a strong influence.

Finally, the Mediterranean countries, including Greece, Italy, Portugal, and Spain, focus their welfare spending on old-age pensions and typically concentrate on employment protection and early retirement to exempt groups of the working age population from participating in the labour market. Strong labour unions in the formal sectors have compressed the wage structure.

3.3 The Threat to the National Welfare State in Europe from Free Factor Mobility

In Europe, there are currently no institutions at the EU level capable of collecting taxes or social contributions to finance welfare transfers so social welfare is provided at the national level. There is widespread concern among politicians and economists alike that increased globalisation, and in particular increased factor mobility related not only to the "internal market" but to the global market as well, will introduce harmful inter-country competition which will threaten the very survival of the welfare state (Sinn, 2002, and Tanzi, 2002).

Two hypotheses are central to these fears. First, countries may be pressured to lower their tax rates, hence reducing tax collections and their means to redistribute, in the competition for increasingly mobile capital and labour. Second, the competition for mobile productive factors may put pressure on nations to adopt fiscal policies strategically favourable to capital and workers rather than providing socially desirable levels of public goods and redistribution (henceforth referred to as fiscal competition).

Tax Competition

An extensive literature suggests that tax competition may lead to inefficiently low tax rates and sub-optimal levels of public spending (e.g., Zodrow and Mieszkowski, 1986, Wilson, 1986, 1991). The resulting underprovision arises because changes in tax rates in one jurisdiction affect tax bases in other jurisdictions, an externality which is not internalised when decisions about tax rates changes are made in the first jurisdiction. That is, when a country chooses its tax rate it ignores the impact on capital and labour location decisions occurring in other countries (positive or negative). Tax rate decreases, thus, may be larger than what is globally optimal had the externality been internalised. Consequently, it becomes increasingly costly to deviate from the tax rates in competing countries, and tax rates, therefore, tend to converge. Furthermore, this competition makes it difficult for countries to maintain desired tax rate levels without loosing dynamic firms and able workers, and lead to a "race to the bottom".

The standard model of tax competition rests on the assumption that there exist a large number of homogeneous jurisdictions. Wilson (1991) and Bucovetsky (1991) relax this assumption to allow for "asymmetric" tax competition between large and small jurisdictions. If the larger jurisdictions are large enough to affect after-tax return on capital, they tend to have higher equilibrium tax rates than smaller jurisdictions because they are less concerned about tax-induced capital outflows since they face lower capital supply elasticities. Thus, in contrast to the standard tax competition, asymmetric tax competition allows different tax rates in small and large countries, respectively, and a tax-induced capital flow from smaller to larger countries.

To make the model more compatible with conditions within the EU, researchers have developed models of tax competition whereby a limited number of countries interact strategically. These models also predict downward pressure on redistribution due to free factor mobility but less drastic than that predicted by the traditional tax competition models. For instance, the equilibrium redistribution levels will depend negatively on the number of countries competing as well as on the mobility of the production factors. When the number of regions and production factor mobility are limited, some measure of redistribution will still be possible.

Proponents of tax coordination or harmonisation have used these results to argue that global welfare would increase if tax reform decisions were taken at a supra-national level in order to internalise external effects affecting other countries' tax bases (e.g., Sinn, 1990, and Tanzi and Bovenberg, 1990). Moreover, the proponents of harmonisation fear that a downward spiral in tax rates will endanger desired government spending. Even if an individual country can gain from tax competition (by winning the race) the losses to the global economy as a whole may be large.

Nevertheless, views differ widely across economists and it is not clear that tax competition is unambiguously harmful and needs to be tamed. Indeed, economists historically have even considered tax competition as healthy and vital for efficiency. The seminal examination of tax competition, Tiebout (1956), for instance, postulates a general equilibrium in which independent jurisdictions compete to attract mobile households by supplying different mixes of taxes and public expenditures, resulting in an efficient provision of public services in all jurisdictions, and household relocation ensures that each household finds a jurisdiction satisfying their preferences. Individuals, "voting with their feet", enforce strict discipline on government leading to efficient outcomes.

Tiebout's hypothesis, originally designed for household mobility, applies equally well to firm mobility (White, 1975, Fischel, 1975, and Wellisch, 2000). Jurisdictions compete to attract firms by providing favourable tax rates and useful public services. In equilibrium, firms locate efficiently across the regions and the tax rates they face reflect the cost of providing "public inputs".

The model is less well-suited for personal capital gains taxation, however, where investors can often avoid taxation by residing in regions/countries where personal income is taxed relatively hard but place their capital in low-tax jurisdictions because of incomplete international control. Where income and capital gains taxation follows the residence principle, that is taxation takes place in the country where the taxpayer resides rather than where the income or gain was made, the model functions better.

In the EU context, the Tiebout hypothesis implies that tax competition will lead the different member states to supply public goods and services efficiently, that equilibrium tax rates and public goods and service levels will generally differ, and that each EU resident will relocate to where her/his preferences are best satisfied. Tax competition within the EU, thus, should lead to efficient provision of public resources and the EU should consequently encourage fiscal competition and avoid coordination.

To realise the positive effects of tax competition predicted by the model, however, a large number of quite unrealistic assumptions must be met. In particular, a large number of jurisdictions must exist permitting each household or firm to find its optimal mix of taxes and expenditures and individuals and firms must be fully mobile,[2] so it is debatable whether the model is applicable for competition between countries. Moreover, the model disregards economies of scale in public production, which can make it inefficient to have many independent jurisdictions each independently supplying public goods and services.

More recently, however, economists have started to question again whether tax competition is harmful and needs to be tamed. The reasons for this are several. First, the result that tax competition leads to a suboptimal small government rests on the assumption that the initial size of government is optimal. If the government is driven by revenue-maximising behaviour of bureaucrats or by the interplay of interest groups rather than a desire to maximise social welfare or satisfy the median voter the resulting government size can be excessive (Brennen and Buchanan, 1980, and Edwards and Keen, 1996). If this is the case, tax competition could have a disciplinary effect on wasteful governments. Second, tax competition may force countries to adopt more efficient tax systems. It is well known, for instance, that taxing mobile tax bases is associated with larger efficiency losses than taxing less mobile tax bases and the welfare gains from efficient taxation can be substantial (Mendoza and Tesar, 2005).

Empirical Evidence of Tax Competition and Alternative Explanations

Whether or not tax competition poses a threat to the welfare state hinges on whether tax competition theory correctly describes reality. Time series of corporate tax rates, for instance, suggest a downward trend. Average OECD corporate tax rates declined by 12 percentage points between 1986 and 2003 (OECD, 2001b, and, 2004) and average EU15 corporate tax rates declined by 3.4 percentage points between 2000 and 2003 (OECD, 2004). The expected reductions in corporate tax revenues have not followed, however. Indeed, despite declining tax rates, they actually increased in the 1990's, though perhaps in part because of favourable business conditions and corresponding increases in the tax base.

Whether this decline in corporate tax rates is caused by tax competition or something else cannot be determined exclusively from these numbers. A vast and growing empirical literature, however, has tried to determine whether tax rates have declined due to tax competition. To briefly summarise, earlier studies generally failed to reach a consensus that increased integration led to lower tax rates on corporate income. Indeed, many studies actually found a positive relationship between corporate tax rates and integration (e.g., Garratt, 1995, Quinn, 1997, and Swank, 2001). This somewhat counterintuitive result has been explained by the compensation hypothesis: increased integration increases the demand for social protection and hence tax rates. More recent studies, using more sophisticated techniques, have generally found relatively robust evidence of a negative relation between integration and tax rates on corporate income (see Griffith and Klemm, 2004 for a recent survey and Winner, 2006), however, even though exceptions exist (e.g., Dreher, 2006). The result is somewhat sensitive to the choice of tax burden studied. Dreher (2006), for example, found that the overall influence of globalisation – including economic, political as well as social integration – on corporate tax rates is positive when using average effective tax rates based on tax revenues while negative when using statutory tax rates. Similarly, Slemrod (2004) obtained a positive relationship between integration and average corporate tax rates (based on revenues collected) but a negative relationship when statutory tax rates were used. The use of tax measures based on historical tax revenues collected can be questioned as they are backward-looking and the investment and location decisions that drive tax competition depend on current and expected future tax rates.

A related literature highlights the interdependence of governments by estimating a reaction function that captures how jurisdictions adjust tax rates depending on the tax policy of its neighbouring jurisdictions, providing further support for the standard tax competition literature (see for instance Besley and Case, 1995, Devereux et al., 2002, and Brueckner, 2003).

The effects of increased integration on other tax bases, in particular labour and capital gains income, have been less well studied, though several papers (e.g., Razin et al., 2002) find that increased labour mobility negatively affects labour tax rates. Even though data point to a downward pressure on labour tax rates, the data are not yet robust and integration is typically not blamed for the downward trend as it took place before labour mobility increased and was primarily driven by tax reforms in the late 1980's and early 1990's aimed at increasing efficiency.

The evidence suggestive of tax competition in the EU has so far been limited primarily to corporate tax rates, which are still far from zero, and the worst fears of a race to the bottom as projected by many have not been realised. This absence of a race to the bottom has sparked a search for alternative explanations. One obvious candidate may be that production factors are not as freely mobile as assumed in theoretical models, especially labour which may be constrained by language and cultural barriers in addition to pecuniary relocation costs. Moreover, even capital does not move seamlessly. Evidence of "home-bias", whereby investors prefer investing financial capital at home abounds (French and Poterba, 1991, and Tesar and Werner, 1995). For corporate capital, there are still means for "home countries" to tax companies located in low-tax countries, for example Controlled Foreign Company taxation, that reduces the gains from relocating. Moreover, attracting firms requires more than low tax rates. For example, it is also important to provide a business friendly climate in general, including working infrastructure and an educated labour force.

Recently, researchers have begun to question whether the relationship between increased integration and taxation must unambiguously be negative. For instance, one consequence of increased globalisation has been an increasing share of foreign ownership, providing governments the ability to increase tax rates and, hence, shift the tax burden from domestic to foreign tax payers, i.e., tax exporting. An empirical study by Huizinga and Nicodemes (2003), for example, found that each one percentage point increase in the share of foreign ownership was associated with an increase in the corporate tax rate of between one-half and one percent.

Burbidge et al. (2006) expand this line of thought and introduce heterogeneous firms earning profits that can be taxed. They argue that tax competition can result in higher taxes and even in overprovision of publicly provided goods with a large share of foreign ownership and a high degree of heterogeneity because governments view the profit accruing to the foreigners as "free money" and are tempted to annex a share through taxation.

Researchers in the field of economic geography offer a perhaps more important explanation of the absence of a race to the bottom (Baldwin and Krugman, 2000). By relaxing the assumptions of constant returns to scale and perfect competition, these models predict that firms tend to concentrate in specific regions, the "core", where production is located close to other producers and consumers in order to realise advantages from linkages in production and consumption. Increased integration, with lower trade and transportation costs, tends to increase the importance of these linkages and strengthen the agglomeration forces to certain regions or countries where industries "lock in", hence limiting factor mobility. As a consequence, the regions where industries and labour choose to locate experienced increased tax bases and may be able (at least to some degree) to raise tax rates. At least theoretically, thus, it is possible for at least some countries (the core) to conduct independent fiscal policy in spite of increased integration.

Whether these agglomeration forces are country-specific and strong enough to affect national tax policy is questionable, however. They are more likely to be local phenomena with little impact on national tax policy, and the few empirical studies that test the insights from economic geography have generally failed to find support for a positive relation between agglomeration forces and tax rates (e.g., Krugstrop, 2004, and Hansson and Olofsdotter, 2005) although some support for this conjecture was found by Dreher (2006).

In summary, even though there is no convincing evidence of a race to the bottom there seems to be robust evidence of a downward pressure on corporate tax rates. It is unlikely however, that we have seen the end of the downward trend and the pressure will likely intensify as labour becomes increasingly mobile.

Fiscal Competition

The Scope for Government

In addition to implications for tax rates and tax revenue collections, increasing integration and the corresponding competition among governments to attract and retain mobile production factors may also have important implications for the composition of public expenditures. Because different types of government spending are valued differentially by the various production factors, nations may be pressured to use their resources in ways favourable to desired factors at the expense of independent fiscal policy. In particular, redistribution may become increasingly costly.

A growing body of literature has delved into this fiscal competition among states. The majority focus on the distinction between expenditures financing public consumption (items like infrastructure and research that primarily benefit firms and items like education, health care and culture that foremost benefit household productivity) and those financing income and wealth redistribution (items like transfers). To the extent that capital is more mobile than labour, it has been postulated that increases in integration lead to a shift in expenditures toward those more likely to attract capital at the expense of those benefiting individuals (e.g., Keen and Marchand, 1997). As labour becomes more mobile, however, this effect will diminish as expenditures that benefit residents may also attract productive labour (Bénassy-Quéré et al., 2005). Indeed, the importance that public spending not directly benefiting businesses plays for firm location has increasingly been realised. For example, Gabe and Bell (2004), found that a rise in educational spending increased the number of firms locating in Maine, a state in the Northeast United States.

Figure 3.1 illustrates how government expenditures benefiting business, labour and primarily welfare recipients, respectively, in constant purchasing Euros per capita have developed over time for the four different welfare state regimes in "old Europe" (Nordic, Continental, Mediterranean and Anglo-Saxon).[3] Specifically, spending on economic affairs, general public services, public order and safety, and defence are categorised as spending benefiting businesses, while spending on education, health, recreation, and environmental protection are assumed to mainly benefit productive labour, and finally government spending on housing and social protection are categorised as spending benefiting "welfare shoppers".

Not surprisingly, the different welfare state regimes spend different amounts on the three categories. The Nordic welfare states generally spend the most in per capital terms on all three categories. The Continental welfare states generally mimic the Nordic spending pattern closely, while Mediterranean and Anglo-Saxon countries spend considerably less with a relative emphasis on expenditures primarily benefiting businesses.

The Nordic and Continental countries increased their expenditures on labour and social welfare between 1990 and 2003 the most (around 80 percent), while they increased their expenditures on businesses by 48 and 29 percent, respectively. The Mediterranean and Anglo-Saxon welfare states, on the other hand, increased

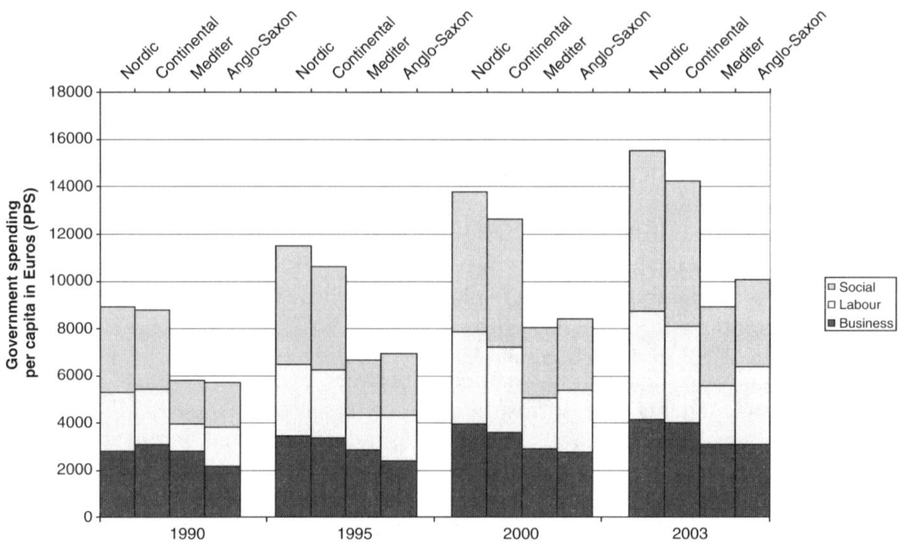

Source: Eurostat

Fig. 3.1. Government spending benefiting business, labour and "welfare shoppers" in constant purchasing power Euros per capita in the Nordic, Continental, Mediterranean and Anglo-Saxon welfare states

their spending on labour the most (approximately 110 percent) but social spending rose considerably as well (around 83 and 91 percent, respectively). Contrary to fiscal competition, thus, the countries in each of the four regimes increased business spending the least and there seem to be no evidence of convergence between the different welfare state blocks. On the contrary, if anything, they appear to have diverged. Moreover, there is no indication that the integration process has so far pressured the Nordic model as would be expected if "welfare shopping" was widespread.

The existing empirical literature aiming at determining how government spending is affected by increased integration is generally consistent with this picture (e.g., Dreher, 2006, and Hansson and Olofsdotter, 2008). Hansson and Olofsdotter (2008), for instance, find no empirical evidence that integration affects public transfers. Public consumption and investment, on the other hand, seems to be negatively associated with integration perhaps because cuts in public consumption and investments are politically easier to undertake than cuts in public transfers.

The Scope of the Welfare State

I now turn to the effects of integration on redistribution, the fastest growing component of government expenditure in most countries and by far the largest component of the welfare state.

The effects of integration on redistribution are hard to predict accurately, and likely vary by type of transfer. The mobility of labour, and in particular the relative mobility of high-skilled versus low-skilled labour, plays a large role. To date, labour mobility in Europe has generally lagged far behind capital mobility, though this is anticipated by many to change as the integration process proceeds. While most theoretical models have assumed that high-skilled labour is more mobile than low-skilled labour, this may not be the case. Indeed, Wildasin (2000), for example, presents data that show that immigration from poorer regions of the world has become an important determinant of today's population and labour force trends in Europe. Some even suggest that the generous welfare programs act as magnet to low-income individuals and attract potential "welfare shoppers" (Razin and Sadka, 2000, 2001 and Borjas, 1999).

It is often assumed in the literature that the threat to the welfare state will arise first when labour becomes more mobile. This is mis-leading, however, as it is enough for capital to be mobile to threaten the welfare state even if its activities are primarily financed by taxes and social security contributions levied on labour income. This would be the case if jobs are driven out of high-tax countries to low-tax countries when firms relocate, with higher unemployment and soaring dependency ratios in the high-tax country as a consequence.

Increased labour mobility may, nevertheless, threaten the survival of the welfare state as redistribution itself provides an incentive for net contributors to relocate elsewhere and potential net beneficiaries to move in (Wilson and Wildasin, 2004). Moreover, even if the welfare states survive redistribution may become ineffective as those supposed to benefit may actually be harmed. To illustrate, consider the following simple example of a small country with three factors of production: high-skilled labour, low-skilled labour and land. Both types of labour are mobile and land is immobile. High-skilled labour is taxed to finance a subsidy to the low-skilled labour. In an integrated world, this tax and transfer policy drives high-skilled labour out of the local economy until the local before-tax return rises to offset the local tax and the net return equals the net return in the rest of the world. Low-skilled labour, on the other hand, is attracted by the subsidy, which drives down the net-of-subsidy return until it equals the net return to low-skilled labour in the rest of the world. Since the real distribution of incomes is unaffected, the tax and transfer policy is inefficient. Nevertheless, the policy alters the returns to high-skilled and low-skilled labour, respectively, thus distorting the equilibrium amount of taxed and subsidised resources consumed in the local economy and harming the welfare of the owners of the immobile resource – immobile land – despite it being neither taxed nor subsidised. Moreover, if low-skilled labourers own the immobile land, it is quite possible that the tax and transfer policy perversely reduces their gross income by an amount greater than the transfer given.

While it may be hard for countries to conduct independent fiscal policies that redistribute between existing cohorts, it may be even harder to do so for policies that redistribute across generations, for example, pensions. Consider, for example, the difficulties in choosing whether to employ a pay-as-you-go or a funded system. First, the two systems have different implications for capital accumulation. In autarchy, for instance, pay-as-you-go systems will generally have higher interest rates. In an integrated world, however, with a given rate of return, capital will flow from countries with funded systems to countries with pay-as-you-go systems, leading to higher welfare in countries employing pay-as-you-go systems.

Pemberton (1999) shows that an individual country should not switch unilaterally to a funded system even though it would be Pareto improving if all countries switched to a funded system simultaneously. Second, young workers have economic incentives to locate in countries with funded systems while older workers benefit from pay-as-you-go systems. Wildasin (1999), for instance, showed that an individual can gain an additional 15 percent or more of his/her lifetime wealth by moving from one public pension program to another, given that the benefits are not contribution based. To overcome this problem, many countries employing the pay-as-you-go system have a contribution based system where pension size depends on how much is contributed and permits amounts to carry over between countries.

With mobile labour, thus, there will be no incentives to institute a pay-as-you-go system as that will attract individuals close to or already retired and drive out younger workers, hence, forcing countries to switch over to funded systems (which none wants to do voluntarily), or all countries have to employ pay-as-you-go systems with equal contributions and benefits. Several researchers (e.g., Homburg and Ritcher, 1993, and Breyer and Kolmar, 2002) have pointed this out and call for harmonisation to increase efficiency. Fiscal independence regarding intergenerational redistribution in the EU will become increasingly limited, whether with or without harmonisation.

Local redistribution, thus, may be doomed to fail, implying that redistributive policies should be carried out by central governments in order to internalise fiscal externalities (e.g., Stigler, 1957, and Oats, 1972). Indeed, redistributive taxes and transfers are typically the responsibility of national rather than local governments. In the EU context, this may argue for coordination of redistributive taxes and policies at a supra-national level.

In addition to economic mechanisms threatening the welfare state several political mechanisms in the face of mobile production factors may threaten the welfare state as well. For instance, Razin et al. (2002) describe a phenomena referred to as the "fiscal leakage effect". In the face of an influx of low-skilled labour, the median as voter will be a native tax payer favouring lower taxes and less redistribution long as the number of medium- to high-skilled native labourers remains larger then the block of pro-transfer voters bolstered by low-skilled immigrants joining at the bottom of the income distribution. Empirically, Razin et al. (2002) found that an increase in low-skilled migration indeed leads to lower taxes and per capita transfers, while the opposite is true for an increase in immigration of medium- and high-skilled labour. Countries may, thus, engage in a "race to the bottom" in which they reduce the generosity of the welfare payments to avoid attracting low-income taxpayers or discouraging high-income taxpayers (Hindriks, 1999).

Moreover, increased factor mobility may also decrease spending if it increases the heterogeneity of the population. Specifically, migration that causes the population to be more heterogeneous may have an anti-social effect (Böheim and Mayr, 2005) and several authors have documented a negative empirical relationship between ethnic heterogeneity and the level of public spending (e.g., Orr, 1976, Ribar and Wilhelm, 1996, Poterba, 1997, Alesina et al., 1999). In practice, ethnic heterogeneity may decrease the utility the median voter derives from public spending because the distance between her/his and the net recipients' preferred types of public spending may increase.

A consequence of increased factor mobility is that the cost of financing the welfare state will increase. The marginal cost associated with financing the welfare state will increase as it gets harder to generate required tax revenues. Provided that current levels of publicly financed social protection is optimal, to justify the status quo the marginal benefit of social protecting must rise accordingly. This may very well happen if increased integration makes us more vulnerable and therefore increase the demand and benefits from social protection. If the increase in marginal costs exceeds the increase in marginal benefits, however, the optimal size of the welfare state from society's point of view naturally shrink.

How has then the four different types of welfare states in Europe developed since 1990? Free factor mobility appears likely to impact the size and the scope for the welfare state and the effect may well be increasing. To determine whether integration has so far affected the welfare state, it is useful to sub-divide social protection expenditures to two categories. The first category consists of redistribution designed to provide public insurance against such risks as unemployment and sickness where private markets function poorly because of adverse selection and moral hazard. The second category consists primarily of intergenerational and inter-class transfers designed to assist the elderly and poor. While these can also be viewed as insurance against risk–for example, longevity and being born to a poor family–they are more commonly viewed as an outcome of the political process in which competing groups attempt to transfer resources toward themselves (Wilson and Wildasin, 2004).

Figure 3.2 shows how these two categories have developed over time for the four different welfare states.[4] Again, the Nordic and Continental welfare states spend considerably more in per capita terms both on redistribution designed to reduce risk and on redistribution directed towards the poor and elderly than the Mediterranean and Anglo-Saxon welfare states. As a share of total social protection expenditures, the welfare states spend a fairly even share on redistribution designed to reduce risk and poverty, however. The increases over time in per capita terms have been substantial, and slightly larger for the risk component for all but the Mediterranean welfare state. There is no suggestive evidence of any systematic differences between the two components or any downward trends or convergence between the different welfare state regimes.

To further illuminate whether increased globalisation has affected the welfare states within "old Europe", the development over time of the different social spending categories benefiting different groups is studied. The four social spending categories are spending primarily benefiting the aged (spending on old age and survivors), spending directed towards working age individuals that are not working (including expenditures on unemployment, sickness and healthcare and invalidity), social spending directed towards families and children and spending on social assistance (including expenditures on housing and social exclusion).[5]

Figure 3.3 illustrates how these different components differ between the various welfare states and have changed over time. The Continental welfare states spend the most in Euros per capita on pensions followed by the Nordic, Mediterranean

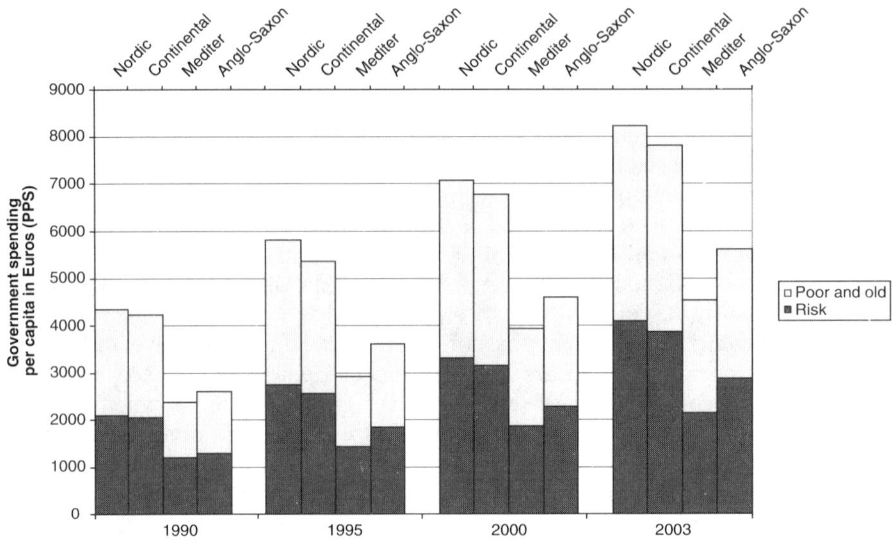

Source: Eurostat

Fig. 3.2. Public insurance against risk and redistribution towards the poor and elderly in constant purchasing power Euros per capita

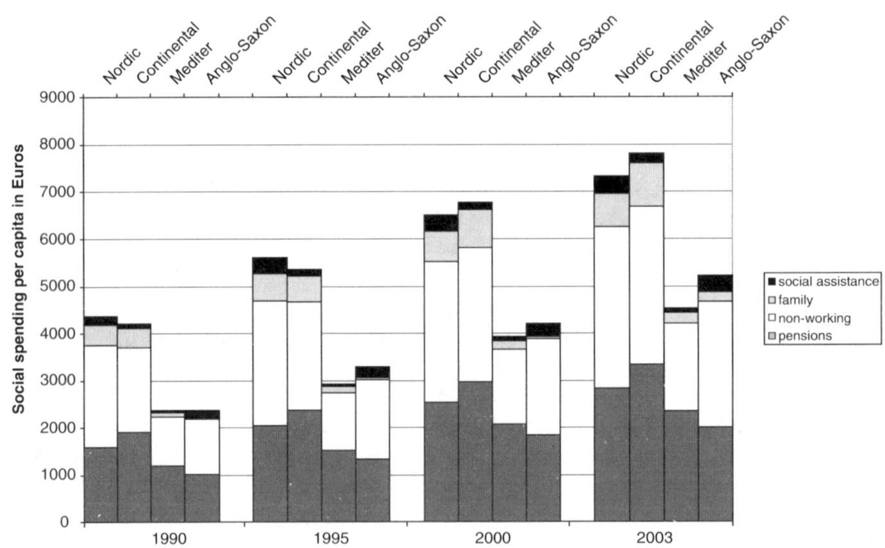

Source: Eurostat

Fig. 3.3. Social spending expenditures on pensions, non-working, family and social assistance in constant purchasing power Euros per capita

and the Anglo-Saxon welfare states. When it comes to expenditures benefiting those not working the Nordic and the Continental welfare states spend about twice as much in per capita terms compared to the Anglo-Saxon and Mediterranean countries. Expenditures on family and social assistance are much lower in per capita terms in all welfare states. As shares of total social protection expenditures the Nordic and Anglo-Saxon welfare states direct the most towards those not-working while the Continental and Mediterranean welfare states direct relatively more towards the elderly. Over time, the Anglo-Saxon welfare states more than doubled their expenditures (total expenditures per capita grew with 119 percent), followed by the Mediterranean, the Continental and the Nordic welfare states who grew with 91, 86 and 67 percent, respectively. Within the different components spending on social assistance and family/child grow the most in percentage terms – partly because of low initial values.

Again, the picture provides no indication that the welfare state is currently threatened. If anything, there seems to be a tendency for increased social protection in per capita terms and the standard deviation between the different welfare states provides no support of convergence. This picture is consistent with a number of empirical studies investigating the effect of integration on social spending. Boeri (2002), for example, finds no evidence for any convergence in social spending between welfare systems but some within groups. He did find a very mild convergence in the size of the welfare state across OECD countries, however, but the EU integration process did not seem to have played a role in this process. Moreover, several studies find social spending to be positively correlated with integration (e.g., Hicks and Swank, 1992, Garrett and Mitchell, 1997, Rodrik, 1998, while others find no correlation (e.g., Castles, 2001, and Dreher, 2006).

3.4 What Can and Should Be Done to Protect The National Welfare State?

How Can the National Welfare State Survive?

The actual development of social protection expenditures in the EU over the last 15 years shows no indication of the welfare state being threatened by increased integration. This is not a reason to conclude that the national welfare state is unthreatened, however. On the contrary, the theoretical discussion gave a generally pessimistic prognosis for the prospects of EU member states to conduct independent redistribution policies in the future, which should be taken seriously.

While it is clear that all member states will need to adapt to a more integrated environment, there are a number of factors that may preserve some degree of sovereign autonomy. First, there are important barriers to labour mobility. For example, it is not costless to move, there are cultural and language barriers that must be overcome, many individuals have strong local ties, and individuals must adapt to new legal and commercial environments. Information barriers and productivity differences due to, for example, language and cultural barriers, make the economic returns uncertain. It is therefore not surprising that mobility is much lower in Europe than in the US. Less than 0.5 percentage point of the European labour force change their residence region each year compared to 2.5 percent of the US labour force (Boeri, 2002). It is important to keep in mind, however, as mentioned before, that it is enough for capital to be mobile for the welfare state to be threatened if firms relocate to low-tax countries and jobs are lost resulting in increasing dependency ratios.

While labour is likely to become increasingly mobile as the integration process proceeds. Economic history suggests that differences in labour returns may persist for some time. For instance, returns to labour and capital narrowed while the returns to immobile land fell in Europe and increased in North America following the movement of labour and capital from Europe to North America in the last half of the 19th and beginning of the 20th century (see e.g., Hatton and Williamson, 1994), but the adjustment process took decades and in some respect continues today. While the costs of moving are less today, given better communication and transportation, they are still substantial.

Moreover, even if labour ultimately becomes quite mobile, the welfare state may still survive if redistribution has the nature of a local public good as suggested by Pauly (1973). He argues that redistribution may have the characteristic of a local public good – that is the welfare of the poor is an increasing function of the rich's utility and the rich care more about the poor that live in close proximity than those that live further away. If this is the case, local redistribution is not only possible but also preferred if regions differ in their taste and income, and, hence, in the amount of redistribution. Nevertheless, the argument for decentralisation is strongest when labour mobility is limited, taste for redistribution is heterogeneous, and there are large potential Pareto gains from redistribution, which may have limited applicability but describe EU better than other regions.

Glazer et al. (2005) argue that redistribution can actually increase because of migration. Because taxes are partially capitalized in property values and rents, a central tenet of urban economics, increased mobility can lead to higher tax rates on the rich in a model where land is heterogeneous and only the rich mobile because emigration by the rich reduces the competition for desirable locations at home and, hence, reduce rents while increasing the competition for desirable location in the new country and hence the price. Their results suggest that accounting for the responses in housing markets can alter the common view that mobility hampers redistribution.

Increased integration, by increasing economic efficiency and better employing production factors, may also reduce the scope of some of the governments' activities naturally. For example, while increased labour mobility may limit government's ability to insure against reduced earnings, greater market efficiency will better employ resources and hence reduce the levels of redistribution needed (Wilson and Wildasin, 2004). In addition, individuals, companies, and governments can each benefit from increased diversification possible in the wider economy. For instance, local risks can be pooled and bundled (for instance, by multinational firms) to achieve better protection against local shocks. In addition, world-wide equity markets make it easier for private investors as well as the public sector to reach preferred exposure to and diversification of local risks and shocks (Asdrubali et al., 1996). Moreover, cross-ownership of immobile resources can achieve gains of diversification of local risks to immobile factors (even though, this may encourage tax exporting, since the tax burden can be shifted to non-residents). This may be especially important as factor mobility may shift the distribution of risks away from mobile resources toward immobile resources. Increased factor mobility may, hence, reduce the need for some types of social insurances while raising overall productivity. It is of great importance that these benefits of globalisation are utilized as the need for other forms of protection due to globalisation may increase.

Even though the demand for some government activities will decline due to increased integration, however, the opposite will be true for others. For instance, individual job losses will likely occur in the short run as the economy adjusts to increased world competition. If fiscal competition constrains local governments from insuring against important risks where the market fails to do so, the social costs of failing to coordinate may be large. As noted already by Domar and Mugrave (1944), social policies that pool otherwise uninsurable risks through the public sector may improve the allocation of resources between more and less risky activities. Failing to coordinate, hence, may undermine important social-insurance mechanisms that help offset market failures. As increased integration may lead to increased vulnerability the need for efficient redistribution and social insurance programs must be met.

Clearly, thus, the EU (perhaps even the OECD) will have to play a major role in designing tax and transfer policies at a supra-national level if public consumption and redistribution are sure to survive (see Chap. 4 for possible ways to do this). The EU is in some respects better prepared than many other regions in the world as the institutional framework is in place and redistribution programs like CAP and the structural funds that redistribute at a supra-national level already exist. Nevertheless, designing tax and transfer policies at an EU level will be a great challenge. Even if some redistribution programs exist already, the EU is not a federation and reforms come about only through negotiation and cooperation. Even if centralised reforms may be Pareto improving, gains and losses are likely to be unevenly distributed and give raise to compensation demands and logrolling. It is unlikely, thus, that centralised tax and transfer policies will continue to be as high as they currently are in many high-tax EU member states. The fact that countries with generous welfare states may actually have incentives to redistribute outside their borders argues that there may be political will to coordinate transfer programs to increase overall efficiency, however.[6]

Reasons Not to Coordinate or Trade-off Between Competition and Coordination

Even if the EU were to succeed in achieving some level of coordination of tax and transfer policies, the gains from that may be limited by external factors. First, the benefits from regional coordination as opposed to global are obviously limited. As capital is mobile not only within the EU but globally, coordination within the EU has limited influence on capital mobility. Several researchers have studied the gains from regional integration and found that the gains from regional as opposed to global coordination are small. Sørensen (2004), for example, shows using a general equilibrium framework that the gains from regional as opposed to global coordination are small if capital is perfectly mobile. If capital is not perfectly mobile between the coordination region and the rest of the world, however, the gains from regional coordination can be greater, though simulations indicate that the gains will not exceed one percent of GDP, the welfare gains are higher in countries with high initial capital income tax rates, and some countries may even lose (an obstacle to agreement on coordination). Several observers have argued that the problems associated with increased globalisation require global institutions as a "World Tax Organization" (Tanzi, 1998) or a "GATT for Taxes" (McLure, 1997) for coordination to be effective.

Second, there is clearly a trade-off between tax policy coordination on EU level and decentralised national tax policy. It may be costly to give up tax policy, one of the few measures left for national governments to influence their own economies in dealing with asymmetric shocks, national externalities and differences in preferences. In addition, competition among national system may enhance efficiency. The benefits from coordination (that is to internalise the external effect) must, hence, outweigh the benefits of competition. Put differently, how bad is tax competition and how advantageous is tax coordination? Several studies have tried to estimate the harm from tax competition. Parry (2003), for example, tried to determine the welfare cost of fiscal competition and find that the welfare costs may be significant under some plausible parameter values, but it can easily be small under others. The size of the welfare cost depends on capital tax elasticity and the capital supply elasticity and for the welfare cost to be sizable the former needs to be substantial and the latter not too large. If governments are assumed to behave in a Leviathan way or if national governments can influence the net return to capital the welfare costs are reduced considerably. Parry finds estimates to be consistent with those from Sørensen (2004), and well below one percent of GDP which cast some doubt on the economic case for harmonisation of capital taxes in the EU.

Similarly, Brueckner (2004) tries to determine whether the "good side" of fiscal competition, as emphasised by the Tiebout literature dominates the "bad side", as studied in the tax competition literature. He finds that a key factor for the outcome is the dispersion of consumer preferences for public goods and the sensitivity of capital to tax rate changes. With identical preferences fiscal competition is undesirable because Tiebout benefits are absent. In many of his scenarios the overall welfare losses of tax competition are less than 1 percent of GDP, and sometimes even negative, though they can be substantial when capital is highly sensitive to tax changes in which case tax competition has significant costs that may offset its benefits.

Mendoza and Tesar (2005) find similar results using a game-theoretical model with two countries. More specifically, they find that the gains to coordination, that is incorporating international externalities, are small and speculates that the lack of tax policy coordination within the EU could reflect that the costs of coordination exceeds the small benefits.

Moreover, Boeri (2002) argues that increasing competition among the European welfare systems may result in better outcomes as it can increase the efficiencies in social spending and suggests that the EU should restrain itself from imposing one particular model over the others and instead let the mobility of the

European workforce drive the political and social policy convergence. He also investigate the effectiveness of the different welfare states and find that the Nordic and Anglo-Saxon models perform better than the Continental and Mediterranean when it comes to reducing poverty and protection against uninsurable labour market risks while at the same time provide reasonable rewards to working.

Centralisation of all tax instruments within the EU is, thus, not only undesirable but also unrealistic. A piece-meal approach, where one or a few taxes are harmonised to help finance supra-national transfer programs, is a more likely alternative. The choice of tax rates to harmonise is not irrelevant, however. Harmonisation of one tax rate, for instance a minimum tax rate on capital income, is likely to lead to fiercer tax competition for other tax instruments as well as slacker enforcement policies in order to re-introduce tax competition through the back-door (see Cremer and Gahvari, 2000, for a discussion of this).

The effects of partial tax harmonisation can even be perverse as countries compete with other tax instruments. Consider a situation with two tax rates: a capital tax that is harmonised at a minimum rate and a tax on low-skilled labour that is free to vary. The tax rate on low-skilled labour is now conditional on the capital income tax and can be used indirectly to attract capital. If the two production factors are complements, a decrease in taxation (a subsidisation) of low-skilled labour will increase the net return to capital and, hence, have the same effect as lowering the capital tax rate. If the two factors are instead substitutes, the net return to capital can be increased if taxation of low-skilled labour is increased, which will perversely reduce the welfare of the poor (Cremer and Pestieau, 2004).

In addition to perverse effects, partial harmonisation may also harm efficiency as it forces countries to raise more distortive taxes to balance the budget (Mendoza and Tesar, 2005). In general, countries with inefficient tax systems competing with countries with relatively efficient tax systems can experience significant welfare losses if forced to raise distortive taxes to remain fiscally solvent. For this reason, Mendoza and Tesar (2005) suggest that it is preferable to harmonise labour taxation over other taxes. Cnossen (2003), on the other hand, strongly disagree with this view as he believes that any "EU-wide coordination of taxes on labour, benefit schemes and labour market regulations would most likely exacerbate the impact of existing distortions and structural rigidities in the labour market" (Cnossen, 2003, p. 634). It is, hence, not straightforward how to harmonise taxes even with the political will.

Coordination should only be undertaken when redistributive tax and transfer policies fail because of fiscal competition, however. Other government activities, with a more public good nature or where private insurance markets against risks function, may benefit from fiscal competition, leading to a better use of public resources. In addition, it is important to increase the link between what residents pay and what they receive wherever possible, for instance by increasing individual unemployment and pensions programs. It is important, however, that these are made mandatory to avoid adverse selection. Local governments should then be allowed to vary in what they provide and permit residents to locate where the mix of taxes and public expenditures reflect their preferences. This will force governments to use its resources efficiently and, in addition, have a disciplinary effect on government waste. Wilson (2005), for example, shows that competition for mobile capital makes government behaviour more efficient. Specifically, he finds that welfare is improved if local governments make the expenditure decisions, even when taxation is conducted centrally.

The European welfare state may in the future be left to provide a basic right of a minimum acceptable level of social assistance, and income and welfare security beyond the basic level may be left for individuals to voluntarily obtain from the market and other non-governmental welfare providers. It is of great importance, however, that individuals can carry with them these social security rights between employers and regions.

3.5 Concluding Remarks on the Survival of the Welfare State in a "United Europe"

Currently, the threat from globalisation to the European welfare state is still hypothetical. The empirical evidence linking integration process within Europe or world wide globalisation to decreased social spending is inclusive. Nevertheless, the theoretical discussion focusing on the prospects of EU member states' ability to conduct independent redistribution policies in the future is pessimistic and should be taken serious. Politicians within the EU face a great challenge as the need to coordinate tax and transfer policies in order to maintain welfare states at current levels likely will become more acute in the future. Not only will it be hard to reach agreement as the gains and costs of coordination will be unequally distributed, but the gains from coordination within the EU are limited. The greatest threat to the national welfare state may very well stem from competition outside EU – for instance, firm outsourcing – that EU authorities have few means to tame.

Without coordination of some tax and transfer policies public social protection expenditures that redistribute from richer to poorer households as well as from one generation to another are likely to diminish both for economic and political reasons. Even with coordination, publicly financed social protection will likely diminish, however. One possible future outcome is that EU will provide a basic level of social protection in the form of a minimum guarantee income scheme and that anything above that will be voluntary and provided by private markets, local governments or through employers and be transferable between regions. This type of arrangement would minimise "welfare shopping" and stimulate migration from countries with inefficient welfare states to more efficient welfare states and "arbitrage away" part of the regional labour market asymmetries.

Other forms of redistribution designed to insure against risk, for example, have a larger chance to survive because they are less income dependent (and hence the gains of relocation less pronounced.) These insurances need to be transferable between regions, however, in order to stimulate mobility. In addition, the demand for redistribution designed to insure against some risks will likely decrease if the gains from integration are redeemed. It is of great important that full advantage is taken of the possibility for individuals to fully diversity and find their preferred exposure to risks and that gains from pooling and bundle risks are utilised by multinational firms as well as by governments as the demand for other forms of risk insurances may increase.

Even if coordination will be necessary, among other things to guarantee an acceptable safety-net for the most vulnerable, coordination should be whenever possible to facilitate better use of public resources that fiscal competition will ensure. Fiscal and political competition is important for efficient resource allocation and economic performance and the gains from region coordination are likely small.

Endnotes

1. I use the same distinction between harmonisation and coordination as in the Chap. 2. That is, harmonisation involves attempts to equalise tax parameters while coordination involves measures that do not lead to equalisation.
2. For firms the number of competing regions can be limited as the bidding process result in efficient firm location (see Black and Hoyt, 1989, and King et al., 1993).
3. Data on government expenditures are classified by function (COFOG) and come from Eurostat.
4. Redistribution designed to reduce risk includes social protection spending on unemployment, sickness and health, invalidity and disability and survivor expenditures, while redistribution towards poverty reduction and the elderly includes social spending expenditures on old age, family and child, housing and social exclusion not elsewhere classified. All data come from Eurostats's ESSPROS database.
5. Data come from Eurostats's ESSPROS database.
6. Indeed, Wildasin (1994) demonstrated that a country may gain by making transfer payments to potential immigrants in order for them to stay home.

References

Alesina, A., Baqir, R. and W. Easterly (1999) Public goods and ethnic divisions, *Quarterly Journal of Economics*, 114(4), 1243-1284.

Asdrubali, P., Sorensen, B. and O. Yosha (1996) Channels of interstate risk sharing: United States 1963-1990, *Quarterly Journal of Economics*, 111(4), 1081-1110.

Baldwin R. and P. Krugman (2000) Agglomeration, integration and tax harmonization, mimeo Graduate Institute of International Studies, Geneva.

Bénassy-Quéré, A., Gobalraja, N. and A. Trannoy (2005) Tax competition and public input, *CEPII Working Paper* , no 2005-08.

Bertola, G., Boeri, T. and G. Nicoletti (2001) *Welfare and Employment in a United Europe*, Cambridge: MIT Press.

Besley, T. and A. Case (1995) Incumbent behaviour: Vote-seeking, tax-seeking, and yardstick competition, *American Economic Review*, 85, 24-45.

Black, D. and W. Hoyt (1989) Bidding for firms, *American Economic Review*, 79, 1249-1256.

Boeri, T, Börsch-Supan, A. and G. Tabellini (2001) Would you like to shrink the welfare state? The opinions of European citizens, *Economic Policy*, 16(32), 7-50.

Boeri, T. (2002) Let Social Policy Models Compete and Europe will win, paper presented at a conference hosted by the Kennedy School of Government, Harvard University.

Böheim, R. and K. Mayr (2005) Immigration and public spending, *IZA Discussion Paper* No 1834.
Borjas, G. (1999) Immigration and welfare magnets, *Journal of Labour Economics*, 17(4), 607-637.
Brennan G. and J. M. Buchanan (1980) *The power to tax: Analytical foundations of a fiscal constitution*, Cambridge: Cambridge University Press.
Breyer, E. and M. Kolmar (2002) Are national pension systems efficient if labour is (im)perfectly mobile, *Journal of Public Economics*, 83, 347-374.
Brueckner, J. (2003) Strategic interaction among governments: An overview of empirical studies, *International Regional Science Review*, 26, 175-188.
Brueckner, J. (2004) Fiscal decentralization with distortionary taxation: Tiebout vs tax competition, *International Tax and Public Finance*, 11, 133-153.
Bucovetsky, S. (1991) Asymmetric tax competition, *Journal of Urban Economics*, 30, 167-181.
Burbidge, J., Cuff, K., and J. Leach (2004) Tax competition with heterogeneous firms, *Journal of Public Economics*, 90, 53-549.
Castles, F. (2001) On the political economy of recent public sector development, *Journal of European Social Policy*, 11(3), 195-211.
Cnossen, S. (2003) How much tax competition in the European Union, *International Tax and Public Finance*, 10, 625-649.
Cremer, H., and F. Gahvari (2000) Tax evasion, fiscal competition and economic integration, *European Economic Review*, 44, 1633-1657.
Cremer, H. and P. Pestieau (2004) Factor mobility and redistribution: a survey, *Handbook of Regional and Urban Economics,* vol. 4, Amsterdam: North-Holland.
Devereux, M., B., Lockwood, and M. Redoano (2002) Do countries compete over corporate tax rates, *CEPR Working Paper* No 3400, London.
Domar,E. and R. Musgrave (1944) Property income taxation and risk taking, *Quarterly Journal of Economics*, 58, 387-422.
Dreher, A. (2006) The influence of globalization on taxes and social policy: An empirical analysis for OECD countries, *European Journal of Political Economy*, 22, 179-201.
Edwards, J. and M. Keen (1996) Tax competition and Leviathan, *European Economic Review*, 40, 113-134.
Emerson, M., Aujean, M., Catinat, M., Coybet, P. and J. Alexis (1988) The Economics of 1992: The E.C. Commission's Assessment of the Economic Effects of Completing the Internal Market, New York: Oxford Univesity Press.
Esping-Andersen, G. (1990) *The three worlds of welfare capitalism*, Cambridge, Policy Press.
Ferrera, M. (1998) The four social Europes: Between universalism and selectivity, in Rhodes, M. and Y. Meny (eds), *The future of European welfare: A new social contract*, Palgrave Macmillan.
Fischel, W. (1975) Fiscal and environmental considerations in the location of firms in suburban communities, in Mills, E. and W. Oates (eds), *Fiscal Zoning and Land Use Controls*, DC Health, Lexington, MA.
French, K. and J. Poterba (1991) Investors diversification, and international equity markets, *American Economic Review*, 81, 222-226.
Gabe, T. and K. Bell (2004) Tradeoffs between local taxes and government spending as determinants of business location, *Journal of Regional Studies*, 44, 44, 21-41.
Garrett, G. (1995) Capital mobility, trade and the domestic politics of economic policy, *International Organization*, 49, 657-687.
Garrett, G. and D. Mitchell (1997) International risk and social insurance: Reassessing the globalization - welfare state nexus, Yale University, mimeo.
Glazer, A., Kanniainan, V. and P. Poutvaara (2005) Income taxes, property values, and migration, paper presented at the IAES meetings in Berlin 2006.

Griffith, R. and A. Klemm (2004) What has been the tax competition experience of the last 20 years?, *The Institute for fiscal studies Working paper* 04/05.

Hansson, Å. and K. Olofsdotter (2005) Integration and tax competition; an empirical study of OECD countries, *Scandavian Working Papers in Economics*, No 2005:4.

Hansson, Å. and K. Olofsdotter (2008) Integration and the structure of public spending, University of Lund, forthcoming *Comparative Politics Studies*, 41(7).

Hatton, T. and J. Williamson (1994) International migration 1850-1939: An economic survey, in T. Hatton and J. Williamson (eds), *Migration and the international labour market 1850-1939*, London: Routledge.

Hicks, A. and D. Swank (1992) Politics, institutions, and welfare spending in industrialized democracies 1960-1982, *American Political Science Review*, 86(3).

Hindriks, J. (1999) The consequences of labor mobility for redistribution: tax vs. transfer competition, *Journal of Public Economics*, 74, 215-234.

Homburg, S. and W. Richter (1993) Harmonizing public debt and public pension schemes in the European Community, *Journal of Economic Supplements*, 7, 51-64.

Huizinga, H and G. Nicodemus (2003) Foreign ownership and corporate income taxation: an empirical evaluation, *CEPR Discussion Paper*, no 3952.

Keen, M. and M. Marchand (1997) Fiscal competition and the pattern of public spending, *Journal of Public Economics*, 66, 33-53.

King, I., McAfee, R. and L. Welling (1993) Industrial blackmail: dynamic tax competition and public investment, *Canadian Journal of Economics*, 26, 590-608.

Krogstrup, S. (2004) Are corporate taxes racing to the bottom in the European Union?, manuscript, The Graduate Institute of International Studies, Geneva.

McLure, C. (1997) Tax Policies for the XXIst Century, in *Visions of the Tax System of the XXIst Century*, Hague: Kluwer.

Mendoza, E., and L. Tesar (2005) Why hasn't tax competition triggered a race to the bottom? Some quantitative lessons from the EU, *Journal of Monetary Economics*, 52, 163-204.

Oates, W.E. (1972) *Fiscal federalism*, New York: Harcourt/Brace/Jovanovich.

OECD (2001a) Public Expenditures, vol 2001, SourceOECD Social Expenditure Database.

OECD (2001b) Economic Outlook, SourceOECD database.

OECD (2004) Recent tax policy trends and reforms in OECD countries, *OECD Tax Policy Studies*, No 9, Paris: OECD.

Orr, L. (1976) Income transfers as a public good: an application to AFDC, *American Economic Review*, 66, 359-371.

Parry, I.(2003) How large are the welfare costs of tax competition?, *Journal of Urban Economics*, 54, 39-60.

Pauly, M. (1973) Income redistribution as a local public good, *Journal of Public Economics*, 2, 35-58.

Pemberton, J. (1999) Social security: national policies with international implications, *Economic Journal*, 109, 492-598.

Poterba, J. (1997) Demographic structure and the political economy of public education, *Journal of Policy Analysis and Management*, 16, 48-66.

Quinn, D. (1997) The correlates of change in international financial regulation, *American Political Science Review*, 91, 531-552.

Razin, A. and E. Sadka (2000) Interactions between international migration and the welfare state, CESifo Working Paper No. 337.

Razin, A. and E. Sadka (2001) *Labor, capital and finance: international flows*, Cambridge: Cambridge University Press.

Razin, A., Sadka, E. and P. Swagel (2002) Tax burden and migration: a political economy theory and evidence, *Journal of Public Economics*, 85, 167-190.

Ribar, D. and M. Wilhelm (1996) Welfare generosity: the importance of administrative efficiency, community values and genuine benevolence, *Applied Economics*, 28, 1045-1054.

Rodrik, D. (1998) Why do more open economies have bigger government, *Journal of Political Economy*, 106, 997-1032.
Sinn, H.W. (1990) Tax harmonisation and tax competition in Europe, *European Economic Review*, 34, 489-504.
Sinn, H.W. (2002) EU enlargement and the future of the welfare state, *Scottish Journal of Political Economy*, 49, 104-105.
Slemrod, J. (2004) Are corporate tax rates, or countries, converging?, *Journal of Public Economics*, 88, 1168-1186.
Sørensen, P. (2004) International tax coordination: regionalism versus globalism, *Journal of Public Economics*, 88, 1187-1214.
Stigler, G. J. (1957) The tenable range of functions of local government, in US Congress, joint economic committee (eds.), *Federal expenditure policy for economic growth and stability*, 213-219, Washington D.C.
Swank, D. (2001) Mobile capital, democratic institutions, and the public economy in advanced industrial societies, *Journal of Comparative Policy Analysis*, 3, 133-162.
Tanzi, V. (1998) The need for tax-coordination in an economically integrated world, in Roberti, P. (ed.), *Financial markets and capital income taxation in a global economy*, New York: Elsevier.
Tanzi, V. (2002) Globalization and the future of social protection, *Scottish Journal of Political Economy*, 9, 116-127.
Tanzi, V. and Bovenberg (1990) Is there a need for harmonizing capital income taxes within EC countries?, in Siebert, H., (ed.), *Reforming capital income taxation*, Mohr, Tübringen.
Tesar, L. and I. Werner (1995) Home bias and high turnover, *Journal of International Money and Finance*, 14, 467-492.
Tiebout, C. M. (1957) A pure theory of local expenditures, *Journal of Political Economy*, 64, 416-424.
Wellisch, D. (2000) *The theory of public finance in a federal state,* New York: Cambridge University Press.
White, M. (1975) Firm location in a zoned metropolitan area, in Mills, E. and W. Oates (eds), *Fiscal Zoning and Land Use Controls*, Lexington: DC Health.
Wildasin, D. (1994) Public pensions in the EU: migration incentives and impacts, in A. Panagariya, P. Portney, and R., Schwab (eds), *Environmental Economics and Public Policy: Essays in Honor of Wallace E. Oats*, London: Edward Edgar.
Wildasin, D. (1999) Theories of tax competition, *National Tax Journal*, 52, 269-304.
Wildasin, D. (2000) Factor mobility and fiscal policy in the EU: policy issues and analytical approaches, *Economic Policy*, 338-378.
Wilson, J. (1986) A theory of interregional tax competition, *Journal of Urban Economics*, 19, 296-315.
Wilson, J. (1991) Tax competition with interregional differences in factor endowments, *Regional Science and Urban Economics*, 21, 423-451.
Wilson, J. (2005) Welfare-improving competition for mobile capital, *Journal of Urban Economics*, 57, 1-18.
Wilson, J. and D. Wildasin (2004) Capital tax competition: bane or boon, *Journal of Public Economics,* 88, 1065-1091.
Winner, H. (2005) Has tax competition emerged in the OECD countries? Evidence from panel data, *International Tax and Public Finance*, 12, 667-687.
Zodrow, G. (2003) Tax competition and tax harmonization in the European Union, *International Tax and Public Finance*, 10, 651-671.
Zodrow, G., and P. Mieszkowski (1986) Pigou, property taxation and the underprovision of local public goods, *Journal of Urban Economics*, 19, 356-370.

Chapter 4
Fiscal Competition and Activist Social Policy

Ulrike Schneider and August Österle[1]

4.1 Introduction

More than a century ago national governments in Europe started assuming responsibility on a broader scale for safeguarding the population against major risks of life, such as sickness and old-age poverty, thus transcending the boundaries of a regulatory minimum state. The second half of the twentieth century witnessed the expansion and maturation of modern welfare states around the two core aims of risk insurance and distributional equity (see Tanzi 2002: 119). As observed by Wildasin (2000: 341), the development of social policy can be seen to "reflect the outcome of a democratic policy making process that has not been prepared to accept the market-determined distribution of income in an unaltered form." Recent survey evidence shows that the welfare state is still well rooted in equity preferences and risk aversion of European citizens at large (Osberg and Smeeding 2005, Heien 2000).

At the same time concern has been expressed that factor market integration and the ensuing fiscal competition in Europe create pressures for a downward adjustment of welfare states. More specifically, it is generally acknowledged that tax competition makes it much more difficult for governments to sustain high levels of redistributive activity. Against this backdrop, the contribution studies how social policies and tax policies in the European Union are related. More specifically, it inquires into potential adjustments when fiscal competition via undermining national social policies creates a downward trend on social standards in Europe. In contrast to the greater part of the public finance literature, the emphasis of this contribution is on active rather than on passive integration of social policy. Active social policy integration results from activities to harmonise or to coordinate social policies at the European level. Passive social policy integration, instead, is an adaptation of welfare systems as a response to indirect pressures on the welfare state arising from, e.g., market requirements or concerns of competitiveness (Leibfried and Pierson 2000).

As a starting point, Section 4.2 will depict cross-national differences in social policy in the EU. Sections 4.3 and 4.4 highlight how these differences might vanish in the context of unlimited tax competition. Against this backdrop, we will discuss the potential of coordination as well as harmonisation of social policy to cope with fiscal competition in the 4.5 Section. In doing so, we will pay particular attention to the extent to which a more concerted approach to social policy might induce a backlash on tax policy. The final section summarizes the discussion and defines an agenda for future research.

4.2 United We Stand – Diverse We Move

At the beginning of the millennium social protection expenditure in the European Union amounted to 26.2% of GDP on average (see Table 4.1). However, expenditure levels varied widely across Europe, with the lowest levels in the Baltic States Latvia (12.2%), Lithuania (12.9%), Estonia (13.2%), in Ireland (below 16.3%) and in Slovakia (16.6%), and the highest level in Sweden (31.7%). The disparities are even larger when comparisons are based on purchasing power standards, again with lowest levels in the Baltic States and with highest levels in Luxembourg, Norway and Sweden (Eurostat 2007; 2006). While the figures indicate differences in social, economic and institutional conditions, they reflect even more so different traditions, policy choices and perceptions of the welfare state in European countries.

According to Esping-Andersen (1990), the different traditions have shaped three categories of welfare states. Each can be characterised by specific basic approaches to offering protection against income and consumption shocks from unemployment, longevity and sickness and to attain equity in society. To begin with, the universal welfare regime prevails in Northern European countries. It emphasises equality and represents a rights and citizenship-based approach in organising welfare. Traditionally, the state has a strong role in this welfare model and taxes are the primary source of funding for social policy. Countries following the corporate welfare model – e.g. Germany and Austria – are characterised by the social insurance principle. The major social risks are organised in para-fiscal institutional arrangements (social insurance funds) with funding based on social insurance contributions rather than taxes. Though coverage is extended beyond those paying contributions in most of these schemes, employment criteria still play a major role in defining the material and personal scope of benefits. Traditionally, family ties are strongly recognised in the organisation of this welfare model. The liberal welfare regime represents the third Esping-Andersen type, where state responsibility only comes into play when all other potential social nets fail. In this case, benefits are organised as social assistance requiring individual means-testing. None of the European countries follows a strict market liberal approach in organising welfare, but the UK, Ireland, as well as some of the new EU member countries, at least in some respects come closer to that model.

While this classification has been scrutinised and slightly adjusted by a number of authors (see e.g. Arts and Gelissen 2002, Esping-Andersen 1999, Castles 1993, Lewis 1992), it still highlights three simple yet important points for the discussion of social policy and tax policy. To begin with, there is a means-end relationship between taxes and social policy, and taxes are used to a differing degree in each of

Table 4.1. Social protection expenditure and funding in the European Union, Iceland, Norway and Switzerland (2004)

Country	Social protection expenditure		Social protection funding (% of total social protection funding)		
	% of GDP	PPS per capita[1]	Taxes	Social contributions	Other receipts
Austria	28.3	7822	34.6	64.0	1.4
Belgium	27.9	7519	27	71.1	1.9
Cyprus	17.5	3348	52.7	35.5	11.8
Czech Republic [p]	18.9	3023	19.6	79.2	1.2
Denmark	29.8	8226	63.5	29.8	6.7
Estonia	13.2	1602	21.2	78.7	0.1
EU15[e]	26.6	6970	37.5	59.5	3.1
EU25[e]	26.2	5951	37.3	59.5	3.2
Finland	25.9	6679	44.3	50.3	5.4
France [p]	29.3	7299	30.4	66.0	3.5
Germany [p]	28.4	6977	34.5	63.8	1.7
Greece	25.2	4680	30.5	60.8	8.7
Hungary	20.3	2810	33.0	59.0	8.0
Iceland	22.6	6523	38.3	34.0	27.7
Ireland	16.3	5015	60.8	37.6	1.6
Italy [p]	25.2	6043	42.4	56.0	1.6
Latvia [p]	12.2	1189	33.4	66.6	0.0
Lithuania [p]	12.9	1402	39.5	60.1	0.4
Luxembourg [p]	22.2	11963	44.6	51.8	3.6
Malta	18.6	2964	32.5	64.2	3.3
Netherlands [p]	26.6	7521	19.2	68.7	12.1
Norway	25.8	8970	56.3	43.7	0.1
Poland [p]	19.6	2167	34.8	51.7	13.5
Portugal [p]	23.2	3810	42.2	47.5	10.4
Slovakia [p]	16.6	1990	28.8	69.8	1.4
Slovenia [p]	23.8	4283	31.6	67.0	1.3
Spain [p]	19.5	4321	30.3	67.2	2.4
Sweden [p]	31.7	8437	48.7	49.4	1.9
Switzerland	27.5	8285	23.5	62.3	14.3
United Kingdom [e]	25.8	6863	49.7	48.7	1.7

[1] Purchasing Power Standards
[p] provisional value
[e] estimated value
Source: Eurostat 2007

the three welfare state models. While in some countries, such as Spain, Belgium or the Czech Republic, social insurance contributions amount to more than two thirds of total social protection financing, taxes account for more than 60% of total funding in Denmark or Ireland (see Table 4.1). So, secondly, tax policy has to be viewed in conjunction with other instruments of social policy. They substitute for and complement social security contributions and regulation. Empirical evidence shows that the redistributive effect of taxes varies quite considerably in the EU. While in countries as diverse as France, Italy or Sweden inequality reduction through taxes amounts to just about 10% of pre-tax income, it is around 20% in Austria, Belgium or Denmark. And, these higher levels do not systematically reflect a larger degree of pre-tax inequality (Verbist 2004). Thirdly, given these basic observations and given the different designs of the European welfare states and their respective funding sources, tax competition will affect each country or welfare regime differently. Impacts will arise in the funding base, in the redistributive effect of taxes and in the pressure these changes create for the provision of state-funded cash and in kind benefits.

In addition to different design principles which have emerged over decades, it is current policy choices that determine the level and scope of benefits. Hence, even when countries follow similar welfare state principles, quite substantial differences may occur in social expenditure and/or in spending on specific programmes, as well as in funding requirements. This is in fact the case in Europe. To offer an example, health care systems in the UK, in Northern as well as in Southern European countries are all tax-funded schemes providing health care to all citizens. Yet, in 2003 the share of public funding in total expenditure on health varied considerably between 85% for Sweden, 83% for the UK and around 70% for Spain and Portugal (OECD 2005).

It is important to note that these differences, while striking, have not been a political concern for EU policies by themselves. Over the past decades a number of initiatives have been taken to increase the reassignment of political responsibilities to the EU level in various policy areas. Social policy, however, has remained a national endeavour. As will be discussed in section five, national governments were much more reluctant to abandon their discretion in shaping this important field of policy, which claims a huge share of the national budget. Advocates of a decentralised approach to social policy point to idiosyncratic risk and equity preferences in the EU member states. Yet, national social policies are increasingly influenced by developments in other policy fields, in particular when focusing on the elimination of "distortions of competition" and the concomitant integration of factor and product markets. As a result, while formally independent of each other, social policy politicians in individual member states increasingly appear to interact strategically in their policy choices (see Chap. 3).

From a welfare-economic viewpoint, social policy choices serve to maximise social welfare in the context of its distributional objectives and resource constraints. Atkinson (2000) highlights the role of different distributional objectives in choosing the level of social benefits on the one hand and tax rates on the other (see also Sørensen 2000: 442 f.). He presents a framework for analyzing how welfare states with differing redistributive objectives can adjust most effectively to budgetary pressures and labour market shocks. Since market integration and fiscal competition have been shown to create budgetary pressures and to generate income risks for low-skilled workers, Atkinson's framework provides a very suitable reference point in the given context, even if his contribution did not explicitly take up the issue of tax competition.

The analysis assumes additive welfare functions which consider the net incomes of the working population, pensioners and the unemployed. If governments were entirely indifferent to distributional outcomes of the market process, gain of one euro of income would count the same irrespective of its recipient. In reality, all governments show some concern for distribution, as reflected in social spending. Yet, as shown in Atkinson's framework, governments may weight the welfare of the working population, the unemployed and pensioners (or young dependent persons) differently. For example, with a "charitable conservative objective," income would be redistributed to the elderly whereas no redistributive action would be taken for the unemployed. By contrast, alternative objective functions do account for the income positions of individuals, irrespective of their working status, and would also consider wage dispersion. With a "rank order social welfare function," as an example, an additional euro of income would count most if it went to the least advantaged person in society, and would be weighted gradually less for recipients who rank higher in society. Governments hence will use more or less progressive income taxation, depending on marginal evaluation of income at different income levels (see Atkinson 2000: 452–454).

Atkinson (2000) shows that different social policy possibility frontiers emerge for governments pursuing different redistributive objective functions, when tax disincentives are considered. Governments choose the level of social benefit rates in conjunction with tax rates in a way that maximises welfare and – depending on the objective function – they sometimes accept unemployment in doing so. It is important to note that from this perspective unemployment is therefore not a matter of policy failure. Even with unemployment, social welfare is maximised, since equity considerations, which are considered significant in the objective functions, can only be met with the appropriate amount (and type) of taxation. Bringing taxes down to a level which abolishes unemployment would have to be considered sub-optimal. We will return to this point in section four.

4.3 When Social Policy Goes Limbo Dancing: Fiscal Competition and the Welfare State

We now turn to repercussions of factor market integration and the ensuing fiscal competition for European welfare states. How does the free movement of mobile factors affect income inequality and risk? Recent evidence suggests that fiscal competition presents a challenge to independent national fiscal policies in general and to national social policy, affecting the revenue and the expenditure side alike (see e.g. Wildasin 2000: 347, Rodrik 1997). Which effects on the welfare state can be expected from the integration of factor markets and the ensuing competition of countries for mobile factors? The discussion of this question has a long tradition in economics, resulting in ever more mature theoretical approaches and a solidifying corps of empirical evidence on the issue. As elaborated in Chap. 3 or in more detailed reviews of literature by Wilson (1999) and Avi-Yonah (2000), while the virtues of competition and market integration are praised, there is also considerable concern about the impact of fiscal competition on income security and equity.

It is widely acknowledged that fiscal competition sets an incentive for governments to reduce the taxation of mobile factors of production, to shift the tax burden to immobile factors of production, to substitute taxes for fees and user charges, or to reduce the amount of revenues raised altogether. All these measures tend to increase inequality, be it that tax progression is moderated or that more regressive forms of raising revenues are used. Looking at the expenditure side, fiscal competition also makes governments more closefisted and leads to a restructuring of the budget to the benefit of "productive spending" (see e.g. Tanzi 2002: 126, Keen and Marchand 1997, Borck et al. 2005). As less is spent on social transfers and social infrastructures, inequality and social exclusion may be aggravated. At the same time, factor market integration, which precedes fiscal competition, has been shown to increase income insecurity, income volatility and hence consumption risks (e.g. Rodrik 1997), resulting in higher wage dispersion and increasing the demand for social protection. In other words, in an environment of unrestrained fiscal competition it appears that European welfare states confront the challenge of doing more with less (see e.g. Gunter and van der Hoeven 2004).

Incentives to reduce taxation – in an environment without legal barriers to migration – will lead to under-provision of insurance, a scenario called "race-to-the bottom" (Drèze 2002, Delsen 2002, Sinn 2002). In the extreme case, the result would be a "bottom" situation with no taxes and no redistribution at all (Cremer and Pestiau 2004). However, Chap. 3 in this book points out that there is no empirical support for the "race-to-the bottom" hypothesis (see also Wildasin 2000, Sørensen 2000). Yet, all of the aforementioned changes directly interfere with the two core objectives of social policy, namely safeguarding the population against major risks of life (including income and consumption shocks from unemployment, longevity, sickness) and attaining equity in society. The fact that these policy objectives still claim relevance on the national and on the EU level, which is supported by the Lisbon agenda as well as by social surveys on attitudes towards the welfare state in Europe (see e.g. Osberg and Smeeding 2005, Heien 2000: 22), raises the question of how to prevent adverse effects from fiscal competition on social policy.

4.4 The Tail Wags the Dog: Passive Integration of Social Policy

The previous section has established a negative relationship between fiscal competition and the attainment of major social policy objectives. Restraining tax competition then appears not only an effective but also the most obvious way to tackling this problem at its roots (see e.g. Sørensen 2000: 447 ff). This option (and its limits) has been discussed in some detail in Chap. 3. What is striking in the economics literature, however, is that many authors do not even carry the discussion of fiscal competition this far. One group of authors, while not welcoming the impending changes in social policy, appears to be at a loss about how to prevent the expected downward adjustment of social policy in scale and scope. A second group of authors even suggests that a rescaling of the welfare state is the appropriate response to the challenges of fiscal competition, for which two lines of reasoning are offered. The first argument points to the efficiency gains from fiscal competition which are likely to foster growth and which should hence increase the tax base in the long-run. Furthermore, factor market integration is also perceived as reducing economic risks in society, which would reduce the demand for social policy. A second line of reasoning maintains that the welfare state tends to be excessive in the first place, reflecting a general tendency of governments to overspend. From this perspective, fiscal competition offers a convenient mechanism to trim away the welfare fat.

Apart from the fact that both lines of arguments lack empirical backing, they are mainly concerned with the issue of (static and dynamic) efficiency. They offer no solution to the problem of rising inequality in the context of fiscal competition. In addition, as pointed out by Avi-Yonah (2000), a claim for democracy has to be considered. This refers to the freedom of countries "to determine the size of the countries' public sector" or to choose a level of (redistributive) taxation which mirrors the preferences of a country's citizenship. Yet fiscal competition could wear away a society's options for choices concerning the degree of income (in)equality or social inclusion, as has been shown for the case of asymmetric competition between larger and small countries (see Avi-Yonah 2000: 1613 and the studies quoted there).

Against this backdrop, it is intriguing to look at the policy prescriptions derived by Atkinson (2000) from his normative analysis of welfare state adjustments in an environment of budgetary pressure and labour market shocks. As briefly outlined above in section two, Atkinson discusses policy choices for governments following specific redistributive objective functions. As can be expected, Atkinson (2000: 456) concludes that governments following different objective functions would want to respond differently to such challenges, even if they would face similar socio-economic conditions (such as old-age dependency ratios or skill distributions). However, confronting this result with social policy reforms across Europe in recent years (see e.g. Andersen et al. 2005, Ellison 2005, Kuhnle 2000), one finds a striking similarity in reform measures taken and reform measures discussed. There are two explanations for this empirical observation. Either risk and equity preferences, which have shaped the welfare regimes in the past, have been converging, bringing about discrete shifts in the redistributive objective functions of those countries that have formerly displayed higher levels of redistributive action. Or some countries have chosen a reform path which is not in accordance with their underlying social welfare function, such that they experience a welfare loss. Which of these explanations can claim more credit?

Attitudinal surveys using data from the International Social Survey Programme (ISSP) from the 1980s and 1990s show that redistributive action is generally valued highly in Continental Europe as compared to the Anglo-Saxon countries, while at the same time offering proof of continuing attitudinal differences across the Continent (see e.g. Osberg and Smeeding 2005, Heien 2000). So there is reason to believe that efforts of some governments to "shape up" social policies for meeting the challenges of fiscal competition are in fact doing a disservice to the redistributive objectives which are still supported by their citizenship at large. Currently, the policy debate focuses on "extensive welfare states" and how they need to be scaled down to overcome unemployment and to secure the gains of growth. By contrast, Atkinson's framework and analyses reveal that budgetary pressures and labour market shocks may require limited welfare states, which are characterized by a narrow interest in redistribution to adjust *upwardly* to even meet their modest redistributive objectives.

4.5 Can the Horse Get Back in Front of the Cart Again? Options for Active Integration

As has been discussed in the previous chapter, tax coordination or tax harmonisation, while a direct and effective way to prevent harmful side effects of factor market integration (see e.g. Sørensen 2000) on social policy, is inhibited by strategic behaviour of governments and is also a matter of academic controversy (see the other contributions in this volume). At the same time, passive integration of national social policy does not systematically account for equity and democracy considerations as pointed out by Avi-Yonah (2000: 1578, 1616 ff). As a consequence, this section investigates the potential of active social policy integration to maintain redistributive activities to the extent that it reflects voter preferences in an environment of open markets and fiscal competition.

Social policies in the European context are often described as national policies. This is still true with regard to legal competences in most welfare sectors. But, as discussed in the previous section, room for national social policies has diminished. European policies increasingly regulate, coordinate or determine macroeconomic policy in general, and tax policy in particular. In the process single member states lose control over fields of policy that traditionally have fostered national social policy (Leibfried and Pierson 2000). But what are the opportunities to face this loss? There are four major approaches to increase the capacity for activist social policy on the European level which will be discussed in more detail below: (a) through coordination of national social policies without completely harmonising (establishing uniformity for) national regulations, (b) through full harmonisation (with a centralisation of competences in social security), (c) through partial harmonisation (a combination of harmonisation and national policy discretion), and (d) through the Open Method of Coordination (OMC).

Harmonisation and coordination are not clear-cut concepts. Following Pennings (2001: 251), the term harmonisation is used when the objective is to change national systems, while coordination formulates rules that should facilitate the interaction of national systems. In accordance with the terminology used for tax policies in Chap. 2, full harmonisation attempts to establish uniformity for all relevant parameters for the entire Union, while partial harmonisation aims at uniformity for some, but not all relevant parameters. Examples for partial harmonisation would be minimum standards or binding frameworks for calculating benefits. Other forms of coordination exist either in the form of coordinating national regulations within the Union, without requiring uniform legislation, e.g. to facilitate migration between member countries, or in very loose forms without any sanctions attached. Both, harmonisation and coordination have an impact on the relation between EU law and national law and they may leave more or less room for national policy. While approaches of harmonisation and legally binding coordination between member countries include at least some "hard law" regulations, the OMC is a voluntary approach where countries agree to exchange information and experiences in a systematic way. This approach is not aimed at harmonisation or coordination, but convergence is a potential outcome.

It seems necessary here to remark briefly on our treatment of the harmonisation and coordination rules. This contribution provides a very general coverage of social security. In a more detailed analysis of activist social policy integration one would have to recognise the differences between various areas of social security. Marked lines of division run between regulatory, allocative and redistributive functions as well as through basic features of social security schemes (including, for example, the sources of funding, cash vs. in-kind provision or target groups). Respective policy differences occur between areas of social security as well as between countries which can put them at very different starting points for any harmonisation or coordination attempt. In what follows, we will first summarize moves on the European level to coordinate social policy, before entering the discussion of (heretofore hypothetical) policy harmonisation.

Coordination Without Uniformity

Coordination of security rights for workers migrating within Europe has a long tradition. The underlying objective of coordination rules in social security is to solve the problems of positive conflict of laws (a migrant falling under the provisions of two or more countries) and of negative conflict of laws (a migrant falling under no country's provisions). Building on earlier bilateral agreements, two of the very first EC regulations (3/58 and 4/58) have addressed the social security of migrant workers. With regulation 1408/71, and a large number of revisions of material, the personal scope of coordination rules has constantly been extended. The personal scope now applies to nationals of the European Economic Area (EU plus Norway, Island and Liechtenstein) and Switzerland and has been extended from workers to their families, the self-employed, students and others not gainfully employed. In terms of the material scope, the regulation covers all major social protection schemes (including sickness and maternity benefits, invalidity benefits or old age benefits), but not social assistance (Fuchs 2005, Pennings 2001). Recognising the developments in national social law as well as ECJ decisions (see below), regulation 1408/71 recently has been replaced by regulation 883/2004 which, however, will only be applicable with the implementation regulation becoming effective.

In summary, coordination without uniformity focuses on securing the rights of cross-border migrants. With the system of social security coordination, free migration neither should be hindered because of the risk of losing social security nor should it be promoted for the sole reason of accumulating social rights. And it should prevent individuals from making double financial contributions to social security systems. On a systems level, consensus relies on a relative balance of incoming and outgoing social rights and related funding requirements. Data on the aggregate financial flows between social security systems, which follow from the application of bilateral or multilateral agreements, have not been made available on the EU level (and is similarly hard to obtain on the national level). However, when the balance is disturbed, be it as a consequence of different benefit regulations, which are dealt with differently in the coordination rules, or as a consequence of benefit shopping or social tourism, national social policies are more likely to adapt their rules. This concern is also recognised by ECJ rulings on patient mobility in Europe. While free movement of patients remains the underlying principle (following the free mobility philosophy of the European Union), the ECJ has referred to the protection of the financial balance of national social security schemes as grounds for justifying a limitation of free movement of patients. (Pennings, 2001)

Full Harmonisation

Whether and how a European Community should attempt to harmonise social policies is not a new debate. Even prior to the Treaty of Rome strong arguments were put forward in favour of harmonisation (including a harmonisation of funding schemes) to prevent negative effects of market integration for those countries with high levels of social protection. Others have stressed the arguments in favour of a competitive approach. Finally, the Treaty adopted a market integration model where social policies by and large are left to the single member states. So far, regulations and directives in social policies with a harmonisation effect have been largely limited to equal treatment of men and women, labour law and specific public health issues. These issues stress the regulatory type of intervention with no or very little financial involvement of public bodies. Potential negative effects of passive integration, as described earlier, are strong in social security areas where the redistributive function involves large amounts of funding. And in these areas there have been no attempts at actively harmonising social policy so far.

According to the public finance literature, centralisation of the redistributive function of governments would ensure that a certain amount of funding is channelled to social policy. Full harmonisation would require member states not only to agree on the level of social security but also on the way it is organised, including the schemes for funding the system. Full harmonisation thus could have a more visible impact on taxation. Even the introduction of a common "EU social tax" might be an option in this approach. Such a political compromise would of course put an end to national social policy traditions. Depending on the harmonisation level, it would exert strong downward pressure on those with social protection spending above average and/or a strong upward pressure for those below the average. This would create disturbing effects on allocation and distribution and it would destroy the innovative power of diversity in welfare systems. In addition, thinking of the welfare traditions, of the way social policies have been dealt with on the European level in the past 50 years or of the principle of subsidiarity that underlies the European integration idea, this would involve a fundamental institutional and value change. As long as risk aversion and equity preferences differ across the member states of the European Union, such a move would also violate the democracy criterion mentioned above, that is the right of the electorate to choose the level of social protection it prefers. Given the current state of the

European Union, it is hard to imagine that full harmonisation and the evolution of new institutions will become a broader option in the short and even in the medium term.

Partial Harmonisation

If full harmonisation is not an adequate option for most parts of social security, partial harmonisation might work as a response to pressures on the welfare state. There are a number of concepts put forward in the literature and in the policy debate, which can be divided into three categories. A first set of ideas attempts not to harmonise an area of social security fully, but to harmonise parts of the system. This would be the case with the introduction of common instruments. For example, with channelling specific tax revenues to specific social policy concerns, such as unemployment, a harmonisation of tax policies could be combined with a major European social policy concern. Partial harmonisation also occurs with the introduction of social standards, e.g. minimum pensions. With this approach one would establish minimum financial social rights for the entire community. However, having such standards at a low level (the only likely consensus) would not at all change the passive integration effects, and might even strengthen these effects in countries with traditionally high levels of social protection. Hence, the tax system would still work as a determinant of passive integration not supporting activist approaches.

A second bundle of partial harmonisation concepts leave considerable room for national variations in social security, while at the same time attempting to shape a European social model. In the social snake model (Dispersyn et al. 1992) EU-indicators are established for specific social security benefits, e.g. old age pension expenditure or public health care expenditure as a percentage of GDP. Countries above the average are asked to keep the level constant, while those below average should increase the expenditure levels. Those countries above the average are only allowed to increase their expenditure levels further when they also make contributions to a redistribution fund that subsidises those countries below average. The funding issue is not addressed in the outline of the model. However, there are strong incentives not to increase social expenditure for those who spend above average (because they would have to pay into the transfer mechanism) and for those who spend below average (because they would lose their opportunity to receive transfers). The social-snake model would effectively introduce lower limits to social spending for the EU member states. In the "below average" group the floor for social spending (relative to GDP) would amount to their current relative level of social spending, while it would correspond to the EU average at the time of the agreement in the case of "above average" countries. This mechanism would hence limit potential harm from fiscal competition.

The corridor model (Busch 1998) takes a broader perspective by relating total social expenditure and economic performance. Clusters of countries (according to economic development) are given corridors of total social expenditure. In such a system, countries with relatively low economic performance would not have to meet higher social standards that could economically pose a risk to their development.

However, moving up in economic performance would require them to spend additional money on social security. By clustering countries by economic performance, the room for social dumping for reasons of competitiveness would be very much limited. Tax competition could lead to a re-arrangement of the tax mix, but not to a substantial reduction of funding for social security below what the corridor allows. At the same time, member states would be free in structuring social security schemes as well as in channelling funds within social security. Similarly, Scharpf (1999, 2002) has proposed framework directives differing for groups of member countries. While the corridor model or the framework model addresses all member states, the idea of "variable geometry" would allow groups of countries to develop common policies for specific issues. The Treaty allows such 'closer cooperation,' but under very strict conditions.

With all these harmonisation proposals a key question is the power with which respective directives are enforced. Linking compliance with this framework with, for example, access to financial means of the European Social Fund could help to better enforce respective corridors. As a current in-depth study on labour law directives has shown, response to adaptation requirements is rather limited in Europe. Falkner et al. (2005) have identified different worlds of compliance ranging from those of law observance to those of neglect. Also, introducing a floor to social spending in some way or another still does not prevent a shift in the tax burden to the detriment of immobile factors and/or low-skilled workers, which is to be expected from tax competition.

Open Method of Coordination

The third partial harmonisation approach neither harmonises instruments nor policy corridors, but objectives. And it does not aim at harmonisation of policies, but convergence is a potential outcome. With the introduction of the Open Method of Coordination (OMC) in the Lisbon Council in the year 2000 this approach has gained some prominence in European social policies. Rather than coordinating or harmonising social policies through legislation, the OMC attempts to facilitate a policy learning process. Following common guidelines proposed by the Commission and a bundle of indicators and benchmarks, a reporting, monitoring and evaluation system is used to discuss plans and developments between member states and at the EU level. The OMC has been used in the areas of social inclusion, pensions and health and long-term care. Currently, a reform aiming at streamlining the OMC in social security is under way. The plan is to integrate a more coherent bundle of objectives and annual reports for all three sectors.

However, the process of the OMC is voluntary in nature with no formal sanctions attached. The question of potential success (or failure) is judged quite differently in the literature (e.g. Scharpf 2002, Eckordt 2005, Zeitlin 2005, Trubek and Trubek 2005), often vaguely pointing more at potential than at concrete effects. There is no doubt that the method helps to improve the information base, but effects on policy formation so far seem very limited. Consequently, the approach does not restrain fiscal competition in a direct way. However, it facilitates the exchange about social policies and preferences regarding respective policies, and, herewith, provides a path for debating coordination that goes beyond this rather loose form.

4.6 Concluding Remarks on European Tax Competition and Social Policy Integration

The history of European integration "... has created a fundamental asymmetry between policies promoting market efficiencies and those promoting social protection and equality" (Scharpf 2002: 665). The lack of legal competence on the EU level, the lack of political consensus, the diversity of welfare traditions and differences in attitudes and values have kept social policies on the national level, while, what so far has emerged as EU welfare dimension is an "...unplanned collage" (de Búrca 2005: 9). Tax policies became a key instrument of market-making policies, aiming at growth and employment in Europe via increasing competitiveness. That is, tax policies are increasingly market driven rather than citizenship-rights driven. While the objectives of growth and employment will find broad consensus in all European countries, the sole focus of tax policies on competitiveness increases pressure on social policies and social standards.

Tax coordination or tax harmonisation both seem to be the obvious ways to limiting harmful tax competition effectively in the first place. However, a sizable number of economists are more inclined to accept the rollback of the welfare state by a process of passive social policy integration. We hold, however, that social policy has a legitimacy of its own. Viewed from this perspective, when suggestions are made to rescale the welfare state, rather than thinking about restraining fiscal competition by way of tax coordination, it seems to us that the tail wags the dog. As long as social objective functions reflect the equity concerns of citizens, solutions to the challenges of market integration should be developed actively and in a "top-down" manner while at the same time allowing for some policy variation across countries.

Given that the support for objectives of equality and social security is still broad in European countries, passive integration with a downward pressure on welfare states may well coincide with a downward trend in identification with the European idea. This calls for a coherent extended EU social policy dimension. However, any such development has to face the challenge of establishing a set of social rights while at the same time respecting the diversity of welfare state developments.

Active integration of European social policy can be achieved by loose forms of coordination, coordination without uniform national legislation, partial harmonisation or full harmonisation. Along this scale of actions, room for idiosyncratic action on the national or sub-national levels is reduced. So far, very few steps in harmonising social policy have been taken, while coordination of social security has long been a key instrument in eliminating barriers to free movement. A novel approach for European Social Policies, the Open Method of Coordination, has been introduced in the Lisbon Council in 2000. Both of these latter approaches improve communication between systems, but they are inadequate approaches if one attempts to prevent the harmful effects of fiscal competition on social protection and equity. Policymakers either need to advance tax coordination or to take effective steps towards social policy harmonisation to maintain a level of redistributive spending that meets the preferences of European citizens.

Endnote

1. This paper is based on research carried out under research grant F-2008 of the Austrian Science Fund (FWF) Special Research Program on International Tax Coordination. Special thanks go to Bruce Murray for proof-reading the text.

References

Andersen, G., Guillemard, A-M, Jensen, P-H and B. Pfau-Effinger (eds) (2005) The Changing Faces of Welfare. Consequences and Outcomes from a Citizenship Perspective, Bristol: The Policy Press.

Arts, W. and J. Gelissen (2002) Three Worlds of Welfare Capitalism or More. A State of the Art Report, *Journal of European Social Policy*, 12, 137–158.

Atkinson, A.B. (2000) The Welfare State, Budgetary Pressure and Labour Market Shifts, *Scandinavian Journal of Economics* 102 (3), 445–462

Avi-Yonah, R. S. (2000) Globalization, tax competition and the welfare state, *Havard Law Review*, Vol. 113, 1575–1676.

Borck, R., Caliendo, M. and Steiner, V. (2005) Fiscal Competition and the Composition of Public Spending: Theory and Evidence. *Discussion Paper* No. 528, DIW Berlin (German Institute for Economic Research), Berlin.

Busch, K. (1998) Das Korridormodell – ein Konzept zur Weiterentwicklung der EU-Sozialpolitik, in J. Schmid & R. Niketta, *Wohlfahrtsstaat: Krise und Reform im Vergleich*, Marburg: Metropolis Verlag.

Castles, F.G. (1993) *Families of Nations. Patterns of Public Policy in Western Democracies*, Dartmouth: Aldershot.

Cremer, H. and P. Pestieau (2004) Factor Mobility and redistribution, in J.V. Henderson & J. F. Thisse (eds) *Handbook of Regional and Urban Economics*, Amsterdam: North-Holland, 2529–2560.

de Búrca, G. (2005) Towards European Welfare?, in G. de Búrca, *EU Law and the Welfare State. In Search of Solidarity*, Oxford: Oxford University Press.

Dispersyn, M. et al. (1992) La construction d'un serpent social européen. Etude de faisabilité, *Revue Belge de Sécurité Social*, 36, 315–656.

Drèze, J.H. (2002) Economic and Social Security: The Role of the EU, *De Economist*, 150(1), 1–18.

Delsen, L. (2003) Are European Welfare States Sustainable?, Research Institute SOM (Systems, Organisations and Management) Research Report No. 03C28, University of Groningen, Groningen.

Eckordt, M. (2005) The Open Method of Coordination on Pensions. An economic Analysis of its Effects on Pension Reform, *Journal of European Social Policy*, 15, 247-267.

Ellison, N. (2005) *The Transformation of Welfare States*, London: Routledge.

Esping-Andersen, G. (1999) *Social Foundations of Post-Industrial Societies*, Oxford: Oxford University Press.

Esping-Andersen, G. (1990) *The Three Worlds of Welfare Capitalism*, Cambridge: Cambridge Policy Press.

Eurostat (2007) *European Social Statistics. Social Protection Expenditure and Receipts. Data 1996-2004*, European Communities, Luxembourg

Eurostat (2006) *Statistics in Focus 14/2006. Social Protection in the European Union*, European Communities, Luxembourg

Falkner, G. et al. (2005) *Complying with Europe. EU Harmonisation and Soft Law in the Member States*, Cambridge: Cambridge University Press.

Fuchs, M. (ed) (2005) *Europäisches Sozialrecht*, 4th Edition, Baden-Baden: Nomos.

Gunter, B. G. and R. van der Hoeven, (2004) The social dimension of globalization: A review of the literature, *International Labour Review*, 143, 7–43.

Heien, T. (2000) Attitudes towards the Welfare State in Europe: Starting Point or Obstacle on the Road to a Social Union? EWV *Working paper* 2/00. Universität Bielefeld, Fakultät für Soziologie.

Keen, M. and M. Marchand (1997) Fiscal competition and the pattern of public spending, *Journal of Public Economics*, Vol.66, 33-53.

Kuhnle, S. (ed) (2000), *Survival of the European Welfare State*, London: Routledge.

Leibfried, S. and P. Pierson (2000) Social Policy. Left to Courts and Markets?, in H. Wallace & W. Wallace (eds), *Policy-Making in the European Union*. 4th Edition, Oxford: Oxford University Press

Lewis, J. (1992) Gender and the Development of Welfare Regimes, *Journal of European Social Policy*, 8, 152–169.

OECD (2005) *OECD in Figures*. 2005 edition, Paris: OECD.

Osberg, L. and T. Smeeding (2005) Social values for equality and preferences for state intervention in the USA and Europe. Syracuse University, Center for Policy Research. Unpublished paper.

Pennings, F. (2001) *Introduction to European social security law,* Hague: Kluewer.

Perotti, R. (2001) Is a Uniform Social Policy Better? Fiscal Federalism and Factor Mobility, *The American Economic Review*, 91(3), 596–610.

Rodrik, D. (1997) Has globalization gone too far? Washington, DC : Institute for International Economics. [abridged version: California Management Review, Spring, Vol. 39 (3), 29–53.]

Scharpf, F.W. (1999) *Governing in Europe. Effective and Democratic?*, Oxford: Oxford University Press.

Scharpf, F.W. (2002) The European Social Model: Coping with the Challenges of Diversity, *Journal of Common Market Studies*, 40, 645–670.

Sinn, H.W. (2002) Der neue Systemwettbewerb, *Perspektiven der Wirtschaftspolitik*, 3(4), 391–407.

Sørensen, P.B. (2000) The case for international tax-coordination reconsidered, *Economic Policy*, 15, 429–471.

Tanzi, V. (2002) Globalization and the Future of Social Protection, *Scottish Journal of Political Economy*, 49, 116–127.

Trubek, D.M. and L.G. Trubek (2005) Hard and Soft Law in the Construction of Social Europe: The Role of the Open Method of Coordination, *European Law Journal*, 11, 343–364.

Verbist, G. (2004) Redistributive Effect and Progressivity of Taxes: An International Comparison across the EU using EUROMOD, EUROMOD Working Paper No. EM5/04, University of Antwerp, Antwerp.

Wildasin, D. E. (2000) Factor mobility and fiscal policy in the EU: political issues and analytical approaches, *Economic Policy*, 15, 337–378.

Wilson, J.D. (1999) Theories of Tax Competition. National Tax Journal, Vol 52 (2), 269–304.

Zeitlin, J. (2005) Social Europe and Experimentalist Governance: Towards a new Constitutional Compromise? In: G. de Búrca, *EU Law and the Welfare State. In Search of Solidarity*, Oxford: Oxford University Press.

Chapter 5
An Optional Common Consolidated Corporate Tax Base in the European Union

Krister Andersson

5.1 Introduction

The governments of the EU Member States agreed in Lisbon to make the European economy the most competitive and dynamic knowledge-based economy in the world by 2010. Reforming the economies must therefore be a top priority. Taxes are one of the most important elements of economic policies and have therefore attracted considerable attention in recent years. A corporation doing business within the EU has to comply with up to 27 different tax systems, administrations and legal systems. This in itself is a considerable obstacle to economic growth and prosperity. Besides the compliance costs, the differences in effective tax rates across investment types and regions may lead to over- or underinvestment.

The lack of provisions for consolidation across borders often results in non-recognition of losses incurred by a subsidiary in one country in assessing the taxable profit of its parent in another country even if the subsidiary is fully owned by the parent company. There are also numerous situations in which double taxation occurs. Applying the arm's length principle in transfer pricing may still lead to conflicting tax claims from different Treasuries. Even though the dispute is between countries, the business entity often must pay taxes on the same income in more than one state.

The uncertainty of the tax outcome is obvious. Furthermore, countries continuously change their tax systems and their interpretation of the existing code. Businesses therefore have to make investment decisions with tax uncertainty added to the market risk they take. The effect of the tax uncertainty on investment has not been discussed much in the economic literature.

Nor has the way countries try to reduce the risk and the possible welfare gains from such policies. This paper addresses some of these issues. Under what circumstances can businesses benefit from a common corporate tax base in Europe? What benefits would be lost and what gains made if an optional common consolidated corporate tax base was introduced?

The paper is divided into seven sections. Section 5.2 gives some background information on the taxation of business activities in Europe. Section 5.3 looks into response measures taken by several countries in Eastern Europe. Section 5.4 reviews some of the challenges in the corporate tax area. Section 5.5 describes the present work Member States in the European Union are involved in, constructing an optional common consolidated corporate tax base. Section 5.6 assesses the economic, legal and cultural barriers to such a tax regime. Finally, Sect. 5.7 summarises the report and makes some suggestions for the future direction of corporate tax policy in Europe.

5.2 Business Taxation in Europe

Most industrial countries have lowered their statutory corporate tax rates in the last two decades (see Fig. 5.1). The main reason behind this development has been their need to increase the number of viable investment projects after tax and thereby to promote job creation and economic growth. However, there has also been an element of tax competition. Competing for a given investment volume, however, would never suffice for governments. Since the tax revenue from corporate profits is a relatively small fraction of overall tax revenue, the lion's share of tax revenues from increased investment comes from the resulting jobs and consumption in the economy. It is from these sources that the government will receive most of the increase in tax revenue. With relatively high tax levels on labour income (payroll taxes, social security contributions and income taxes) and consumption, a reduction in corporate tax revenues may therefore easily be recouped from these tax revenue sources.

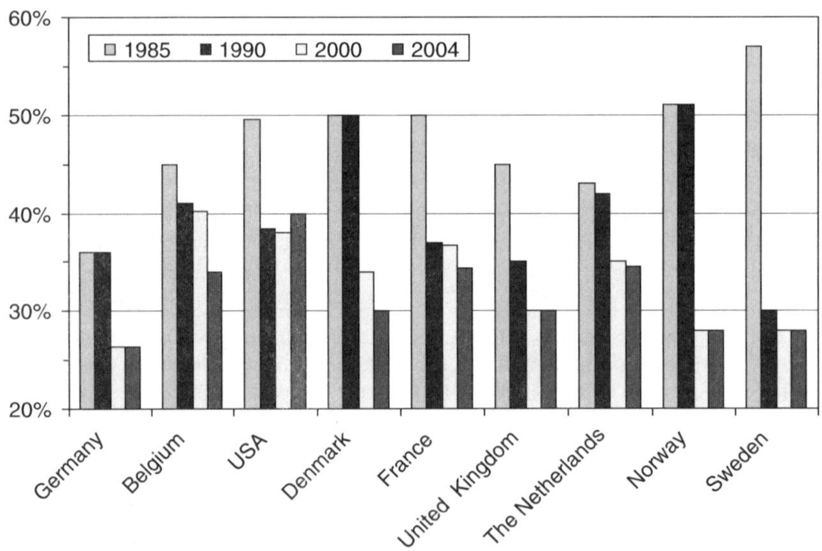

Source: Eurostat

Fig. 5.1. Statutory corporate tax rates

According to a study published by KPMG in April 2006, tax competition within Europe has forced corporate tax rates down to levels well below the rest of the world. Average statutory corporate tax rates in the European Union stood at 25 percent in 2005, compared with an average of 28 percent for the Organisation of Economic Co-operation and Development (OECD) countries, 28 percent for Latin America and 30 percent in the Asia-Pacific region.

According to the study, the average European tax rate fell by 0.28 percent to 25.04 percent in 2005, as a result of rate cuts in six EU Member States including France, Greece and the Netherlands. The average rate in the Asia-Pacific region was unchanged, while the regional average for Latin America fell very slightly, by less than a tenth of a percentage point.

Tax competition between EU Member States has increased as a result of the accession of 10 new members to the EU in 2004 and efforts by the EU judicial system to remove barriers to the free movement of capital, KPMG said. The majority of the 86 countries surveyed had either kept their tax rates unchanged since 2004 or had reduced them. The countries with the highest tax rates were Japan, with 40.69 percent, and the US with 40 percent. At the bottom of the scale was the Cayman Islands with a zero corporate tax rate.

Countries were becoming wary of aggressively cutting rates because of fears that neighbouring countries would follow suit. Increasingly, they were competing on other grounds, such as the "business friendliness" of their tax regimes. Favourable factors included the simplicity and stability of the tax system, the willingness of tax authorities to make rulings ahead of transactions and the absence of an aggressive approach to enforcing tax law.

The regional averages calculated by KPMG do not take account of the size of the constituent economies. As a result, the EU average is significantly below the rates charged in its largest economies, such as France (33.33 percent), Germany (38.34 percent), Italy (37.25 percent) and the UK (30 percent). Smaller countries tend to charge low corporate tax rates to compensate for the smaller size of their markets and other disadvantages, and to attract new investment without significantly jeopardising tax revenues from existing companies. Although Europe's largest economies have been reluctant to risk damaging their short term public finances by making drastic cuts in their tax rates, they are gradually coming under pressure from companies considering moving part of their operations or making new investments in lower tax regimes. The KPMG report said: "The progressive lowering of trade barriers, particularly in the EU, and the increasingly sophisticated supply chain options available to large, global companies provide credible alternatives for locating investments, so exerting constant downward pressure on headline rates."

While lower statutory corporate tax rates make more investment projects viable, they are not the only factor in an investment decision. The market size and a number of factors also play a crucial role. Nevertheless, a number of countries with low statutory corporate tax rates have experienced rapid investment growth while larger economies with higher rates have experienced relatively low levels of investment.

Four of the new Member States top the investment league in 2003 – Estonia, Slovak Republic, Latvia and Czech Republic. The challenge for all Member States to reduce unemployment and increase growth has received much more attention after the Lisbon agreement was reached but much more needs to be done. The role of taxes has become evident and after an initiative from the Commission in July 2004 (when two non-papers were issued)[1] all 27 Member States have decided to participate in a working group looking into the possibility of creating an optional common consolidated corporate tax base (CCCTB) (see Section 5.5).

In an economic union, whether it is just a country or a larger economic union consisting of many countries, it is important to try to achieve a tax system that does not unduly distort investment decisions.[2] Prevailing tax systems often distort decisions about what type of investment to undertake or where to locate it. They also influence the legal form of the investor and the decision on how to finance the investment. If Member States have a national perspective only, there is considerable risk of double taxation and misplacement of investments. It is therefore important to underline the need for generally applying Capital Import Neutrality (CIN) within an economic union.

Many countries have conversely focused on achieving Capital Export Neutrality (CEN) in the tax code. The tax treatment has thus been identical, irrespective of in which country the return on an investment came from. However, this often meant that identical investments in a country carried a different total tax burden since the tax rates at the investor level across countries vary. It is a challenge for Europe to extend the concept of capital import neutrality beyond the national borders. Capital export neutrality, however, may still be a principle that could be applied to activities in third countries, countries outside the union.

Some researchers have extended the analysis beyond CIN and CEN to CON, Capital Ownership Neutrality.[3] Differences in the taxation of owners will affect the ownership structure and may therefore distort investment decisions. The different tax rates and levels in Member States play a role, as well as imputation systems or partial inclusion systems. Besides the taxation of dividends, the tax treatment of capital gains is also important when assessing CON. So far, most of the academic literature on CON has focused on the "quality" of owners. With different tax burdens, the actual owners may not be the most efficient owners, and therefore the overall efficiency and growth of the economy will suffer.

However, there is also another implication which Member States may find particularly interesting. Since Member States retain the right to tax capital owners not only at the corporate level but also at the investor level, the ownership structure will have revenue implications. Countries with high tax burdens on capital income and gains will tend to have a reduced ownership share (which could lead to reduced overall investment level in the union since the most productive owners are suppressed) and these countries will collect less in taxes as well. Some owners will in reality be taxed only through the corporate tax since their home country does not tax long-term capital gains or even dividends. Domestic owners may have to pay capital gains taxes and dividend taxes, leaving them at a competitive disadvantage in relation to foreign owners. The revenue implication should be of particular importance to Member States. I therefore believe that it is important to include this factor in the analysis.[4]

Besides raising revenues for public spending, national taxes are used to correct for market failures and to influence consumer behavior. However, great care is often taken not to distort allocation decisions between various consumption commodities and investments in various assets. The ability to pay taxes, vertical equity as well as horizontal equity are other essential principles in most tax systems. Despite the considerable efforts to make the tax systems neutral and equitable, we experience large differences not only between countries (applying similar principles), but also within countries.

The comprehensive corporate tax study published by the European Commission in 2001 highlighted the tax distortions of cross-border investment in particular and the large variations of effective tax rates across countries as well as within countries.[5] By summing up some 11,000 investment combinations (type of investment, financing mode, locations etc) a summary table was presented showing considerable differences also between Member States (see Fig 5.2).

The impact of taxation on growth and national welfare is hard to assess with great accuracy. Clearly, countries with a less distorting tax system will do better than countries with highly distortive tax systems. Many other factors do, however, influence growth and welfare as well. To my knowledge, there is no ranking of how complex or distorting national tax systems are. Instead, the focus has been on tax competition and attracting foreign investment. As mentioned above, most industrial countries have reduced their statutory corporate tax rates substantially during the last decades. The main reason for these reductions has been to make more investment opportunities economically viable by reducing the tax wedge. To keep the reforms revenue neutral even in the very short term, tax bases have been broadened. In the longer term, revenues increase both since the tax rate reductions improve economic viability, and as a result of increased employment.

One country that has attracted much attention in the area of taxation is Ireland. As late as 1990, Ireland was the 21st wealthiest country in terms of per capita

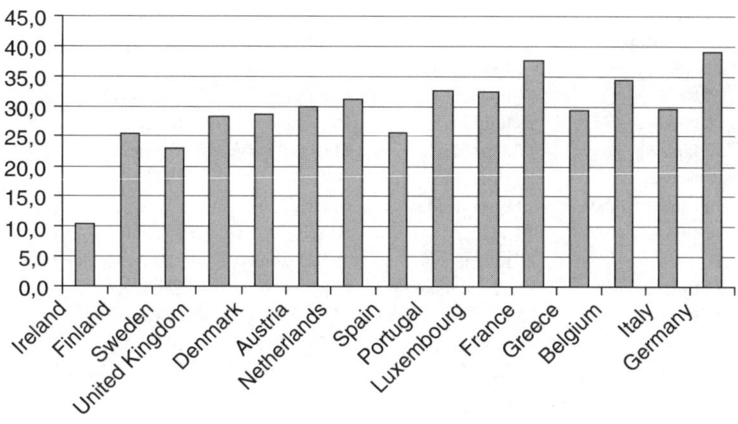

Source: Company taxation in the internal market, European Commission (2001).

Fig. 5.2. Effective company tax rates (Average marginal tax rate, 20 percent pre-tax rate of return, 1999)

income (see Table 5.1). Ten years later, Ireland had reached a position of the 7th wealthiest country. Data for 2004 indicate that Ireland has moved up further, to a 5th position in the OECD welfare league. Contributions from the EU budget may certainly have played a role, but most likely the changes of the Irish tax code are even more important. Ireland is now a net contributor to the EU budget.

Several of the new Member States have introduced proportional taxes, so called 'flat taxes' (see section 5.3). They have found it important to use national tax policies to attract foreign investments and to foster a growing domestic investment demand. Estonia is often singled out as the country with the most strategic tax policy. Retained earnings in the corporate sector are not taxed, while distributions are. Such a tax system tends to reduce the debt-equity ratio in the corporate sector, limiting the credit risk to lenders. However, the tax system also tends to lock in profits to the disadvantage of investment projects in new businesses.

Table 5.1. Per capita income in OECD-countries 1970–2004

1970	1980	1990	2000	2004
1 Switzerland	1 Switzerland	1 Luxembourg	1 Luxembourg	1 Luxembourg
2 United States	2 United States	2 Switzerland	2 Norway	2 United States
3 Denmark	3 Iceland	3 United States	3 United States	3 Norway
4 Luxembourg	4 Canada	4 Iceland	4 Switzerland	4 Ireland
5 Sweden	5 Luxembourg	5 Canada	5 Austria	5 Switzerland
6 Canada	6 Denmark	6 Austria	6 Denmark	6 Iceland
7 Australia	7 Austria	7 Japan	7 Ireland	7 Austria
8 Netherlands	8 Sweden	8 Sweden	8 Iceland	8 Denmark
9 New Zealand	9 Netherlands	9 Denmark	9 Canada	9 Canada
10 France	10 Belgium	10 Finland	10 Netherlands	10 United Kingdom
11 Germany	11 Australia	11 Germany	11 Sweden	11 Australia
12 Austria	12 France	12 Belgium	12 Australia	11 Netherlands
13 Belgium	13 Germany	13 Norway	13 Belgium	13 Belgium
14 United Kingdom	14 Norway	14 Netherlands	14 Japan	14 Finland
15 Iceland	15 Italy	15 France	15 France	15 Sweden
16 Italy	16 Finland	16 Italy	16 Finland	16 Japan
17 Finland	17 Japan	17 Australia	17 United Kingdom	17 France
18 Japan	18 New Zealand	18 United Kingdom	18 Germany	18 Germany
19 Norway	19 United Kingdom	19 New Zealand	19 Italy	19 Italy
20 Spain	20 Greece	20 Spain	20 Spain	20 Spain
21 Greece	21 Spain	21 Ireland	21 New Zealand	21 New Zealand
22 Ireland	22 Ireland	22 Czech republic	22 Portugal	22 Greece
23 Portugal	23 Portugal	23 Greece	23 Korea	23 Korea
24 Mexico	24 Mexico	24 Portugal	24 Greece	24 Portugal
25 Turkey	25 Korea	25 Korea	25 Czech republic	25 Czech Republic
26 Korea	26 Turkey	26 Mexico	26 Hungary	26 Hungary
		27 Poland	27 Slovak republic	27 Slovak Republic
		28 Turkey	28 Poland	28 Poland
			29 Mexico	29 Mexico
			30 Turkey	30 Turkey

Source: OECD.

5.3 Tax Policy in the New Member Countries

When the countries of Eastern and Central Europe (ECE) became market economies they had to make considerable adjustments to their tax systems. Some of the countries had the option of reintroducing a pre-WW II tax code, often with a considerable influence from the German tax code. The early reformers, like Hungary, embarked on an ambitious reform of the existing tax code while applying a high tax rate, and modernised some of its dormant elements – like taxation of exchanges of listed stocks and corporate profits. Others chose to make a drastic overhaul and used tax policy including tax rates as a strategic tool for attracting investment, both domestic and foreign.

It was important for these countries to signal a new orientation and a business-friendly environment. To promote rapid growth and modernisation of the economy, internal as well as external resources were badly needed. Despite large gains for some individuals during the period of transition to a market economy, most countries decided to implement low tax rates, also on capital gains. The risk of stifling the economy was seen as too great and efficiency considerations outweighed short term distributional considerations.

It was also important to signal to foreign investors that investments could be undertaken in these countries without political risks of nationalisation or drastic tax increases. Rather than embarking on tax holidays, many countries opted for broad tax bases and a proportional income tax system (see Fig. 5.3). These flat tax systems, however, developed further and some tax systems did not only encompass proportional income taxes but also equal tax rates on various types of other bases than income.

The benefit of having a top marginal tax rate on labour income at par with the corporate tax rate is obvious since there will be no incentives to convert labour income to capital income. Also, with proportional income taxes, the tax rates on businesses and individuals could be the same. Some countries, such as Slovakia, have, however, gone even further and introduced a complete flat tax regime. This is, however, not the full picture, social security contributions playing an important role. Although there are few, if any, reasons for having the same corporate tax rate as the VAT rate, Slovakia has simplified the tax rate to only one number.

Even in a country like Slovakia, however, the tax rates on dividends and capital gains are zero in order to avoid double taxation of business income. There is therefore no distortion of the intertemporal consumption decision by households and the tax system in this respect is as efficient as an Expenditure Tax would be.[6]

Countries like Estonia have attracted some criticism for having no corporate tax on retained earnings (only on profits distributed). However, it is in the interest of all Member States that the new members have a rapid economic development. That will increase export opportunities and benefit the region as a whole. Furthermore, the effective tax rates of the new Member States are still sizeable, even if they are often lower than in EU15. The most significant difference between the tax systems of old and new Member States is the lower level of complexity of the tax code in the new Member States. Considering the obstacles created by the complexity of current tax systems, it would be worthwhile for EU15 countries to pay as much attention to that circumstance as some countries now pay to the tax rates of the new members.

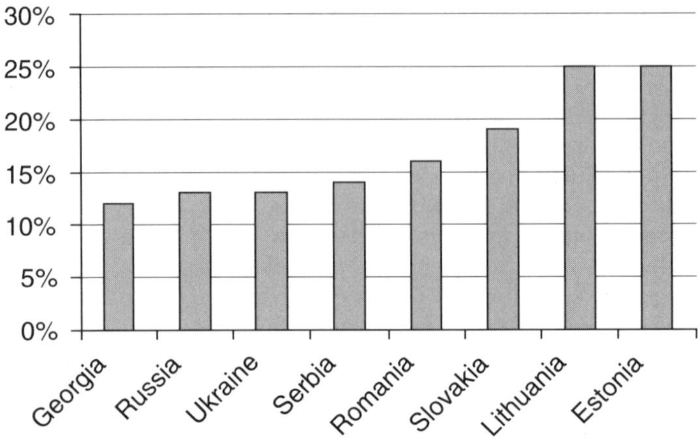

Sources: Various national tax codes.

Fig. 5.3. Flat rate countries, 2005

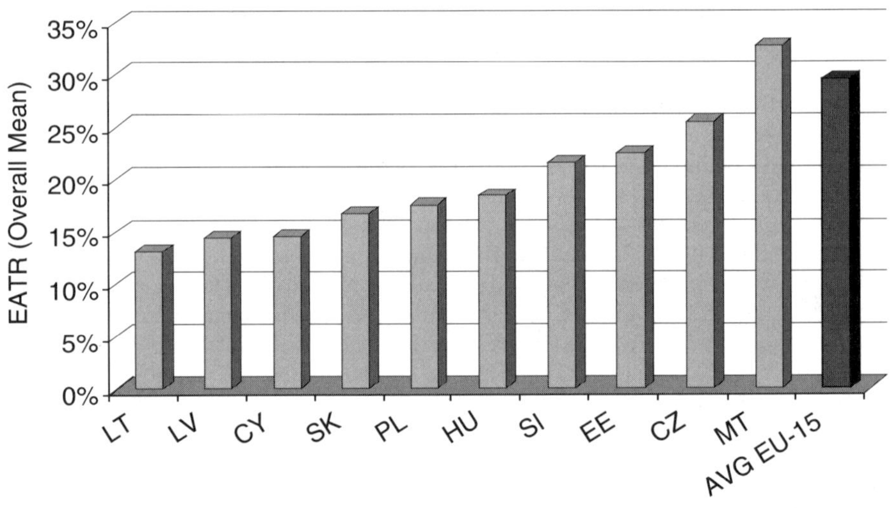

Sources: Finkenzeller and Spengel, 2004 and the European Commission (2002).

Fig. 5.4. Effective average tax rates for domestic investments in the new member states. Pre-tax rate of return, 20 percent

Despite the broad tax bases and generally low tax rates in the new Member States, there are significant differences within countries as well as across countries in the effective tax rate (see Fig. 5.4 and Table 5.2).

Table 5.2. Effective Tax Rates (%). Pre-tax rate of return, 20 percent.

Countries	Overall Mean	Overall Rank	Sources of Finance			Types of Assets				
			Retained Earnings	New Equity	Debt	Buildings	Intangtibles	Machinery	Financial Assets	Inventories
CY	14.5	3	16.3	16.3	11.0	13.7	14.9	14.6	14.7	14.7
CZ	25.5	9	28.8	28.8	19.0	23.4	27.8	23.0	27.5	26.1
EE	22.5	8	19.5	28.5	19.5	22.5	22.5	22.5	22.5	22.5
HU	18.4	6	20.2	20.2	14.6	22.2	18.8	17.4	17.6	15.8
LT	13.1	1	14.9	14.9	9.6	13.1	11.0	12.1	14.7	14.7
LV	14.4	2	16.1	16.1	10.9	18.7	12.3	12.1	14.7	14.0
MT	32.8	10	36.9	36.9	24.7	31.2	34.7	29.4	34.4	34.4
PL	17.5	5	19.7	19.7	13.1	18.2	14.5	19.2	18.7	16.8
SI	21.6	7	24.5	24.5	15.8	20.7	20.5	20.2	24.6	22.1
SK	16.7	4	18.9	18.9	12.3	15.5	15.6	15.9	18.7	17.7

Sources: Finkenzeller and Spengel, 2004.

It is likely that the need to increase investment played a major role in the design of tax regimes in Eastern and Central European countries. With broad bases and relatively low tax rates, or even flat taxes, the countries managed to signal to investors that a new business climate was at hand. This was a drastic and sometimes complete break with the past. Tax uncertainty needed to be avoided at all costs. The old Member States have basically had to react to this development and are now embarking on a reform process.

5.4 Challenges in the Corporate Tax Area

An obvious effect of having to apply 27 tax systems in the European Union is high compliance costs. The European Commission uses a questionnaire concerning company taxation and VAT compliance costs, the *European Tax Survey.*[7] In a report from such a survey the European Commission found that a parent company with subsidiaries in other EU Member States appears to have significantly (about 5 times) higher compliance costs than a company without subsidiaries.

- annual compliance costs are about 202,000 for the average SME (Small and Medium sized businesses) compared with 1,470,000 for a large company, corresponding to an estimated cost-sales ratio of 2.6% for SMEs compared to 0.02% for large companies
- the principal company tax compliance problems relate to transfer pricing, with an estimated 81.9% of companies indicating difficulties linked to documentation requirements
- the top VAT compliance problem is difficulties in coping with the procedures relating to the repayment and refund of VAT expenditures in other Member States, in particular for a company registered in a Member State where it does not have a permanent establishment. An estimated 53.5% of large companies

have not requested refunds to which they were entitled at some point due to these problems
- taxation is a factor for investment location decisions and affects company structure decisions.

The high compliance costs and the tax obstacles to cross-border investments translate into sub-optimal levels of investment and growth. In addition, the risk of double taxation, the uncertainty of implementation of existing rules and the risk of changing tax rules once an investment is undertaken, all adds up to a need for tax reform and increased transparency in the field of taxation.

Given the importance of investment in explaining economic performance, it comes as no surprise that national tax policy often aims at promoting investments. One key element in investment decisions is to reduce uncertainty. An important factor in assessing the desirability of national tax policies therefore is to what extent they reduce, or increase, uncertainty. The level of the tax rate will certainly have an impact on which investments are sufficiently profitable pre-tax to deliver a sufficiently high net of tax rate of return. In an open economy, many investment projects will have to yield the world market rate of return. However, capital markets are not perfect and since information is costly, not all investments in a country will yield this rate of return. The specific tax treatment of various investment projects, the way they are undertaken and by whom, may also influence the required rate of return.

Earlier reviews of the empirical research on the role of uncertainty have been provided by the classic surveys of Jorgensen (1971) and by Chirinko (1993) who surveys the literature since Jorgensen.[8] However, only in the last couple of decades has the irreversibility of investment decisions been fully incorporated into the analysis of investment decisions, and the negative impact of uncertainty on investments been fully recognised. The earlier conclusions that increased uncertainty would raise the marginal profitability of capital and therefore increase investment,[9] have broadly been replaced with the opposite conclusion – a view business economists and business leaders advocated all along.

The literature emphasizing the irreversibility of most fixed investment projects considers each investment as firm-specific, with specific installation costs, bankruptcy risks and commitment to engage labour. It makes investment adjustment costs asymmetric – larger for downward than for upward adjustments of the capital stock. This creates a range of inaction – investment takes place only when expected profitability exceeds a certain threshold. The more inflexible the labour market is, the more costly a downward adjustment becomes and the threshold rate of return turns correspondingly higher. Many have viewed the corporate investment decision as a call option. The potential investment to be made then corresponds to an option's exercise price and the length of time the company can wait before it has to decide is like the call option's time to expiration.

Various methods have been used to investigate the empirical implication of irreversibility in investment, the majority focusing on the relationship between investment flows and proxy measures of uncertainty. A general conclusion is that increased uncertainty, at both aggregate and disaggregate levels, leads to lower investment rates.[10]

A number of research papers have come to this conclusion. A paper by Carlsson (2004) derives the firm-level uncertainty indicator from a neoclassical investment model.[11] Its main findings are that uncertainty has a negative effect on capital accumulation in the short as well as in the long run. The estimates imply that an increase of one standard deviation in the uncertainty measure reduces investment by 16 percent on impact and, if the increase is permanent, the long-run stock of capital will decrease by 2 percent. Although there is considerable variation in the literature across the measures for capturing uncertainty, the overall evidence points towards a negative investment-uncertainty relationship.

However, in Hassett and Metcalf (1994) the type of tax uncertainty is shown to play a role for whether the investment impact is positive or not.[12] If an investment tax credit is introduced and stays for some years, the uncertainty about when it will be repealed may actually increase investment. Then, the results from models with irreversible investment in which increasing uncertainty about prices has been shown to increase the required rate of return (hurdle rate) and delay investment may not hold. This is because tax uncertainty has an unusual form that distinguishes it from price uncertainty: tax rates tend to remain constant for many years, and then change in large jumps.

Bittlingmayer (2001) uses a different approach.[13] He wonders what is missing in the investment literature. Arguably, politics is missing. In particular, political uncertainty poses substantial risks to investment. That uncertainty can take various forms. In extreme cases, a shift in the political climate will threaten property rights, the enforceability of contracts, the repatriation of profits, and the integrity of the monetary standard. He uses antitrust case filings as a measure of regulatory uncertainty. The resulting estimates imply that the low investment of the late 1950s and early 1960s in the US was due at least in part to a resurgence of aggressive antitrust and related initiatives seen as "anti-business". He concludes that some of the unexpectedly low investment of the 1970s may have had a similar origin.

In an empirical study, Edmiston (2001) reports that volatility in effective tax rates on capital income has a significant negative impact on investment per worker.[14] In all of the five models under consideration in the study, the negative effect of tax rate volatility on investment per worker was significant at the 95 percent confidence level or better, and in one case the effect was significant at the 99 percent level. According to this study, a unit increase in the volatility of effective tax rates on capital income in the OECD countries will, on average, lead to a decline in investment per worker of between 0.26 percent and 0.30 percent.

In another paper, Edmiston, Mudd and Valev (2003) explore the effect of tax uncertainty on Foreign Direct Investment (FDI).[15] In this study, they examine the connection between the different experiences of the transition countries in attracting foreign direct investment and their diverse experiences in transforming their tax structures to be consistent with a market economy. In particular, they study whether complexity and uncertainty in tax laws have deterred FDI by increasing transaction costs, the compliance burden and the unpredictability of tax liabilities. Their results indicate that complexity and uncertainty, in the sense of multiple tax rates, indeterminate language in the tax law and inconsistent changes in the tax laws, have a significant negative effect on inward FDI.

The countries of Eastern and Central Europe and the Former Soviet Union (FSU) have been undergoing monumental changes in every aspect of their society and economy. Reforming the tax structure, which is both an important tool for policy and a reflection of ideology, has deservedly occupied substantial attention in that process. Over the last decade, the 24 countries studied in this paper have chosen various paths in terms of tax law. The results suggest that, in the transition economies, more complex and vaguely worded legislation has a negative effect on the decisions of firms. This may be due to high compliance costs or simply because it adds to the already high level of uncertainty in that region. Tax complexity may be especially problematic in countries with underdeveloped tax administration where the staff is ill equipped to clarify and communicate appropriate interpretations of the existing legislation.

The authors conclude that given the evidence they have presented and analyzed, it is not at all clear that policy makers are aware of and fully recognize the costs of complexity and uncertainty in their deliberations on tax policy. Multiple rates and vague language can impose costs on firms and deter business activity. However, a shorter tax code does not necessarily imply a better business environment. If a more extensive and detailed tax law provides more precision, it may actually encourage business activity by reducing uncertainty and transaction costs associated with determining tax liability.

The question they address is whether these choices have had an impact on business activity through complexity and uncertainty. In particular, they examine whether complex and uncertain tax structures have reduced the magnitude of FDI. Their results suggest that a greater number of special provisions and ambiguities in the tax law has indeed had such an impact.

Stasavage (2000) also addresses the role of institutions for private investment across countries.[16] He points out that recent theoretical and empirical work has demonstrated a clear negative link between macroeconomic and political uncertainty and levels of private investment across countries. This result raises the question what institutions might help reduce this uncertainty, in particular, by allowing host governments to limit their own power to act opportunistically with respect to investors. Some have argued that governments might benefit from joining a multilateral investment agreement, but there remain doubts both about the enforceability and the desirability of such an accord. Stasavage proposes a modified version of this hypothesis and tests it using new cross-country data on political institutions. He finds that the average long-run effect of moving from a parliamentary system with one veto player in government to one with three veto players would be a 14% increase in private investment. Political checks and balances are associated with higher levels of private investment.

A paper by Lensink, Bo and Sterken (1999) examines the effect of different uncertainty measures on per capita GDP growth for a cross section of 138 countries for the 1970–1995 period.[17] Their results clearly confirm the relevance of uncertainty for economic growth. Four out of the six measures of uncertainty considered appear to have a robust and negative effect on economic growth. The uncertainty measures directly related to government policies, i.e. the uncertainty with respect to government expenditures, taxes and the budget deficit, are highly significant and have a robust negative effect on per capita growth. Sales uncertainty, as measured by exports, also has such an effect on economic growth.

They also find some evidence for a significant and negative effect of inflation uncertainty on economic growth. According to the authors, their results support the notion that predictability of government policy and credibility of governments stimulate economic growth by lowering uncertainty. This typically holds for fiscal policy, but also for monetary policy. A policy that stabilizes trade also helps in creating more growth per capita. These outcomes underline the extreme importance of a stable macro-economic environment for per capita economic growth.

This review of the literature on tax uncertainty and investment is by no means exhaustive. The effect of tax uncertainty will need further exploration. In the meantime governments have their own views on the importance of tax rates, tax burden and volatility of effective tax burden on investment. Many countries in Eastern Europe seem to have come to somewhat different conclusions than the old Member States of the EU when it comes to tax policy design.

By harmonising tax systems across Europe, tax uncertainty as well as compliance costs would decrease. Tax induced distortions would be reduced but the opportunity to use taxes to counteract national market failures would likewise be substantially reduced. Whether the net outcome on investment will be positive or not also depends on the actual set of rules in the new common tax system as compared to existing national systems. How competitive a uniform tax system would be depends largely on the tax rates applied and the rates of depreciation etc. as well as provisions and other tax code details. From a purely allocative perspective within the Union, a welfare enhancing improvement would materialize as tax induced distortions are reduced. It is very much the latter effect which has persuaded Member States to embark on a process to design a common consolidated corporate tax base in Europe (CCCTB).

5.5 Reforming Corporate Taxation in the EU – CCCTB

General Remarks

The Member States have increasingly become aware of the distortions caused by their tax systems. The role of the European Court of Justice (ECJ) can not be underestimated in this respect. In a number of judgments, the ECJ has found that national tax rules (often with a capital export neutrality approach to taxation) violate the EC Treaty. The number of potential problems for individual Member States is large. To some extent judgments by the ECJ have added to tax uncertainty, at least in the short run. Businesses do not necessarily know the outcome of a prospective ECJ judgment and, in particular, how Member States will react to the judgment. There is always a risk for short term revenue protecting measures, creating a level playing field by treating everyone as the ones the Court considered disfavoured.

If the profits were calculated according to common rules, country specific differences would disappear. This would reduce tax uncertainty and lower compliance costs. It would, however, cut down the options for Member States to grant specific provisions and incentives in the definition of taxable income. The competitiveness of a CCCTB would have to rely on general tax principles such as simplicity and efficiency as well as competitive tax depreciation rates for assets etc.

The lack of cross-border loss offset is a major obstacle in group taxation today. In particular for small countries, not allowing for cross-border loss relief is a competitive disadvantage. This has been recognised by countries like Austria that on Jan 1, 2005 introduced the right for an Austrian parent company to offset losses in a foreign subsidiary. If the loss later on also is claimed in the country of the subsidiary, the loss becomes taxable for the parent company in Austria.

Although similar schemes have been introduced in a few other countries (e.g. Denmark), group consolidation is restricted to domestic companies in the vast majority of the EU Member States. This limitation was subject to scrutiny by the ECJ in the case *Marks & Spencer Group Plc* (M&S), C-446/03, where M&S had been denied the offset of losses incurred in foreign subsidiaries.

In its judgment, the ECJ concludes that Articles 43 and 48 EC do not, as a general principle, preclude the Member States from denying cross border loss relief. According to the Court such a restriction can be justified by imperative reasons in the public interest. Referring to the principle of proportionality, the ECJ nevertheless established that a Member State must not refuse cross-border relief if the possibilities to offset losses in the country of the subsidiary are exhausted.

Thus, even after the M&S case, the lack of cross-border consolidation to a large extent remains a fact. As a result, groups are not taxed on their net income and may experience double taxation. Disputes with tax authorities over conflicting tax claims between countries leave the company in the middle – often having to pay taxes according to the claims of both countries.

A CCCTB would substantially reduce these problems by allowing for a cross-border consolidation within the EU. Resolving transfer pricing problems within the EU by eliminating all intra-group transactions before calculating taxable profit (consolidation) is a key factor behind the idea of a CCCTB. Provided the current concept of a CCCTB is recognized it would moreover:

- reduce the cost of compliance with the present 27 tax systems,
- resolve transfer pricing problems,
- simplify EU corporate restructuring, and
- increase tax transparency.

On these grounds, the European Commission has embarked on a project to provide for a legislative CCCTB proposal by 2008. The 27 Member States have agreed on a work program on a CCCTB with a three year agenda comprising four meetings each year. The project is structured in a Working Group including the Commission and all Member States as well as Sub Groups dealing with specific topics. The main objective of the Working Group is to examine from a technical perspective the definition of a CCCTB. It is important to underline that tax rates are not discussed and will remain the responsibility of individual Member States. This also applies to the tax rate applicable to the allocated profit according to the CCCTB. The national corporate tax rate and the corporate tax rate for the CCCTB may very well differ. The tax base between the national corporate tax system and the CCCTB will differ.[18]

Even though each Member State would retain the right to set its own statutory corporate tax rate, some kind of allocation mechanism of group profits would be needed. Much remains to be done but the work has made significant progress in the technical area. However, countries have not committed themselves to introduce the CCCTB. Some 20 of the 27 Member States have expressed their support for the work, while a few others have expressed their opposition to the project as such.

One reason for the opposition seems to be the risk of reduced tax competition that these countries perceive. That could certainly be the case, in particular if countries would embark on imposing restrictions on the tax rates. By making the system voluntary to the businesses, leaving the option of using the national tax systems – with their merits and shortcomings – the risk of reduced tax competition would be less. One could certainly argue that tax competition may increase rather than decrease, since tax systems would become more transparent and easy to compare.

With a uniform optional CCCTB tax uncertainty would certainly decrease in the EU. Whether such a system would be sufficiently competitive to boost investment and growth, however, would depend on its features in comparison to taxation elsewhere in the world. It would also depend on the technical design of the CCCTB and how it is implemented in the Member States. Under all circumstances, if the CCCTB is not to become an "additional layer" of rules, it is imperative that countries implement tax rules in a uniform way and that local deviations are excluded.

Important Elements in the Design of the CCCTB

The Commission has embarked on the CCCTB process by using an 'issue by issue' approach. Although this approach is supported as such by Member States and the business community, it makes it difficult to get an overview over the links between tax rules in various areas. Nevertheless, four main areas of work can be identified:

I. General Tax Principles: to be used to guide the development of a CCCTB and evaluate the treatment of the different structural elements

- General economic principles that can serve as criteria for a tax system e.g. equity, efficiency, effectiveness, simplicity, certainty and transparency
- Tax accounting principles such as: Valuation or measurement of assets and liabilities, separation of assets and liabilities, timing or recognition of income and expenses, materiality, substance over form, prudence, and the possible distinction between capital and revenue expenditure

II. Traditional Structural Elements of the Tax Base

- Depreciation, types of assets, rates and methods of tax deductible depreciation.
- Provisions
- Capital Gains

- Inventories
- Expenses
- Losses
- Inter-company dividends
- Special incentives, e.g. Research and Development
- Tax accounting rules
- Mergers & Acquisitions

III. Additional Elements of a Common Consolidated Corporate Tax Base

- Method of consolidation
- Legal and administrative framework, including auditing etc
- Anti-avoidance regime (including Controlled Foreign Company legislation)
- 'Water's Edge' – definitions and rules for EU/non EU delineation
- Double Taxation Agreements – EU and non-EU
- Mechanism for 'sharing' the consolidated tax base between individual Member States

IV. Application of the Common Consolidated Corporate Tax Base

- Technical Implications of partial implementation by Member States (enhanced cooperation)
- Compulsory or optional
- Restriction to certain categories of companies, e.g. by size, by sector.

Below, I comment on some of the most important aspects indicated above. Indeed, comments should preferably be given on a complete set of rules. Given the many outstanding issues yet to be resolved, this is, however, not possible at the present stage.

General Tax Principles

Any design of a tax base must of course be based on sound tax principles. Many countries have developed more or less ambitious targets in the design of their tax systems, both in terms of equity-efficiency trade off and neutral treatment of various forms of income from capital. All Member States now face a challenge in re-thinking what neutrality means in terms of a single market and of working together towards an internal market that can withstand the ever fiercer competition from non-European markets. Considering the commitment made by the Member States in signing the Lisbon agenda, each tax principle relied upon when designing the CCCTB should reasonably contribute to the achievement of these objectives. To achieve economic efficiency taxes should distort investment decisions as little as possible. Modes of financing, ownership and legal form of the business entity should preferably not influence an investment decision. Therefore, the CCCTB would need to be generally designed to apply Capital Import Neutrality (CIN).

This would provide for a level playing field in relation to third countries, allowing European businesses to compete on an equal footing with domestic businesses in new and rapidly growing markets outside the EU. Such a regime would also attract and strengthen the position of head offices within Europe.

The Tax Base in Terms of Depreciation Allowances

The issue of tax depreciation has been subject to extensive discussion between Member States as it constitutes an essential factor for the calculation of the tax base and thus the effective level of taxation. A considerable effort has been made to find out how countries depreciate fixed assets and intangibles and which provisions and reserves they allow. One of the core issues raised is whether assets should be depreciated on an individual or on a pool basis. Under the former approach, each asset is depreciated individually according to an individual depreciation scheme. Under the latter, all assets, or larger groups of assets, are depreciated together in a 'pool'. When the expressions 'pooling' and 'individualized' depreciation are used there is a sliding scale between two extremes where a certain method might feature more or less of the characteristics of either of those.

A depreciation regime should, to the extent possible, fulfil two main objectives. First of all, it is essential that the system promote *simplicity* and thereby promote growth. As has been pointed out by the European Commission, a CCCTB should lead to the simplification of the tax environment in the EU.[19] This would endorse business activity and entrepreneurship in Europe, something that is of utmost importance in the ever more competitive global market. At the same time, however, the depreciation method should provide for a *proper reflection of the economic lifetime of an asset*.

There appears to be a certain tension between these objectives. It seems likely that a pooling method is simpler for both the business community and the tax authorities. Under this approach it is, for example, not necessary to keep records of the economic value of each individual asset, documents that may be required to be kept for many years under an individualised approach. An individualised depreciation method, on the other hand, seems to give room for a more accurate forecast or assumption with respect to the economic lifetime of different types of assets. It is hard to see a pooling system with only one pool resulting in a proper reflection of the economic lifetime of an individual asset, although likewise it must be recognised that it is not possible to achieve a precise forecast of the economic lifetime of an individual asset.

The choice of depreciation method therefore seems to depend considerably on how one regards the respective importance of these two objectives. To the extent they cannot be achieved concurrently, a compromise position between the two extremes might be sought.

Since price stability is ensured in the European economy, a minor deferral or acceleration of tax payment should be less of a concern than when the inflation rate is high. This fact, in combination with the arbitrariness of expected economic lifetime, points in the direction of emphasizing simplicity over accuracy.

Simplicity of the tax system is crucial to promote business activity and to create a competitive tax system for the European market. With respect to administrative costs, simplicity is essential from the perspective of both the business community and the tax authorities. The perceived additional precision offered by a differentiated system based on an individualized scheme must be carefully weighed against the cost of managing such a system and the potential for tax arbitrage it may open up.

Furthermore, the complexity of an individualized approach appears increasingly difficult when adopted within the context of a CCCTB (compared to when used within the domestic context of one single country). The more depreciation groups that are created (or in the extreme case, a single depreciation assessment for each individual asset) the more room there is for countries to apply the depreciation regime differently with respect to individual assets. That is, it becomes more difficult to ensure that each individual asset is depreciated equally by all Member States. This suggests that the number of pools should be kept as few as possible.

With this in mind, a system developed around the principles of pooling might be appropriate.

In this context, it should also be noted that the difference between an individualized depreciation scheme and a pooling approach is not one of objective accuracy versus rough estimates. Both approaches are based on a forecast of the expected economical lifetime *ex ante*. The *ex post* outcome might be very different. No system will thus provide for an 'accurate' result. It should also be noted that there is an offsetting mechanism inherent in a pooling approach where some assets inevitably will be depreciated more quickly and some more slowly than accords with their 'actual' economical life. Whether a pooling approach provides for sufficient accuracy from an 'overall perspective' therefore largely depends on the depreciation rate chosen.

Nevertheless, it could be argued that an approach based on pooling, at least in its purest form, might still not provide an acceptable level of 'economic reality'. As pointed out by the European Commission, a "good balance between reflecting as closely as possible economic reality in the tax base and creating a system which can work effectively and efficiently across the EU has to be found".[20]

To ensure such a balance, some sort of intermediate system is conceivable. Such a scheme could be based on the concept of pooling but allow for a more individualized scheme with respect to a limited number of specific assets. As a point of departure, this could be based on the distinction between assets that typically represents large quantities and relatively low values (such as inventories) and assets characterized by low quantities and high values (such as buildings). The rationale behind such an approach would be that assets of the latter group are not excessively burdensome to document but at the same time, due to their relatively higher values, essential to depreciate at a 'correct' economic rate. With respect to the former group, the circumstance is the reverse.

Considering the characteristics of immovable property, a separate depreciation scheme could be used for this asset group. Other (movable) assets should preferably be depreciated under one or a very limited number of pools. Demarcation of such pools by reference to estimated economic life would be possible provided that the categorisation uses broad estimates, e.g. economic life less than 25 years or greater than 25 years. In any case, for reasons of simplicity, straightforward demarcation criteria should be sought.

In addition, under a simple and cost-effective system, assets that have a marginal value only and/or a very short economical lifetime (such as computers, mobile phones etc.) should be expensed. It should also be recognized that under modern environmental considerations land, previously considered as never loosing its value, in fact not only loses its value, but eventually becomes a liability (for example when a chemical plant is built and operated on it and there are environmental spills). Finally, the unique characteristics of intangibles (such as patents, trademarks and goodwill) might call for a differentiated treatment in relation to other movable assets.

To summarize on Asset and Tax Depreciation:

- all acquired assets should be depreciable. With the possible exception of unquoted closely held companies, the CCCTB must not feature a business purpose test
- the CCCTB must be comprehensive and include all assets, also existing depreciable assets
- for reasons of simplicity and compliance costs, the pooling method is preferred over individualized depreciation. Regarding the argument of accuracy, even the best estimation made *ex ante* is very different from the outcome *ex post*. Also, there is an offsetting mechanism in the pooling approach where some assets will be depreciated more quickly and some more slowly than their 'actual' economic lifetime
- nevertheless, an intermediate solution is conceivable. A distinction between movable and immovable assets would not make the system complicated. With regards to movable assets, any division in more than one pool must be kept to a minimum and be made using clear demarcation criteria. Provided the categorisation uses broad estimates (e.g. more or less than 25 years) demarcation based on economic lifetime is conceivable
- a depreciation period of 3–5 years for movable assets is suitable
- low value assets or assets with short economic lifetime should be expensed

Intangible Assets and Tax Depreciation

The treatment of intangible assets in the CCCTB raises some of the same issues as depreciation of tangible assets. For reasons of simplicity, depreciation of assets, tangible or intangible, should be based on the same principles. A diverging treatment will inevitably lead to demarcation problems and should therefore be avoided to the extent possible. For example, intangible assets of smaller value and/or short life should be expensed as incurred. This would promote simplicity and provide for similarity with respect to previous suggestions regarding the treatment of tangibles.

A distinction between internally generated and externally acquired intangibles is nevertheless necessary. Considering the great difficulty of identifying and valuating internally generated intangibles, it appears appropriate that the CCCTB is based on the main rule that they are not activated as assets for tax purposes. As a consequence, they should, also as a main rule, not be depreciated. Conversely, intangibles that are externally acquired should in principle be activated as assets at cost and depreciated. Whether internally generated or externally acquired, costs attributable to intangibles should always be deductible. In this respect, it should be underlined that intangibles, such as trade marks, like any other assets lose value if not maintained. Therefore, any intangible that is recognised as an asset must be depreciated.

R&D is a key driver for the economic growth and the competitiveness of the European Union. This may call for an accelerated depreciation scheme.

Finally, the establishment of value and economic life time should be based on the principle of prudence. The company possessing the asset is reasonably best equipped to make such judgements. If itemised, the CCCTB should be founded on a system where the depreciation is based on a fixed period of time rather than an *in casu* estimation of the life time. Again this is motivated by reason of simplicity and coherent applicability in relation to tangible assets.

Reserves, Provisions and Liabilities

In this area, Member States at present have very different rules. Therefore, current policies among Member States should not be the guiding star. A few remarks may be made.

Under the principle of net taxation, all costs must be deductible. On this basis, legally required provisions or transfers of reserves should as a minimum be deductible. This is furthermore motivated by the fact that such provisions or reserves inhibit a company's freedom to allocate profits and to use them in the most efficient way.

Another important matter refers to the treatment of provisions and reserves upon the transfer of businesses from one Member State to another. In order to remove tax obstacles for companies operating within the EU market and to comply with the principles of free movement of persons and freedom of establishment as they have been carved out by the ECJ (e.g. N-case),[21] it is imperative that reserves and provisions as regulated under the CCCTB rules are not subject to any forms of exit taxes.

Finally, provisions and reserves are closely linked to several "elements of judgment" such as timing and amount. In order to achieve a truly *common* tax base, attention must thus be paid not only to the adoption of uniform rules but also to a coherent application thereof. As has been indicated above, this is essential if the CCCTB is to *replace* the current situation of 27 parallel systems with one, rather than adding a new layer on top of existing ones.

Capital Gains and Losses

Also in this area, Member States have very different rules at present. In the CCCTB system it is important to follow some guidelines.

To promote simplicity, A CCCTB should be based on the principle that profits or losses arising in a business shall be treated the same way for tax purposes irrespectively of how they have materialized, be it from working capital or from other assets. Capital gains should thus be treated as ordinary business income.

In line with this, ring-fencing should be avoided. Apart from being questionable from a principle perspective, ring-fencing gives rise to substantial differentiation problems. This does for example imply how to distinguish between capital gains (and losses) and other business profits (and losses). Such a differentiated treatment also infringes on the principle of neutrality. As a general rule, capital gains should therefore be fully taxed (except if roll over treatment or specific incentive rates apply) and capital losses be fully deductible.

It shall furthermore be noted that ring-fencing creates specific problems for small businesses that possess only one or a few high net-worth ring-fenced assets (such as land or buildings). Where such businesses make capital losses, there is a substantial risk that they can not recoup these losses within a reasonable time frame.

A well-founded and internationally accepted principle is that taxation shall be levied only upon realization. It is essential that this principle be recognized within a CCCTB, as a system that provides for taxation of unrealized gains would give rise to unacceptable consequences both from a business perspective and from a government revenue stability perspective. For reasons of simplicity, administration costs and the stability of public finances, accrual taxation is not desirable. For this reason, it is essential that capital gains are taxed only upon realization.

To the extent capital gains are reinvested, it is furthermore desirable that roll-over relief be granted within a CCCTB. This is important to promote reinvestment and growth. Also, if no such relief is available, there is a risk that assets are used longer than appropriate from an economic efficiency perspective. Roll-over relief is furthermore structurally important in order to uphold the principle that tax shall be levied only on income and not on substance.

Finally, with respect to disposal occurring between related companies, it is important that any documentation requirements and related rules are minimized and that they are based on the principles of simplicity and prudence. Also, to promote simplicity, indexation for inflation should preferably be avoided and monetary policy should ensure price stability. The negative effects of a low but stable inflation rate could be taken care of by increasing depreciation rates and by lowering tax rates. Inflation is also dealt with by allowing for roll-over relief.

Taxable Income

Since the CCCTB does not necessarily follow the accounting rules, there is a need to define taxable income and costs. In doing so, it is crucial to adhere to the principles of simplicity, tax capacity and net taxation.

To achieve this, the taxable income (profit or loss) must be founded on the difference between *all income* and *all expenses* arising within a business. Any deviations, for example by taxing income or gains not yet realized or by disallowing expenses, depart from net taxation. Indeed, out of policy considerations, it might be appropriate to disallow deduction of expenses connected to criminal activities such as bribes, fines and penalties. With respect to other expenses, however, there should in principle be no limitation of the right to deduct them.

Apart from complying with the principle of net taxation, it would avoid the many problems connected to business purpose tests or similar complex regimes.

In this context it shall be noted that specific difficulties might occasionally arise with respect to closely held companies. This might, for example, be the case where the owner and the management coincide. For such companies, it can sometimes be difficult to draw a clear line between business expenses and expenses for personal consumption as the control that the owners exercise in widely held companies may be insufficient. As such conflicts exclusively relate to closely held companies, the discussion on whether to adopt special rules for this should be limited to such businesses. For widely held companies no special rules should apply and costs must be deductible without restrictions.

As established above, to promote simplicity and net taxation, all income should be treated the same way regardless how it has materialized. Nevertheless, dividends and gains from participations in subsidiaries should be exempt for structural reasons. This is crucial in order to avoid chain taxation.

In general, the principle of prudence should be adhered to. Income can only be recognized once it is certain, whereas costs should be recognized as soon as they are probable and can be measured. It is therefore important to tax only such income or gains that have been realized in as much as they have been generated by a transaction in the market. Only then is the capacity to pay taxes sufficiently proven. It is not enough that it is probable that future economic benefits will flow to the enterprise. The benefit has to be certain and the taxpayer has to have control over it.

Finally, even though the economic performance of a business is measured periodically for fiscal reasons (i.e. at the end of each fiscal year), the principle of net taxation is not limited to this period. It extends over a business's lifetime. From a principle perspective, an unlimited loss carry back should hence be allowed to make sure that not more than the net profit of a company is taxed. If this is not accepted by the Member States, unlimited loss carry forward must as a minimum be allowed as any limitation of this right infringes on net taxation.

International Aspects and Territorial Scope

The objective of efficiency can be achieved in several ways. Following the principle of net taxation, it is essential that the CCCTB adequately removes international double taxation which occurs in relation to third states and that any lack of recognition of costs or losses is avoided. In achieving this, the CCCTB could principally be drafted based on either the principle of Capital Export Neutrality (CEN) or Capital Import Neutrality (CIN). To promote efficiency and competitiveness, there is a strong preference for the latter approach since it would result in an efficient and simple double tax relief as well as an equal tax treatment (or neutrality) for different types of investment and ownership. This would provide for a level playing field with respect to business located in third countries, something that is particularly important if European businesses are to be competitive in the global economy. Such a regime would also attract and strengthen the position of head offices within Europe.

To ensure uniformity and to foster simplicity, double taxation relief should be given as an element of the CCCTB itself, rather than at the national level by bilateral tax treaties. A reason for such a system is the difficulty to identify the origin of an income element in the profit allocated to an individual Member State. Apart from fostering efficiency, such an approach would also minimize the difficulties of having to apply bilateral double tax treaties in the context of the CCCTB. As double tax treaties can only reduce the tax liability, their applicability is limited to situations where the underlying tax legislation (i.e. the CCCTB) provides for a less favourable relief than the treaty. Thus, where the CCCTB provides for a comprehensive relief by means of exemption, the problems of having to apply and/or re-negotiate existing treaties are kept to a minimum.

In achieving CIN, there are great benefits in designing the CCCTB around the principle of territoriality (i.e. source taxation) *provided* there will be no underlying domestic taxation of any exempt income.[22] As mentioned above, the CCCTB must be comprehensive and exclusive in relation to domestic systems if it is in fact to replace the current parallel imposition of 27 different tax systems with one. No taxation must thus be levied under domestic (national) rules. For reasons of competitiveness, the CCCTB should also allow for the deduction of foreign losses, possibly accompanied with a recapture mechanism. Such an approach would be simple, competitive and resolve many of the double tax problems currently arising due to overlapping tax jurisdictions. As a matter of fact, the proliferation of worldwide taxation systems in combination with insufficient double taxation relief has substantially reduced an efficient global allocation of investment capital. The European Union could play an instrumental role in reversing this trend (even if tax proposals in the US already have moved in this direction) by ensuring full double taxation relief.

The suggested approach would resolve many of the double tax problems arising from lack of consolidation. International double taxation is one of the most hampering obstacles against economic efficiency and growth. Under current tax systems, it frequently occurs either because of double residence or because of two countries adopting source and residence taxation simultaneously on the same income. Under a single taxation approach, double taxation of *outbound investment* would generally be resolved through exemption, without having to rely on the complex and often unsatisfactory application of national double tax treaties.

Provided the non-EU state does not likewise use a single taxation approach with exemption, double taxation on *inbound investment* could still be an issue that has to be resolved by traditional means (i.e. double tax treaties). Following the concept of CIN, this could be done by exemption. Currently, many treaties are developed around the principle of CEN by allowing for a credit of the foreign tax. Given the merits of CIN, it is desirable that a common approach for CCCTB purposes is established by developing a common EU tax treaty based on the exemption approach.

The tax base is best protected by ensuring that the CCCTB is competitive and attractive for foreign investors. Anti-avoidance rules are typically very complex and provide for substantial tax uncertainty. They frequently also give rise to sub optimal investment decisions. This must be prevented. Any such rules should therefore be included in the CCCTB with great care and must not obstruct valid business transactions.

Some measures may be considered necessary by Member States to ensure that the appropriate distribution of the right to tax is upheld. This particularly refers to the adoption of a common transfer pricing regulation. In line with current Member

State rules, it should be developed around the arm's length principle. Many of the current difficulties follow from the fact that the current rules among the Member States vary. This could be significantly remedied by the implementation of a common transfer pricing regime vis-à-vis third countries. Following international practices, this regime as well should preferably be based on the arm's length principle and be accompanied by a clear dispute resolution mechanism.

To summarize, in the specific design of the CCCTB in the area of international taxation, the following issues should be considered:

- investments in the union should be based on the principles of *Capital Import Neutrality* (CIN). A system based on source taxation (territoriality) is preferred provided there will be no underlying domestic taxation of any exempt income. Also for reasons of competitiveness, the CCCTB should allow for a deduction of final losses attributable to subsidiaries outside the CCCTB-jurisdiction.
- Under a world-wide regime, foreign source income should be exempt to avoid double taxation
- double taxation should be avoided by means of exemption through an explicit rule within the CCCTB-regulation itself
- anti-avoidance rules should only be included if absolutely necessary and must not obstruct valid business transactions
- in the relation to third states, the CCCTB should provide for common transfer pricing rules based on the arm's length principle and be accompanied by a clear dispute resolution mechanism
- parallel to the CCCTB, the development of a common EU tax treaty would be desirable
- the CCCTB shall only cover entities (tax subjects) situated within a CCCTB-state
- the CCCTB must be comprehensive and exclusive in relation to domestic systems. No taxation must be levied under domestic (national) rules on those opting for CCCTB.
- if taxation is to be levied on a world-wide basis, both income and losses attributable to foreign sources shall be included
- the exemption of foreign source income should not infringe on the possibility to deduct foreign losses. It could, however, also under a world-wide regime, be accompanied with a recapture mechanism to ensure taxation of net profits
- dividends must under any regime be exempt to prevent economic double taxation
- all other income/losses (most notably business profits, royalties and interest income) should be included in the CCCTB
- the source of an income refers to the place where the income creating activity is carried out (royalties e.g. where the licensor is situated, interest income where the lender is situated, dividends where the subsidiary is residing and business profits where the business is performed)
- income/sources held indirectly by a resident through a third country intermediate should be included in the CCCTB

- income covered by the CCCTB should not be subject to withholding tax within the CCCTB jurisdiction
- allocation of profits and losses to a permanent establishment (PE) should follow the arm's length principle established in the OECD Model Tax Convention (MTC)
- anti-avoidance rules must only be adopted where absolutely necessary and ensuring that they do not infringe on the principle of net taxation.

Group Taxation

An issue linked to the international aspects of the CCCTB is group taxation. Here, it is important to recall that a CCCTB offers three core benefits:

1. removal of *double taxation* due to conflicting tax claims (e.g. transfer pricing-issues),
2. reduction of compliance costs by allowing for a *single compliance* of a single set of rules in a single location, and
3. assurance of net taxation through *consolidation*.

These considerations result in a strong preference for the CCCTB to be consolidated from the beginning. Without consolidation, two of these fundamental advantages would fail, essentially depriving the project from its chances to contribute to the much needed growth in the EU economy. A two step approach (i.e. an approach with first a common base, and then, later on, consolidation across participating countries) would be detrimental to the process and face the risk of creating a system which is not removing tax obstacles or designed to operate efficiently in a consolidated tax environment. It would also remove much of the incentive to create a truly competitive system that will cope with international competition.

The definition of a group is essential for the application of the CCCTB as it will determine which companies will be covered by the CCCTB rules and thus enjoy the benefits of the scheme. If the group opt for the CCCTB, all entities in the group must enter the system, i.e no "cherry picking". It is crucial that the CCCTB provides for a simple and straightforward group concept.

For this reason, a definition based on the legal relationship between two companies rather than economic criteria such as economic or managerial control is preferred. However, the CCCTB nevertheless needs to recognize that there are a number of significant dual structures operating in the EU. To ensure that such structures can facilitate the CCCTB-regime, it might be suggested to allow groups that show a significant and sufficient economic link and which are operating under common management, to be allowed to opt in as one group.

An important issue is how consolidation is to be calculated. For reasons of simplicity, there is a clear preference for a system where the consolidation is based on the companies' entire profits or losses. A proportional scheme where the consolidation is based on the level of legal ownership would be overly complex. The more detailed design of the consolidation method is indeed a very difficult issue and it is hard to make any detailed comments at this stage in the process. As a general remark, however, it is important that the consolidation regime adopted for the CCCTB be designed to reduce compliance costs and prevent double taxation arising from transfer pricing. As argued above, one of the core benefits of a CCCTB is to reduce compliance costs by allowing for a single compliance in a single location. The consolidation method would obviously need to be designed to comply with this objective.

A consequential question is what type of legal ownership should qualify for CCCTB treatment (e.g. voting and/or non-voting shares). In this respect it is crucial that the CCCTB regime recognize that Member States under general law adopt a large range of differentiated regimes, enabling different voting rights, 'golden shares' etc. Recognizing the holding of the voting rights as a key factor for company control and decision making, a dual requirement between shares/capital and voting rights could also be considered.

To maximise the benefits of the CCCTB it should cover as many entity types as possible, including both opaque and transparent entities. It is essential that the CCCTB, to the extent possible, respect the principle of neutrality and not interfere with the most efficient way of structuring business activities by using appropriate entity forms. Neither should it require current groups to restructure in order to benefit from the regime.

In this context, it is important to underline that all entities in the same group should be included in the CCCTB regardless of the activity pursued. As has been repeatedly stated, the CCCTB must be a comprehensive system that is "exclusive" and not "supplementary" to the domestic tax regimes. The aim of the CCCTB is to replace 27 parallel tax systems with one common scheme, which should be the only one a business has to comply with. Therefore, eligible entities should be included in the CCCTB, regardless of the type of activity carried out. In rare cases, where a differentiated treatment might be justified for a certain sector, this should be provided for within the CCCTB regime itself and not under domestic law.

Administrative and Legal Framework

The design of the administrative and legal framework naturally attracts much attention by Member States. The importance of adopting well functioning administrative rules for the CCCTB cannot be overemphasized. Correctly implemented, it will promote *simplicity*, reduce *compliance costs* and ensure a streamlined and *common application* of the CCCTB in all countries. Improperly designed, however, it could lead to increased complexity and compliance costs. If this were to be the case, the very purpose of the CCCTB regime would be unfulfilled.

With this in mind, it shall be underlined that one of the most fundamental benefits of a CCCTB is to reduce the compliance cost of having to deal with up to 27 systems monitored by 27 tax authorities by replacing it with the option for a group to choose to be taxed according to a common and consolidated tax base. For the CCCTB to have any significant impact on the compliance burden, however, it must not only provide for a single set of rules, but also allow for a *single compliance* in a *single location*. If the system were to require the corporate group to continuously deal with the tax administration in each Member State, the fact that there is a common set of rules would not significantly reduce compliance costs. It is therefore essential that the administrative framework follows the CCCTB concept and that it is developed around a *one-stop-shop* approach where a single Member State is responsible for handling all tax affairs of a given group.

Notably, this approach would mean that the taxpayer has to file one tax return only in one country for the entire group. Most reasonably this would be to the tax authority in the Member State were the ultimate EU-parent is residing. Similarly, the approach would mean that the 'one-stop-shop' authority is alone responsible for the audit of the books. It must be recognized that under the CCCTB, the computation of the tax base in no longer a local matter with respect to the individual entity. Consequently, the tax audit of a separate company is not to be carried out by the individual local authority in each Member State where the group is active.

The 'one-stop-shop' approach must equally apply to the apportionment of the calculated profit or loss. For obvious reasons, it is not acceptable that an apportionment decision made by the appointed tax authority (i.e. the one in the parent state) can be ignored or overruled by the tax administration of another Member State. The 'one-stop-shop' authority shall be able to make an apportionment ruling which is authoritative for the taxpayer. Any disagreement between the Member States shall be resolved at a common and single point of authority. This is absolutely crucial if the CCCTB is to resolve the problem of double taxation and avoid disputes between Member States to the ultimate detriment of the taxpayer.

Finally, it should be emphasized that the introduction of a CCCTB needs to be made by means of a regulation. Given the experience in the VAT-area, where the Community legislation has been introduced in the Member States through national laws imposed in implementation of directives, it is clear that such an approach is inferior in establishing a common EU-legislation which is implemented and enforced in the same way in all Member States. To ensure that the CCCTB becomes a truly *common* tax base, it would therefore be important if it could be introduced through a regulation, directly applicable as such in the Member States.

Personal Scope

The issue of who should be eligible for the CCCTB is of course a crucial one. To be competitive and attractive, the CCCTB should be applicable as widely as possible with respect to the definition of eligible entities. In line with this, the general approach for defining eligible entities should be to identify what business vehicles to exclude rather than what business vehicles to include. An entity type should only be excluded where it is motivated by non-arbitrary and very convincing reasons. Nevertheless, some demarcation is necessary.

The fundamental purpose of the CCCTB is to provide for a common tax base for *corporate income tax* purposes throughout the EU. That is, the aim is to create a common base on which the Member States levies their corporate taxation. As has been underlined repeatedly, it is essential that the CCCTB materializes in a comprehensive corporate tax system that when elected replaces current domestic systems.

With this in mind, the CCCTB should reasonably cover all entities that trigger corporate income tax, either directly (i.e. opaque entities) or indirectly (i.e. transparent entities), in their respective Member States. Conversely, activities carried out in entities that do not trigger corporate income tax should be excluded. This "corporate tax nexus" approach would promote clarity and simplicity and provide for a logical delimitation of the personal scope. Moreover, a CCCTB that would include some "corporate entities" but not others would deviate from the objective of creating a common and comprehensive tax base for corporate tax purposes in the EU. The exclusion of certain entity types liable to corporate taxation would lead to situations where the CCCTB and current domestic tax rules have to be applied concurrently. This would defeat the very purpose of the CCCTB and provide for considerable complexity both for taxpayers and tax administration.

In this regard, it should be underlined that the CCCTB must not be based on a "business purpose test". Such a subjective test would provide for harmful uncertainty and lead to complex evaluation processes both for business and for tax administrations. Instead, the CCCTB should be based on the presumption that an entity which is liable to corporate taxation is carrying on a business activity for CCCTB purposes.

Under the suggested "corporate tax nexus"-approach, there is a need to clarify what is a corporate income tax for CCCTB purposes. This issue does not appear to create any major difficulties. All Member States impose corporate income taxes of some sort and they are relatively easy to identify. To ensure certainty and predictability, however, the CCCTB should provide for a list where the various domestic taxes are clearly defined. Such a list already exists in the parent/subsidiary directive (90/435/EEC) and in implementing national legislation.

In addition, it is necessary to clarify when an entity is liable to such a corporate tax and thus eligible for CCCTB-treatment. In this respect, it is necessary to make a distinction between opaque and transparent entities. An opaque entity, such as most typically a limited liability company, is liable to corporate tax as such and should thus undoubtedly be covered by the CCCTB.

Based on the arguments of a wide application, transparent entities should, however, also be included in the CCCTB. Transparent entities, such as partnerships, are very commonly used in current business structures and the exclusion of this entity type would frequently require difficult and costly reorganizations to allow for a common CCCTB-treatment. Compliance costs of entering into the system must be kept to a minimum, meaning that business should be able to opt for CCCTB-treatment with a minimum need of restructuring. Also, for the efficiency and neutrality reasons mentioned above, it should be possible to run a business through a transparent entity without being disallowed CCCTB-treatment. It should furthermore be noted that an exclusion of this entity type would open the door for so-called "cherry picking".

Although transparent entities should be included as such, the "corporate tax nexus" implies that the income of such entities would be included in the CCCTB only where the owner is liable to corporate income tax for that income. Thus, an income generated by a transparent entity held (either directly or indirectly through other transparent legal entities) by an opaque entity (such as a limited liability company) would be covered. Conversely, to the extent the transparent entity is held by individuals, the CCCTB would generally not apply, as the income then typically is subject to individual rather than corporate income tax.

Finally, to maximize the benefits of a simple and competitive CCCTB, the system should not be available only with respect to groups conducting cross-border trade, but also with respect to activities carried out in only one Member State. This would reduce the problem of having to shift systems upon the expansion or reduction of the group's cross-border activities.

Allocation Key

The possible revenue implications of the CCCTB for Member States make the allocation of tax revenues a key issue. There is a considerable risk that short term revenue implications will attract so much attention that longer term revenues and growth generating aspects of the CCCTB are not recognised. Since the CCCTB is set to eliminate transfer pricing issues for participating companies in these countries, the sharing mechanism is important. Without consolidation, there are few benefits with the new corporate tax system. With consolidation there is a need to find a suitable key to allocate tax revenues. This issue must therefore be resolved.

The Commission has identified three different approaches. One would be to apply a formula apportionment. This system would to some extent resemble the system used in federal states. There would however be only *one* formula and it would identify factors important for generating profits. In a globalized economy, it is not easy to identify where profits have materialised in the production chain. It is equally difficult to find one formula allocating the profit in such a way that all Member States agree. Key elements in the formula are likely to be the production factors (labour and capital) and sales. Needless to say, Member States will have different views on the relative importance of the factors included in the formula.

The second approach would be to allocate revenues according to Value Added. However, since value added is dependent on prices, an element of transfer pricing issues will resurface. Since one of the most important issues to be resolved with the CCCTB is the elimination of transfer pricing, any reintroduction of tax difficulties due to shift of profits across countries would probably be very objectionable. This is unfortunate, since there is much experience in the VAT area in the European Union and value added in theory is a good and reliable concept. There are however transfer pricing problems – even though they are much reduced compared to the present situation where net profits potentially are shifted rather than value added. Nevertheless, it seems more likely that Member States opt for a formula apportionment approach than opting for a value added approach.

A third approach would be to apply a macro-economic formula. Profits would simply be distributed to Member States in relation to their GDP or some other macro economic variable. Such a method would not be subject to manipulations by companies but the distribution of tax revenues would no longer mirror actual economic activities. Taxes would have to be paid to participating Member States in the CCCTB even in the case when the Group has no economic activity in the country. This could in turn create an adverse incentive structure for governments to increase the tax rate for profits taxable under the CCCTB. In theory they might as well adopt a tax rate of 100% since there would not be any significant effect on the revenue base from a higher tax rate. However, as Member States increase their tax rates, economic activity in Europe would decrease (at least for companies that opted for the CCCTB) and revenues would be reduced for all governments. To avoid any temptation unduly to increase the corporate tax rate for the CCCTB, restrictions may be needed. Tax rates, however, are not discussed in the work of the CCCTB. They remain a strictly national area of competence and it is hard to see how any restrictions on rates could be agreed upon. Instead, it is likely that some kind of formula apportionment will be chosen. Once there is an agreement on the formula, it is likely to be very stable since it would be easy to identify winners and losers if the formula were to change. Under all circumstances, the formula must be identical for all Member States.

Key Principles to Make the CCCTB Attractive and Successful

To sum up, the development of a CCCTB should refer to general tax principles and each principle relied upon must contribute to the achievement of the Lisbon objectives. By making the CCCTB optional to businesses, national tax systems will face institutional competition in a transparent way. The CCCTB regime will be attractive to businesses since it will resolve transfer pricing problems in participating countries and allow for increased simplicity.

However, for the CCCTB regime to be successful a number of key features are important:

- competitiveness in the design ensuring economic efficiency,
- simplicity,
- consolidation from the beginning
- optional for businesses
- one-stop-shop (single tax return filed in a single location),
- Capital Import Neutrality (source taxation/exemption),
- net taxation,
- removal of double taxation (both economic and juridical),
- comprehensive and exclusive (i.e. no parallel domestic taxation),
- low compliance costs,
- based on realization
- resolve transfer pricing problems
- no tax rate harmonization or minimum rate,
- no room for domestic flexibility/deviation,
- pooling as method for tax depreciation, and
- deduction of foreign losses as an incentive (recapture mechanism).

A CCCTB regime which fails to fulfil these objectives will not contribute sufficiently to make it possible to achieve the Lisbon objectives. Although the issue has not yet been tabled, it is desirable that the CCCTB could be introduced by means of a regulation. A directive would carry the risk of falling short of reaching a *common* tax base.

Future Work

The European Commission will continue to issue progress reports. There is still considerable work to be done on tax incentives and anti-avoidance rules as well as on the administrative aspects. Then there is the whole issue of transition rules. The political process is likely to focus on consolidation and the mechanism of sharing revenues. It remains to be seen how many countries are willing to allow the introduction of a completely new and competing tax system to their national systems. The European Commission is expected to present a comprehensive Community legislative measure by the end of 2008.

5.6 Economic, Legal and Cultural Barriers to a Common Business Taxation

Country specific conditions can probably be more easily addressed with a national tax policy. A cost disadvantage may be partially offset by a lower effective tax burden and areas important for development, like research and development spending, can be promoted by the tax system. However, the resulting complexity and borderline cases may require a considerable administrative effort with correspondingly high compliance costs. In an economic union like the EU, some of the tax concessions may furthermore constitute illegal state aid.

To the extent specific tax rules are not exactly matching externalities, welfare will indeed deteriorate rather than improve. In practice, it is impossible to apply specific tax rates to each good or activity, furthermore according to consumer or investor. Most countries have therefore opted for broad tax bases and lower tax rates. However, the level and rate structures differ across Member States. There will therefore be tax induced changes as markets are opened up.

For the union as such, a reduction of tax induced behaviour will result in increased economic efficiency and welfare. On the negative side is the lost opportunity to tailor counter-measures to negative externalities. However, the economic efficiency arguments broadly speak in favour of a common tax policy. With less tailored national tax policy, it will also be more difficult to satisfy political requests based on equity and distributional considerations. However, the increased growth rate and prosperity will tend to be favourable to disadvantaged groups like the unemployed, in particular if the increased growth rate leads to lower levels of unemployment.

The legal barriers to national tax policy are mainly the agreements made between Member States. Most countries are against ring-fencing tax provisions and unfair tax competition. The recognised merits of free movements of labour, capital and goods also result in limitations on national policies, including national tax policies. These limitations are the corner-stones of a single market. In combination with a non-discrimination policy, a forceful mechanism is in place for fulfilling the Member States' ambition to establish a single market.

However, there are clearly cultural barriers to becoming the "United States of Europe". These barriers are important and may very well allow countries to fail rather substantially in the implementation of tax coordination. Politicians may find it favourable to distance themselves from decisions made in Brussels while at the same time reaping benefits from a single market. There is also a substantial grey zone between taxes and fees. By connecting specific benefits to tax payments, fees are in reality collected and by limiting the recipients of the benefits, national tax rules may indeed prevail also in a single market. The distortionary effects of these levies may, however, be reduced, if alternative systems or opt out clauses are available.

An optional CCCTB would not necessarily infringe on the scope for national tax policies. It would however introduce institutional corporate tax competition since businesses would be able to vote with their feet – by choosing the CCCTB over the national corporate tax base – without having to relocate their headquarter or production facilities. It is an open question to what extent countries are willing to introduce such a new concept of tax competition. It may be perceived as a threat to national tax policies. However, it should be seen as a complement to national tax policies, enabling necessary tax coordination to remove cross-border tax obstacles without having to harmonize or abandon national tax policies and priorities.

5.7 Concluding Remarks on a Common Consolidated Corporate Tax Base in Europe

The role of national business taxation in an economic union like the EU is limited but certainly there is some room for it. The desirability of such policies largely depends on the extent to which they are used to correct for national market failures. It is important that tax policies are transparent and that the effect of national tax rules deserves more attention than it has received. The fact that a pan-European business has to work with 27 different tax systems and tax administrations result not only in double taxation and high compliance costs, but also in considerable tax uncertainty. The effects on investment decisions of tax uncertainty caused by national tax policies have not been given sufficient attention by EU Member States.

An important reason why the countries in Eastern and Central Europe as well as in the Former Soviet Union streamlined their tax systems was an awareness of the negative impact of tax uncertainty and the need to demonstrate that a new business climate now prevailed. Some countries even introduced flat taxes to further reduce tax uncertainty. Neither flat taxes, nor simple tax systems are necessarily good or bad for private sector investments, but their simplicity and transparency certainly seem to have been helpful in attracting investments. With low tax rates and stable rules implying increased predictability in tax matters, tax uncertainty has been reduced.

The Member States of the EU have now embarked on a reform process trying to reduce tax distortions, provide for consolidation and alleviate administrative burdens. The compliance costs of adapting to 27 different tax systems, administrations and legal systems are huge. By allowing corporations to opt for calculating corporate profits in a uniform way, consolidation can be achieved, reducing the risk of double taxation. The way forward in designing a new corporate tax system is complicated but certainly worth the effort. The old Member States could learn much from the new members when it comes to tax rates and simplicity. Broad bases and equal treatment go quite some way in reducing tax uncertainty, fostering investment and growth in Europe. The competitive pressure is likely to reduce tax rates further, making more investment opportunities viable. There will be room for

Member States to pursue national tax policies but for cross-border activities common rules could enhance economic efficiency. The area of direct taxation is therefore likely to follow a similar development to that which indirect taxes have taken. There will be national differences, based on historical, cultural and economic reasons, but the need to create a single market calls for giving businesses the option to be taxed on a common set of rules.

The EU Commission is expected to present a legislative proposal for an optional common consolidated tax base. It remains to be seen how many countries will be willing to allow the introduction of a completely new corporate tax system which will compete with the national system. Tax competition will then become transparent, both between countries since the tax base is identical and between the national system and the common system – perhaps too transparent for some Member States. The extent to which countries are willing to introduce this type of tax competition, even if tax rates are strictly national, is an open question. It may be perceived as a threat to national tax policies. However, it should be seen as a complement to national tax policies. It will allow member states to achieve the tax coordination which is necessary to remove cross-border tax obstacles without abandoning national tax policies and priorities.

Endnotes

1. European Commission (2004).
2. There could of course be a need to use taxes to take externalities into account.
3. See for example Desai and Hines J:r (2003).
4. A historical overview and analysis of the impact of taxes on owners can be found Bank and Cheffins (2006).
5. European Commission (2001).
6. It is worth noting that also in the Western countries we see a development towards consumption taxation within the framework of the income tax system, since the tax rate on capital income is reduced. This is particularly noticeable in a country like the US, where the dividend tax rate has been sharply reduced. Among the member states of the EU, reducing capital income taxes is often the way to mitigate the double taxation of corporate income. The need to do so increased drastically when imputation systems could no longer be used (since countries gave relief for domestic corporate taxes only and not for foreign corporate taxes, thus violating Art. 56 and 58 of the EC Treaty).
7. The survey is available on the Europa internet site: http://europa.eu.int/comm/taxation_customs/whatsnew.htm
8. See Jorgenson (1971) and Chirinko (1993). There is an extensive review of the literature on tax policy and investment in Hassett and Hubbard (1997).
9. See e.g. Hartman (1972) and Abel (1993).
10. For a review of the literature, see Carruth, Dickerson and Henley (2000).
11. See Carlsson (2004).
12. See Hassett and Metcalf (1994).
13. See Bittlingmayer (2001).
14. See Edmiston (2001).
15. See Edmiston, Mudd and Valev (2003).
16. See Stasavage, (2000).

17. See Lensink, Bo and Sterken (1999).
18. The only way the tax bases will be identical is to abolish the national corporate tax system or to change it to the same tax base as the CCCTB has.
19. CCCTB/WP/012, p. 5.
20. CCCTB/WP/012, p. 4.
21. Case C-470/04.
22. Most notably of income from third country sources.

References

Abel, A.B. (1983) Optimal investment under uncertainty, *American Economic Review*, 72, 228–233.

Abel, A.B. and J.C. Eberly (1994) A unified model of investment under uncertainty, *American Economic Review*, 84, 1369–1384.

Andersson, K. (2005) En gemensam konsoliderad skattebas för företag i EU, *Svensk Skattetidning,* 72, 5–17.

Arrow, K.J. (1968) Optimal capital policy with irreversible investment, in J.N. Wolfe (ed.), *Value,Capital and Growth, Essays in Honour of Sir John Hicks*, Edingbourg: Edinburg University Press.

Bank, S. and B. Cheffins (2006) Taxation and the Separation of Ownership and Control, *Conference paper,* Max Planck Institute, December.

Barro, R.J. (1991) Economic growth in a cross-section of countries, *Quarterly Journal of Economics*, 106, 407–443.

Bernanke, B.S. (1983) Irreversibility, uncertainty and cyclical investment, *Quarterly Journal of Economics*, 98, 85–106.

Bittlingmayer, G. (2001) Regulatory uncertainty and investment: Evidence from antitrust enforcement, *Cato Journal*, Vol. 20, No. 3 (Winter 2001).

Brunetti, A. and B. Weder (1998) Investment and institutional uncertainty: a comparative study of different uncertainty measures, *Weltwirtschaftliches Archiv*, 134, 513–533.

Böhm, H, Funke, M. and N.A. Siegfried (1999) Discovering the Link between Uncertainty and Investment – Microeconometric Evidence from Germany, Quantitative Macroeconomics Working Papers Series, No 5, Hamburg Universität.

Caballero, R.J. (1991) On the sign of the investment-uncertainty relationship, *American Economic Review*, 81, 279–288.

Caballero, R. J. (1999) Aggregate investment, in J. Taylor and M. Woodford (eds)., *Handbook of Macroeconomics*, vol. 1B, Amsterdam: North–Holland.

Carlsson, M. (2004 Investment and Uncertainty: A Theory-Based Empirical Approach, *Working Paper* 2004:17, Department of Economics, Uppsala University (October 6).

Carruth, A., Dickerson, A. and A. Henley (2000) What do we know about investment under uncertainty?, *Journal of Economic Surveys* 14: 119–153.

Chirinko, R. S. (1993) Business fixed investment spending: modelling strategies, empirical results and policy implications, *Journal of Economic Literature*, 31 1987–1911.

Desai, M. A. and J. R. Hines (2003) Economic Foundations of International Tax Rules, *Conference paper,* American Tax Policy Institute, Washington D.C., December.

Dixit, A. K. and R. S. Pindyck (1994), *Investment under uncertainty*, Princeton: Princeton University Press.

Edmiston, K. D. (2001) Tax Uncertainty and Investment – A Cross Country Investigation, International Studies Program, Working Paper 01-5, April, Georgia State University.

Edmiston, K. D. (2004) Tax Uncertainty and Investment: A Cross-Country Empirical Examination, *Economic Inquiry*, 42, No 3, 425–440.

Edmiston, K.D., Mudd, S. and N. Valev (2003) Tax Structures and FDI – The Deterrent Effects of Complexity and Uncertainty, William Davidson Working Paper No. 558, April, William Davison Institute, University of Michigan Business School.

European Commission (2001) *Company taxation in the internal market.*

European Commission (2004) Non-Paper to informal Ecofin Council, 10 and 11 September 2004; A Common Consolidated EU Corporate Tax Base, 7 July.

Feldstein, M. (1983) *Inflation, Tax Rules and Capital Formation*, NBER, Chicago: University of Chicago Press.

Feldstein, M., Hines, J.R. and R.G. Hubbard, R.G. (eds) (1995) *The Effects of Taxation on Multinational Corporations*, NBER, Chicago: University of Chicago Press.

Finkenzeller, M. and C. Spengel (2004) Measuring the effective levels of company taxation in the new member states: A quantitative analysis, *Working paper* no 7, European Commission.

Giovannini, A., Hubbard, R.G. and J. Slemrod (eds) (1993). *Studies in International Taxation*, NBER, Chicago: University of Chicago Press.

Hartman, R. (1972) The effects of price and cost uncertainty on investment, *Journal of Economic Theory* 5: 258–266.

Hassett, K and G. E. Metcalf (1994) Investment with Uncertain Tax Policy: Does Random Tax Policy Discourage Investment? NBER Working Paper no. 4780.

Hasset, K. and R. G. Hubbard (1997) Tax Policy and Investment, in Auerbach, A (ed) *Fiscal Policy: Lessons from Economic Research,* Chicago: MIT Press, pp. 339–385.

Hubbard, R.G. (1994) Investment under Certainty: keeping one's options open, *Journal of Economic Literature*, 32, 1816–1831.

Huizinga, J. (1993) Inflation, uncertainty, relative price uncertainty, and investment in US manufacturing, *Journal of Money, Credit and Banking*, 25, 521–554.

Jorgenson, D. (1971) Econometric studies of investment behaviour: a survey, *Journal of Economic Literature*, 9, 1111–47.

Leahy, J. and T.M. Whited (1996) The effects of uncertainty on investment: some stylized facts, *Journal of Money, Credit, and Banking*, 28, 64–83.

Lensink, R., Bo, H. and E. Sterken (1999) Does Uncertainty Affect Economic Growth? – An empirical Analysis, Research Report 99E23, University of Groningen.

Pindyck, R. (1988) Irreversible Investment, Capital Choice, and the Value of Firm" *American Economic Review*, 78(5) 969–85.

Pindyck, R. (1991) Irreversibility, uncertainty and investment, *Journal of Economic Literature*, 29, 1110–48.

Pindyck, R. (1993) A note on competitive investment under uncertainty, *American Economic Review* 83: 273–277.

Razin, A. and J. Slemrod (eds), (1990). *Taxation in the Global Economy*, NBER, Chicago: University of Chicago Press.

Shiller, R. (1989) *Market volatility*, Cambridge: MIT Press.

Stasavage, D. (2000) Private Investment and Political Uncertainty, *Discussion Paper* No. DEDPS 25, July, London School of Economics and Political Science.

Tanzi, V. and L. Schuknecht (2000) *Public Spending in the 20th Century – A Global Perspective,* Cambridge: Cambridge University Press.

Tobin, J. (1969) A general equilibrium approach to monetary policy, *Journal of Money, Credit and Banking*, 1, 15–29.

Chapter 6
The Influence of the European State Aid Rules on National Tax Policy

Franz Philipp Sutter[1]

6.1 Introduction

Art 87 of the Treaty of Rome reads: "Save as otherwise provided in this Treaty, any aid in any form whatsoever granted by a Member State or through State resources which distorts or threatens to distort competition by favouring certain undertakings or the production of certain goods shall, insofar as it affects trade between Member States, be incompatible with the common market."

The underlying purpose of a principal ban on State aid in Art 87 EC lies in guaranteeing fair competition, functioning markets and economic efficiency within the European Union. In the words of the Commission's recent State Aid Action Plan 2005 its competition policy "rests upon the idea that a market-based economy provides the best guarantee for raising living conditions in the EU to the benefit of citizens. ... Competition is furthermore essential to enhance the competitiveness of the European economy, as it creates an environment in which efficient and innovative companies are rewarded properly".[2] Against this background the Commission emphasizes that "State aid control comes from the need to maintain a level playing field for all undertakings active in the Single European Market, no matter in which Member State they are established. There is a particular need to be concerned with those state aid measures, which provide unwarranted selective advantages to some firms, preventing or delaying the market forces from rewarding the most competitive firms, thereby decreasing overall European competitiveness. It may also lead to a build-up of market power in the hands of some firms, for instance when companies that do not receive state aid (e.g. non-domestic firms) have to cut down on their market presence, or where state aid is used to erect entry barriers. As a result of such distortions of competition, customers may be faced with higher prices, lower quality goods and less innovation".[3] Moreover state aid would "not come for free", as taxpayers in the end have to finance state aid and there are opportunity costs to it. Giving aid to undertakings would "mean taking funding away from other policy areas".[4]

Without questioning the reasonableness of these economic considerations of the Commission in principle, it must however be noted that it would be an illusion to think that the EC State Aid rules alone can ensure a "level playing field" on the European Market, as the EC State aid control has to start from an unequal general legal setting in the European Union. An illustrative example is the procedure against the Austrian Energy Tax Rebate system that was installed in Austria in package with the first introduction of a new energy tax.[5] The rebate system was then attacked because it provided for a selective advantage for huge energy consumers that were granted a rebate of a certain percentage of their energy tax debt establishing a sort of ceiling of the maximum energy tax costs. To the Austrian industry the reproaches of being "subsidized" by the energy tax package came as an "economic surprise" since the introduction of the energy tax package meant a huge additional financial burden for them, while many other European Member States still did not have any energy taxation at all at this time. Therefore one should not forget: As the choice of tax events lies within the sovereignty of the Member States, the European State aid rules cannot do anything against such general differences between the Member States – a structural deficiency that has to be kept in mind when talking about the economic function of State aid control.[6]

As the wording of Art 87 EC already shows (arg "any aid in any form whatsoever"), Art 87 EC is characterized by a very broad notion of State Aid[7], also referred to as "form neutrality" of the EC State aid surveillance. This form neutrality has already been stressed by the Spaak Report preparing the draft of the EC Treaty in 1956[8] and shall prevent Member States from easily circumventing the prohibition by simply changing the form of their individual business support. As the Treaty of Rome does not contain any legal definition of the term "aid", its borderlines had to be determined by the ruling practice of the ECJ. According to the Court the term embraces every "measure which, in various forms, reduces the charges normally borne by an undertaking and which is not therefore a subsidy in the strict sense of the word but is equivalent to one by reason of its nature and effect".[9] This early ruling in the Case De Gezamenlijke Steenkolenijnen has remained the landmark decision in the definition of the scope of Art 87 EC and is thus still the starting point of any examination of indirect State aid including cases of preferential tax measures. Later rulings of the ECJ have further stressed the broad concept of Art 87 EC and its effect-orientated definition approach. On the occasion of the Case Italy v Commission of 1974, in which the ECJ had to examine a temporary and partial reduction of social charges for the benefit of the textile and garment-making industry and small craft, the Court held: "The aim of Article 92[10] is to prevent trade between Member States from being affected by benefits granted by the public authorities which, in various forms, distort or threaten to distort competition by favouring certain undertakings or the production of certain goods. Accordingly, Article 92 does not distinguish between the measures of State intervention concerned by reference to their causes or aims but defines them in relation to their effects. Consequently, the alleged fiscal nature or social aim of the measure in issue cannot suffice to shield it from the application of Article 92".[11]

Tax privileges do not go hand in hand with direct funding, but they put the beneficiaries in a clearly better position than their competitors who pay the full amount of taxes and hereby fulfil the De Gezamenlijke-formula. Fiscal privileges could consist of "a reduction in the tax base (such as special deductions, special or accelerated depreciation arrangements or the entering of reserves on the balance sheet); a total or partial reduction in the amount of tax (such as an exemption or a tax credit) or a deferment, cancellation or even special rescheduling of tax debt."[12] Due to the progressive element of direct taxation it is, however, typical for this form of aid that its exact amount cannot be fixed at a certain sum a priori. It varies case by case depending on the exact profit situation of the individual undertaking in the relevant fiscal year, which can logically just be determined a posteriori. In a loss situation it might even be nil.[13] For enterprises this makes it often difficult to plan extra-investments on the mere grounds of tax advantages attainable. That's why economics rather prefer direct subsidies over tax reductions as means to reach important political goals.[14] From an economic point of view another fundamental peculiarity of fiscal aid is that it is normally designed as so-called operating aid. This means that the aid measures "are not linked to the carrying out of specific projects and reduce a firm's current expenditure without it being possible to assess the precise volume involved when the Commission carries out its ex ante examination".[15] As such aid is not proportionate to and directly targeted to new investments, job creation or other Community objectives, the Commission is very reluctant to authorise it at all. If it does so, the aid must be degressive, limited in time and applied outside sensible sectors of disrupted competition.[16]

If a Member State plans to introduce new State aid measures, it has to notify its plans to the Commission that can authorize these measures under a catalogue of reasons (Art 87 para 3 EC), if the proposed aid scheme has a beneficial impact "in overall Union terms". This possibility of being declared compatible with the Common Market has been included in the Treaty because State aid measures can – in the words of the Commission - "sometimes be effective tools for achieving objectives of common interest. They can correct market failures, thereby improving the functioning of markets and enhancing European competitiveness. They can also help promote e.g. social and regional cohesion, sustainable development and cultural diversity, irrespective of the correction of market failures".[17] As the allegedly "clearly defined"[18] objectives of common interest in Art 87 para 3 EC are in fact not that clearly defined, but leave a huge room of discretion to the Commission, they have given the Commission a very strong political position in co-shaping the Member States' economic policy.[19]

The rest of this chapter is organized in four main sections: Section 6.2 will shortly describe the evolvement of the EC State aid policy and the development of Art 87 EC into a sort of European Principle of Equality Test for national business legislation demonstrating that there are no areas of tax law spared from its grasp. In Sect. 6.3 I will elaborate on the specific procedural concept of the European State aid rules as failures to duly notify State aid measures have – despite the uncertainty of the material EC State aid test - far-reaching immediate consequences including possible recovery claims on the motion of competitors. In this context I will also demonstrate that many core procedural issues are still not settled by European case law. Sometimes undertakings therefore even ended up being given additional money when unlawful State aid was detected.[20] The procedural uncertainties make it also difficult to assess the political dimension of the EC State aid rules comprehensively. In Sect. 6.4 I will nonetheless try to sum up the political implications arising from the material and procedural characteristics of the European

State Aid Rules for national tax legislators and finally give a concluding evaluation on the topic in Sect. 6.5.

6.2 The State Aid Prohibition af Art 87 EC and its Development into a Sort of European Equality Test for National Business (Tax) Legislation

The Code of Conduct on Business Taxation As Political Turning Point

Against the background of the early wide definitions of the scope of Art 87 EC one might have imagined that tax provisions had always played a major role in the State Aid review practice of the EC Commission. However, up to the 1990s tax cases have been very rare among European State aid procedures. This was probably due to a certain self-restraint of the Commission being reluctant to plunge into the complex field of national taxation while its personal resources were still heavily occupied with more obvious cases of direct transfers to individual undertakings.

This attitude of the Commission changed fundamentally with the adoption of the Code of Conduct for business taxation on 1 December 1997.[21] The Code has its background in an intense discussion about unfair tax competition among OECD and EC Member States in the late 1990s showing that national tax individualism ultimately leads to a harsh fiscal race to the bottom in attracting "mobile" foreign industries and businesses. As tax-dumping can not be won by the States in the long run, the EC Member States have eventually agreed upon a merely political commitment[22] to restrict intra-community tax competition. The Code of Conduct has however also pointed out that some elements of unfair tax competition could already be targeted by the legally binding EC State Aid rules. In Point J of the Code the Commission was therefore explicitly urged to "commit itself to the strict application of the aid rules concerned, taking into account, inter alia, the negative effects of aid that are brought to light in the application of this code". Furthermore it was noted "that the Commission intends to examine or re-examine existing tax arrangements and propose new legislation by Member States case by case, thus ensuring that the rules and objectives of the Treaty are applied consistently and equally to all".

Backed up by this political mandate of the Council and the Representatives of the Governments of the Member States, the Commission issued a Notice on the application of the State aid rules to measures relating to direct business taxation (hereinafter: Notice Business Taxation) on 12 December 1998 and started to take a closer look on preferential tax regimes of the EC Member States in its daily control practice. This crack down on national tax provisions was commented upon as "dramatical change" in the Commission's State Aid Policy.[23] Since then the Commission has initiated a wide range of tax procedures.[24] In parallel, national bodies have opened several national proceedings against preferential tax regimes and also forwarded several tax requests for preliminary rulings to the ECJ.

In February 2007 the Commission eventually decided to target Swiss company tax regimes under which the Cantons may fully or partially exempt profits generated abroad from cantonal and municipal company tax.[25] Following complaints by Member States, Members of the European Parliament and businesses, the Commission reviewed some of the cantonal tax regimes to assess their compatibility with the State aid provision in Article 23(1) of the Agreement between the European Economic Community and the Swiss Confederation of 22 July 1972.[26] If the efforts of the Commission are successful, State Aid Rules could even prove to be an effective tool against unfair tax provisions of a Third State loosely linked to the European Union.

The Selectivity Test - Development of Art 87 EC into a Sort of European Principle of Equality Test for National Business Legislation?

In order to trigger the European ban on State aid, a national measure must meet all tests of Art 87 para 1 EC.[27] The heart of every State aid examination is, however, the so-called selectivity test examining if the national measure is targeted at "certain undertakings or the production of certain goods".[28] If there is no specific group of addressees, the measure is a general economic programme that falls - when causing any market distortions – solely within the scope of Art 96 EC. Under this provision the Commission can – in contrast to its competences under Art 88 EC – not take any decisions on its own, but can only make suggestions to the Council that has to adopt measures at unanimity. Due to this hurdle Art 96 EC has not played any significant role so far. This underlines the importance of the selectivity test as watershed between Art 87 and 96 EC.

In its Notice on Business Taxation the Commission held that a selective tax measure favouring specific undertakings in the sense of Art 87 EC "may derive from an exception to the tax provisions of a legislative, regulatory or administrative nature or from a discretionary practice on the part of the tax authorities".[29] Leaving aside discretionary measures of the national tax authorities[30] this makes it necessary to define the benchmark tax system in every State aid review in the first place because without a reference framework it is impossible to identify a beneficial "exception".[31] If a tax measure also implies and pursues evidently other than fiscal aims such as socio-political purposes, this can be seen as an indication of a subsidy element in a tax measure and thus of a beneficial "exception".[32] Non-fiscal aims could however also form part of the logic of a tax scheme installed and are then not harmful if pursued consistently.[33] In practice, the definition of the borders of the benchmark tax system is quite difficult and involves a certain latitude in the evaluation by the competent authorities. In the long run it is always up to the ECJ to melt the latitude of theoretically possible assumptions down to one solution. Following an obiter dictum in an elder ECJ ruling of 1974[34] the Commission has stressed an additional examination level after the identification of an exception. Accordingly, it must still be examined whether "the exception to the system or differentiations within that system are justified 'by the nature or general scheme' of the tax system, that is to say, whether they derive directly from the basic or guiding principles of the tax system in the Member State concerned. If this is not the case, then State aid is involved".[35]

Consequently, a selectivity review by Commission and ECJ consists of three steps:

1. What is the benchmark tax system defining the relevant reference framework?
2. Is the measure at issue an exception to this system?
3. Can it still be justified "by the nature or general scheme" of the tax system?

As an incriminated beneficial State measure has always to be set into comparison to the benchmark tax system for checking its "exceptional" status,[36] the State aid review resembles in its comparability technique the patterns of national equality tests. This resemblance can also be observed in the reasoning of the ECJ. In its ruling on the Adria Wien Pipeline Case the ECJ held for instance: "The only question to be determined is whether ... a State measure is ... to favour 'certain undertakings or the production of certain goods' ... in comparison with other undertakings which are *in a legal and factual situation that is comparable in the light of the objective pursued by the measure in question*".[37] After examining the purpose of the Austrian energy taxation the ECJ concluded: "ecological considerations ... do not justify" different treatment of "undertakings supplying services" and "such ... manufacturing goods", as "energy consumption by each of those sectors is equally damaging to the environment".[38] This ruling shows that the ECJ does not only consider internal technical tax justifications, such as the necessity to limit tax avoiding, but also accepts references to an external, eg ecological, underlying logic of the tax scheme scrutinized.[39] Justification in this context means to examine whether the derogation of the benchmark system is still proportionate to the external objective pursued by the installed tax sub-system. The burden of proof for such a justification is attributed to the Member States.[40]

The selection of a comparator, ie the definition of the group of taxpayers still sufficiently comparable to be necessarily equally treated, is certainly a decision which is eventually up to the individual assessment of the competent body.[41] It leaves much room for divergent positions on the scope of Art 87 EC in an individual case. This deficiency of clear borderlines of the EC State aid Prohibition becomes especially obvious in the field of tax legislation as tax law provisions are often not governed by a single clear-cut principle, but serve several goals making it hard to identify "unsystematic" exceptions. Therefore a considerable amount of uncertainty is inherent in the application of the EC State Aid Prohibition in tax matters.[42]

Nonetheless, it is important to stress that neither the comparison nor the justification test applied by the competent national authorities must involve any balancing consideration of completely external political reasons which do not already form part of the logic of the installed tax scheme itself – such as the political goal to counteract economic depression or high regional unemployment rates. They might well be reasonable motives of the legislator when introducing the aid measure, but do not absolve the legislator from the national duty of notification and asking for the Commission's clearance. The Treaty of Rome clearly ascribes this totally external balancing competence exclusively to the Commission under Art 87 para 3 EC. Therefore the justification level in the above State Aid Examination Pattern can - in contrast to its role in cases on the European fundamental freedoms or the national constitutional principles of equality – only serve for fine-tuning the definition of the specific benchmark tax (sub-)system as the relevant reference framework.[43]

Due to the outstanding importance of the selectivity test and its resemblance to national equality tests one could describe the ECJ jurisprudence as a development of the EC State Aid Prohibition into a sort of European Principle of Equality Test for national business legislation. As far as this development leads to a growing insignificance of the other tests of Art 87 para 1 EC, it wears away important other demarcations of the State aid Prohibition.[44]

The Areas of Tax Law on the Radar of the EC State Aid Rules

National provisions of direct business tax law have been in the spotlight of the EC State aid control since the adoption of the Code of Conduct on Business Taxation and the issue of the Commission's Notice Business Taxation. Nonetheless, all business related taxes are, in principle, on the radar of Art 87 EC. National tax policy makers have therefore to understand that no field of national business taxation – even if coined by secondary EC law - is spared from the grasp of the EC State Aid Prohibition. In its follow-up-report of 2004[45] the Commission has already pronounced to equally scrutinize other fields of national tax law and has stressed that "the principles" of its Notice Business Taxation seemed "largely applicable" to indirect taxation as well.[46]

A review of national indirect tax measures however brings up interesting questions about the relationship and interaction of secondary law directives and the primary EC law of Art 87 seq as indirect taxation is widely determined by EC directives in the European Union. Although the Commission presumes potential infringements of Art 87 EC rather in areas of indirect taxation that have not been codified so far or that have even been explicitly left to the discretion of the Member States by the European directives,[47] it is certainly also imaginable that conflicts between the requirements of the directives themselves and Art 87 EC do emerge. The assessment of such conflicts need not necessarily fall within the exclusive State aid surveillance responsibility of the Commission: If the implementation of a directive into national law has started over after the accession of a Member State, it falls within the new aid control regime of Art 88 EC. Consequently it is then the national bodies of the Member States applying those national implementation rules that have to scrutinize their conformity both with the EC directives and with the primary EC State aid provisions.[48]

Hence, the European Court of First Instance has just recently taken a large number of secondary-EC law-driven national tax measures out of the scrutiny of the European State aid rules. In the Case T-351/02, Deutsche Bahn AG/Commission the Court held on 5 April 2006 that Art 87 EC just referred "to the decisions of Member States by which, *in pursuit of their own economic and social objectives*, they give, *by unilateral and autonomous decisions*, resources to undertakings or other persons or procure for them advantages intended to encourage the attainment of the economic or social objectives sought".[49] In transposing exemptions of secondary EC law directives into national law, Member States would therefore be "only implementing Community provisions in accordance with their obligations stemming from the Treaty".[50] Such a tax exemption is in the eyes of the European Court of First Instance thus, not imputable to the German State, but in actual fact stems from an act of the Community legislature. Although the exemption remains financed by State budget, "the imputability of aid to a State is separate from the question whether aid was granted through State resources. It is clear from the case-law that they are separate and cumulative conditions".[51] Therefore the German railroad company Deutsche Bahn AG could not challenge the exemption of excise duties on mineral oils used as fuel for the purpose of air navigation although this tax privilege might cause distortions of competition between its railroad operations and the air travel industry.

Under this jurisprudence of the Court of First Instance national tax measures transposing EC directives can only be challenged under Art 87 seq EC if the transposition has filled in areas left undetermined by the directive or if the national tax measure is the result of making a choice under several transposition options offered by the directive. As this interpretation result of art 87 EC is not the only possible interpretation result, it would be certainly desirable if the European Court still had a word on the issue. The ruling unfolds however the special nature of the State Aid Prohibition as a primarily politically important pressure instrument on the Member States: In substance, there will probably be little difference for a disadvantaged undertaking if its competitors are strengthened by national or European tax law without justification out of the logic of the tax system installed. From an integration perspective one might however argue that the Commission was already involved in the creation of EC directives and thus gave an implicit clearance of their advantageous provisions. Insofar the ruling of the Court of First Instance might well be consistent with the underlying concept of Art 87 seq EC that do not create an absolute ban on national State aid, but just demand a compulsory notification of national measures that might then still be cleared by the Commission for political reasons. The ruling thus shows impressively that the European State aid rules must not be misunderstood as noble European protection measures of free and fair competition in any event, but that they shall primarily ensure a European instead of a merely national balancing of the interests at stake guaranteeing the necessary flow of information to Brussels and giving the Commission the possibility of some sort of (tax) coordination via its approval practice.

National Tax Treaty Policy Under European State Aid Scrutiny

The influence of the EC State Aid Prohibition reaches even beyond purely national tax policy, as it may also have a major impact on the shaping of the international tax policy of the EC Member States: The inclusion of bilateral Double Tax Conventions (DTC)[52] into the European State aid debate starts from the observation that according to the form neutrality of Art 87 EC it could make no fundamental difference whether a tax advantage limited to a selective group of undertakings is granted within the frame of a bilateral treaty or of domestic tax law. Otherwise Member States could easily escape the grasp of the EC State Aid Prohibition.

On the Third Summer Conference on International Tax Law 2003 in Rust I therefore presented a case study discussing a possible aid element of an unrestricted application of the Exemption Method in DTC because this method regularly leads to tax advantages in comparison to the national tax level.[53] Its evaluation under Art 87 EC is however quite difficult and the relevant reference framework could either be the national tax level on its own or the national tax level including unilateral relief mechanisms for international double taxation and/or a (standard) DTC constellation.[54] Therefore the classification of the exemption method as aid measure[55] eventually depends on the definition of the benchmark tax system.

In principle, the exemption method should however be justifiable as it serves the internationally recognized principle of capital-import-neutrality: By guaranteeing a tax resident engaged in business abroad the same tax level as a foreign-based company it establishes competitive equality *on the foreign market.*[56] It thus serves the same aim as the European State aid rules, ie guaranteeing a level playing field for market participants from different countries. Nonetheless, it would be well arguable for the Commission to set certain limits to the application of the exemption method as this method also allows an unlimited import of excessively low foreign tax levels and might therefore lead to disturbances *on the home markets* of the capital origin. The exemption method thereby favours (1) national businesses partly engaged in low tax countries vis-á-vis solely national suppliers[57] and (2) national import-export undertakings vis-á-vis European exporters whose home country has not concluded an unlimited exemption DTC with the foreign tax haven. Moreover, an unlimited acceptance of the import of – possibly even ringfenced[58] – low foreign tax regimes would counteract the European struggle against harmful tax competition and threaten to distort the competition on the European home markets. Therefore the Commission could, in my view, require DTCs under the heading of Art 87 seq EC to have the insertion of an exemption method always accompanied by special reservation clauses - such as subject-to-tax-clauses hindering cases of double non-taxation, the import of foreign unfair tax competition or even the import of extremely low foreign general tax levels.[59]

The grasp of the EC State aid rules, however, need not be restricted to the question of a possible aid qualification of the exemption method, but can also seize other provisions of DTC.[60] Although the core structure of DTC is very similar worldwide as they are largely based on a common model developed by the OECD, there are lots of differences in the details - among the various treaties of a country on the one hand side and among the various distribution rules of an individual treaty on the other hand side. Consequently, two State aid examination directions would be imaginable and could be distinguished: First, the question could be raised whether differences between the various bilateral DTC and differences between DTC and unilateral relief mechanisms can trigger State Aid concerns. Secondly, the various rules within an individual DTC could be compared with other provisions of the same DTC.

If – under the above premise - one defines the main distribution rules such as Art 7 or Art 15 OECD-Model Convention as DTC-benchmarks for all related sorts of income, then deviations from their distributionary concepts within a DTC would already have to be justified. Under this premise such a justification is to be doubted if different groups of undertakings are in comparable situations and are nonetheless treated differently. In this context, Luja (2004) has illustratively pointed at the construction of Art 8 OECD-Model Convention ("Shipping, inland waterways transport and air transport") by the official OECD-Commentary expanding Art 8 OECD-MC also to transfer hotels run by airlines. Thereby the OECD-Commentary attributed the taxing right to the effective home country of the airline and not to the PE State of the transfer hotel. This deviation from the PE-principle of Art 7 OECD-Model Conventions leads to a different treatment threatening to distort competition between airline hotels and ordinary hotels as the latter have to pay taxes in their PE State, while the airline-hotels can easily escape the taxing claims under Art 8 OECD-MC choosing a low tax country as overall home State.[61] Several other constellations are imaginable.[62] Such a content control would also embrace the challenge of a mix of credit and exemption method within a single DTC: Under Art 87 EC one could not mix the two methods of avoiding double taxation arbitrarily. Even if such a mix was eventually in line with the OECD-model and the inner logic of a consistent double tax law policy, there would at least remain an additional justification pressure under Art 87 EC.

Via its potential influence on DTC the EC State aid rules could even affect third countries like the US: A study of Panayi (2004) has come to the conclusion that the ownership/base erosion tests of the Limitation of Benefits-Clauses regularly included in European DTC with the US were incompatible with Art 87 EC because they restricted the treaty benefits to the selective group of corporations with strong ties to the Contracting States.[63] Accordingly, EC Member States would not be allowed to agree to their adoption in bilateral treaties with the US. If one goes even further, one might also doubt the authority of Member States to conclude tax treaties on a national level as they segment the Common Market into bilateral relationships. As long as those relationships are not treated completely alike, DTC will always contain selective incentives for an increase of certain economic exchanges and thereby foster certain undertakings over others. Such an effect could only be ruled out by shifting the competence to conclude DTC from the national to the supranational level.[64]

Currently, it is not foreseeable how far European State aid rules will plunge into the law of DTC. Hence, the above excursus into the young debate about EC State aid aspects of DTC should not only show their potential impact on the future treaty policy of European countries restricting their room for autonomous treaty negotiations. It ought also highlight *pars pro toto* the far reaching and comprehensive intrusion into the inner circle of national tax sovereignty by Art 87 seq EC and illustrate the possible radiation of the State aid rules on Non-Member States.

Regional Tax Autonomy Under European State Aid Scrutiny

One of the recently most contentious issues is the impact of the European State aid rules on the system of regional tax autonomy existing in several Member States, as regional tax laws could always be considered as "selective" in the sense of Art 87 EC. The Commission finds itself in a difficult situation in this context: If it regards the reference to tax autonomy as a justification automatism, Member States could be inclined to defer their taxing rights to small federal entities in order to grant regional aid without the need of Brussel's consent. If it, however, ignored federal tax constitutions totally, it would target the heart of national tax sovereignty and submit the complete exercise of fiscal autonomy of a federal Member State to the Commission's approval policy giving Member States a good pretext for centralizing taxing rights. Such an exercise of Art 87 EC would run foul the commitment of the European Union to subsidiarity[65] and respect of federal constitutionalism.[66] While literature has therefore cautioned against a harsh application of Art 87 para 1 EC against local tax laws, the Commission has always been sceptical about State aid privileges in local tax laws.[67] Hence, the regional tax laws scrutinized in the past did not involve any spectacular State aid issues, as they were regularly already selective within their territorial scope favouring just certain regional undertakings and thus constituted undoubtedly Sate aid.[68]

In recent decisions of the Commission the role of regional tax autonomy has, however, become crucial. The first case pertained to the Azores which enjoy – like Madeira - administrative and financial autonomy under the Constitution of the Portuguese Republic. Due to this fiscal autonomy the regional legislative assemblies of the Azores and of Madeira are authorised to reduce the rates of income and corporation tax applicable up to a maximum of 30% of those laid down by national legislation. This general rebate shall allow companies in the Azores – inter alia – to overcome the structural handicaps resulting from their location in an insular and outermost region. The Azores used this competence and adopted a reduction in the rate of personal income tax (IRS) of 20% (15% for 1999) and a reduction in the rate of corporation tax (IRC) of 30% for taxpayers in the region – both applying automatically to all economic operators (natural and legal persons). In an investigation of the measure the Commission remained unimpressed by the justification argument of the regional tax autonomy, found the measure to fulfil Art 87 EC denying it a justification out of the logic of the tax system. According to the Commission the economy of the Member State as such should exclusively constitute the relevant framework in which comparisons for State aid examinations should be made.[69]

This decision of 2002 meant a serious strike against the independence of national tax autonomy, because the Azores' tax law was not reproached with favouring certain undertakings within its territory. It applied automatically to all economic operators therein and was a general regional measure in the Azores. Nonetheless it was found to constitute State aid in respect to the national tax level.[70] Yet, the Commission still kept a back-door open by highlighting that the measure at issue was defined in explicit reference to national taxation and was therefore not a completely independent regional tax measure.[71] Likewise AG Geelhoed stressed in his opinion in the subsequent annulment procedure that the Azores' tax scheme "takes the form of a regional exception to the otherwise applicable general Portuguese tax system".[72]

In 2004 the Commission issued another decision on regional tax measures and classified the reorganization of the Gibraltar tax system as State aid. This decision meant a further setback for regional tax autonomy. One of the reasons for this decision was that the tax reorganization shifted the major tax burden onto other tax subjects than before.[73] Moreover the Commission objected to the total absence of a tax (in casu the corporation tax).[74] Such tax law structuring issues are however the core elements of national tax sovereignty. Although it is comprehensible that the Commission seeks to ensure the effectiveness of the EC State aid regime and fears circumventions by deferring fiscal competences to infra-State-authorities,[75] the Commission's Gibraltar decision raises serious concerns that Brussels has already surpassed its competences under Art 87 EC.[76] The decision has been challenged by the government of Gibraltar.[77]

A possible settlement of the dilemma about the exercise of regional tax autonomy could lie in a closer content-analysis of the autonomy of the establishing body: If the infra-State authority enjoys a broad amount of autonomy also in various other fields apart from tax law establishing a considerable independence from the central authority, then regional tax sovereignty should also be recognized under European State aid rules. The government of Gibraltar argued that it should even be sufficient, if at least the regional tax autonomy of a region was designed in a way that its exercise formed a separate tax jurisdiction that was independent from the one of the rest of the Member State and paid attention to special characteristics of the region's economy.[78]

In its Azores' case the European Court of Justice has finally taken a differentiated and Solomonic approach vis-à-vis regional tax autonomy. In its judgment of 6 September 2006 the Court held that "the very existence of an advantage may be established only when compared with 'normal' taxation. The 'normal' tax rate is the rate in force in the geographical area constituting the reference framework", which however "need not necessarily be defined within the limits of the Member State concerned".[79] In cases of tax laws issued by regional bodies it is - according to the Court - crucial "to examine whether that measure was adopted by that body in the exercise of powers sufficiently autonomous vis-à-vis the central power and, if appropriate, to examine whether that measure indeed applies to all the undertakings established in or all production of goods on the territory coming within the competence of that body".[80]

Following its Advocate General the Court distinguishes three constellations that might lead to different tax rates within a state territory and that have to be treated differently:[81]

1. "The *central government unilaterally decides* that the applicable national tax rate should be reduced within a defined geographic area". This will normally lead to the necessity of a State aid notification.[82]
2. "The second situation corresponds to a *model for distribution of tax competences in which all the local authorities at the same level (regions, districts or others) have the autonomous power to decide,* within the limit of the powers conferred on them, *the tax rate applicable in the territory within their competence.* The Commission has recognised ... that a measure taken by a local authority in the second situation is not selective because it is impossible to determine a normal tax rate capable of constituting the reference framework".[83]
3. "In the third situation, *a regional or local authority adopts, in the exercise of sufficiently autonomous powers in relation to the central power, a tax rate lower than the national rate* and which is applicable only to undertakings present in the territory within its competence". In this situation, the legal

framework appropriate to determine the selectivity of a tax measure may – according to the Court - be limited to the geographical area concerned if three core conditions are met:[84]

a) The tax measure "has been taken by a regional or local authority which has, from a constitutional point of view, *a political and administrative status separate from that of the central government*". The infra-State body must occupy "in particular on account of its status and powers, ... a fundamental role in the definition of the political and economic environment in which the undertakings present on the territory within its competence operate".[85]
b) "Next, it must have been *adopted without the central government being able to directly intervene as regards its content*".
c) "Finally, the *financial consequences* of a reduction of the national tax rate for undertakings in the region *must not be offset* by aid or subsidies from other regions or central government". According to the Court sufficient "political and fiscal independence of central government ... presupposes ... that the infra-State body not only has powers in the territory within its competence to adopt measures reducing the tax rate, regardless of any considerations related to the conduct of the central State, but that in addition it assumes the political and financial consequences of such a measure.[86] This condition is, in my view, only consistent, as a complete financial offset by the central State makes the third situation economically correspond to the first situation of a federal law directly granting a regional tax privilege by itself.

In the light of these conditions the Court finally held that the Azores Tax System was selective, because the "reduction in tax revenue ... is in any event offset by a financing mechanism which is centrally managed". The Court pointed at the Portuguese "constitutional principle of national solidarity" and stressed that financing would be provided for in the form of *"budgetary transfers managed by central government"*.[87] Consequently the Court did not see all its conditions for autonomous tax laws fulfilled and decided to assess the tax measures in relation to the whole Portuguese territory making them selective.

While the general approach of the European Court in drawing a reasonable borderline between due exercise of regional (fiscal) autonomy and the dangers of circumventing Art 87 EC via regional tax laws and the general criteria defined seems quite adequate, the role ascribed to the budgetary transfers in the Azores' judgment is not completely convincing as the ECJ did not demonstrate that the reductions were fully financed by compensatory transfer payments.[88] The mere existence of a „constitutional principle of national solidarity" and of transfer payments alone can, in my view, not already cover State aid reproaches. A scrutiny of autonomous regions in the EU will probably show that many enjoy on the one hand a certain amount of fiscal autonomy, but that almost none can finance themselves from these sources alone. Therefore the ECJ would have had to demonstrate more precisely the special link between the tax reductions at issue and the Portuguese budgetary transfers. It can't be the necessary conclusion of the ECJ that regional tax laws are just in such cases outside Art 87 EC where they derive from fiscally completely autarkic regions as this would almost demand an economic independence of separate States – an independence which mere regions normally cannot fulfil by definition. The exact role of budgetary transfers from the central State in an Art 87 EC scrutiny should therefore still be further developed and clarified by the Court in future case law. One of the first test cases of the new criteria set out in the Azores' ruling will be the annulment procedure T-211/04 on the Commission's decision on the reorganization of the Gibraltar tax system pending before the Court of First Instance.

If one tries to measure the tax policy impact of the Azores' judgment, it must, however, be conceded that the judgment reflects both the consciousness of the European Court of the sensitive question referred to Luxembourg and the serious attempt to find a golden means solution. Thus the judgment is – despite possible objections - a viable starting point for further legal discussions. Moreover, it is important to stress that the Azores' judgment just targets regional reductions to a "normal" tax system designed and installed by the central State. It does neither concern independently set up regional tax laws nor constellations of regional tax autonomy involving all the local authorities at the same level (regions, districts or others) and giving them autonomous options in the design of certain elements of the central legislation (eg in the definition of the tax rates without federally fixed "normal" figures). In this latter constellation the Court even seemed to accept the Commission's point of view that such merely optional schemes are non-selective in the sense of Art 87 EC because of missing "normal" reference rates.[89]

In any case, the debate about the permissibility of independent general regional tax laws under the European State aid rules demonstrates quite lively the far reaching consequences of an extensive application of the European State aid rules for national tax policy, as the Commission can also invade into the rules of fiscal constitution of the Member States via Art 87 EC and thereby coin a Member State's constitutional system considerably. Hence, one ought not ignore that the allurements of its ample powers under the European State aid rules also create a special momentum for the Commission to broaden the State aid notion excessively examining more and more national measures under Art 87 EC instead of Art 96 EC because the latter just vests the Commission with comparably negligible rights. It is therefore the constant responsibility of the European Courts to reasonably set out the necessary demarcation lines.

6.3 The EC State Aid Control and its Direct Impact on National Law

The Procedural Concept of Art 88 EC and Its "Explosive" Element

The procedural aspects of the State aid control system are contained in Art 88 EC. Under its scheme a clear distinction must be made between existing and new aids as the Treaty provides for two completely different procedures for these two categories. Existing aids are such that had already been in operation when the EC-Treaty came into force on 1 January 1958 or on a later accession date of the particular Member State. They are exclusively monitored by the Commission that can ban them just pro futuro if they appear no longer compatible with the Common Market under Art 87 para 3 EC. Reclaims are not possible.[90] All other aids - including alterations of existing aids[91] - are "new aids" and must be notified to the Commission already before their implementation. If the Commission authorises them or at least does not raise any objections within a certain period of time,[92] they turn into "existing aid".

The "explosive" element of the EC State Aid control regime is in the back-up of the notification requirement for new aids by the "standstill clause" of Art 88 para 3 last sentence EC.[93] This unambiguous and absolute clause is - in contrast to Art 87 EC itself that is exclusively addressed to the Member States[94] - directly applicable.[95] Via this provision national courts and administrative bodies thus take directly part in the EC State aid review. This system shall hinder Member States to introduce aid systems clandestinely and applies to all un-notified aid measures - irrelevant of possible justifications in content and approval perspectives. The ECJ has repeatedly highlighted the importance of the direct applicability of Art 88 para 3 last sentence EC for the functioning of the EC State aid surveillance system and pointed out that the Member States would otherwise create *faits accomplis* for the Commission by ignoring their notification obligations without effective penalty.[96] In the following chapters I will therefore take a closer look upon the very specific provision of Art 88 III 3 EC and explain its genuine consequences for national tax policy.

The Role of the Standstill Clause in the National Legislative Process

The national tax policy of a Member State is outlined and worded within the frame of the national legislation process that has to balance divergent social interests. Tax privileges have therefore normally their point of origin in the passing of a beneficial tax scheme in national parliament.[97] Hence, it would be completely wrong if one assumed that national legislators didn't have to care about the European State aid rules. The opposite is true: If a Member State intends to introduce new aid measures, it must notify the planned measure to the Commission in advance - irrespective of whether the measure is an individual aid to be granted by an administrative body to a single enterprise or an aid scheme[98] enshrined in a legal bill that introduces an explicit right for certain groups of enterprises to claim individual aid grants. Consequently, it is regularly already the tax legislator that has to deliberate about possible aid elements in its planned new tax measures.[99]

The determination of the right point of time for a due notification of legislative aid schemes however still causes some difficulties. New aids have to be notified to the Commission "in sufficient time to enable it to submit its comments" (Art 88 para 3 first sentence EC). From the wording of Art 88 para 3 first sentence EC stipulating that "the Commission shall be informed ... of any plans to grant or alter aid",[100] it can be derived that the notification of national legislative acts fulfilling the definition of Art 87 EC has to be submitted still before their formal adoption (arg: "plans"). This result is also affirmed by the Commission's interpretation of the standstill clause of Art 88 para 3 last sentence EC that backs up the notification requirement and reads: "The Member State concerned shall not put its proposed measures into effect until this procedure has resulted in a final decision".[101] In a letter to the Member States of 27 April 1989 the Commission referred to this wording and pointed out "that a Member State has failed to fulfil its obligation to notify it where the process of putting aid into effect has been initiated. By 'putting into effect' it means not the action of granting aid to the recipient but rather the prior action of instituting or implementing the aid at a legislative level according to the constitutional rules of the Member State concerned. Aid is therefore deemed to have been put into effect as soon as the legislative machinery enabling it to be granted without further formality has been set up."

In its "Guide to procedures in State Aid Cases" the Commission has further clarified its standpoint and presented an alternative to a halt of the legal machinery for a timely notification of legal aid schemes: "By 'putting into effect' is meant not only the actual granting of aid but the conferment of powers enabling the aid to be granted without further formality. To avoid breaching this requirement when passing aid legislation, Member States can either notify the legislation while it is still at the drafting stage or, if not, write into it a clause whereby the aid granting body can only make payments after the Commission has cleared the aid".[102] Accordingly, Member States could also include special reservation clauses in their "advantageous" legal bills emphasizing therein the missing approval of the Commission still necessary for the entry-into-force of the national measure.

In my view, the adoption of such caveat-clauses is, however, quite problematic as a standard notification pattern for legal aid schemes: Given the broad concept of aid in Art 87 EC, such a legislative practice would permanently produce legal acts whose entry into effective force still remains doubtful after their publication in the national Official Journal. The adoption of caveat clauses as a regular legislative tool would therefore provoke a structural uncertainty about the binding character of published legal acts putting the effectiveness of the national jurisdiction at stake and raising both constitutional and EC law concerns of legality. Above that, national reservation clauses do not even withstand a critical functionality analysis, as a mere call of the Commission for minor amendments of the notified bill is already sufficient to hamper its coming into force completely. Consequently every Commission intervention would make a laborious and long winded restart at the very beginning of the national parliamentary process necessary. This shows that caveat clauses do not only meet legality concerns, but also lack the essential flexibility to pay proper attention to the cooperative relationship between Commission and Member States in passing new national aid schemes. They are therefore – if permissible – at least no convincing alternative to the notification of an aid scheme on its drafting stage.

Wondering about the best timing for a notification during the national drafting process of legal bills, one should neither choose a date too early nor a date too late. As long as the political opinion about a legal bill has not been fully developed and significant amendments are still very likely, the dispatch of a notification is not reasonable, because otherwise the Member States would regularly have to re-notify their planned measures several times. A duly notification therefore ought not take place *before* the pre-parliamentary review process involving interested parties (ie the phase of informal discussion of the ministerial or governmental draft) has been completed and the planned bill has definitely been forwarded to parliament. The notification date should however neither be chosen too late in the parliamentary process, as amendments required by the Commission should still be easily includable into the bill. A reasonable notification process must therefore still be initiated (and completed) *before* the start of the last parliamentary session that can adopt textual amendments of the notified bill.[103] From the angle of economy of time it might however be better not to await this final date, but to notify the measure some time earlier,[104] because Commission review and national legislative machinery could then run in parallel saving time in the overall introduction process of the measure. Unfortunately most national rules governing the legislative process at the parliamentary stage do not contain any provisions regulating at which stage and by whom national bills should be forwarded to the Commission in order to ensure a proper notification of planned aid schemes. This lack of clear responsibilities on the national parliamentary level leads to avoidable failures in notifying national bills and should therefore be addressed by the national parliaments themselves.[105]

If a national parliament does not respect the notification requirements of Art 88 EC, the question arises whether the national (administrative) body responsible for the publication of the legal acts in the national Official Journal is the first person hit by the direct blocking effect of the standstill clause of Art 88 para 3 sentence 3 EC. In other words: does this person - in Germany that's the President of the Republic, in Austria it is the Federal Chancellor, ie the prime minister of the government – have to refuse the publication of the national bill infringing the standstill clause? If one highlights the special nature of Art 88 para 3 sentence 3 EC as a requirement of form that obliges Member States to inform the Commission about all their beneficial legislative plans, such a consequence is at least not out of imagination. If the "publishers" of the parliamentary bill therefore detect (or more precisely: presume to have detected) a (serious and evident) notification failure of parliament, they could consider such a refusal. For constitutional reasons the publishers will however - at the utmost - just be able to halt the legislation machinery in order to start a notification of the bill to the Commission on their own motion. Otherwise a misuse of the EC State aid rules as pretext for arbitrary interventions of executive bodies into parliamentary powers would be possible. A definitive turn down of the publication of a parliamentary bill would subsequently require a negative result of the Commission's State aid review.[106]

The Role of the Standstill Clause in Administrative and Court Procedures

In the monitoring of new aid national courts and administrative authorities play an important role, as they both have to respect the direct effect of the standstill clause of Art 88 para 3 sentence 3 EC when applying national provisions.[107] If an aid scheme therefore manages to pass the legislative process without prior notification, national courts and administrative authorities have to ask themselves if the national provisions to be applied at issue constitute State aid in the sense of Art 87 para 1 EC and – if the answer is affirmative - whether the contended provisions have been put aside by the supremacy of European law, ie by the standstill clause of Art 88 para 3 last sentence EC for new aids.[108] In this context they must also take into account that since the adoption of several exemption regulations some new aid schemes do not need to be notified anymore.[109] This makes it necessary to check the preconditions of the relevant regulations rendering the surveillance more complex. If a national *court* has doubts, if all criteria of Art 87 para 1 EC (or of the exemption regulations) are fulfilled, it may refer preliminary questions to the Court of Justice pursuant to Article 234 of the EC Treaty and indeed must do so if being the last instance.[110]

In the supervision of new aid measures the Commission thus shares its surveillance competences in a triangle of power with the national bodies in the Member States and with the European Court of Justice. However, these co-players in the State aid arena can just rule on the scope of Art 87 para 1 EC (and on the new exemption regulations), but not on the final compatibility of the aid measure with the Common Market, because the competence to authorize national aid measures after an overall balancing of interests under Art 87 para 3 EC lies exclusively in the hands of the Commission that enjoys a broad range of discretion in its assessment.[111]

Via the standstill clause of Art 88 para 3 last sentence EC the tax administration, however, sets up a second national net against unlawful aid grants after parliamentary negligence: In pending procedures they have to observe the direct "blocking effect" of Art 88 para 3 last sentence EC on their own motion and must not grant any individual aids on the grounds of unlawful national aid schemes. A breach of the EC State aid rules by the tax legislator can consequently never become effective in the purses of the deemed beneficiaries of an illegal aid scheme if the stand still clause is at least duly respected on the executive level.[112]

Refusal vs Extension as Appropriate Consequences for Unlawful Aid Schemes?

In its order of 10 March 1999 referring to the ECJ for a preliminary ruling in the so-called Adria Wien Pipeline Case the Austrian Constitutional Court (Verfassungsgerichtshof) pointed out that it saw generally two possibilities to bring illegal aid grants to an end by reference to the direct effect of the standstill clause: First, a national body confronted with such a case could regard the whole aid scheme conferring a selective fiscal advantage as inapplicable and suppressed by the supremacy of European law and thus grant no more aid to any claimant (refusal of individual aid grants). Alternatively, the national body could just consider the restriction of the beneficial scheme to the group of certain undertakings as inapplicable and thus grant the tax privilege to any undertaking (extension of the aid scheme). In the latter case the illegal aid scheme would be extended - by court ruling - to all undertakings and then constitute no longer an aid measure in the sense of Art 87 EC, but turn into a general economic measure not granted to specific undertakings anymore.[113] In its subsequent judgment the ECJ did, however, not comment on the Austrian "innovative", but certainly arguable construction of the standstill clause and just held that the current national tax rebate system at issue infringed Art 87 EC. Therefore the Austrian Constitutional Court chose the extension as the consequence more suitable to the case at issue.[114] Despite the revolutionary concept and far-reaching dimension of this judgment it has *not* attracted much attention in literature and has soon been accepted by the Commission as a legitimate reaction.[115] Some authors also welcomed it because it renders reclaims unnecessary and thus avoids *ab ovo* conflicts with good faith of the original beneficiaries.[116]

In contrast to these authors I took the position that the Austrian extension model did not fit into the procedural concept of Art 88 EC.[117] One just has to draw the parallel to the classical aid situation where a State grants a certain cash amount to an individual undertaking (what has been the historical common pattern in 1958), to grasp the peculiarity of the Austrian approach. In the classical aid situation nobody would come to the idea that a national court could also grant the money to all other undertakings in order to satisfy the standstill clause of the EC. Why should there be a difference when aid is granted indirectly?

In my view, the approach of the Austrian Constitutional Court already overdoes the role ascribed to the national courts within the review machinery established by Art 88 EC: When a national court draws the conclusion to grant an aid measure to all undertakings, it does no longer just safeguard the notification to the Commission, it renders it unnecessary![118] This seems in contradiction with the ECJ-jurisprudence that the national courts must not rule on the compatibility of aid measures with the Common Market but have to leave this issue to the Commission to decide upon:[119] If a State measure is enlarged to a general economic measure by a national judge, the Commission is already put out of the game, as its approval is then no longer necessary. Moreover, the wording of Art 88 para 3 last sentence EC is clearly negative stating that a Member State "*shall not put* its proposed measures *into effect*" before the end of the review procedure of the Commission. It does not say that national authorities and courts shall alter unlawful measures in order to bring them outside the grasp of the European State aid system.[120] National bodies that draw this conclusion arrogate a competence normally solely contributed to the national legislator - without any necessity out of EC law. Thereby they are already leaving the role ascribed to them in the triangle of powers of Art 88 EC, as their task is just an interim one and not a definite one securing the non-application of the unlawful aid scheme until the Commission has ruled on the State aid case.

An ambiguity in the application of the standstill clause would also make its handling much more complicated and weaken the EC State aid review system remarkably. National administrative authorities and courts that detect an infringement of Art 88 para 3 sentence 3 EC could no longer draw a clear and fast consequence out of their findings. Under the Verfassungsgerichtshof's premise they have to consider both alternative reactions and give reasons for choosing the refusal or the extension path in the individual case. If they have chosen to extend the unlawful aid scheme, things become even more complex as they must be very careful in correctly extending the national measure: If the national judges or tax officers extend it too cautiously, the measure might persist to fulfil Art 87 para 1 EC so that they have eventually even enlarged the infringement of the standstill clause and created a bigger unlawful aid than before![121] This huge risk of unintentional amplification of the EC law infringement is probably the major weakness of the Austrian extension solution.[122] The solution of the Austrian Constitutional Court thus creates several new problems and adds to the existing uncertainty about the exact material scope of Art 87 para 1 EC a second uncertainty about the consequences out of a breach of the standstill clause. It thereby makes the impact of the EC State aid rules on national tax law even more incalculable. Due to the various forms of reaction imaginable (refusal of the aid or its variably far reaching extension) a uniform response of the local tax administrations to unlawful national aid schemes would become unlikely.

The greatest advantage of the Austrian extension model, however, is that it opens a sensitive path out of a harsh roll-back spiral for unlawful aid grants and can thus pays attention to the good faith and legitimate expectations of the beneficiaries of unlawful aid schemes. Under the extension model it's the Member State that has to pay for its own non-notification fault (by bearing the extension costs) sparing the deluded beneficiaries from repayments. Such a protection of the beneficiaries seems at least welcome if the aid element in the legal scheme was hard to detect. This end can however also be reached by other means: The harsh roll-back-spiral could have for instance equally be mitigated by allowing requests for retroactive approval of the Commission that would have fitted better within the European State aid system than the Austrian extension model.[123] Alternatively the interests of the beneficiaries can still be paid attention to in the national recovery procedures themselves – on a then merely national level.[124]

As the Austrian construction of the standstill clause touches vital questions for the relationship of national tax law and the EC State Aid Prohibition and for the balance of power in the triangle of competences between the Commission, national bodies and the European Courts of Luxembourg, the missing European debate of the objections against the Austrian extension model has been a great deficit in the last years. When the Austrian Administrative Court lodged – against a different background[125] - a second request for a preliminary ruling on the Austrian Energy Tax Rebate Act, literature characterized this procedure as the last opportunity for the ECJ to break its silence on the Austrian extension model. Although the Austrian construction of the standstill clause extension was not questioned by the index a quo anymore, it was obviously taken as a basis of the case, so that an ignorance of the issue would have had to be interpreted as silent consent. Against this background AG Jacobs did address the issue in his Opinion of 29 November 2005 on his own motion. In his analysis he shared most of the critics mentioned above and found an extension of the circle of beneficiaries via Art 88 para 3 last sentence EC at odds with the system of the European State aid rules.[126] As the Austrian Constitutional Court's construction of Art 88 para 3 sentence 3 EC makes a homogenous solution of conflicts between national law and EC State aid rules almost impossible, bears great failure risks and puts both the national legislator and the Commission out of the game, the ECJ was right to eventually follow this position.[127]

Minor Use of Un-Notified Aid Schemes – a Case of De-Minimis-Aid?

De-minimis-aid,[128] ie aid below a certain threshold for individual grants, is regarded as negligible and thus not able to affect intra-community trade so that Art 87 seq EC do not apply. De-minimis-aid can therefore be granted to undertakings without prior notification to the Commission and the standstill clause of Art 88 III 3

EC does not apply. According to European de-minimis-rules in force until the end of 2006 aid not surpassing an overall ceiling of EUR 100 000 within a three-year period qualified as de-minimis aid.[129] In the hearing of the Heiser Case the question was raised whether beneficiaries could invoke this de-minimis-privilege also for the use of an unnotified aid scheme if they actually just took minor advantage of it, although the aid scheme was neither openly identified as such nor did possess any safeguard mechanism ensuring the respect of the overall de-minimis-ceiling. An affirmative answer would limit the number of cases hit by the standstill clause of Art 88 para 3 last sentence EC considerably and thereby restrict the impact of the EC State aid Prohibition on national tax law remarkably, but bring up several review problems.

In its preliminary ruling of 2005 the ECJ held that in the Heiser Case "it was not apparent form the case-file [...] that the amount of the deductions which [an individual undertaking] may be able to make under a measure such as that at issue is, in all circumstances, less than the *de minimis* amount, which is set at EUR 100 000 over three years. [... As] the national legislation ... does not lay down any limit on the amount ... an individual undertaking may receive [...] it is not established that such a measure can be covered by the *de minimis* rule".[130] As the ECJ just pointed at the missing precautions against cumulations of *de-minimis*-aid beyond the 100.000 EUR limit in the aid scheme, one can conclude that the ECJ examines the de-minimis conditions exclusively on the level of the aid scheme itself. If the scheme can not establish the respect of the de-minimis limit "in all circumstances", the standstill clause seems to remain applicable in any case. Apparently it is not necessary in such a situation to measure case by case the amount of aid cumulated by an individual undertaking.

This ruling of the ECJ has however still been delivered on the grounds of the Commission's De-minimis-Notice of 6 March 1996 and not on the basis of the subsequent De-minimis-Regulation 69/2001. In this regulation de-minimis-aid is solely defined by reference to the maximum threshold of EUR 100 000 over any period of three years (Art 2 leg cit). The obligations of the Member States to ensure appropriate monitoring and information of the beneficiaries to hamper illicit cumulations of de minimis aids above the overall limit are laid down outside the definition clause in the subsequent Art 3 leg cit.[131] This could be seen as an indication that these obligations shall be merely procedural obligations of the Member States not affecting the definition of "de-minimis-aid" itself. On the grounds of this setup of the regulation one might argue that even an undertaking that has just by chance not received aid above the de minimis threshold could be classified as recipient of de-minimis-aid and spared from recaptures. According to this position an unnotified aid scheme could produce both de-minimis aid and unlawful, reclaimable aid – depending on the amount actually distributed to the individual undertaking. Under this approach the standstill clause would not apply to recipients of small aids out of an unnotified aid scheme as they would also enjoy the de-minimis-protection despite the omission of cumulation precautions in the scheme. A close up on the wording of Art 2 De-minimis-Regulation 69/2001 however also allows the contrary position, because Art 2 subpara 2 first sentence precisely stipulates that a de-minimis-exemption requires that "the total de minimis aid *granted to any one enterprise* shall not exceed EUR 100 000 over any period of three years".[132] Applied to aid schemes as such this definition is not fulfilled if cumulations over 100.000 EUR are not banned in any event. The crucial question now remains whether unnotified aid schemes must always be examined as such under Art 2 subpara 2 of the Regulation 69/2001 or if a split up into a case by case analysis is permissible.

If one leaves the unclear wording and structuring of the Regulation aside, there are also good teleological arguments against a possible de-minimis defence in case of the application of an unnotified and undeclared aid scheme. First one shouldn't abstract away from the fact that the easements for de-minimis aid can only be justified in a trade-off for maximal transparency: If Member States could introduce hidden aid schemes without facing more severe consequences than in case of the introduction of open de-minimis-schemes, there would be no incentive for them to declare de-minimis aid schemes as such and thereby ensure a possible control of the overall ceiling. Moreover, an acceptance of de-minimis excuses in case of minor uses of unnotified and undeclared aid schemes would make the de minimis concept collapse, as this concept stands and falls with the possibility to easily add up the de minimis sums already received. If the computation of the 100.000 €-treshold would however have to take all receipts of hidden aid of an undertaking into account as well, every turn in the ECJ-jurisprudence settling a disputed conflict about the aid nature of a State measure, would make reassessments of the de-minimis grants necessary, as the overall amount of explicit de-minimis-aid and unconscious aid grants could suddenly rise over the ceiling. The inclusion of the use of unnotified aid schemes into the de-minimis Regulation would therefore not always be to the advantage of the minor beneficiaries of this scheme. If they have taken advantage of other legal provisions involving "hidden" de-minimis aid, it could even be to their detriment jeopardizing all their ordinarily received explicit de-minimis aid ex post. Therefore the better arguments speak against the recognition of a de-minimis-privilege for minor uses of an unnotified aid scheme that has neither been expressly declared as de-minimis scheme nor secured against illicit cumulations of de-minimis aid.[133] The Austrian Administrative Supreme Court followed this position obiter dictu in June 2005.[134]

On 15 December 2006 the Commission eventually adopted the new De-minimis-Regulation 1998/2006.[135] This new Commission Regulation increases the general de-minimis-threshold to 200.000 € over a period of three fiscal years.[136] In the new text the Commission also stresses a strict ex post "mathematic" approach in the definition of de-minimis aid and holds in Art 2 para 2 second subparagraph:[137] "When an overall aid amount exceeds this ceiling, that aid cannot benefit from this Regulation, even for a fraction not exceeding that ceiling. In such a case, the benefit of the Regulation cannot be claimed for this aid measure either at the time it is granted or at any subsequent time."

In order to ensure the controllabilty of such a de minimis system the Commission Regulation also empasizes the mutual information obligations between Member State and beneficiary. In its reasoning it therefore holds: "To that end, when granting *de minimis* aid, Member States should inform the undertaking concerned of the amount of the aid and of its *de minimis* character, by referring to the regulation. Moreover prior to granting such aid the Member State concerned should obtain from the undertaking a declaration about other *de minimis* aid received during the ficals year concerned and the two previous years and carefully check that the *de minimis* ceiling will not be exceeded by the new *de minimis* aid" (mn 17). Alternatively Member States could set up a central register of de minimis aid. The Commission Regulation also clarifies that "for the purposes of transparency, equal treatment and effective monitoring, this Regulation should apply only to *de minimis* aid which is transparent. Transparent aid is aid for which it is possible to calculate precisely the gross grant equivalent *ex ante* without a need to undertake a risk assessment. Such precise calculation can, for instance, be realised as regards grants, interest rate subsidies and *capped* tax exemptions" (mn 13, emphasis added).

For the first time the new Commission Regulation also explicitly addresses the use of aid schemes without ex ante defineable individual aid amounts – a situation, which is typical for beneficial tax provisions: "Where the *de minimis* aid is granted to different undertakings on the basis of a scheme and different amounts of individual aid are granted to those undertakings under the scheme, the Member State concerned may choose to fulfil this obligation by informing the undertakings of a fixed sum corresponding to the maximum aid amount to be granted under the scheme. In such case, the fixed sum shall be used for determining whether the ceiling laid down in Article 2(2) is met" (Art 3 para 1 second and third sentence of the Regulation).

The new Commission Regulation has thereby eventually paid attention to the problems identified in literature concerning the use of unnotified aid schemes lacking explicit de-minimis labelling and safeguard mechanisms against illicit cumulations. Limiting the scope of the de minimis rule now clearly to transparent types of aid, ie such measures where it is possible to determine in advance the precise aid amount or where the maximum aid amount is capped, the new Commission Regulation is defintetly a step forward to more transparency in state aid granting procedures and also an important prerequisite for national courts to ensure an effective review of the de-minimis-block exemption. For tax policy makers it means that tax provisions have to include caps if they shall be able to take advantage o the de minimis privileges. The risks of notification failures have correspondingly risen again.

Recovery Consequences Before National Courts and Possible National Competitors' Claims

One of the most difficult – and if dealt with – most disputed issues of EC State aid law is the question which recovery consequences national bodies and courts still have to draw from a breach of the standstill-clause of Art 88 para 3 sentence 3 EC *after* the deliverance of the individual final tax assessment containing the grant of the tax advantage. In the SFEI-Case the ECJ has ruled in that context that "national courts *must in principle allow an application for repayment of aid paid in breach of Article 88(3) of the Treaty*"[138] and that "a national court requested to order the repayment of aid must grant that application if it finds that the aid was not notified to the Commission, unless by reason of exceptional circumstances repayment is inappropriate".[139] Consequently disadvantaged competitors should, in principle, be able to trigger recapture claims – even before any compatibility examination of the national aid measure by the Commission under Art 87 para 3 EC has taken place.

The exact preconditions for such national recovery claims of competitors are, however, still unclear in many respects, as the ECJ has not taken a clear stand on this issue and broadly referred to the national laws. In its famous FNCE-formula the ECJ held: "National courts must offer to individuals the certain prospect that all appropriate conclusions will be drawn from an infringement of that provision, *in accordance with their national law*, as regards the *validity* of measures giving effect to the aid, the *recovery* of financial support granted in disregard of that provision and possible *interim measures*".[140] The interpretation of this crucial ECJ-formula is widely unclear. If one looks back at the past jurisprudence of the ECJ, it stands out that the ECJ has so far not stated any obligation of national authorities to recover unlawful aid already granted on their own motion.[141] In the SFEI-Case the ECJ has just stressed the responsibility of national courts for the claims of disadvantaged competitors.[142] National law is therefore, in my view, not obliged to provide for an ex-officio-recapture automatism. Hence, it is - despite the broad reference of the ECJ to domestic law in the *FNCE*-formula ("in accordance with their national law") – neither allowed to exclude competitors completely from lodging national recovery claims either. Literature that has interpreted the vagueness of the *FNCE*-formula in this way[143] should not be followed.

Instead, the reference of the ECJ to national law should be understood in the same way as other references of the ECJ to national procedural law. Accordingly, "normal" national restrictions such as time-limits for lodging claims before national courts are permissible if they are not more restrictive than the ones for other (comparable) national claims and if they do not render the chances of a national recovery claim almost nil. AG Jacobs has just recently pointed out that this also implies a competence of national law "to determine an individual's standing and legal interest in bringing proceedings". In other words: national law might also require the existence of a "competitive relationship" for an entitlement to bring proceedings against unlawful beneficiaries.[144] Further restrictions of competitors' claims might, however, result from the individual circumstances of an illicit aid receipt that might be considered by the national courts in recovery procedures.[145]

Things look however completely different if the Commission has examined an unlawful aid scheme and reached the conclusion that it could neither be declared compatible with the Common Market under Art 87 para 3 EC. In this case the Commission itself has to reclaim the illicit aid according to Art 14 EC Regulation 659/99, while the mere breach of the notification requirement does – in contrast to possibly available national recapture claims of competitors - not authorize the Commission to recall the granted aid.[146] A recovery decision of the Commission reaches back 10 years and must be executed by national bodies regardless of any contrary or missing procedural provisions including national constitutional obstacles.[147]

Can the Commission Deliver a Retroactive Authorization of Unlawful Aid and Thereby Stop National Recoveries?

Another important recovery issue is the question whether the Commission can deliver a retroactive authorization of unlawful aid and which effects such a retroactive authorization would have on pending national recovery claims of disadvantaged competitors. In August 2004 the Austrian Administrative Supreme Court has asked the ECJ for a preliminary ruling on this issue.[148] This case has been registered before the ECJ as Transalpine Ölleitung and has its background in the same statutory law as the Adria Wien Pipeline proceedings: After the classification of the Energy Tax Refund Act as "State aid" by the ECJ the Austrian tax administration has notified the Act to the Commission obtaining a retroactive authorization of the aid scheme. As a consequence out of this approval the tax administration took the position that it no longer had to follow the ruling of the Constitutional Court and need not extend the grant of an energy tax refund to all undertakings anymore.[149] In the eyes of the tax administration the retroactive authorization had removed the direct effect of the standstill clause so that the energy taxation could be applied in its original preferential form again.

In the Case C-368/04, *Transalpine Pipeline* AG *Jacobs* has however argued *against* a competence of the Commission to issue *retroactive* authorizations pointing out that they had a harmful healing effect for past grants of unlawful aid and would thereby undermine the respect for the European aid rules.[150] *The arguments pro and contra retroactive authorizations are in my view, however, not that clear cut.* First, it has to be noted that the opponents of retroactive approvals falsely proceed on the assumption that aid grants can easily and indisputably be attributed to certain periods of time. In fact, it is extremely difficult to clarify whether the application of an aid scheme has been "put into effect" still before or already after an authorization by the Commission. In case of indirect aid grants several points of time could be regarded as decisive for this categorization - namely the issuing date of the administrative decision (eg of the tax assessment), the date of its legal effectiveness or the date a waived tax claim belongs to substantively. In domestic tax law the latter date often varies. In Austria it is once determined as the date of the underlying business transaction, once as the end of the fiscal year of the transaction – depending on the sort of tax applied.[151] Consequently, one should keep in mind that it is already quite unclear for which aid grants a Commission approval is retroactive and for which ones not.

Above that, one has to emphasize that the safeguarding role of the standstill clause for the notification obligation of the Member States is – contrary to the assumption of AG Jacobs in his Opinion in the Transalpine Ölleitung Case[152] - *not* jeopardized at all by the allowance of retroactive approvals: As long as the grant of such authorizations remains in the sole discretion of the Commission after considering the individual facts of the case, there is no incentive for the Member States to intentionally ignore the notification obligation. The reason for this is simple: Member States can never be certain to get a retroactive approval of the Commission for their unlawful aid measures, while a correct notification spares them from being exposed to the "mercy" of the Commission. A prudent approval practice of the Commission could thus easily ensure that retroactive authorizations do not run foul the surveillance system of Art 88 EC.[153] Moreover, a retroactive authorization of an un-notified, but compatible aid only cuts short the alternative way of applying to the Commission for re-granting the aid again after its recapture.[154]

Retroactive authorizations would just open up a way out of a harsh roll-back spiral solely based on a procedural EC law infringement (ie the breach of the notification obligation of Art 88 III 1 EC) and help get around a potential disproportionality between the uncertainty of the borderlines of Art 87 EC on the one hand side and a relentless roll-back-automatism on the other hand side. If a Member State applies for a retroactive approval and the Commission eventually finds the measure to be compatible with the Common Market under Art 87 para 3 EC, it could then additionally consider the reasons and circumstances of the non-notification in the individual case and limit the financial risk for the recipients of unlawful aid grants if appropriate. Such a limitation would for instance be reasonable in those constellations, where the failure of the Member State to notify its measure can be explained as a consequence of the uncertainty of the notion of State aid and does not involve gross negligence of the Member State and/or the beneficiary.

Unfortunately, the ECJ did not see these arguments and followed the conclusions of AG Jacobs banning retroactive authorizations of the Commission categorically. Thereby it closed an important window for possible individual case evaluations on the European level. Nonetheless, the judgment should not be interpreted as an imperative to national roll-back automatisms. It will now be up to the national authorities and courts to pay proper attention to the individual circumstances of the illicit State aid cases in order to prevent disproportionality concerns about the European State Aid Rules.[155] A common European steering of this balancing of interests has, however, become much more difficult after the exclusion of the Commission from this process by the Transalpine judgment.[156]

6.4 The Political Dimension of the European State Aid Rules and Their Implications for National Tax Policy

While the influence of the Council on national *direct* tax legislation has remained quite limited due to the unanimity-requirement of Art 96 EC, the extensive application of Art 87 EC in tax matters has given the Commission a far-reaching influence on all fields of national business taxation and boosted European tax coordination. Although the EC State aid rules attribute no *initiative* legislative rights to the Commission in the field of tax law, they have become one of the most powerful tools for Brussels to shape national business tax legislation. As the introduction of new national tax acts regularly can't go without various - economically or politically necessary - deviations from the benchmark tax system favouring certain groups of taxpayers, national tax policy requires regular cooperation with the Commission. By threatening not to authorize national preferential tax provisions, the Commission can push its own ideas on a common tax policy more easily, while the room for independent and autonomous exercise of national tax sovereignty has become very narrow for Member States.[157] This strong European influence does not exclude any field of national business taxation and reaches from direct over indirect taxation to international tax treaty policy. Even constitutional rules in the Member States – such as traditional concepts of regional tax autonomy – can not abscond themselves from the grasp of the European State aid Prohibition.

This silent shift in legislative competence in tax matters via Art 87 EC would probably have surprised the founders of the EC-Treaty. Hence, the European State aid rules mustn't be mistaken as full substitute for the lacking unanimity in tax coordination efforts by legislative European acts. This can be demonstrated by reference to the example of energy taxation where the Commission has cracked down on preferential national exceptions for certain industries of some Member States, but could not oblige other Member States to introduce any energy taxation at all. It is therefore an illusion to think that the EC State aid rules alone can guarantee equal (tax) conditions on the European market because such an assumption ignores the existing general differences between the Member States in the first place. Under the EC State aid rules the Commission can only require amendments from Member States willing to introduce a new tax package involving preferential features, but it can not actively force other Member States in the same direction or hinder Member States from totally abolishing a certain tax. Its coordinative powers under Art 87 seq EC are therefore clearly limited.

With the evolvement of an extensive application of the EC State aid rules in tax matters national tax policy makers are certainly facing new challenges: The amorphous borderlines of Art 87 EC often require complex legal deliberations – just to find out whether a national tax measure meets Art 87 para 1 EC and must be notified to the Commission or not. Sometimes clear results can't be reached at all in the light of the vagueness of Art 87 para 1 EC. Unfortunately, the European law situation is even double incalculable, as national tax policy makers are also left in doubt about the exact (procedural) consequences of potential infringements of the State aid provisions. On the grounds of this legal uncertainty, Member States often rely upon ventured justification arguments for the systematic coherence of their new tax measures[158] instead of submitting precautionary notifications to Brussels. The reluctance to forward such precautionary notifications is probably due to the fact that they can slow down the national legislation process considerably involving laborious formalistic and explanatory efforts that simply seem unnecessary, if there are justification patterns at hand anyway. Unfortunately precautionary notifications are currently the only reliable tool to avoid legal uncertainties and possible recapture consequences under the ambiguous notion of State Aid in Art 87 EC.

This dilemma becomes especially evident for the regular accumulative tax updates proposed to parliament: National tax legislators often try to pack all tax amendments of a year into an annual Tax Amendment Act as such acts can politically be justified as balanced development of the tax system containing both "goodies and badies" for the tax paying electorate. These tax packages regularly contain urgent measures to close unintentional loopholes in the tax system detected by resourceful tax practitioners or opened up by tax jurisprudence in the last months. These bills thus largely consist of mere readjustments and "maintainance work" resulting out of the experience with the daily application of the various tax acts. The potential-slow down-effect now becomes quite evident if one imagines the efforts necessary to provide the Commission with background information on all the tax updates in the Member States in order to have the Commission itself decide whether any slight amendment or legislative re-interpretation of a former contentious issue is still in line with the national benchmark tax system. An over-cautious notification practice could thereby in fact both tie up the Commission completely and prolongate national legislation considerably as several separate notification procedures would have to be awaited. It seems therefore inevitable for Member States to try to find a responsible notification practice that does include a certain national pre-assessment of the tax measures and their justifiability out of the logic of the tax system.[159]

The duality of the EC State aid surveillance procedure stipulating notification and stand still obligation just for new aids enhances however also a certain petrification of existing national tax structures. Member States will often shy at fine-tuning and reshaping their existing beneficial tax schemes because they don't want to expose them to the directly applicable stand still clause after an alteration[160] or to point the Commission unnecessarily at their existing tax privileges and then submit themselves to the Commission's approval discretion for a continued application of the altered scheme. This petrification effect in the sense of an understandable "just-don't-touch-existing-aid-schemes"-approach is certainly a considerable downside of the EC State aid concept as it can hamper necessary modifications and modernizations of national tax laws and reduces the response abilities of Member States to factual developments in society.

To some extent, notification failures of the Member States might have their reasons not only in the vague European State aid doctrine, but also in missing precautions for a proper notification of legislative aid schemes on the Member States' parliamentary level[161] and in the ironical sanction mechanism of the EC State aid regime:[162] Although the correct notification clearly falls within its responsibility, the Member State itself does not have to fear any penalty payments for wrongful non-notifications. Instead, it is exclusively the recipients of unlawful aid grants that have to fear far-reaching consequences as they run the risk of having to pay back all the sums received - either upon request of the Commission or upon request of competitors before national courts.

In the long run the un-notified introduction of economic incentives targeted at a small group of undertakings could however also trigger additional costs for the Member State's budget rendering the introduced measure finally more expensive than primarily planned and thereby forming also a sort of sublime financial punishment of the State for its notification omission. Such budgetary consequences could either result from political pressure calling for retroactive legislative repair of unlawful aid schemes[163] or for the adoption of costly substitute future measures for the disappointed target groups of the illegal aid measures.[164] Even if such budgetary consequences don't show up, the political damages of State aid infringements will in any event be very painful for the Member States as there's no interest on their side to deliberately disappoint legitimate expectations of business investors and their confidence into national tax legislation.

After the Transalpine Judgment of the European Court in late 2006 national tax policy makers can no longer start penitential *"journeys to Canossa"* asking for retroactive remission in Brussels in order to keep the financial and economic consequences of unlawful aid grants limited.[165] Hence, this judgment does, in my view, not trigger an obligatory national roll-back automatism either, but rather shifts the burden of balancing the respective elements pro and contra national reclaims in an individual case to the national courts instead of allocating it to the Commission. Thereby this new model bears the risk of disparate ruling practice in the Member States, while the alternative concept of retroactive remissions of the Commission would have allowed a common steering of this balancing on the European level.

Despite all these major problems in the current implementation of the European State Aid rules and the necessity to challenge some of them still before the European Courts for disproportionality examinations the (deliberately) *clandestine* introduction of economic incentives via beneficial tax measures should, eventually, decrease significantly in the Member States facing the irreversible evolution of a stricter European State aid control system. Nonetheless the scrutinizing process of the European national tax laws will still take years. In this process the national tax administrations and tax courts have become the key "field agents" of the Commission in the Member States in the control of the national tax legislators – vested by art 88 para 3 sentence 3 EC with a European mandate and obligation to question all un-notified parliamentary tax policy decisions. It thus turns out that the European State aid rules have created a new and complex system of mutual check-and-balances-relationships *within* the Member States. National tax policy has to be aware of that. One ought however not to forget to keep also an eye on the daily application of the national tax laws and thereby on the local tax administrations themselves, as the best legal system is of no value if it is not also exercised in the light of the European law in daily practice.[166]

6.5 Concluding Remarks on the Role of European State Aid Rules on National Tax Policy

Aims of national welfare can not only be pursued by spending the tax money collected, but also by shaping the national tax law in a way that supports the development of crucial and sensitive areas of the national economy. Due to the extensive application of the European State aid Prohibition in tax matters the Member States have however been confronted with a narrowing room of national tax sovereignty in recent years rendering national business tax policy undoubtedly by far more complex. Correspondingly, the position of the Commission has been strengthened allowing it to set forth a certain direction in European taxation by its approval practice under Art 87 para 3 EC. Despite rising criticism about the new interference of the Commission in national tax policy the sublime form of "tax coordination" via the European State rules should not be judged by categories such as black or white and good or bad. Instead it ought to be seen – in principle - as a sort of golden means between a complete European laisser-faire of national State interventions on the Common Market through national fiscal measures and a far-reaching European tax harmonization eliminating also the possibility of fair tax competition between the Member States. Above that, taxpayers might find it quite healthy if national tax policy has to face a certain justification pressure rendering privileging tax spending more laborious.

Despite the important coordinative role of Art 87 seq EC, the current deficiencies in daily State aid practice must not be blanked out either. Firstly, it is evident that the allurements of its ample powers under the European State aid rules create a special momentum for the Commission to broaden the State aid notion in its decision practice excessively narrowing the room for national tax policy to an inadmissible extent and wearing away the distinction of the Treaty of Rome between Art 87 EC and Art 96 EC. This makes it all the more important that the European Courts elaborate clearer borderlines of Art 87 EC and vigilantly control the Commission's State aid practice without showing too much judicial self-restraint. Secondly, the procedural consequences of unlawful State aid grants are still widely unclear in many respects and impose considerable risks for national tax policy makers and business operators. Facing a rather incalculable State aid notion the rigid threat of recapturing all unlawful aid grants from the recipients seems too undifferentiated and disproportionate. It is therefore high time that the ECJ gives up its cautiousness in addressing procedural State aid issues. Instead of referring the most sensitive procedural issues to national law for settlement it is up to the ECJ to give clear and prudent guidelines for a uniform minimum procedural standard in the European Union.

Due to the existing huge uncertainties in the operation of the European State aid rules the interim balance sheet on the influence of the EC State aid rules on national tax policy is – despite a considerable downward trend in subsidizing in the European Union from 3,42% in 1981 down to 0,59% of the European GDP in 2005[167]- still very ambiguous: It must not be forgotten that the European State aid rules should serve business development in the European Union by contributing to a transformation of the European Market into a level playing field. Hence, they ought not create new, incalculable risks for business operators making them solely bear the current shortfalls of a clear State aid doctrine, a transparent procedural concept and a sober notification discipline by the Member States. A prudent case law development of the European Court of Justice must therefore ensure that the European State aid rules remain broadly accepted as a balanced, proportionate and well-operating tax policy-coordination mechanism between national tax sovereignty and welfare responsibility and the Single Market requirements.

Endnotes

1. I want to thank Paolo Rossi, DG Competition of the Commission, for his valuable remarks on the paper. For further comprehensive thoughts on legal (material and procedural) issues arising in the relationship between the EC State aid rules and national tax law provisions see my book *Das EG-Beihilfenverbot und sein Durchführungsverbot in Steuersachen* (available under www.lindeverlag.at).
2. Commission, *State Aid Action Plan 2005* mn 6.
3. Commission, *State Aid Action Plan 2005* mn 7.
4. Commission, *State Aid Action Plan 2005* mn 8.
5. I will elaborate on this case in detail in Sect. 6.3.

6. *Sutter* (2003), p. 172 et seq.
7. *Baudenbacher* (1997), 8.
8. Chapitre 2 Section 1 – Les distorsions, 57: "Les aides accordées par les Etats doivent être examinées de très près, indépendamment de la forme extérieure qu'elles revêtent : l'exemption accordée à une catégorie d'entreprises ou à une branche d'industrie au regard des charges de droit commun comporte les mêmes effets et relève des mêmes critères d'examen qu'une subvention sur fonds publics".
9. ECJ, 23 February 1961, 30/59, *De Gezamenlijke Steenkolenijnen in Limburg v High Authority,* ECR 1961, 3 seq., 43. The definition was originally rendered in respect of the comparable provision of Art 4 c ECSC Treaty, but regularly referred to in later rulings on Art 87 EC.
10. Article 87 was numbered Art 92 before the Treaty of Amsterdam that employed a general renumbering of all EC Treaty provisions in order to adjust the numbering chaos after the regular inclusion of new articles in the course of time.
11. ECJ 2 June 1974, ECR 1974, I-718, mn 13.
12. Commission, "Notice on the application of the State aid rules to measures relating to direct business taxation", 12 December 1998 (OJ C-384/3) mn 9.
13. Apart from fact that the possibility of a loss carry forward would still habe to be examined.
14. *Surrey* (1983), pp. 705–738; *Sutter* (2005a), p. 81 et seq.; Sometimes you can even find national options between tax concessions or direct premiums. Cf Art 108 f Austrian Income Tax Act on a premium or Art 124 nr 31 Austrian Income Tax Act on a tax allowance – both rewarding alternatively the hiring and training of young apprentices throughout all business sectors.
15. Commission, Notice Business Taxation mn 32. Due to the missing link to a specific project operating aid just reduces the beneficiaries' current costs and does not contribute *in a measurable and provable way* to the achievement of any EU objectives. Cf also *Jaeger* (2005), mn. 297 et seq.
16. Commission, Notice Business Taxation mn 32.
17. Commission, *State Aid Action Plan 2005* mn 10.
18. Commission, *State Aid Action Plan 2005* mn 10.
19. See in detail on the procedural concept of Art 88 EC and the resulting role of the Commission in Sect. 6.3.
20. See Sect. 6.3.
21. Resolution *of the Council and the Representatives of the Governments of the Member States,* meeting within the Council of 1 December 1997, on a code of conduct for business taxation (OJ 1998 C 2, p 2, emphasis added).
22. Also stressing the *political* nature of the Code AG *Léger*, Opinion, 2 May 2006, C-196/04, *Cadbury Schweppes,* mn 57.
23. *Pinto* (1999), p. 295 et seq.
24. Just cf press release 11 July 2001, IP/01/982 "Commission launches large scale state aid investigation into business taxation schemes".
25. Cf Commission Press Release from 13 February 2007, IP/07/176: "Under Swiss law, the Cantons may fully or partially exempt profits generated abroad from cantonal and municipal company tax. All Swiss Cantons have made use of this provision, although in different forms. Over the years, this has proved to be a formidable incentive for the headquarters, co-ordination and distribution centres of multinationals to be based in Cantons such as Zug and Schwyz, in order to minimize their tax liabilities. As these multinationals are mostly active in the EU market, such tax regimes may directly or indirectly affect trade between the EU and Switzerland. While the Commission is not against tax competition or low tax rates, it cannot accept schemes that differentiate between domestic and foreign source income. [...] Tax regimes similar to those in

Switzerland are not allowed inside the EU under the State aid provisions of the EC Treaty (Article 87), and the Commission has taken action against Member States."

26. OJ L 300, 31.12.1972, p. 189.
27. On the various tests in detail *Sutter* (2001), p. 239 et seq.
28. Cf in detail *Aldestam* (2005), p. 241 et seq. Certainly, one must not forget the various other tests of Art 87 EC (such as the test of distortion of competition and affect on intra-community trade) over the examination of the potential pairs of comparisons for the selectivity test.
29. Notice Business Taxation (supra FN 12) mn 12.
30. On EC State aid elements of discretionary powers and their different possible categorizations cf in detail *Sutter* (2005a), p. 52 et seq.
31. Cf *Ross* (2000), 407: "no advantage can be identified without a comparator first being found as a benchmark for treatment"; *Kepenne* (1999), p. 23 et seq. mn 26: "Pour déterminer s'il y a avantage, il est donc indispensable de déterminer un point de référence pour la comparaison. Il faut apprécier la mesure par rapport au traitement appliqué aux opérateurs se trouvant dans la même situation factuelle et juridique que la société prétendument favorisée".
32. The Commission speaks of "external objectives assigned to a particular tax scheme" which might be "difficult to justify by the logic of a tax system" (Notice Business Taxation [see supra FN 12] mn 26).
33. See below.
34. ECJ 2 July1974, 173/73, *Italy/Commission*, ECR 1974, 709 seq. where the ECJ concluded that "the partial reduction of social charges pertaining to family allowances devolving upon employers in the textile sector is a measure intended partially to exempt undertakings of a particular industrial sector from the financial charges arising from the normal application of the general social security system, *without there being any justification for this exemption on the basis of the nature or general scheme of this system"* (mn 15, emphasis added).
35. Notice Business Taxation (supra FN 12) mn 16.
36. *Rossi* (2005), p. 111: "It was impossible for the Commission to identify a benefit or advantage without identifying the group in relation to which such advantage was enjoyed."
37. ECJ, 8 November 2001, C-143/99, *Adria Wien Pipeline*, mn 41.
38. ECJ, 8 November 2001, C-143/99, *Adria Wien Pipeline*, mn 52.
39. *Rossi* (2005), p. 112 et seq. speaks of a "two-pronged justification by the nature of the system" – considering first justifications of an internal tax logic, and then of an external or economic logic of the system. Similarily AG *Geelhoed*, Opinion, 20 October 2005, C-88/03, Portugal/Commission, mn 76. In its State aid control practice the Commission often applies a multiple steps approach and divides its State aid analysis into several questions such as: 1) Is the measure State aid or a mere tax measure? (meaning: is the effect due to a fundamental exclusion in the tax system?); is there a derogation from ordinary tax jurisdiction? 2) Is the tax measure selective or general? 3) Is the selectivity justified by the nature of the tax system? (meaning: is the exception proportionate to the tax objective it wants to reach? - this requires to define the *general,* tax-inherent exemptions in a tax system) and 4) Is the selectivity justified by an external objective pursued by the specific tax system? (meaning: is the derogation proportionate to the external objective pursued?). Such an approach might be useful when opening a case file. From a theoretical point of view, it makes however no difference whether you concentrate the State-aid-testing in a two step-test of a comparative rule of reason examination or expand it into a 4 or more partly overlapping sub-steps test, as it will always come down to the latitude of individual evaluation of the competent authority – either of the "logic" of the system or of the

proportionality of the external/internal objectives or of tax inherent "fundamental exclusions".

40. AG Geelhoed, Opinion, 20 October 2005, C-88/03, Portugal/Commission, mn 75.
41. Cf also *Aldestam* (2005), p. 241 et seq. with reference to *McIntyre* (1980), pp. 83–89 and his example of the difficulties to distinguish "weed" from "flowers" due to the subjective nature of the judgment.
42. Against this background it seems to be quite reasonable to give a Member State the possibility to apply for a retroactive authorization before the Commission in such cases in which the State aid element has not been evident. See in detail below Sect. 6.3.
43. Strictly logically speaking, the justification level could thus be even seen as tautological and superfluous, because an exact determination of the benchmark tax system and of the deviating exception character of a national measure already requires a thorough pendular analysis of the "nature or general scheme" of the tax system. Therefore the justification level could also be seen as already comprised in the first and second level of the selectivity review (see *Sutter* (2005a), p. 96 et seq.). The phrases "is still part of the tax system without exceptional character" and "the exception is justified by the logic of the tax system" are thus exchangeable.
44. Critical on the definition of the "effect on competition" test by the ECJ jurisprudence that has led to such an insignificance *Sutter* (2005a), p. 130 et seq.
45. Report on the implementation of the Commission notice on the application of the state aid rules to measures relating to direct business taxation, Box 15.
46. Cf just recently the negative decision of the Commission on a German real estate transfer tax exemption for housing companies in Berlin (Art 4 nr 8 GrunderwerbsteuerG), IP/05/1465.
47. Cf Commission, Implementation Report (supra FN 45) mn 72 seq.: "VAT reductions are subject to strict Community rules and conform to the principle of equality of taxation for similar products. Such reductions are therefore usually not caught by Article 87 (1). As a general rule, the same is not true of excise duties, which directly affect businesses" as the rules in this field were not codified. Moreover, the Commission has pointed at the entry into force of the Energy Tax Directive that continues to allow Member States to grant specific tax exemptions.
48. The detection of an aid element in an EC directive would however trigger bona fide arguments against roll-backs.
49. ECI 5 April 2006, T-351/02, *Deutsche Bahn AG/Commission*, mn 100.
50. ECI 5 April 2006, T-351/02, *Deutsche Bahn AG/Commission*, mn 102.
51. ECI 5 April 2006, T-351/02, *Deutsche Bahn AG/Commission*, mn 103.
52. Cross-border activities are often subject to the fiscal claims of two or more States. To reduce the massive obstacle this poses to the free movement of labour, goods and capital, many countries have concluded bilateral double-taxation conventions (DTC) which suppress the fiscal claim of one of the parties to the agreement by means of detailed regulations on the distribution of taxing rights involved.
53. This case study has been published: *Sutter* (2004a), p. 4 et seq. For a possible classification of the exemption method as export subsidy it is also rewarding to take a closer look on similar thoughts discussed at the WTO level, as the WTO Agreement on Subsidies and Countervailing Measures is also confronted with the argument that the exemption method incorporated in bilateral tax treaties can bring about similar effects as unilateral exemptions supporting the export industry. Cf the so-called tax legislation cases of the Netherlands, GATT-Expert Panel, Document L/4425 of 2 November 1976, intertax 1977, 111 seq. Similarly Document L/4423 of 2 November 1976, intertax 1977, 68 ff on France and Document L/4424 of 2 November 1976, intertax 1977, 103 ff on Belgium.
54. *Sutter* (2005c), p. 94 et seq.

55. On a possible aid qualification of tax exemptions of cross-border-income cf Commission, 17 March 2003, Irish Foreign Income Scheme, OJ 2003 L 204/51.
56. On the economic effects of the capital import and export concepts see illustratively *Hubbard* (2002).
57. The exemption method allows an unrestricted repatriation of the foreign business profits and thus an import of excessive tax advantages which could then be used by the crossborder undertakings on the national home market for financing a cut-throat competition strategy on the home market. Cf also *Commission*, 30 March 2004, C(2004) 928, OJ 2005, L 029/24 seq., *Gibraltar Qualifying Companies*, mn 62: "Even if some Qualifying Companies are established by individuals for tax planning purposes and do not trade, produce or compete in the market, they are not precluded from doing so".
58. "Ringfencing" means that the foreign preferential tax regime is "partly or fully insulated from the domestic markets of the country providing the regime. The fact that a country feels the need to protect its own economy from the regime by ring-fencing provides a strong indication that a regime has the potential to create harmful spillover effects." See OECD, Harmful Tax Competition - A emerging global issue (1998).
59. Younger Member States can, of course, observe this development calmly as most of their DTC would probably still be existing aids, which can only be by suppressed the Commission itself pro futuro. The other Member States could, in my view, however invoke Art 1 lit b sublit v of the Procedural Regulation 659/99 for the exclusion of recapture claims.
60. *Sutter* (2005c), p. 104 et seq.
61. *Luja* (2004), p. 235 et seq. referring at OECD Model Commentary Art 8 mn 11. This provision has however been dropped by the 2005 Update of the OECD leaving it open, if this drop should result in another DTC handling of transit hotels. According to the prevailing opinion an update of the OECD-Model Commentary can however in any case just unfold consequences for new DTCs and not for DTC still concluded already under the old Model.
62. Cf my examples in *Sutter* (2005c), p. 108 et seq.
63. *Panayi* (2004), p. 83 et seq. Opp *Luja* (2004), 237 pointing out that it should be "acceptable to try and limit reciprocal benefits in a bilateral tax treaty to those persons with strong ties to the contracting states".
64. Such a development can be observed at the moment in the field of bilateral air transport agreements as a reaction to the "Open Skies" rulings of the ECJ. See *Kofler* (2004), p. 51 et seq.
65. *Bacon* (1997), p. 301 with further reference to *Wishlade* (1997): "However, a distinction must be drawn between a regional aid programme initiated by central government, and a measure taken by regional authority extending to all undertakings within its territorial jurisdiction. Whereas former, even if it favoured equally all undertakings within a given region, would fall in principle within Article 92 (1), the latter in the same circumstances would not. Any other result would conflict with the principles of subsidiarity and decentralisation which are an increasingly important part of Community policy".
66. Cf also ECJ 1 June 1999, C-302/97, *Konle*, mn 61 ff, 63 (against a non-state aid background).
67. *Commission*, 11 December 2002, Reductions in the rates of income and corporation tax in the Autonomous Region of the Azores, notified C (2002) 4487, OJ 2003, L 150/52 seq., mn 31: "In the Commission's approach the tax autonomy of the regional authority that grants the benefits has never been considered as a factor that would make it possible not to regard measures as aid." Similarily AG *Saggio*, 1 July 1999, Conclusions, C-400/97, C-401/97 und C-402/97, *Administración del Estado/Juntas*

Generales de Guipúzcoa ua, mn 37. The procedure on this case has, however, been suspended by order of 16 February 2002.
68. Cf ECI 6 March 2002, T-127/99, T-129/99 and T-148/99, *Territorio Histórico de Álava – Diputación Foral de Álava,* Slg 2002, II-1275 seq.
69. *Commission*, 11 December 2002, Reductions in the rates of income and corporation tax in the Autonomous Region of the Azores, notified C (2002) 4487, OJ 2003, L 150/52 seq., mn 26 where the Commission also points at the discretionary exemptions of article 87 para 3 lit a and c EC which also indicated that benefits whose scope is limited to part of the territory of the State subject to the rules on aid may constitute selective benefits.
70. Critical thereupon Strüber (2005), p. 168 et seq., 172 et seq. - also with further references to the WTO-Agreement on Subsidies and Countervailing Measures.
71. *Commission*, 11 December 2002, Reductions in the rates of income and corporation tax in the Autonomous Region of the Azores, notified C (2002) 4487, OJ 2003, L 150/52 seq., mn 31: "It should also be noted that the present Decision does not concern a mechanism that would allow all local authorities of a particular level (regions, districts or others) to introduce and levy local taxes with no reference at all to national taxation. On the contrary, the case in point involves a reduction applicable solely in the Azores in the rate of tax established by national legislation and applicable on the mainland of Portugal. Under the circumstances, the measure adopted by the regional authorities clearly constitutes a derogation from the national tax system." Cf also Commission, Implementation Report (supra FN 45) mn 33 and Box #6 ("In a case where a local authority introduced a specific reduction in a tax that was part of the national tax system as selective").
72. AG Geelhoed, 20 October 2005, Opinion, C-88/03, Portugal/Commission, mn 77. Cp also Joined Cases T-346/99, T-347/99 and T-348/99 *Diputación Foral de Álava* [2002] ECR II-4259, mn 62 seq. on tax aid in the form of a reduction in the tax base for firms in certain Spanish provinces, esp the Basque region. The Court of First Instance held in this context that "the fact that the Basque authorities were granted certain powers in matters of taxation under the Spanish Constitution does not mean that any and every tax concession they might be granted would be justified by the nature or structure of the tax system".
73. *Commission*, 30 March 2004, Gibraltar tax reform, C (2004) 929 fin, OJ 2005, L 85/1 seq. and thereupon Horacek, *Commission's negative decision on Gibraltar corporation tax reform: findings on regional and material selectivity*, Competition Policy Letter 2/2004, 97 ff.
74. Cf *Commission*, 30 March 2004, Gibraltar tax reform, C (2004) 929 fin, OJ 2005, L 85/1 seq. mn 143: "A payroll tax under which all undertakings are liable in the amount of a fixed sum per employee per year can at least under certain circumstances be considered as selective when it is applied in the absence of a general system of taxation of company profits and replaces such a system. This is the case when one takes into account the specific features of the Gibraltar economy and in particular the existence of a large offshore sector without any fiscal presence, which would escape any taxation under the payroll and property tax system. Even though such a system formally applies without discrimination to all enterprises, de facto it benefits the current 'exempt companies' that do not have any employees in Gibraltar. It constitutes a specific advantage in favour of these undertakings with no real presence in Gibraltar."
75. Cf *Commission*, 30 March 2004, Gibraltar tax reform, C (2004) 929 fin, OJ 2005, L 85/1 seq. mn 105.
76. Critical on the Gibraltar decision also *Luja* (2005), p. 566 et seq.; *Jaeger* (2005), mn. 450 et seq.
77. Application for annulment T-211/04, published in OJ C 217, 28.08.2004, p. 27.

78. Cf the argument of the Government of Gibraltar against the Commission's State aid decision emphasizing that "the Commission's regional selectivity principle cannot apply to Gibraltar. According to the applicant, the decision concerns *two tax jurisdictions which are entirely separate and mutually exclusive* so that Gibraltar's tax laws cannot be treated as derogations from tax law in the United Kingdom" (T-211/04, emphasis added - application published in OJ C 217, 28.08.2004, p. 27). Moreover, the Government of Gibraltar submitted that its "tax reform could not be considered selective because its nature, general scheme and essential features were designed to suit the special characteristics of the economy in Gibraltar and in particular its limited size, scarcity of labour, service dominated industry and operational simplicity for a small administration".
79. ECJ 6 September 2006, C-88/03, Portugal/Commission (annulment procedure) mn 56 seq.
80. ECJ 6 September 2006, C-88/03, Portugal/Commission (annulment procedure) mn 62 (emphasis added). Cf also mn 58: It is possible that an infra-State body enjoys a legal and factual status which makes it sufficiently autonomous in relation to the central government of a Member State, with the result that, by the measures it adopts, it is that body and not the central government which plays a fundamental role in the definition of the political and economic environment in which undertakings operate. In such a case it is the area in which the infra-State body responsible for the measure exercises its powers, and not the country as a whole, that constitutes the relevant context for the assessment of whether a measure adopted by such a body favours certain undertakings in comparison with others in a comparable legal and factual situation, having regard to the objective pursued by the measure or the legal system concerned.
81. ECJ 6 September 2006, C-88/03, Portugal/Commission (annulment procedure) mn 64 seq.
82. This stems already from Art 87 para 3 lit a and lit c EC. Cf also ECJ 19 September 2000, C-156/98 *Germany* v *Commission* [2000] ECR I-6857 mn 23.
83. Cf the German Gewerbesteuer (Special Business Tax) that allows the local communities to define the ultimate tax rate autonomously. This specific of the tax shall enhance a form of "good" competition between the local municipalities to explain costs of their business place in relation to the public services offered and to set an incentive for efficient public management.
84. ECJ 6 September 2006, C-88/03, Portugal/Commission (annulment procedure) mn 67 with explicit reference to the Opinion of the Advocate General, mn 54.
85. ECJ 6 September 2006, C-88/03, Portugal/Commission (annulment procedure) mn 68.
86. ECJ 6 September 2006, C-88/03, Portugal/Commission (annulment procedure) mn 68.
87. ECJ 6 September 2006, C-88/03, Portugal/Commission (annulment procedure) mn 75 seq. Cf also mn 76: "It follows that the two aspects of the fiscal policy of the regional government, namely the decision to reduce the regional tax burden by exercising its power to reduce tax rates on revenue and the fulfilment of its task of correcting inequalities deriving from insularity, are inextricably linked and depend, from the financial point of view, on budgetary transfers managed by central government."
88. In fact the ECJ-judgment of 6 September 2006, C-88/03, Portugal/Commission (annulment procedure) mn 75 referred to "Article 5(2) of Law No 13/98" for the relevant budgetary transfers. This Portuguese provision is quoted by the Court in its judgment above (mn 11) and reads: "National solidarity requires, notably, in the financial sphere, budgetary transfers provided for in this Law and which must adapt continuously to the level of development of the autonomous regions and seek above

all to create conditions for better financial coverage by own resources." The provision does therefore apparently not guarantee any full compensation payments for tax cuts.

89. For an example of such a constellation cf FN 83. On the issue of missing "normal" reference frameworks and the possible theoretical concepts in addressing this situation under Art 87 EC cf *Sutter* (2005a), p. 125 et seq.
90. For an example see the examination of Luxembourg's 1929 legislation exempting certain holding and financial companies. See on the pending procedure *Rossi* (2006), p. 513 et seq.
91. On the term "alteration" of existing aids cf *Sutter* (2005a), p. 173 et seq.
92. Cf Art 4 para 6 of the procedural Regulation of the Council 659/1999 of the 22 March 1999.
93. It reads: "The Member State concerned shall not put its proposed measures into effect until this procedure has resulted in a final decision." Cf also Art 3 of the procedural EC Regulation 659/1999.
94. ECJ, 22 March 1977, Case 78/76, *Steinike und Weinlig vs Germany* ECR 1977, 595, 609 and 11 July 1996, C-39/94, *SFEI*, ECR 1996, I-3547, 3589, mn 36; for the general requirements of direct applicability of Treaty provisions see the fundamental ECJ decision 5 February 1963, 26/62, *Van Gend en Loos,* ECR 1963, 1.
95. ECJ, 15 July 1964, Case 6/64 *Costa vs E.N.E.L,* ECR 1964, 1253, 1273 obiter dictu and 11 December 1973, Case 120/73, *Lorenz,* ECR 1973, 1471 mn 8. See in detail below.
96. ECJ, 8 November 2001, C-143/99, *Adria Wien Pipeline*, mn 23 seq: "In order to ensure the effectiveness of that prohibition, Article 88 EC places on the Commission a specific duty to monitor aid and imposes on the Member States specific obligations to facilitate the Commission's task and to prevent *faits accomplis* for that institution. As regards plans to grant or alter aid, Article 88 (3) of the Treaty requires, first, that the Commission be informed in sufficient time to enable it to submit its comments. Article 88 (3) then requires the Commission to initiate without delay the procedure provided for in Article 88 (2) of the Treaty if it considers that the plan notified is not compatible with the common market. Finally, the last sentence of Article 88 (3) of the Treaty unequivocally prohibits the Member States from putting the proposed measure into effect until that procedure has resulted in a final decision. [...] The final sentence of Article 93(3) of the Treaty is the safeguard of the review machinery established by that article which, in turn, is essential for protecting the proper functioning of the common market."
97. Certainly, there are also cases, where the underlying tax provision could be interpreted in conformity with the European State aid rules, but is interpreted otherwise by the national tax administration. Moreover, there are the cases of beneficial exercise of discretion provisions. On these forms of "administrative" tax aid see *Sutter* (2004b), p. 56 et seq. and 64 et seq. and *Sutter* (2005a), pp. 47–72.
98. According to Art 1 lit e Reg 659/99 „aid scheme shall mean any act on the basis of which, without further implementing measures being required, individual aid awards may be made to undertakings defined within the act in a general and abstract manner and any act on the basis of which aid which is not linked to a specific project may be awarded to one or several undertakings for an indefinite period of time and/or for an indefinite amount"
99. If the tax measure is to be introduced by administrative regulation it's regularly the Minister of Finance that has to start such deliberations. On a notification requirement of the adoption of new regulations that are still covered by the framework of existing statutory tax law cf *Sutter* (2005a), p. 174 et seq.
100. Emphasis added.
101. Emphasis added.

102. Commission, *Guide to procedures in State Aid Cases* mn 27 (available under: http://europa.eu.int/comm/competition/state_aid/legislation/notif_en.html).
103. Accordingly it would be imprudent to initiate notifications on a stage when the notified bill can just be dropped totally, as Commission interventions would then always require a restart of the parliamentary process. The Austrian parliamentary procedure rules install such an exclusive turn-down competence for the third lecture of a proposed bill.
104. Eg after an intense discussion of the bill in the responsible parliamentary committee.
105. On the consequences of Art 87 seq. EC on national legislation procedures cf extensively *Sutter* (2005a), p. 185 et seq.
106. Also affirming a possible surveillance competence of the prime minister: *Thienel*, mn 19. Opp *Chojnacka* (2005), p. 263 et seq. as she sees in such a competence of the publishers already a too far-reaching risk for the constitutional priciples of democratic legitimacy and of separation of power. Indeed the Austrian parliament itself could not directly challenge the Commission's decision before the ECJ.
107. On the commitment of national *administrative* bodies to direct EC law cf fundamentally ECJ, 22 June 1989, 103/88, *Fratelli Constanzo*, ECR 1989, 1839 seq., mn 31: "It would, moreover, be contradictory to rule that an individual may rely upon the provisions of a directive which fulfil the conditions defined above in proceedings before the national courts seeking an order against the administrative authorities, and yet to hold that those authorities are under no obligation to apply the provisions of the directive and refrain from applying provisions of national law which conflict with them. It follows that when the conditions under which the Court has held that individuals may rely on the provisions of a directive before the national courts are met, all organs of the administration, including decentralized authorities such as municipalities, are obliged to apply those provisions."
108. In literature it has been a contentious issue for some time if the notion of aid incorporated in Art 88 para 3 is the same as the one in Art 87 para 1 EC. Some authors believed that the notion of aid in Art 88 EC was broader requiring the Member States to notify every *potential* aid measure, while the case law of the ECJ and the Commission supposed a terminological identity (cf ECJ *Steinike and Weinlig*, ECR 1977, 610 and *Commission*, Notice on cooperation between national courts and the Commission in the State aid field, OJ C-312, 23 November 1995, 7 seq. IV.20). The procedural regulation 659/1999 has clarified this issue by defining "aid" as „any measure fulfilling all the criteria laid down in Article 92 (1) of the Treaty" (Art 1 lit a EC Reg 659/1999).
109. Cf *Sutter* (2005b), mn 34 et seq.
110. In its Notice on cooperation between national courts and the Commission in the State aid field the Commission points out that national courts "must also request assistance *from the Commission* by asking it for 'legal or economic information' by analogy with the Court's *Delimits* judgment in respect of Article 85 of the EC Treaty" (OJ C-312, 23 November 1995, p. 7 seq., mn 95, emphasis added).
111. ECJ 17 September 1980, Case 730/79, Philip Morris, ECR 1980, 2691 seq. mn 24.
112. National claims for damages of competitors can therefore always be based on negligence of the administration and need not be founded on negligence of the legislator. In Austria this opens up a possible tort claim under the Amtshaftungsgesetz (*Sutter* (2005a), p. 364 et seq.). If the national administrative bodies do not refuse unlawful aid grants the question arises if competitors can trigger a recovery claim once they detect the grant. Cf thereupon below.
113. The background of the *Adria Wien Pipeline* Case lay in a newly adopted energy tax package of Austria that introduced a new energy taxation, but granted industrial undertakings a rebate if they surpassed a certain limit in their energy tax burden. This

Energy Tax Rebate Act excluded the service sector completely. See in detail on the background of the case *Sutter* (2001), p. 248 et seq.

114. Verfassungsgerichtshof 13 December 2000, B 2251/97-45.

115. In the Case C-136/00, *Danner* the Commission has taken a similar standpoint in its observations : «Le fait de conclure qu'un traitement qui diffère selon les cas constituerait une aide d'Ètat illicite ne serait pas non plus nécessairement à l'avantage du contribuable concerné. Cette différence de traitment pourrait être éliminée de deux facons: ou bien en faisant bénéficier de la déductibilité l'ensemble des cotisations et prestations d'assurance retraite, ou bien en supprimant entièrement le droit à déduction. Cette dernière solution placerait M. Danner dans une situation moins favorable. Quant à la première solution, il n'est nullement certain que M. Danner profiterait de cette modification, car l'Ètat finlandais devrait décider quelles règles de déductibilté seraient applicables à l'ensemble des cotisations de retraite» (mn 51). Cf also AG *Geelhoed* summarizing the Commission's position in 18 September. 2003, C-308/01 Gil Insurance mn 55 as follows: "According to the Commission there are two types of aid: The classic type of aid granting a specific benefit or a specific fiscal derogation. The classic remedy provided for in terms of eliminating the exceptional benefit is for the Member State concerned to recover the amount of aid granted, together with interest, from the person concerned. An alternative, though not available for budgetary reasons, is to generalise the aid; the second type of aid is where an exceptional fiscal burden is imposed on a part of a sector. In that case the aid is eliminated by eliminating the exceptional fiscal burden. In that connection the course of action decided upon could be to pay back to the undertaking concerned the specific charge paid in order in that way to restore competition with undertakings which were not subject to it. That is the solution proposed by the applicants. However, an alternative remedy would be to generalise the specific charge and thus recover the aid from all concerned." Similary Opinion of AG *Geelhoed* 4 March 2004, C-174/02 SWNB and C-175/02 FJ Pape, mn 72 where he rapports that the Commission has even highlighted the advantage of the "inverse solution" for evading protection of good faith problems.

116. *Jaeger* (2003), 646; *Arnold* (2002), S 52; *Potacs* (2002), 87

117. *Sutter* (2002), 217 mn 11; *Sutter* (2003), p. 176; *Sutter* (2005a), p. 241 et seq.; *Sutter* (2005b) mn 76; consenting *Chojnacka*, (2003), p. 52 et seq. Also critical *Ardolino* (2002), p. 73 seq.

118. Cf already *Sutter* (2003), p. 176.

119. ECJ, 8 November 2001, C-143/99, *Adria Wien Pipeline*, mn 29. See also ECJ, C-354/90 *FNCE* mn 14.

120. *Sutter* (2003), p. 177. Alike AG *Jacobs*, Opinion, 29 November 2005, C-368/04, *Transalpine Ölleitung* mn 77.

121. This was even the consequence out of the extension of the Energy Tax Rebate Act by the Austrian Constitutional Court, because the court just set aside the contended restriction of the tax rebate to productive undertakings, but did not set aside the restriction of the rebate system to huge energy consumers defined by a 0.35% threshold of net production costs. Thereby the aid scheme still remained selective, extended to a further, but still limited, class of beneficiaries. This led to a second State aid procedure of the Commission against Austria: cf OJ C 164/2 of 15 July 2003 and the incompatibility decision of 9 March 2004, C 33/2003.

122. Cf also AG *Jacobs*, Opinion, 29 November 2005, C-368/04, *Transalpine Ölleitung* mn 74. Alike ECJ 15 June 2006, C-393/04, *Air Liquide Industries Belgium SA*, mn 45 seq.

123. The ECJ however denied this possibility in C-368/04, *Transalpine Pipeline* on ECJ 5 October 2006. Thereupon see below.

124. See below Sect. 6.3. last paragraph.

125. See thereupon below.
126. On the AG's Opinion cf *Sutter* (2006a), p. 321.
127. ECJ 5 October 2006, C-368/04, *Transalpine Pipeline* = EuZW 2006, 725 seq. (with case note Sutter) = EStAL 2007, 105 seq. with case note *Retter* and *Bielesz*. In the parallel case C-393/04, *Air Liquide Industries Belgium SA* the ECJ already uttered its scepticism concerning the extension solution on 15 June 2006: "Finally, it should be pointed out that an extension of the circle of potential recipients to other undertakings would not make it possible to eliminate the effects of aid granted in breach of Article 88(3) EC but would rather, on the contrary, lead to an increase in the effects of that aid". For a special case pattern the ECJ however does not rule the extension out (ECJ 15 June 2006, C-393/04, *Air Liquide Industries Belgium SA,* mn 45 continuing in mn 46, emphasis added) : « It would be otherwise *if the tax and the envisaged exemption were an integral part of an aid measure*. For a tax to be regarded as forming an integral part of an aid measure, it must be hypothecated to the aid measure under the relevant national rules, in the sense that the revenue from the tax is necessarily allocated for the financing of the aid and has a direct impact on the amount thereof and, consequently, on the assessment of the compatibility of that aid with the common market (see *Streekgewest*, paragraph 26, and Joined Cases C-266/04 to C-270/04, C-276/04 and C-321/04 to C-325/04 *Casino France and Others* [2005] ECR I-9481, paragraph 40). However, a tax cannot be hypothecated to an exemption from payment of that same tax for a category of businesses. Application of a tax exemption and its extent do not depend on the tax revenue (see *Streekgewest*, paragraph 28, and *Casino France and Others*, paragraph 41)".
128. Cf the Roman saying: "De minimis non curat praetor."
129. For certain sensitive areas of harsh intra-community competition the de-minimis rules do not apply.
130. ECJ 3 March 2005, C-172/03, *Heiser*, mn 34.
131. Cf also the informal, not strictly mandatory tone of the preliminary remarks of the Reg 69/2001 in mn 7: "The Commission has a duty to ensure that State aid rules are respected and in particular that aid granted under the *de minimis* rules adheres to the conditions thereof. In accordance with the cooperation principle laid down in Article 10 of the Treaty, Member States should facilitate the achievement of this task by establishing the necessary machinery in order to ensure that the total amount of aid, granted to the same beneficiary under the *de minimis* rule, does not exceed the ceiling of EUR 100 000 over a period of three years. To that end, *it is appropriate* that Member States, when granting a *de minimis* aid, should inform the enterprise concerned of the *de minimis* character of the aid, receive full information about other *de minimis* aid received during the last three years and carefully check that the *de minimis* ceiling will not be exceeded by the new *de minimis* aid. Alternatively respect of the ceiling may also be ensured by means of a central register" (emphasis added).
132. Emphasis added.
133. *Repplinger-Hach* (2003), § 5 mn 10 et seq.; *Rüffler* (2004), 169 FN 143; *Sutter* (2005a), p. 141 seq.; *Sutter* (2005d) p. 577 mn 5.
134. VwGH 29.6.2005, 2005/14/0024 with explicit reference to my doctoral thesis. Cf also my Case note in AnwBl (Journal of the Austrian Bar Association) 12/2005. The issue would however be worth an explicit clarification by an amendment of the regulation 69/2001 or by a subsequent ECJ ruling.
135. OJ 28 December 2006, L 379/5 seq.; *Berghofer* (2007), p. 11 et seq.
136. Before the three year period was determined by reference to calendar years.
137. Art 2 para 2 of the Draft Reg reads in whole: "The total de minimis aid granted to any one undertaking shall not exceed EUR 150000 gross over any period of three fiscal years. This ceiling shall apply irrespective of the form of the aid or the objective pursued and regardless of whether the aid granted by the Member State is

financed entirely or partly by resources of Community origin. The period shall be determined by reference to the fiscal years used in the Member State concerned. *When an overall aid amount exceeds this ceiling, that aid cannot benefit from this Regulation, even for a fraction not exceeding that ceiling, either at the time it is granted or in respect of a later period.*"

138. ECJ, 11 July 1996, C-39/94, SFEI, ECR 1996, I-3547 seq. mn 70.
139. ECJ, 11 July 1996, C-39/94, SFEI, ECR 1996, I-3547 seq. mn 71 (= 4th ruling).
140. ECJ, 8 November 2001, C-143/99, *Adria Wien Pipeline*, mn 27 ; cf also ECJ 21 November 1991, Case C-354/90, *Fédération Nationale du Commerce Extérieur des Produits Alimentaires and Syndicat National des Négociants et Transformateurs de Saumon*, ECR 1991 I-5505, mn 12 .
141. Certainly it cannot be ruled out that this is just due to missing preliminary answers of corresponding content.
142. Cf also ECJ, 11 July 1996, C-39/94, *SFEI*, ECR 1996, I-3547 seq. mn 67 seq: "The role of a national court seised of an application based on the last sentence of Article 88(3) goes beyond that of a judge ruling on an application for interim relief. The national court is under a duty to provide protection in the final judgment it gives in such a case against the consequences of unlawful implementation of aid. [...] A finding that aid has been granted in breach of the last sentence of Article 93(3) must in principle lead to its repayment in accordance with the procedural rules of domestic law. Any other interpretation would encourage the Member States to disregard the prohibition laid down in Article 88(3). Thus, if national courts could only order suspension of any new payment, aid already granted would subsist until the Commission's final decision finding the aid incompatible with the common market and ordering its repayment. Having regard to the importance for the proper functioning of the common market of compliance with the procedure for prior review of planned State aid, national courts *must in principle allow an application for repayment of aid paid in breach of Article 88(3) of the Treaty*" (emphasis added).
143. *Frank* (2000), p. 574 et seq. and *Eilmansberger* (1997), p. 91 FN 303
144. AG *Jacobs*, Opinion, 29 November 2005, C-368/04, Transalpine Ölleitung mn 91seq. In this sense already before: *Sutter* (2005a), p. 274 et seq. and 281 et seq.
145. See below, last paragraph of Sect. 6.3.
146. Under special conditions the Commission can however already adopt a provisional recovery injunction before its examination process is concluded. Cf Art 11 Reg 659/99.
147. Cf in detail *Sutter* (2005b), mn 92 to 112 with further references.
148. The preliminary questions of this request (with reference to a discussion of mine in the Journal of the Austrian Bar Association) read as follows: "1. Does the prohibition on putting measures into effect under Article 88 (3) EC preclude the application of a national legal provision which excludes businesses whose activity is not shown to consist primarily in the manufacture of goods from energy tax rebates and which must therefore be classified as aid within the meaning of Article 87 EC, but which was not notified to the Commission prior to the national entry into force of the rules, even where the Commission has found the measure to be compatible with the common market under Article 87 (3) EC for a period in the past and the application for reimbursement relates to taxes payable for that period? 2. If so, in such a case does the prohibition on putting measures into effect require a rebate even in cases where the applications were made by service businesses after the adoption of the Commission's decision for assessment periods prior to that date?"
149. On this peculiar consequence out of the standstill clause of Art 88 para 3 sentence 3 EC see above.
150. AG *Jacobs*, 29 November 2005, Opinion mn 49 seq. Cf also ECJ, 11 July 1996, C-39/94, SFEI, ECR 1996, I-3547 seq. mn 67: "The national court is under a duty to provide protection in the final judgment it gives in such a case against the

consequences of unlawful implementation of aid. Its decision cannot be challenged by the Commission. The latter's final decision does not have the effect of regularizing ex post facto the measures unlawfully implementing aid."

151. Cf Art 4 Austrian Federal Fiscal Code (Bundesabgabenordnung). In Detail on the uncertainties of an attribution of State aid grants to a precise date *Sutter* (2005a), p. 300 et seq.
152. AG *Jacobs*, Opinion, 29 November 2005, C-368/04, Transalpine Ölleitung mn 46 seq. Critical on this part of the opinion *Sutter* (2006a), 321.
153. A retroactive approval does however not mean a complete healing of the notification omission. First one could consider that the interest advantages for the *premature* grant should remain reclaimable in any event. Second, aid already recaptured on the national level upon request of disadvantaged competitors need not be re-granted automatically after a retroactive approval.
154. Cf however the harsh attitude of the ECJ on identical re-grants of illegal aid in cases of a conflinging State aid authorization by the Council under Art 88 para 2 subpara 3 EC. Cf thereupon Sutter (2005b), mn 141 et seq.
155. *Sutter* (2006b), p. 730 mn 11.
156. It is a pity that the issue was not discussed in a larger composition of the Court, as it just sat as a Chamber of five judges in this case which would have justified in my view a Grand Chamber.
157. The ECJ has declared in various rulings that the Commission enjoys a wide discretion in its approval practice under the discretionary exemptions of Art 87 para 3 EC.
158. Cf *Lopez-Mata* (2001), p. 577 seq: "The creativity of national governments ... in some cases resembles the creativity of individual tax planners. Even though they pursue different objectives, both try to find the loopholes in the system and attempt to avoid anti-subsidies rules or taxes, respectively".
159. Prof *Gassner* has once held polemically in a presentation on European State Aid Law that Member States would have to react to the Commission's stiffening State Aid Practice by simply sending all drafted tax acts without any comment to Brussels to avoid later recaptures. In practice this would however not only paralyse the Commission, but also the Member States as they would have to laboriously explain every tax amendment separately in the course of this notification process in detail.
160. For the question *which* alterations of existing aid schemes have to be notified as new aid measures see Sutter (2005a) 173 et seq.
161. See in detail above.
162. Cf *Vajda* (2001), p. 90: "The Court (and the Commission) are in effect seeking to employ aid recipients as policemen to ensure compliance by Member States of their obligations under Article 88 (3). While the approach of the Court is understandable in the light of the well-known problem of disregard by Member States of the pre-notification obligation in Article 88 (3), one is entitled to question whether the policy objective of seeking recovery of aid in order (as far as possible) to restore the *status quo ante* leaves too little scope for recognition of any potential legitimate expectation of the recipient of the aid. The irony of this policy approach is that if anyone is to blame for a failure to notify, it is the Member State but the Member State does will in effect escape without any sanctions. The only obligation on the Member State is that it will have to recover the aid granted together with interest thereon. In financial terms that is hardly a sanction. In commercial terms it may well not be a sanction either. In many cases the Member State may have achieved the commercial objective of the aid (for example the start-up of a new industry or the staving off of bankruptcy of a failing firm) and the repayment of the aid from the recipient will not in reality restore the *status quo ante*".
163. Cf also AG *Jacobs*, Opinion, 29 November 2005, C-368/04, Transalpine Ölleitung mn 80.

164. In the past, they could also result from an acceptance of the disputed Austrian extension model that set aside the selective limitations of unlawful aid schemes instead of the aid scheme as such via Art 88 para 3 last sentence EC. On the objections against this model see above Sect. 6.3.
165. Both the permissibility of the Austrian extension model and of a national request for retroactive Commission remission are actually discussed before the ECJ. See above Sect. 6.3.
166. This is also a requirement in the light of equal treatment of the Member States. On the criteria of an application of Art 87 para 1 EC on the exercise of national tax law by local tax administrations see *Sutter* (2005a), p. 63 et seq.
167. Cf respectively Annex I, Table E of the Commission's First State Aid Report of 1981 and the European State Aid Scoreboard of autumn 2006.

References

Aldestam, M. (2005) *Article 87 (1) EC applied to taxes - An analysis of the selectivity criterion*, Uppsala: Iustus Förlag.

Ardolino, D. (2002) The Adria-Wien case: how the EC legislation on State aid can prove useless and, in some cases, even harmful, *Rivista di diritto tributario internazionale*, 73 et seq.

Arnold, W.-D. (2002) Die Regelung der Energieabgabenvergütung gilt für alle Unternehmer, *Steuer und Wirtschaftskartei*, S 52 et seq.

Bacon, K. (1997) State Aids and General Measures, *Yearbook of European Law*, 269 et seq.

Baudenbacher, C. (1997) *A brief guide to European State Aid Law*, The Hague: Kluwer Law International.

Berghofer, M. (2007) The New De Minimis Regulation: Enlarging the Sword of Damocles?, *EStAL 1/2007*, 11 et seq.

Chojnacka, Z. (2003) Das Verbot der Durchführung von formell rechtswidrigen Beihilfenmaßnahmen und seine tatsächliche Effektivität, in Eisenberger, I./Golden, I./ Lachmayer, K./Marx, G./Tomasovsky, D. (eds.) *Norm und Normvorstellung*, Wien: Springer, 31 et seq.

Chojnacka, Z. (2005) *Notifikationsverfahren für technische Vorschriften und Normen,* Vienna: Verlag Österreich, 263 et seq.

Eilmansberger, Th. (1997) *Rechtsfolgen und subjektives Recht im Gemeinschaftsrecht*, Baden-Baden: Nomos.

Frank, St. L. (2000) *Gemeinschaftsrecht und staatliche Verwaltung*, Vienna: Verlag Österreich.

Hubbard, R. G. (2002) *Tax Policy and International Competitiveness*, Speech on the International Tax Policy Forum in Washington DC, 9 December 2002 (available under http:\\www.whitehouse.gov/cea and http://www0.gsb.columbia.edu/faculty/ghubbard/ other.html).

Jaeger, Th. (2003) Durchführungsverbot und rückwirkende Beihilfengenehmigung, *Zeitschrift für Verwaltung*, 646 et seq.

Jaeger Th. (2005) *Steuern und parafiskalische Abgaben im EG–Beihilferecht*, Graz: NWV - Neuer Wiss. Verlag.

Kepenne, J. P. (1999) *Guide des aides d'Etat en droit communautaire*, Bruxelles: Bruylant.

Kofler, G. (2004) European Taxation Under an 'Open Sky': LoB Clauses in Tax Treaties Between the U.S. and EU Member States, *Tax Notes International*, 45 et seq.

Lopez-Mata, R. (2001) Income Taxation, International Competitiveness and the World Trade Organization Rules on Subsidies: Lessons to the U.S. and to the World from the FSC Dispute, *The Tax Lawyer*, 577 et seq.

Luja, R. (2004) Tax Treaties and State Aid: Some Thoughts, *European Taxation*, 235 et seq.

Luja, R. (2005) State Aid Reform 2005/09: Regional Fiscal Autonomy and Effective Recovery, *European Taxation*, 566 et seq.

McIntyre, M. (1980) A Solution to The Problem of Defining a Tax Expenditure, *University of California, Davis, Vol 14/1980*, 83-89.
Panayi, Ch. (2004) Limitation on Benefits and State Aid, *European Taxation*, 83 et seq.
Pinto, C. (1999) EC-State Aid Rules and Tax Incentives: A U-turn in Commission Policy, *European Taxation*, 295 et seq.
Potacs, M. (2002) Case note, *Österreichische Zeitschrift für Wirtschaftsrecht*, 82 et seq.
Repplinger-Hach, R. (2003) De minimis-Beihilfen, in Heidenhain (editor) *Handbuch des Europäischen Beihilfenrechts*, München: C. H. Beck, Chapter 5.
Ross, M. (2000) State aid and national courts: definitions and other problems – a case of premature emancipation?, *Common Market Law Review*, 401 et seq.
Rossi, P. (2005) The Italian tax premium in favour of newly listed companies and the notion of selectivity relative to direct business taxation, *Competition Policy Newsletter 3/2005*, 109 et seq.
Rossi, P. (2006) Luxembourg's Holding Regime Under EC Review, *Tax Notes International*, 513 et seq.
Rüffler, F. (2004) Rechtsfolgen gesetzwidriger Beihilfengewährung, in WiR - Studiengesellschaft für Wirtschaft und Recht (editor) *Beihilfenrecht*, Vienna: Linde Verlag, 141 et seq.
Strüber, M. (2005) *Steuerliche Beihilfen. Eine kritische Analyse der Anwendung des Beihilfeverbots im Bereich der direkten Steuern*, Frankfurt: Peter Lang Verlag.
Surrey, St. (1983) Tax Incentives as a Device for Implementing Government Policy: A Comparison with Direct Government Expenditures, *Harvard Law Review 1970 (vol 4/1983)*, 705 – 738.
Sutter, F. Ph. (2001) The Adria Wien Pipeline Case and the State Aid Provisions of the EC Treaty in Tax Matters, *European Taxation*, 239 et seq.
Sutter, F. Ph. (2002) Case note on the Adria Wien Judgement, *EuZW*, 217 mn 11.
Sutter, F. Ph. (2003) National Report Austria, in Schön (editor) *Tax Competition in Europe*, Amsterdam: IBFD, 153 et seq.
Sutter, F. Ph. (2004a) Die DBA-Freistellungsmethode als unzulässige Beihilfe iSd Art 87 EG?, *SWI*, 4 et seq.
Sutter, F. Ph. (2004b) Beihilfen im materiellen Steuerrecht – Steuergesetze und Verwaltungshandeln der Steuerbehörden im Spannungsfeld zum EG-Beihilfenverbot, in WiR - Studiengesellschaft für Wirtschaft und Recht (editor) *Beihilfenrecht*, Vienna: Lindeverlag, 37 et seq.
Sutter, F. Ph. (2005a) *Das EG-Beihilfenverbot und sein Durchführungsverbot in Steuersachen*, Vienna: Linde Verlag.
Sutter, F. Ph. (2005b) Art 88 EG, in Mayer, H. (editor) *Kommentar zu EU und EG-Vertrag* (Austrian Commentary on European Law), Vienna: Manz Verlag.
Sutter, F. Ph. (2005c) Die abkommensrechtliche Verteilung der Besteuerungsrechte zwischen Ansässigkeits- und Quellenstaat aus beihilfenrechtlicher Sicht, in Gassner, W. and Lang M. and Schuch, J. and Staringer, C. (editors) *Die abkommensrechtliche Verteilung der Besteuerungsrechte zwischen Ansässigkeits- und Quellenstaat*, Vienna: Linde verlag, 83 et seq.
Sutter, F. Ph. (2005d) Case note, *Anwaltsblatt*, p. 574 et seq.
Sutter, F. Ph. (2006a) Guest Editorial, *EuZW*, p. 321.
Sutter, F. Ph. (2006b) Case note, *EuZW*, p. 725 et seq.
Thienel, R. (1999) Art 48 and 49 B-VG, in Korinek, K. and Holoubek, M. (editors) *Österreichisches Bundesverfassungsrecht - Textsammlung und Kommentar* (Commentary on the Austrian Constitutional Act), Vienna: Springer.
Vajda, Ch. (2001) Unlawful State Aid: What is it and what are its legal consequences?, *EC Tax Journal*, 77 et seq.
Wishlade, F. (1997) *When are Tax Advantages State Aids and when are they General Measures*?, European Policy Research Paper Nr 20 (http://www.eprc.strath.ac.uk/eprc/publications_eprp.cfm).

Chapter 7
The European Court of Justice and Direct Taxation: A Recent Change of Direction?

Mattias Dahlberg

7.1 Introduction

The importance of the fundamental freedoms of the EC Treaty for shaping the national tax system of the Member States cannot be enough emphasised. This is contrasted by the problems of the Council to reach the required unanimity to adopt common legislation in the field of direct taxation.[1]

The general objective of this chapter is to examine whether, and if so to what extent, there have been major developments of the case law of the European Court of Justice, here also referred to as the Court. Because this field of law is based on case law, it is necessary to be relatively thorough when analysing the cases, especially recent cases.[2]

This chapter will examine some topical issues in the case law of the European Court of Justice in the field of direct taxation. Three main issues will be discussed. First, the Court's (possible) turn from a discrimination analysis to a restriction analysis. A highly related issue is the meaning of "objectively comparable situations", which is the second issue covered.[3] Traditionally, the identification of objectively comparable situations has been the stepping stone for the discrimination analysis. Whether this still holds true will be subject to analysis. Third I will discuss grounds of justification in the general interest.

In relation to these three issues, three hypotheses will be tested.[4] The first hypothesis is that regarding companies, the European Court of Justice has departed from a discrimination analysis to a restriction analysis. The second hypothesis is that regarding individuals the Court still upholds a discrimination analysis, whereby maintaining the requirement of identifying objectively comparable situations, even if anomalies exist in its case law. The third hypothesis is that the Court has become more amenable with regard to grounds of justification in the general interest.

In the final part of the chapter I attempt to make two alternative tax-policy explanations for the direction of the Court's case law identified. The first one is the cul-de-sac explanation, which means that negative integration through the case law of the Court has come to a point where it cannot go any further. Thus, the Court will continue to apply its previous case law, but it will not go beyond this point. The second explanation is the U-turn explanation. According to this explanation the Court is now reversing its previous "integrationist" case law, permitting Member States a wider margin of sovereignty in the field of direct taxation.[5]

The chapter has the following outline. Section 7.2 gives a general background to the issues discussed. Fundamental freedoms and the meaning of discrimination are introduced. From a general perspective, the function of the European Court of Justice is also discussed. Section 7.3 deals with the meaning of "objectively comparable situations". In a discrimination analysis it has been a precondition that the situations compared are "objectively" comparable. The meaning and development of this concept is discussed. Section 7.4 covers grounds of justification in the general interest. There are only a few grounds in the area of direct taxation that in principle have been accepted by the Court. Recent developments are considered, including the case C-446/03 *Marks & Spencer*. In the case C-374/04 *Test Claimants in Class IV of the ACT Group Litigation* the Advocate General (AG) Geelhoed in his opinion made an attempt outline a framework to the Court's case law in the field of direct taxation. This structural attempt is subject to critical analysis in Sect. 7.5. A few cases that the European Court of Justice will decide in the future are discussed in Sect. 7.6. Concluding remarks are given in Sect. 7.7.

7.2 Background

It is clear that the fundamental freedoms of the EC Treaty prohibit restrictions, even if Article 39 on the free movement of workers refers to discrimination.[6] "Discrimination" means the application of different rules to comparable situations or the application of the same rule to different situations. One relevant distinguishing criterion in the field of taxation is nationality.[7] This form of discrimination is usually labelled direct or overt discrimination. Another form of discrimination is indirect or covert discrimination. This can be defined as the application of other criteria of differentiation that in fact lead to the same result, which also is relevant in tax-law cases.[8]

The first phase of case law from the European Court of Justice predominantly dealt with cases on discrimination. Moreover, the early cases dealt with infringement of fundamental freedoms that took place in the host state; the state where for example an establishment had been made. The second phase of case law in the field of direct taxation was instead focused on infringements taking place in the home state, the state where for example the investor was a resident. It seems as if the Court has stepped away from its previous discrimination analysis. Rather, the Court identifies whether the national measure at issue constitutes a "barrier" or likewise. This more vague language has been subject to criticism.[9]

A hallmark of discrimination is, as previously noted, that two situations are compared and one situation is treated worse than the other. In my view, it is possible to identify such comparable situations in a large number of cases were the Court has chosen to apply a restriction analysis.[10]

It has been debated whether or not the European Court of Justice takes political considerations when deciding its case law. For example, it has been suggested that the Court "deliberately" decides its cases with the aim of providing a higher degree of integration within the European Union. Recently the opposite view has been advanced. When analysing the cases from the Court in the field of direct taxation I have found little evidence of such an "agenda".[11] Of course, the fundamental freedoms which the Court interprets in this case law, have the purpose of creating an internal market. The former Finnish judge of the Court Leif Sevón explains: "Before arriving at the Court I had observed from writings that the Court has an agenda for the promotion of integration within the EC. Like the crusaders set out in the search for the Holy Grail I set out in search for that agenda. After three and a half year of search I have come to the conclusion that prospects for the crusaders were more favourable than mine even if the crusader's efforts never brought any result. If there is an agenda it is so secret that no one knows of it."[12] Of course the fundamental freedoms of the EC Treaty have been agreed upon by the Member States with political objectives, but that is not any different from national rules on taxation or any other rule of law.

What is special with the area of direct taxation in relation to the European Union is that there have so far been few acts of law decided upon by the Member States. There are a few directives, but they affect only fragments of the tax law of the Member States, albeit important fragments. Such "positive integration" has proved difficult for the Member States to agree upon. In stark contrast, there are well over one hundred cases decided by or pending at the Court where measures of direct taxation are questioned in relation to the fundamental freedoms of the EC Treaty. In the large majority of the decided cases the outcome has been that national tax laws have been found to be in breach of fundamental freedoms. This has been labelled "negative integration". Such integration is problematic. The complex solutions needed for the facilitation of cross-border movement also in the area of direct taxation requires general Community measures like directives. The Court can only respond to the isolated questions put before it. General tax policy issues neither could nor should be the task of the Court to model.[13]

7.3 Objectively Comparable Situations

The Schumacker Doctrine

As previously mentioned, to expressively identify comparable situations is a fundamental component of the discrimination analysis. A common distinguishing criterion in tax law is between residents and non-residents. As regards individuals, nationality is not necessarily, albeit frequently, identical with residence for tax purposes.

In the case C-279/93 *Schumacker* the Court made the following principal consideration. As a starting point, the income received by a non-resident person in a Member State is in most cases only part of his total income. Instead, the major part of the income is concentrated to his state of residence.[14] The Court declared: "Moreover, a non-resident's personal ability to pay tax, determined by reference to his aggregate income and his personal and family circumstances, is more easy to assess at the place where his personal and financial interests are centred. In general, that is the place where he has his usual abode." Interestingly, the Court finds support for this view in what it refers to as "international tax law". The Court explains: "Accordingly, international tax law, and in particular the Model Double Taxation Treaty of the Organization for Economic Cooperation and Development (OECD), recognises that in principle the overall taxation of taxpayers, taking account of their personal and family circumstances, is a matter for the State of residence."[15]

Recent Developments Regarding Individuals

In several recent cases there have been developments on the meaning of objectively comparable situations. Here I will discuss three such cases. An important recent case from this aspect is C-234/01 *Gerritse*. Mr Gerritse was a Dutch national who was resident for tax purposes in the Netherlands. He was a professional drummer and jazz musician, and in 1996 he made a performance at a radio station in Berlin. He earned about 6,000 DEM for that performance. His business expenses for that engagement were about 970 DEM. In Germany his income was taxed at a flat rate of 25 percent on the gross amount of his earnings. The tax was withheld at source. The Court considered whether this legislation was in breach of the freedom to provide services according to Article 49 of the EC Treaty. In its decision, the Court divided the issue into three parts. It did separate assessments of the meaning on objectively comparable situations in relation to each part, which will be discussed subsequently.

a) *The deductibility of business expenses.* Mr Gerritse argued that there were serious consequences for non-resident artists on tour in Germany whose business expenses were generally very high. In this context the Court made the following vital statement: "... the business expenses in question are directly linked to the activity that generated the taxable income in Germany, so that residents and non-residents are placed in a comparable situation in that respect".[16] It should be noted that the Court found this difference in treatment to constitute an indirect discrimination.

b) *The tax free allowance and c) the flat tax rate of 25 percent.* Regarding the tax-free allowance the Court found that such benefits should be granted by the state in which the person receives the greater part of his income. Therefore, Mr Gerritse was not granted that right in Germany, which he instead was granted in the Netherlands.

To conclude, I find it somewhat strange why the Court did not uphold the distinction between residents and non-residents and their family circumstances when it comes to the deductibility of business expenses, but upholds it when it comes to the tax free allowance. The only reason that I find possible is that the national law at issue had as its motive to take personal and family circumstances into account. That seems to be the case with the German tax free allowance. In the following we will see how the Court decided on this matter in the originally Swedish case C-169/03 *Wallentin*.

The Wallentin case concerned Swedish taxation of employment income earned by non-residents. Mr Wallentin was a German national who was resident in Germany where he was studying. He received money from his parents (monthly 650 DEM) and a grant from the German state (monthly 350 DEM). Because of their nature, those payments were not taxable in Germany. He worked for a month in 1996 with the Church of Sweden where he earned about 8,700 SEK (about 1,000 euro). The Swedish income of Mr Wallentin was subject to the Swedish SINK[17] taxation. Taxation according to this law meant a flat tax rate of 25 percent on the gross amount. No cost deductions were allowed, and the basic allowance granted according to the regular Swedish Income Tax Act[18] was not granted either. The basic allowance, should Mr Wallentin's income have been covered by the Swedish Income Tax Act, would have amounted to 8,600 SEK.

The basic allowance denied was, according to Mr Wallentin, a breach of the free movement of workers according to Article 39 of the EC Treaty. In its answer on the interpretation of that fundamental freedom, the Court referred to its general findings on comparable situations in the Schumacker case. The starting point, according to the Court, is that the situations of residents and non-residents are not comparable. That is, however, different where a non-resident receives no significant income in the state of residence and he receives the major part of his taxable income from an activity in the state of employment. In such a situation the result is that the state of residence "... is not in a position to grant him the benefits resulting from the taking into account of his personal and family circumstances". The Court emphasised that the present situation was "exactly" the same as in the Schumacker case. In the Court's view the basic allowance according to the Swedish Income Tax Act had the same objective as the one contained in German law (*Grundfreibetrag*).[19]

In conclusion the Court found that Mr Wallentin's situation was comparable to the one of a resident in Sweden who was covered by the benefit of the tax-free allowance. In Germany, he did not earn enough income to be covered by the German basic allowance. His family and personal circumstances could not be considered in Germany. Therefore he was to be covered by the Swedish allowance. However, in my view, the Wallentin case is based on a wrong assumption – at least currently – on the objectives behind the Swedish tax-free allowance. Subsequently, I will return to that issue. From 1 January 2005 the Swedish *SINK*-legislation was amended in this respect. A non-resident taxpayer subject to *SINK*-taxation may opt to be covered by the general Income Tax Act instead. If he chooses that option he will be granted a basic allowance, but will be subject to a progressive tax rate spanning between (about) 32 percent and a maximum 57 percent.

The recently decided case C-376/03 *D* has predominantly been discussed in relation to the question if EC law requires a most-favoured-nation treatment in tax treaty law. The way in which the Court in that case considered what constitutes "objectively comparable situations" is also interesting, and that issue will be dealt with here.

Mr D was a German national and he was also resident for tax purposes in that Member State. Ten percent of his wealth consisted of real property located in the Netherlands. The remaining part of his wealth was held in Germany. In the Netherlands, he was as non-resident subject to wealth taxation. Even if he was non-resident in the Netherlands he wanted to be covered by Article 14 (2) of the *Wet B*, the Dutch tax code. That provision granted resident taxpayers the right of an allowance from their net worldwide assets when calculating the taxable wealth. Non-resident taxpayers were not granted this allowance. Still, Mr D claimed that according to Community law and the free movement of capital he was entitled to this allowance.[20]

The situations of residents and non-residents have been considered by the Court to be comparable under certain circumstances according to the Court's case law. That is the case where the non-resident receives no significant income in the Member State of residence and obtains the major part of his taxable income from an activity performed in the state of employment. Consequently, the state of residence cannot grant him the benefits from considering personal and family circumstances.

According to the Court's previous case law, the prerequisite for granting non-residents such benefits are that they earn at least 90 percent of their income in that state. This case law concerns income taxation. To be able to rely on it the Court decided that income taxation is similar to wealth tax in several aspects:

- both are direct taxes,
- wealth tax is often regarded as a complement to income taxation, and
- a person liable to wealth tax as a rule holds the greater part of his assets in the state where he is resident.[21]

Next, the Court examined the specific circumstances of the case to decide whether the situations of residents and non-residents were comparable. It was noted that residents in the Netherlands were liable ("subject") to taxation on their world-wide wealth, whereas non-residents were liable to tax only on their wealth held in the Netherlands.[22] However, in Germany there was no wealth tax because it had been abolished altogether. Germany was Mr D's state of residence, but his personal and family circumstances could accordingly not be taken into account in that state. In view of Mr D, he was therefore discriminated against in the Netherlands because he was not entitled to the basic allowance regarding wealth taxation.

The Court did not accept this reasoning. The fact that Germany had abolished its wealth tax had no bearing on the factual situation. The Member State in which Mr D held only a proportion of his wealth was not required to grant him the benefits which it granted Dutch residents.[23] The present case was in this respect different from the Wallentin case, according to the Court. The reason was that "… sums as the subsistence allowance paid to Mr Wallentin by his parents and the grant which he received from the German State did not of their nature constitute taxable income under German tax legislation. Accordingly, the sums received by Mr Wallentin in Germany and the wealth held by Mr D in that Member State cannot be regarded as comparable for the purpose of determining whether, with regard to taxation of the wealth possessed by him in the Netherlands, Mr D must be eligible for the allowance provided for by Netherlands legislation."[24]

I disagree with this outcome. In my view, the general situations of Mr Wallentin and Mr D are comparable in all important aspects. The income of Mr Wallentin and the wealth of Mr D, in Sweden and the Netherlands respectively, is taxable in the source state, and not taxable in the state of residence. The taxation of non-residents in the source state is more burdensome than the corresponding taxation of residents. There is in neither case any possibility, according to national law, for the state of residence to take personal and family circumstances into account. In the case of Mr Wallentin the reason is that the relevant German income is not taxable, and in the case of Mr D the relevant tax in Germany has been abolished.

In my view, the reason why personal and family circumstances cannot be taken into account in the state of residence should be of no relevance. The fact that they cannot, should be sufficient for the state of residence to grant the non-resident Mr Wallentin and Mr D equal treatment with residents.[25]

Companies and "Objectively Comparable Situations"

The meaning of "objectively comparable situations" in relation to companies has not been extensively analysed by the Court in its case law on direct taxation. I will discuss this issue in relation to two cases: C-311/97 *Royal Bank of Scotland* and C-253/03 *CLT-UFA SA*.

Case C-311/97 *Royal Bank of Scotland* dealt with Greek tax law on the taxation of banks. The Royal Bank of Scotland, resident in the United Kingdom, had a branch in Piraeus, Greece. The profits of the UK branch were subject to a higher tax rate than the profits of a bank resident in Greece. The Court repeated its definition of discrimination contained in the Schumacker case-law, even if that case-law deals with individuals. It stated that "... it is necessary to ascertain whether, for the purposes of the taxation of profits earned in Greece, a company having its seat in Greece and a branch established in Greece of a company having its seat in another Member State are in an objectively comparable situation".[26] Regarding the method of determining the taxable base, there was, according to the Court, no difference in treatment of the two categories of companies. The fact that resident companies were taxed on their world-wide profit and the branches of non-resident companies on the profits attributable to the branches did not alter the decision that they were in objectively comparable situations regarding the determination of the taxable base.[27]

However, most of the cases regarding companies do not contain a discrimination analysis where two objectively comparable situations are established and compared. Rather, the Court merely establishes that a cross-border situation is treated worse than a strictly national situation, albeit not being very articulate when making that comparison. This is the "restriction approach".[28]

The facts of the recent case C-253/03 *CLT-UFA SA*[29] strongly resemble classic cases such as 270/83 *avoir fiscal* and C-311/97 *Royal Bank of Scotland*, and the case is therefore an excellent touchstone of any recent changes in the practice of the Court in the area of direct taxation. The company CLT-UFA had its seat and central administration in Luxembourg, and it also had a branch in Germany. Accordingly, CLT-UFA was subject to limited tax liability in Germany. The tax rate applicable to the profits of the German branch was 42 percent. A German subsidiary of a foreign company would have been subject to a tax rate of 33.5 percent or even 30 percent. The tax rates for subsidiaries applied if they distributed all profits to their parent company. The Court declared that the refusal to apply the reduced tax rate to branches "… renders the possibility, for companies having their seat in another Member State, of exercising the right to freedom of establishment through a branch less attractive".[30] The Court also found that the national law at issue "… restricts the freedom to choose the appropriate legal form in which to pursue activities in another Member State".[31] Seemingly, the Court has decided not to make a discrimination analysis. In my view the case is not different in this respect from the *avoir fiscal* and *Royal Bank of Scotland* cases, where the Court in fact labelled the national measures discriminatory. However, there are other interesting parts of the Court's reasoning. Next, the Court examined whether the differential treatment was objectively justified. The German tax authority (*Finanzamt*) and the German government argued that the situations of a branch of a foreign company and the subsidiary of a foreign company were not objectively comparable. In the light of previous case law, the Court rather unsurprisingly came to the conclusion that the different forms of establishment were objectively comparable.

In my view, one could argue whether this line of reasoning is somewhat different from the reasoning in previous case law. In the present case the Court establishes that the national law at issue constitutes a restriction. Previous case law contained a discrimination analysis, which meant that objectively comparable situations were identified. In the present case the issue of comparable situations is discussed in relation to justifications. The case supports the view that the Court has moved from a discrimination analysis to a restriction analysis.

In addition it seems as if the Court considers fewer circumstances when determining whether the situations of companies are objectively comparable or not. Regarding individuals, however, a wide scope of personal and family circumstances are considered. The reasons for this are not clear. One possible explanation could be the following. Several of the cases regarding individuals have dealt with national law granting allowances when calculating the taxable income. An objective of national law granting such an allowance is to take personal and family circumstances into account. However, the objective behind basic allowances in one Member State may not be the same as in another Member State. Swedish law on basic allowances does not, anymore at least, have the objective of granting individuals a minimum income. Rather it exists in order to reduce the taxation of taxpayers with low income.[32]

Recent Cases on the Free Movement of Capital

Recently there have been several cases decided on measures of direct taxation in relation to the freedom of capital. It should be recalled that Article 58 (1)(a) of the EC Treaty stipulates that the provisions of Article 56 shall be without prejudice to the right of Member States "…to apply the relevant provisions of their tax law which distinguish between taxpayers who are not in the same situation with regard to their place of residence or with regard to the place where their capital is invested". This is similar to what the Court stipulated in the previously discussed Schumacker case in relation to the concept of "objectively comparable situations". In for example the case C-35/98 *Verkooijen* the Court declared the basic similarity between Article 58 (1)(a) of the EC Treaty and what here is referred to as the Schumacker doctrine.[33]

Case C-512/03 Blanckaert (8 September 2005)

The first case is C-512/03 *Blanckaert*. It dealt with the compatibility of Dutch tax law with the free movement of capital. Mr Blanckaert was a Belgian citizen also resident in Belgium. He and his wife had a summer house in the Netherlands. According to Dutch income tax law, Mr Blanckaert was considered as a non-resident taxpayer in the Netherlands, taxable on income from savings and investment relating to his (and his wife's) summer house in the Netherlands. Still, he received less than 90 percent of his income there. According to Dutch tax law there was a possibility for non-residents to make an option to be treated as residents, which meant that they would be granted a tax-free capital allowance and special tax credits (although not on such income as earned by Mr Blanckaert). Such an option would also result in an unlimited tax liability in the Netherlands. However, according to the 1970 tax treaty between Belgium and the Netherlands, Mr Blanckaert was still granted the tax-free capital allowance and certain tax credits. Yet, he was not according to the treaty granted a tax credit in the Netherlands in respect of national insurance, which residents in the Netherlands were entitled to. The reason for this denied tax credit was that he did not pay any social contributions in the Netherlands, which he did in Belgium. Mr Blanckaert considered the denial of that particular tax credit to be in breach of the free movement of capital.

Initially the European Court of Justice decided that the free movement of capital applied: the investment in real property on the territory of a Member State by non-residents is according to settled case law covered by this freedom.[34] The law provision at issue granted a tax credit for contributions to the Dutch social security system. This tax credit was only granted those who were covered by that social security system. The Court declared: "The criterion of insurance chosen by the Netherlands legislation favours, in the majority of cases, persons resident in that Member State. Taxpayers who are not insured under that system are more often than not non-residents." This way of establishing a difference in treatment is in line with the way in which the Court previously has identified "covert discrimination", also referred to as "indirect discrimination". For example in the case C-330/91 *Commerzbank*, dealing with the freedom of establishment, the Court explained: "/.../ the rules regarding equality of treatment forbid not only overt discrimination by reason of nationality or, in the case of a company, its seat, but all covert forms of discrimination which, by the application of other criteria of differentiation, lead in fact to the same result".[35] However, that is not the final approach taken by the Court in the Blanckaert case. The Court states: "Less favourable tax treatment for non-residents only might deter the latter from investing in property in the Netherlands. That legislation is therefore capable of hindering the free movement of capital."[36] This seems to be evidence of the Court's step from a discrimination analysis to a broader restriction analysis.

The next step in the reasoning of the Court is whether such a restriction can be justified. The Court tries whether there is an objective difference between the objective situation of a non-resident, as Mr Blanckaert, and that of a resident who as Mr Blanckaert only receives income from savings and investments. The Court notes that the specific tax credit only is granted those who are covered by the Dutch social security system. If a non-resident as well as a resident is not covered by that system, then the tax credit is not granted. If Mr Blanckaert were to be granted the tax credit that would according to the Court be to treat different situations in the same way.[37] In addition the Court finds that the Dutch provisions of the social security system are consistent with Regulation No 1408/71 on social security within the European Union. The conclusion of the Court is that the denial of the tax credit at issue can be justified in the light of Article 58(1)(a) of the EC Treaty by the objective difference between a person that is insured according to the Dutch social security system and a person that is not insured according to that system.

In my view the outcome of this case is reasonable. Dutch tax law make a connection between the tax credit and whether one was covered by the social security system or not. Both residents and non-residents were denied the tax credit if they were not covered by that system. The compatibility of Dutch law on social security with the Community Regulation seems to have been important for the outcome. The case clearly illustrates the step away from the discrimination analysis to a broader restriction analysis. When dealing with the free movement of capital the question whether objectively comparable situations are at hand forms part of the justification issue, which follows from the wording of Article 58. It has been suggested by several scholars that in reality there is no difference between a discrimination analysis and a restriction analysis in the sense that a restriction analysis also requires the comparison between different situations, for example one strictly national situation and one cross-border situation. In the Blanckaert case the Court identifies a restriction, which in my view presupposes a comparison between different situations, but finds it justified because the situations are not objectively comparable according to Article 58. This is an interesting outcome, and it suggests that there are indeed differences between the two approaches.

Case C-513/03 Van Hilten (23 February 2006)

The second case is C-513/03 *Van Hilten* which dealt with Dutch inheritance taxation and its compatibility with the free movement of capital. Mrs Van Hilten was of Dutch nationality and had been resident in the Netherlands until 1988, when she moved to Belgium. In 1991 she moved to Switzerland where she died in 1997. Her estate consisted of immovable property in the Netherlands, Belgium and Switzerland. It also contained other assets in different Member States of the European Union, Switzerland and the United States. Her heirs were assessed to inheritance tax in the Netherlands. Dutch inheritance law stipulated that the value of all assets of a deceased individual should be subject to Dutch inheritance tax if the deceased at the time of death was resident in the Netherlands.

In addition Dutch tax law provided that an individual should be considered to have been resident in the Netherlands ten years after ceasing to reside there. The tax treaty regarding gift and inheritance taxation between the Netherlands and Switzerland was also relevant to the case. Article 2 of the tax treaty stipulated that immovable property should be subject to inheritance taxation only in that state in which it was situated. Article 3 stipulated that other assets should be subject to tax only in the state where the deceased resided at the date of death. Yet, the state where the deceased was a national had, according to a declaration annexed to the tax treaty, a right to levy inheritance tax if the deceased had been resident there during the ten years before death and was a national of that state at the time of ceasing to reside there. If a deceased person in such a way was deemed to have been resident in the Netherlands, the estate would be granted a relief from inheritance taxation, provided that the tax levied by the other signatory state was similar to the Dutch inheritance tax. The right to tax relief in this situation followed from a decree in internal Dutch tax law.

At the time of death, Mrs Van Hilten was according to Dutch law considered to be resident in the Netherlands and her estate, including all real property irrespective of where it was situated, was subject to Dutch inheritance taxation. A precondition for such inheritance taxation in the Netherlands was that the foreign inheritance taxation was lower abroad than in the Netherlands. In the Netherlands a credit was granted relating to the inheritance tax paid in Switzerland. It follows that the Swiss inheritance taxation was lower than the one in the Netherlands.

The main question dealt with by the Court was whether the Dutch legislation at issue was in breach of the free movement of capital. Initially the Court decided whether inheritances constitute movements of capital in the meaning of the EC Treaty. On the basis of the directive 88/361/EEC the Court answers that question in the affirmative. Next the issue was whether the national legislation constitutes a restriction on the free movement of capital. The answer of the Court was no. The reason is that the Court finds the taxation provisions identical for those nationals who have transferred their residence abroad and those who remain resident in the Netherlands. It declared: "Since it [i.e. the Dutch legislation at issue] applies only to nationals of the Member State concerned, it cannot constitute a restriction on the movement of capital of nationals of the other Member States."[38]

The fact that an exclusive taxation in Switzerland would have resulted in a lower inheritance tax was not of relevance according to the Court. Such a difference "... cannot be regarded as constituting discrimination prohibited by Article [56] of the Treaty".[39] In view of the Court that difference flows "... in the absence of any unifying or harmonising measures adopted in the Community context, from the Member States' power to define, by treaty or unilaterally, the criteria for allocating their powers of taxation".[40] It is a bit surprising that the Court decided to use the term "discrimination" in relation to Article 56, which prohibits "restrictions", but it may be a consequence of Article 58 (3) which prohibits the justification of measures constituting "arbitrary discrimination".

The Court also emphasised that the allocation of taxing powers at issue in the present case is in line with the OECD MTC (on gift and inheritance taxation), which is a similar point to what it made in the Gilly case.[41]

The legislation at issue in this case has similarities with exit taxation in the area of income taxation. So far only one such case has been decided by the European Court of Justice, case C-9/02 *de Lasteyrie*. That case dealt with the freedom of establishment and French legislation on exit taxation of shares when the shareholder changed residence for tax purposes. The French law was lenient because French taxation could be suspended according to certain conditions.[42]

The outcome of the Van Hilten case gives support for the position that "disparities" between tax systems are accepted under the fundamental freedoms. The fact that Switzerland had lower inheritance taxation did not restrict the free movement of capital.[43]

The European Court of Justice has recently developed an approach to the relationship between the freedom of establishment and the free movement of capital in relation to third countries. It was first developed in a non-tax law case, C-452/04 *Fidium Finanz,* why I refer to it as the Fidium Finanz doctrine. Basically, the Fidium Finanz doctrine means the following. The freedom of establishment is the dominant freedom in relation to the free movement of capital. The territorial scope of the two freedoms differ: the free movement of capital applies in relation to third countries, whereas the free movement of capital only applies within the European Union. In several tax cases recently decided by the Court, the question has been whether the national tax measure constitutes a restriction on the free movement of capital in relation to a third country. As regards a situation strictly within the European Union, the Court has come to the conclusion that the measure is in breach of the freedom of establishment. However, in relation to a third country the freedom of establishment does not apply, and therefore the measure is not in breach of the fundamental freedoms. But does not the national measure constitute a breach of the free movement of capital? No, says the Court. Even if the measure in principle breaches the free movement of capital, the freedom of establishment is dominant in relation to the free movement of capital, and since the freedom of establishment does not apply in relation to third countries, there is no breach of fundamental freedoms. In my view, this way of reasoning is absurd. The freedom of establishment cannot be dominant to the free movement of capital if it does not apply. It would have been better if the Court had dealt with the third-country issue by altering the way in which grounds of justification apply, for example a wider definition of the ground of preventing tax avoidance, or by applying a more lenient proportionality test in relation to third countries. Recent tax law cases where the Fidium Finanz doctrine has been applied are, for example, C-102/05 *Skatteverket v. A and B and C-524/04 Test Claimants in the Thin Cap Group Litigation v. Commissioners of the Inland Revenue..*

7.4 Grounds of Justification in the General Interest

The Court has developed the rule-of-reason doctrine, according to which national measures of law can be justified even if they constitute a hindrance to one or more fundamental freedoms. In the case C-55/94 *Gebhard*, the Court explained that national measures liable to hinder or make less attractive the exercise of fundamental freedoms must fulfil four conditions: (i) they must be applied in a non-discriminatory manner, (ii) they must be justified by imperative requirements in the general interest, (iii) they must be suitable for securing the attainment of the objective which they pursue, and (iv) they must not go beyond what is necessary in order to attain it.[44] In the present context it is the first condition that is the most important one. The fact that only non-discriminatory restrictions are covered means that a measure that constitutes discrimination, or at least is labelled discriminatory, never can be justified according to the rule-of-reason doctrine.

A problem with the notion of non-discriminatory restrictions is that they do not explicitly include a comparison of "objectively comparable situations". Therefore, a national measure that constitutes discrimination may never be justified according to the rule-of-reason doctrine. That is also what the Court explicitly stated in the previously mentioned case C-311/97 *Royal Bank of Scotland*: "According to settled case-law, only an express derogating provision, such as Article 56 of the EC Treaty, could render such discrimination compatible with Community law".[45]

For some time it has been argued that the Court indeed accepts the application of the rule-of-reason doctrine in relation to measures that constitute indirect discrimination, where the case C-204/90 *Bachmann*, is such a case. In that case the ground of fiscal coherence was accepted as an imperative requirement in the general interest.

A characteristic of discrimination is, as previously mentioned, that two "objectively comparable situations" are compared and the one with a foreign element is treated worse than a strictly internal situation. It is also possible to model two cross-border situations as objectively comparable.

The first criterion of the rule-of-reason doctrine as manifested in the Gebhard case means that it could never apply where the Court has identified objectively comparable situations and found that the one with a foreign element is treated worse. That would considerably limit the scope for Member States to justify national measures. This was focused on in the decision by the Special Commissioners in the Marks & Spencer case.

In the case C-446/03 *Marks & Spencer* the Court accepted the national measure, under certain conditions, even if it constituted a restriction. The Court did in this case accept two new grounds of justification and also applied a third previously acknowledged ground. The grounds of justification were the following. First, that profits and losses must be treated symmetrically.[46] Second, that it should be prevented that losses could be taken into account twice.[47] The third ground was the prevention of tax avoidance. If a cross-border loss-relief was permitted, there was a risk that the losses would be transferred to the company subject to the highest rate of taxation in the corporate group. It should be underlined that the three grounds were applied cumulatively.

It is likely that Member States will advance those grounds in a number of subsequent cases. This is of course a major development of the rule-of-reason doctrine in the field of direct taxation. Still, what form of infringement did the United Kingdom legislation constitute? The case concerned the UK system for group consolidation of profits and losses. It was possible for a UK parent company to take into account the losses of a UK subsidiary, but not the losses of a foreign subsidiary. In the view of the Court, this difference in treatment constituted a restriction on the freedom of establishment.[48] Therefore the rule-of-reason doctrine could apply and the hindrance could potentially be justified, which it also turned out to be under certain conditions.[49]

However, could it not be said that the UK legislation at issue was discriminatory? If discrimination is the same treatment of different situations or the different treatment of similar situations, could that not apply in this case? Did not the UK refusal of group consolidation in a cross-border situation, with the acceptance in a strictly national situation, constitute discrimination? In my view, one could very well come to such a conclusion. In the case C-311/97 *Royal Bank of Scotland*, which was, according to the Court, a case of direct discrimination there was a comparison between the treatment of a branch of a foreign company and a resident company. One of the situations had a cross-border nature and the other was strictly national. There is one difference: the *Marks & Spencer* case concerns the home state, and the *Royal Bank of Scotland* case the host state. In my view, that should not be of any significance.

There is little support for the view, that the meaning of the fundamental freedoms should be different concerning the perspective. The wording of the fundamental freedoms contained in the EC Treaty, as interpreted by the Court, does not make any difference in treatment between host- and home-state restrictions.[50] Can any conclusion be drawn? In my view it seems as if the Court has stepped away from the discrimination approach, and now applies the restriction approach. Suppose that it does constitute an important factor that the *Marks & Spencer* case concerned the home state, a possible conclusion could be that a difference in treatment in that state is more easily justified than in the host state, because the rule-of-reason doctrine applies to restrictions and not to discrimination.

The same question regarding the meaning of discrimination and restriction is relevant for cases on CFC legislation in relation to fundamental freedoms. One pending case is C-169/04 *Cadbury Schweppes*. The referring national court, UK Special Commissioners John F. Avery Jones and Malcolm Gammie, address as an uncertainty of the case whether a discrimination or restriction approach should be applied.[51] Maybe the European Court of Justice will take the opportunity to express its principal view on the two approaches.

Recently the Court decided case C-152/03 *Ritter-Coulais* (21 February 2006). The decision is complex and the interesting parts are perhaps those dealing with procedural matters, which go beyond the scope of this chapter. The referring German court (*Bundesfinanzhof*) had wrongly understood national tax law and also referred to wrong fundamental freedoms. Yet the Court decided to try the case and not to reject it. The case concerned German law provisions on the computation of the applicable tax rate. Mr and Mrs Ritter-Coulais were German nationals but lived in their private house in France. They both worked as teachers in a state school in Germany. Mrs Ritter-Coulais was also a French national.

When computing the applicable tax rate in Germany, Mr and Mrs Ritter-Coulais wished to take into account negative income relating to their house (real property) in France. However, German tax law only permitted negative income of a passive nature to be taken into account if it concerned a private dwelling in another Member State and there were no corresponding positive income that was taxable in Germany.[52] The Court concluded that even if the national legislation was not specifically directed at non-residents, they were more likely to own a home outside of Germany than resident nationals. Accordingly, the treatment of non-resident workers according to German law was "less favourable" than that granted workers resident in Germany with houses of their own.[53] This legislation was found to be in breach of Article 39 (previous Article 48) of the EC Treaty and the free movement of workers.

The German government had argued that an eventual breach could be justified by the need for fiscal coherence. The Court answered that since German law permitted the taxation of foreign positive income resulting from the use of a dwelling in another Member State, fiscal coherence was not "... a suitable justification on any ground for refusing to take into account, for the same purposes, income losses of the same kind arising in the same State".[54] One may wonder whether fiscal coherence would have been accepted as a ground of justification if foreign positive income had not been taxable in Germany. Maybe the Court would have accepted fiscal coherence in that circumstance. How does that relate to the somewhat similar *Marks & Spencer* case? According to UK tax law losses of foreign subsidiaries were not taken into account and profits of foreign subsidiaries were as a general rule not taxable in the hands of their UK parent.[55] Could not fiscal coherence have been a permissible ground of justification in the Marks & Spencer case? Even if the comparison between the cases is intriguing my answer is no. The Court has spelled out that fiscal coherence only applies for one and the same tax subject,[56] which by the way was fulfilled in the Ritter-Coulais case. In principle, the Marks & Spencer case dealt with two tax subjects, the parent company and its subsidiary.

7.5 Critique of the Structural Attempt by AG Geelhoed

There has been a recent attempt by AG Geelhoed in case C-374/04 *Test Claimants in Class IV of the ACT Group Litigation* to give a structure to the Court's position on direct taxation in relation to the fundamental freedoms.[57] One could perhaps say that AG Geelhoed is trying to give a conceptual framework for the position that the Court as a general rule should not interfere with Member States' sovereignty in the field of direct taxation. The case concerns the now abolished UK imputation system for the taxation of corporate profits. Here I will only deal with the general issues dealt with by the Advocate General on the relationship between fundamental freedoms and direct taxation.

Restrictions and "Quasi-restriction"

Initially the Advocate General finds that there are no practical differences between the meaning of a "restriction" and "discrimination" in the case law of the Court in the field of direct taxation. I agree with this view. Concerning "restrictions" it is possible in the Court's case law to identify two comparable situations where one is treated worse than the other.[58] In addition AG Geelhoed makes a distinction between "restrictions" (or "discrimination") and "quasi-restrictions", which is rather novel terminology, even if the concepts are previously known.[59] Quasi-restrictions refer to restrictions inevitably resulting from the co-existence of national tax systems. "True restrictions" go beyond those restrictions that are the mere outflow of the co-existence of national tax systems. AG Geelhoed divides quasi-restrictions into three categories, which will be discussed here.

Greater Administrative Compliance Burden

The fact that Member States have separate national tax systems means that persons involved in cross-border activities will have to comply with administrative burdens in several Member States. Member States have their own tax authorities, their own procedure for submission of tax returns and their own subsequent investigations of those returns.

To some extent one must agree with the Advocate General, but it shows from the Court's case law that also provisions constituting an administrative burden may be in breach of the fundamental freedoms. A clear example is case C-250/95 *Futura Participations* where the obligation in Luxembourg for branches of foreign companies to keep accounting according to Luxembourg law, was in breach of the freedom of establishment. The reason was that such non-resident companies also were obliged to keep accounting according to the law of their state of residence, France in the particular case.

Existence of Disparities

Moreover, the existence of disparities between the national tax systems of the Member States gives rise to acceptable "quasi-restrictions". Such disparities follow from different macroeconomic circumstances in the Member States, and at the present status of integration of national economies they differ considerably. The Advocate General gives several examples of such differences. For example, some Member States have a larger labour force in relation to capital, which may incline such states to place a greater tax burden on capital than on labour. Some Member States may choose to have a better public service and to redistribute to "lower levels of society".[60] Moreover, regarding the taxation of companies, some Member States with lower tax rates may opt for the classical system regarding the taxation of corporate profits, whereas Member States with higher tax rates may opt for an imputation system. In conclusion, differences between Member States' tax systems resulting from such disparities as previously mentioned do not, in the view of the AG Geelhoed, interfere with the freedom of establishment.

I find this reasoning of the Advocate General to be difficult to relate to any concrete (potential) "quasi-restriction". If in every case a Member State could argue that the differences in tax treatment were due to, for example, a certain position on public spending, few, if any, tax provisions would be in breach of the fundamental freedoms. The case law of the Court in the field of direct taxation would not be valid anymore.

The Advocate General finds support in the Court's decision in the case C-403/03 *Schempp*, albeit dealing with the citizenship of the European Union. He considers the case to be relevant also to the freedom of establishment, which was at issue in the present case. I will briefly discuss the Schempp case. Mr Schempp was a German national and he paid alimony to his former wife, for convenience's sake here referred to as Mrs Schempp. He wished to deduct the cost for the alimony in his German tax return, which he was denied. German tax law contained the condition for such a cost deduction that the recipient was taxable for the alimony obtained. It seems that the alimony was tax exempt in Austria, at least Mr Schempp could not verify that the alimony had been subject to tax in Austria. In relation to the general prohibition against discrimination in Article 12 of the EC Treaty, the Court declared that it did not prohibit divergences existing between Member States so long as they affected all persons subject to them in accordance with objective criteria and without regard to their nationality.[61] The Court concluded that there was no case of discrimination according to Article 12 of the EC Treaty.

Furthermore the Court considered whether the national law at issue was in breach of the citizenship of the European Union contained in Article 18 (1) of the EC Treaty. The Court found that the German law at issue did not in any way obstruct Mr Schempp's right as a citizen of the European Union to move or reside in other Member States. Even if the transfer of Mrs Schempp's residence to Austria had had an impact on the tax situation of Mr Schempp, that did not affect his rights following from the citizenship of the European Union. Moreover, the Court meant that the different tax treatment in Austria was an expression of disparities between the tax legislation of the Member States, which are allowed.[62] In my view this is a reasonable outcome and it seems to be in line with the Court's case law on the (other) fundamental freedoms of the EC Treaty.

The Advocate General finally notes that Member States may take action also against distortions if they wish (cf. Articles 94, 96 and 97 of the EC Treaty), even if they are acceptable in relation to the freedoms contained in the EC Treaty.[63]

Division of Tax Jurisdiction (Dislocation of Tax Base)

Finally, AG Geelhoed mentions the division of tax jurisdiction as an inevitable consequence of the co-existence of national tax systems. This means, in particular, that a state must choose a criterion by which it decides which part of an economic operator's income that falls within its tax jurisdiction.[64] He identifies that states usually apply worldwide taxation and territoriality taxation (source-country taxation). The application of these principles may give rise to juridical double taxation.[65] In this respect the Advocate General makes a statement that is somewhat controversial: "Under international tax law, the generally accepted rule of taxation priority is that of 'source country entitlement': that is, priority of taxation right over source country income lies with the source State."[66]

This statement is questionable from several aspects. To begin with, what is "international tax law"? A sovereign state no doubt has the right to levy taxes. Member States of the European Union have agreed, among other matters, to abide by the fundamental freedoms of the EC Treaty, which limit the scope of the freedom of the Member States to completely design their tax laws as they wish. Still, the fundamental freedoms are not "international *tax* law". Another element of tax law is tax treaty law, which consists of international agreements. According to tax treaties, the concluding states agree to limit the effects of international juridical double taxation, prevent tax avoidance and tax avoidance, and to exchange information.[67] The OECD Model Tax Convention and its commentary (OECD MTC) is an important tool for interpreting tax treaties, even if the interpretative value of the OECD MTC has been subject to immense discussion. In my view, the Court has accepted the OECD MC too uncritically. Is it a valid opinion that the OECD MTC constitutes "international tax law"? To some extent my answer is yes. When interpreting tax treaties between Member States of the OECD, the OECD MTC is vital, and to some degree even outside of the OECD community. Is it possible to say that the principles of world-wide taxation ('residence taxation') and territoriality taxation ('source-country taxation') follow from the OECD MTC and that this justifies them as principles of "international tax law"? My answer is no. Residence taxation and source-country taxation are techniques for tax law design that sovereign states can apply if they so wish. In contrast, the principle of legality is manifest in the constitution of many states. In the area of tax law that means that tax may only be levied according to law provisions. To phrase the core question in a drastic manner: Which taxpayer would accept a tax inspector who makes a tax claim according to the residence principle or source-country tax principle as manifest in international tax law?

It is true that the OECD MTC refers to residence- and source-country taxation, but that is because those principles are manifest in the national law of the Member States of the OECD. The OECD MTC does not in itself constitute a legal basis for those principles.

Moreover, is it as the Advocate General states, that the generally accepted rule of taxation is that of 'source country entitlement'? It follows already from my scepticism vis-à-vis the meaning of "international tax law" that my answer is in the negative. To rephrase the question: Is the priority of 'source country entitlement' a principle contained in tax treaty law and also manifested in the OECD MTC? My answer is no. A tax treaty divides the taxing rights between the signatory states. In general both treaty-concluding states can be both source state and residence state. In a specific case of international juridical double taxation both states may be state of residence according to national law, even if the application of Article 4 of the OECD MTC will mean that only one state will be state of residence for tax-treaty purposes. If one analyses the distributive articles of the OECD MTC one notices that most of the articles primarily grant the state of residence either an exclusive taxing right or a taxing right shared with the source state.[68] When applying the treaty article on the elimination of double taxation ("method article") it is generally the state of residence[69] that shall eliminate (mitigate) the remaining double taxation. Even so, the outcome of the method article may still be that the residence state also will be granted some tax revenue.[70] It is true that Vogel among others considers source-country taxation to be in principle more legitimate and just than residence taxation (global taxation), but not even Vogel considers source-country taxation to be superior to residence taxation in any legal sense.[71]

AG Geelhoed also states that under Community law, the power to choose criteria of, and allocate, tax jurisdiction lies purely with the Member States. He refers in this instance to the case C-336/96 *Gilly*. I agree in full with this view and the interpretation of the Gilly case.

Regarding the supposedly predominant source-country tax-principle one could mention the recent interest/royalty directive (2003/49/EC). This directive grants sole taxing right to the residence state – a Community measure in stark contrast to the view of AG Geelhoed on the status of the source-country tax-principle.

True restrictions in the field of direct taxation do, according to AG Geelhoed, result from the tax jurisdiction of one Member State. In his view, the concept of discrimination ("true restriction") is different between the residence- and the source-state perspectives. He states: "Quite simply, as the nature of the tax jurisdiction being exercised in each case differs fundamentally, an economic operator subject to home State jurisdiction cannot per se be considered to be in a comparable situation to an economic operator subject to source State jurisdiction, and vice versa."[72] His conclusion is that Article 43 of the EC Treaty imposes two different categories of obligations on a state: one relates to the home state and one relates to the source state.

According to the Advocate General it is for the home state to treat foreign-source income of its residents consistently with the way it has divided its tax base.[73] To the extent the home state has decided to include foreign-source income in its taxable base, it must not discriminate between foreign and domestic income.

Here only one of the cases referred to by the Advocate General will be discussed and that is the case C-168/01 *Bosal Holding*. In brief, the case dealt with Dutch legislation on the right to deduct costs for the financing of subsidiary companies. Such deductions were only allowed if the subsidiary was resident in the Netherlands.[74] However, the Court found this condition to be in breach of the freedom of establishment and no grounds of justification were applicable. The Advocate General considers this to be a wrong decision.[75] In his view the Court did not sufficiently recognise the Member States' division of tax jurisdiction. He also identifies a risk that the outcome of the Bosal case could lead to a situation where costs are taken into account twice: once in the Netherlands and once in the other state at issue. The Advocate General compares the Bosal case with the Marks & Spencer case and considers the outcome of the cases not to be compatible. The Court's decision in the Marks & Spencer case meant that it was permissible only in very limited situations to take foreign losses into account in the home state (the United Kingdom). That was when all possibilities of considering the losses ceased to exist in the source state (host state). I agree with the analysis of the Advocate General regarding both the Marks & Spencer case and the Bosal Holding case. The two decisions are in my view difficult to reconcile.

In the view of the AG Geelhoed, source states are subject to a more limited obligation under Article 43 of the EC Treaty. This means, in his view, that the source state has an obligation to treat all non-residents in an equal way to residents to the extent that they fall within its jurisdiction. He exemplifies with case-law from the Court in the field of direct taxation.

Regarding the UK legislation at issue in the present case, which deals with the now abolished imputation system, I will not go into detail on the analysis of the Advocate General. Yet, it should be noted that he finds that the UK legislation was not in breach of Community law. He states that the difference in quality of tax jurisdiction results from the manner in which states have chosen to allocate (divide) taxation power.[76]

7.6 On Pending and Forthcoming Cases Before the European Court of Justice

There are several cases pending before the European Court of Justice which deal with areas of tax law that previously have not been dealt with by the Court. A few Swedish cases are such "frontier cases".

The Swedish Council for Advance Tax Rulings (*Skatterättsnämnden*) has interpreted the free movement of capital in relation to third states in several decisions. Two decisions from 2005 deal with CFC legislation and fundamental freedoms.[77] The decisions confirm the restriction approach of the European Court of Justice, which is of interest. Moreover, the Council for Advance Tax Rulings considers the prevention of tax avoidance as a ground of justification to be more generally applicable in relation to third states. The European Court of Justice has so far not decided on that issue in any similar case.

Still, it should be noted that there are also such cases pending at the level of the European Court of Justice. Two of the Swedish cases decided by the Swedish Council for Advance Tax Rulings have been made public. The present Swedish CFC legislation was introduced 1 January 2004. According to this legislation it is, under specific circumstances, possible to tax the Swedish owners of foreign low-tax companies. This legislation does not contain any subjective requirement regarding the reason for the establishment of the foreign entity. Instead, the legislation contains detailed conditions regarding ownership and control, as well as the minimum effective tax rate of the foreign entity. In a decision of the 4 April 2005 the Council for Advance Tax Rulings decided that the Swedish CFC legislation was in breach of the freedom of establishment in relation to an establishment made in Luxembourg. The reason was that this legislation treated a cross-border situation worse than a strictly national situation. The more burdensome treatment due to the CFC legislation was partly because it meant an earlier taxation in time of foreign profits, partly because the calculation of profits was less favourable to the taxpayer. According to the Council for Advance Tax Rulings, it was not possible to justify this difference in treatment according to the rule-of-reason doctrine, not even on the ground of preventing tax avoidance. In another decision of the 4 April 2005 the Council for Advance Tax Rulings considered the same CFC legislation in relation to the free movement of capital and a subsidiary located in Switzerland. All general considerations made in the first case were found to apply also in this case. However, when it came to grounds of justifications, the Council for Advance Tax Rulings decided that it is possible to justify infringements to a wider extent in relation to third countries than within the European Union. Therefore, the ground of preventing tax avoidance could be applied in this situation.[78] In my view, the decision in the case C-169/04 *Cadbury Schweppes* makes it clear that also the Swedish CFC legislation is in breach of fundamental freedoms, especially since it does not contain any subjective criterion whatsoever.

7.7 Concluding Remarks on the Change of Direction of the European Court of Justice

In the first section of this chapter I put forward three hypotheses that would be examined in relation to the case study. The first thesis was that regarding companies, the European Court of Justice has departed from a discrimination analysis to a restriction analysis. The cases discussed in this chapter have more or less confirmed this thesis; see for example case C-253/03 *CLT-UFA SA*.

The second thesis was that regarding individuals the Court still upholds a discrimination analysis, thereby maintaining the requirement of identifying objectively comparable situations, even if anomalies exist in its case law. It seems that the Court applies a restriction analysis also regarding individuals, for example in case C-152/03 *Ritter-Coulais* and C-513/03 *Van Hilten*.

The third thesis was that the Court has become more amenable with regard to grounds of justification in the general interest. On this issue it is only the case C-446/03 *Marks & Spencer* that is of relevance. Together three grounds of justification applied; in special circumstances they even met the proportionality test. Even if it is rare that grounds of justification are found to apply in the area of direct taxation, it has occurred previously. Moreover, the outcome of the Marks & Spencer case is in my view reasonable. If the foreign subsidiary had the right in its state of residence to take the losses into account either in the period concerned or for future periods, the parent company was not entitled to any loss relief. However, one could very well argue that the outcome of the Marks & Spencer case is not in line with the Court's decision in the case C-168/01 *Bosal Holding* concerning the deduction of costs relating to foreign subsidiaries. This difference has also been noted by AG Geelhoed in his opinion to the case C-374/04 *Test Claimants in Class IV of the ACT Group Litigation.*

The first section of this chapter also contained two alternative labels to the recent case law of the European Court of Justice in the field of direct taxation. The first one was the cul-de-sac explanation, which means that negative integration through the case law of the Court has come to a point where it cannot go any further. Thus, the Court will continue to apply its previous case law, but it will not go beyond this point. The second explanation was the U-turn explanation. According to this explanation the Court is now reversing its previous "integrationist" case law, permitting Member States a wider margin of sovereignty in the field of direct taxation.

After the analysis of recent case law I cannot conclude that either of these labels apply. There have been amendments to the Court's case law, but they are hardly dramatic. The number of cases before the Court in the area of direct taxation is exploding. It is natural that some of the national law provisions at issue will be found not to be in breach of fundamental freedoms, be it either because they do not constitute a restriction or because they are justified.

Even if amendments to the case law of the European Court of Justice have been recorded, there has not been any change of direction.

Endnotes

1. This Chapter was discussed at a seminar held at the Faculty of Law, Uppsala university. I am grateful to the participants for valuable comments.
2. In general this is a difference in relation to the legal method applied when analysing national tax law, which is characterised by detailed law provisions.
3. In my study *Direct taxation in relation to the freedom of establishment and the free movement of capital*, Kluwer Law International, The Hague, 2005, I dealt with, among other matters, the meaning of discrimination and restrictions and grounds of justification in the general interest. The meaning of "objectively comparable situations" had to some extent to be delimited from the study (cf., however, *op.cit.*, pp. 100–107).
4. It should be noted that I do not attempt to use the hypothetical-deductive method developed by Popper, which in my view is more adequate for social sciences. The hypotheses are instead used to make the Chapter more readable.

5. A third explanation may of course be a combination of the two explanations. With the previously used metaphors: the Court has entered a cul-de-sac and is now making a U-turn! I am not using the metaphors in any scholarly way. They are used in order to give understandable labels to my policy explanations.
6. Cf. case C-415/93 *Bosman*.
7. Cf. *e.g.* cases C-279/93, *Schumacker*, para. 30 and C-80/94, *Wielockx*, para. 17.
8. Cf. case C-330/91, *Commerzbank*, para. 14.
9. Dahlberg, Direct taxation in relation to the freedom of establishment and the free movement of capital, pp. 327–336 (with further references).
10. Cf. *e.g.* case C-324/00 *Lankhorst-Hohorst*.
11. In my view one could in this instance perhaps discuss the Court's interpretation of Article 58(1) (a) of the EC Treaty. Originally it was introduced with the 1992 Maastricht Treaty and was by some regarded as measure to exclude the Court from the area of direct taxation, cf. Terra/Wattel, European Tax Law, 4th ed., Kluwer Law International, The Hague, 2005, pp. 23–24. However, in the case C-35/98 *Verkooijen* the Court declared that this provision did not add anything new to its previously developed rule-of-reason doctrine. Was this a political decision in favour of a higher degree of integration? All in all, I do not believe so. From legal systematic reasons, it would be very difficult if the scope of application differed between the fundamental freedoms. For example, the material scope of the freedom of establishment and the free movement of capital are highly parallel. Then it would be strange if the rule-of-reason doctrine applied differently regarding the free movement of capital.
12. Sévon, (1999), p. 74.
13. This is also how I read the Swedish judge of the Court, Stig von Bahr, expressing his personal view in a recent festschrift article: Ytterligare om EG-domstolen och skatterätt, in *Festskrift till Nils Mattsson*, Ståhl & Thorell (2005) p. 80.
14. Case C-279/93, *Schumacker*, para. 32. It has been strongly questioned whether the OECD MC or "international tax law" stipulates such an obligation for the residence state. Cf. Lang, Ist die Schumacker-Rechtsprechung am Ende?, RIW, 2005, pp. 336–344.
15. Case C-279/93, *Schumacker*, para. 32. See also Mattsson, (2003).
16. Case C-234/01, *Gerritse*, para. 27.
17. *Lagen (1991:586) om särskild inkomstskatt för utomlands bosatta* [Act on Special Income Taxation for Non-Residents].
18. *Inkomstskattelagen (1999:1229)*.
19. Case C-169/03, *Wallentin*, para. 19.
20. In its decision the Court recapitulated its findings in the previous Schumacker case. Referring to that case the Court declared that the state of residence generally has available all the information needed to assess the taxpayer's overall ability to pay, taking into account his personal and family circumstances. Moreover, the situations of residents and non-residents are generally not comparable (case C-376/03, *D*, para. 27–28).
21. Case C-376/03, D, para. 32–33.
22. Case C-376/03, *D*, para. 35.
23. Case C-376/03, *D*, para. 41.
24. Case C-376/03, *D*, para. 42.
25. This view is supported by the opinion of the AG Colomer in the case C-376/03 *D*. According to AG Colomer, Mr D was in the same situation as a resident in the Netherlands since, in reality, 100 percent of his taxable wealth was located in the Netherlands (para. 64).
26. Case C-311/97, *Royal Bank of Scotland*, para. 26.

27. Case C-311/97, *Royal Bank of Scotland*, para. 29.
28. Cf. *e.g.* cases C-200/98 *X AB and Y AB* and C-168/01 *Bosal Holding*.
29. Decided 23 February 2006.
30. Case C-253/03, *CLT-UFA SA*, para. 17.
31. *Ibid.*
32. Cf. Lodin *et al.*, Inkomstskatt. En läro- och handbok, Studentlitteratur, 10th ed., Lund, 2005, p. 59.
33. Case C-35/98, *Verkooijen*, para. 43.
34. Cf. *e.g.* case C-222/97 *Trummer and Mayer*.
35. Case C-330/91, *Commerzbank*, para. 14.
36. Case C-512/03, *Blanckaert*, para. 39.
37. Once again the Court applies a classic phrase of the discrimination analysis, but without using the word "discrimination". Case C-512/03, *Blanckaert*, para. 47.
38. Case C-513/03, *Van Hilten*, para. 46.
39. Case C-513/03, *Van Hilten*, para. 47.
40. *Ibid.* In this instance the Court refered to the cases C-336/96 *Gilly* and C-307/97 *Saint-Gobain*.
41. The European Court of Justice also declares that the mere transfer of residence is in itself not enough for the free movement of capital to apply, case C-513/03, *Van Hilten*, para. 50.
42. There is a Dutch exit case pending which resembles the *de Lasteyrie* case, C-470/04 *Van Dijk*. See on this case Kemmeren, Pending Cases Filed by Dutch Courts I: The Van Dijk and Bujura Cases, in ECJ – Recent Developments in Direct Taxation, ed. M. Lang, Linde Verlag, Vienna, 2005, pp. 221–243.
43. The general outcome of the case C-265/04 *Bouanich* (decided 19 January 2006) was different from the *Blanckaert* and *van Hilten* cases. The Bouanich case dealt with Swedish withholding taxation on dividends paid to non-residents, *kupongskattelagen (1970:624)*. A Swedish company repurchased its own shares from Mrs Bouanich, who was a shareholder resident in France. The purpose of the repurchase was a reduction of the corporate share capital. Swedish withholding tax was levied on the capital payment made by the Swedish company. The tax was calculated on the gross amount with no cost deductions permitted. Had Mrs Bouanich been resident in Sweden, a cost deduction would have been allowed. The European Court of Justice concluded that the Swedish law at issue was in breach of the free movement of capital. No justifications applied. The Court also dealt with implications following from the application of the French-Swedish tax treaty, but left it to the referring court (the Administrative Court of Appeals in Sundsvall) to decide on that issue. I have largely delimited this Chapter from tax treaty issues, and will therefore not deal with that part of the Court's decision.
44. Case C-55/94, *Gebhard*, para. 37. On these criteria see *e.g.* Kingreen (1999) p. 67.
45. Case C-311/97, *Royal Bank of Scotland*, para. 32.
46. Case C-446/03, *Marks & Spencer*, para. 43.
47. Case C-446/03, *Marks & Spencer*, para. 47.
48. Case C-446/03, *Marks & Spencer*, para. 34.
49. Cf. case C-446/03, *Marks & Spencer*, para. 35.
50. Cf. *e.g.* case 81/87, *Daily Mail*, para. 16.
51. The question referred to the ECJ in the *Cadbury Schweppes* case is, however, more general: "Do articles 43, 49 and 56 of the EC Treaty preclude national tax legislation such as that in issue in the main proceedings, which provides in specified circumstances for the imposition of a charge upon a company resident in that Member State in respect of the profits of a subsidiary company resident in another Member State and subject to a lower level of taxation?"

52. Case C-152/03, *Ritter-Coulais*, para. 35.
53. Case C-152/03, *Ritter-Coulais*, para. 39.
54. Case C-152/03, *Ritter-Coulais*, para. 40.
55. Here I am not taking into account UK CFC legislation and the fact that profit distributed as dividends is taxable for the UK parent company.
56. AG Juliane Kokott has convincingly argued that fiscal coherence in exceptional circumstances could be applied also to the taxation of more than one tax subject, see her opinion in the case C-319/02 *Manninen*. See also Mutén, ECJ Advocate General Issues Opinion on Finland's Imputation System, Tax Notes International, 2004, pp. 1154–1157.
57. The opinion was issued 23 February 2006.
58. Dahlberg, *op.cit.*, pp. 112–113 (Chap. 3) as well as the case-law analysis of Chapters 4 and 6.
59. Terra/Wattel, European Tax Law, pp. 57–64.
60. Opinion of AG Geelhoed in case C-374/04, *Test Claimants*, para. 44.
61. Case C-403/03, *Schempp*, para. 34.
62. Case C-403/03, *Schempp*, para. 45–46.
63. Opinion of AG Geelhoed in case C-374/03, *Test Claimants*, para. 47.
64. Opinion of AG Geelhoed in case C-374/04, *Test Claimants*, para. 49.
65. AG Geelhoed is brief in this part of his opinion. It should be noted that juridical double taxation may occur not only by the clash of (i) residence- and source-country taxation. In principle, two other possibilities exist: (ii) residence taxation in two states, and (iii) source-country taxation in two states. Cf. para. 3 of the commentary to Articles 23A-B of the OECD MC.
66. Opinion of AG Geelhoed in case C-374/04, *Test Claimants*, para. 51.
67. Other objectives behind tax treaties can be advanced, but these are the predominant from a legal point of view.
68. It should be noted that the "source state" when applying a distributive article may base its underlying tax claim on the residence principle of taxation. There can only be one state that is the state of residence when applying a tax treaty.
69. As determined according to Article 4 of a tax treaty based on the OECD MTC.
70. The following example may serve as an illustration. A company resident in state A distributes dividends of 100 to a shareholder resident in state B. State A levies a withholding tax of 30 per cent and the dividend income is subject to a 30 per cent income taxation in state B. Article 10 of the tax treaty between states A and B reduces the withholding tax in state A to 10 percent. The tax treaty applies the credit method. The dividend will be fully taxable in state B, but the individual is granted a tax credit equal to the 10 percent paid in state A. The outcome is that state A ("source state") will levy a 10 percent tax and state B ("residence state") will levy an effective 20 per cent tax on the dividend income.
71. Vogel/Lehner et al., (2003), Einl., marg.no 23–26. This part of the referred commentary is written by professor Klaus Vogel (Munich).
72. Opinion of AG Geelhoed in case C-374/04, *Test Claimants*, para. 57.
73. Opinion of AG Geelhoed in case C-374/04, *Test Claimants*, para. 58.
74. According to a Government decree in the Netherlands this right was also granted non-resident companies on the condition that they had a permanent establishment in the Netherlands.
75. Opinion of AG Geelhoed in case C-374/04, *Test Claimants*, para. 63–64.
76. Opinion of AG Geelhoed in case C-374/04, *Test Claimants*, para. 81. It is worth noting that AG Geelhoed considers a limitation-on-benefits article in the UK-Netherlands tax treaty to be in line with the freedom of establishment.

77. See also Brokelind, Group taxation and CFC rules in Swedish tax cases, Tax Notes International, 2005, pp. 237–241.
78. On this issue see Ståhl, Free movement of capital between Member States and third countries, EC Tax Review, 2005, pp. 49–58.

References

von Bahr, S. (2003), Ytterligare om EG-domstolen och skatterätt, in *Festskrift till Nils Mattsson*, Ståhl & Thorell (ed.), Uppsala: Iustus Förlag, pp. 79-91.

Brokelind, C. (2005) Group taxation in Swedish tax cases, *Tax Notes International*, pp. 237-241.

Dahlberg, M. (2005) *Direct taxation in relation to the freedom of establishment and the free movement of capital*, Hague: Kluwer Law International.

Kingreen, T. (1999) Die Struktur der Grundfreiheiten des Europäischen Gemeinschafts-recht, Berlin: Duncker & Humblot.

Lang, M. (2005) Ist die Schumacker-Rechtsprechung am Ende?, RIW, 2005, pp. 336-344.

Lodin, S., G. Lindencrona, P. Melz, and C. Silfverberg (2005), *Inkomstskatt – en läro- och handbok,* 10th ed., Lund: Studentlitteratur.

Mattsson, N. (2003) Does the European Court of Justice understand the policy behind tax benefits based on personal and family circumstances?, European Taxation, pp. 186-194.

Mutén, L. (2004) ECJ Advocate General issues opinion on Finland's imputation system, Tax Notes International, pp. 1154-1157.

Sévon, L. (1999) The role of the Court in assisting the transition process in Finland, *Europarättslig Tidskrift*, pp. 72-77.

Ståhl, K. (2005) Free movement of capital between Member States and third countries, *EC Tax Review*, pp. 49-58.

Terra, B. and P. Wattel (2005), European tax law, 4th Ed., Hague: Kluwer Law International.

Vogel, K and M. Lehner, (2003) Doppelbesteuerungsabkommen der Bundesrepublik Deutschland auf dem Gebiet der Steuern vom Einkommen und Vermögen: Kommentar auf der Grundlage der Musterabkommen, 4. völlig neubearb. Aufl., Munich, Beck.

Case Law

81/87 Daily Mail and General Trust plc [1988] ECR 5483.

C-330/91 Commerzbank AG [1933] ECR I-4017.

C-279/93 Roland Schumacker [1995] ECR I-225.

C-415/93 Bosman [1995] ECR I-4921.

C-55/94 Reinhard Gebhard [1995] ECR I-4165.

C-336/96 Epoux Gilly [1998] I-2793.

C-222/97 Trummer and Mayer [1999] ECR I-1661.

C-307/97 Compagnie de Saint-Gobain [1999] I-6161.

C-311/97 Royal Bank of Scotland plc [1999] I-2651.

C-35/98 Verkooijen [2000] I-4071.

C-324/00 Lankhorst-Hohorst GmbH [2002] I-11779.

C-168/01 Bosal Holding BV [2003] I-9409.

C-234/01 Arnoud Gerritse [2003] I-5933.

C-319/02 Petri Manninen [2004] ECR I-7477.

C-152/03 Ritter-Coulais [2006] ECR I-1711.

C-169/03 Wallentin [2004] ECR I-6443.

C-253/03 CLT-UFA SA [2006] ECR I-1831.

C-376/03 D. [2005] ECR I-5821.

C-403/03 Schempp [2005] ECR I-6421.

C-446/03 Marks & Spencer [2005] ECR I-10837.

C-512/03 Blanckaert [2005] ECR I-7685.

C-513/03 Van Hilten [2006] ECR I-1957.

C-169/04 Cadbury Schweppes [2006] ECR I-4027.

C-265/04 Bouanich [2006] ECR I-923.

C-374/04 Test Claimants [2006] not yet reported.

C-470/04 Van Dijk [2006] not yet reported.

C-524/04 Test Claimants in the Thin Cap Group Litigation V. Commissioners of the Inland Revenue. [2007] not yet reported.

C-102/05 Skatteverket V. A and B. Order of the Court dated 10 May 2007.

Chapter 8
Tax Treaty Policy

Michael Lang

8.1 Introduction

Tax treaty policy is part of a State's domestic tax policy. However, States are not free to determine the contents of their tax treaties. First, they need the consent of the other Contracting State. Second, if they are EU Member States, they are bound by EC law. Third, in reality the OECD Model Convention plays an important role and it is difficult for States to deviate from the OECD Model Convention. For these reasons, most States do not have too much room to develop their own tax treaty policy.

On the other hand, tax treaties concluded by a State determine to a certain extent the rest of its domestic tax policy. As far as a State is in the position of a Residence State, tax treaties have relatively little impact on domestic tax policy. However, the taxation of non-residents is much more influenced by tax treaty provisions. This will be shown in more detail in this contribution.

8.2 Room for Tax Treaty Policy under EC Law

Obligation to avoid Double Taxation under Art 293 EC?

Art. 293 EC explicitly makes reference to double taxation: "Member States" shall, so far as is necessary, enter into negotiations with each other with a view to securing for the benefit of their nationals:

- the abolition of double taxation within the European Community.

Scholars have considered whether it might constitute an infringement of this EC Treaty provision if double taxation were still to exist in an intra-Community cross-border situation, due e.g. to the lack of a tax treaty. However, in the *Gilly* case the ECJ rejected this idea[1]: "Article 220 [now Art. 293 EC] is not intended to lay down a legal rule directly applicable as such, but merely defines a number of matters on which the Member States are to enter into negotiations with each other 'so far as is necessary'. Its second indent merely indicates the abolition of double taxation within the Community as an objective of any such negotiations. Although the abolition of double taxation within the Community is thus included among the objectives of the Treaty, it is clear from the wording of that provision that it cannot itself confer on individuals any rights on which they might be able to rely before their national courts".

It should be emphasized that the ECJ recognized the abolition of double taxation as part of the objectives of the EC Treaty. Although Art. 293 EC does not confer any rights on individuals, the avoidance of double taxation is nevertheless not completely outside the scope of the EC Treaty. On the contrary, the ECJ seems to be of the opinion that other provisions of the EC Treaty should be interpreted in such a way that double taxation can be avoided. This may have some impact on the interpretation and application of the fundamental freedoms.

Furthermore, it is worth mentioning that the ECJ seems to distinguish between the conclusion of tax treaties and the objective of abolishing double taxation. According to the wording of Art. 293 EC, Member States should enter into negotiations with each other. However, the ECJ interprets this provision in a broader way by referring to the objective of abolishing double taxation as such, not necessarily by means of concluding a treaty. Therefore, the ECJ is obviously not of the opinion that avoiding double taxation is reserved to tax treaties.[2] While an obligation to abolish double taxation may not be derived from Art. 293 EC, the ECJ does not rule out that the abolition of double taxation may be required in certain circumstances under other provisions of the treaty.

Since Art. 293 EC emphasizes the role of the "Member States", some authors have drawn the conclusion that taking measures to avoid double taxation is reserved to the Member States. However, the wording of Art. 293 EC does not support this opinion: Art. 293 EC mentions the obligations of Member States to "enter into negotiations", but in no way prevents the EC from also taking measures to avoid double taxation.[3] Furthermore, the ECJ has mentioned repeatedly that the Member States could take such measures "in the absence of Community measures".[4] It should not be forgotten that the Community has already taken action in this field: The Parent-Subsidiary Directive is a perfect example of a Community measure that intends to avoid double taxation. Nobody has ever argued that these directives infringe Art. 293 EC.

Obligation to avoid Double Taxation under the Freedoms?

The *Schumacker* case is a well-known ECJ decision for several reasons.[5] One reason is closely related to the objective of avoiding double taxation: Mr. Schumacker was a resident of Belgium and was an employee in Germany, where he received all his income. The tax treaty between Germany and Belgium provided for the exemption method as far as employment income was concerned. Therefore, Belgium could not levy any taxes. It was thus not in a position to take into account Mr. Schumacker's personal and family circumstances. In Germany, on the other hand, Mr. Schumacker was treated as a non-resident and therefore was treated differently compared to resident taxpayers: He and his wife did not qualify for the tax benefit of "splitting" that married couples who are residents usually enjoy and he was not entitled to deduct his social security expenses (premiums in respect of old age, sickness or invalidity insurance).

The ECJ viewed this situation as discrimination: "In the case of a non-resident who receives the major part of his income and almost all his family income in a Member State other than his residence, discrimination arises from the fact that his personal and family circumstances are taken into account neither in the State of residence nor in the State of employment."[6] It is worth mentioning that the ECJ does not think that the discrimination arises exclusively from the fact that Mr. Schumacker was not treated in the state of employment in the same way as resident taxpayers even though he was in the same position. For the ECJ it is crucial that Mr. Schumacker could take his personal and family circumstances into account neither in the State of residence nor in the State of employment. As Advocate General Léger has pointed out, "overtaxation" would arise if the personal and family circumstances are nowhere taken into account.[7] The ECJ concluded that the fundamental freedoms require that the personal and family circumstances have to be taken into account in one Member State, either in the State of residence or in the State of source, or even to a certain extent here and to a certain extent there.[8]

The Advocate General's Opinion and the ECJ's judgment are very interesting because not allowing deductions in either state and taxing income in both states are two sides of the same coin. The Advocate General has expressed this idea by describing a situation in which allowances are nowhere taken into account as "overtaxation". Therefore, one could infer from this decision that the fundamental freedoms require the avoidance of "overtaxation" by allocating the taxation rights for every type of income to one of the Member States. This would mean that the fundamental freedoms require the Member States to avoid double taxation.

However, one has to be very careful about deriving such far-reaching conclusions from the *Schumacker* judgment and some other more recent decisions that are in the same line.[9] They all deal with personal and family circumstances or social and similar expenses. The ECJ only requires the avoidance of "overtaxation" in this area, but not in general.[10] Even with respect to personal and family circumstances or social expenses, the ECJ has been heavily criticized for taking this position.[11] The ECJ does not give convincing reasons for assuming an obligation to take into account personal and family circumstances in one of the Member States. The ECJ refers to the OECD Model Convention but seems to have misunderstood its provisions:[12] The Court expressly mentions Art. 24 para. 3 OECD Model Convention.[13] The first sentence of this provision states that "the taxation on a permanent establishment which an enterprise of a Contracting State has in the other Contracting State shall not be less favorably levied in that other State than the taxation levied on enterprises of that other State carrying on the same activities." The second sentence makes clear where the scope of this provision ends: "This provision shall not construed as obliging a Contracting State to grant to residents of other Contracting States any personal allowances, reliefs and deductions for tax purposes on account of civil status or family responsibilities which it grants to its own residents." However, the second sentence of Art. 24 para. 3 OECD Model Convention in no way obliges the State of residence to grant those allowances, reliefs and deductions. The State of residence is completely free not to allow any deductions at all, if e.g. this State prefers to have a flat tax rate system with a broad tax base, which does not allow any deductions.

It is true that it is difficult to find arguments why the *Schumacker* case law is restricted to personal and family circumstances. It would be consistent to also apply these ideas to other deductions and all types of income in general. This would lead to the exact result that double taxation has to be avoided in general. However, it is much harder to argue that there is a legal basis for the *Schumacker* case law at all:[14] It is clear that double taxation is an impediment to the internal market. However, one must not forget that double taxation arises because of measures taken by two different countries. Since it is not possible to blame one single country for a situation of double taxation, it is very difficult to argue that a certain country is responsible for eliminating double taxation. There is no logical reason for making either the source state or the residence state responsible.

It is true that in social security law similar problems arise. However, according to the basic principles of social security law, contributions to a system and benefiting from a system are more or less closely linked. This idea gives some guidance identifying one state that can be held responsible for avoidance of social security contributions in two (or more) countries. In tax law the benefit the taxpayer may get in return for the taxes paid is usually not at all linked to the levy. In a world of globalization it is very difficult or even impossible to link the taxes levied to the amount of publicly financed benefits one gets from different countries.

Of course, double taxation could be avoided if one can assume that under Community law the taxation rights of Member States are split among themselves on the basis of certain criteria. If e.g. either the person or the source of income has a kind of "genuine link" to a certain Member State, the other Member States could be prevented from levying taxes. Thus, principles of residence or territoriality could be guiding principles. However, ECJ case law does not support such an approach: In the *Gilly* case the Court held that it is up to the Member States to decide which connecting factors are relevant for the allocation of taxation rights. In the *van Hilten-van der Heijden* case Advocate General Léger and the ECJ went so far as to accept that a state which used to be the State of residence some years ago is still able to levy taxes on a worldwide basis on its former resident taxpayers.[15] It is true that at least the Advocate General assumed that it is the obligation of this state to avoid double taxation, in case such a state does go that far. However, the main reason for this assumption seems to be the fact that in the case of other taxpayers who are liable to worldwide taxation, double taxation would also be avoided under Dutch tax law. It is not certain that a Contracting State that goes so far as to levy world-wide taxation on non-residents has to provide for avoidance of double taxation. Interestingly enough, the ECJ itself did not mention such an obligation.

If one assumes that EC law requires the Member State to provide for the avoidance of double taxation in intra-Community cross-border situations, one would have to make clear what has to be understood by the term "double taxation". There are different types of juridical and economic double taxation. A certain type of double taxation can also arise in transfer pricing cases and whenever income is allocated to different taxpayers, e.g. in the case of CFCs, partnerships or group taxation systems. Taxing income both at the level of a corporation and a shareholder could even be viewed as double taxation. It seems to be very difficult to determine which situations of double taxation should be considered to conflict with the EC Treaty. It is therefore not surprising that AG Geelhoed has stated that there is no obligation to avoid double taxation:[16] "It is for this State to choose whether and how it wishes to provide such relief [...] – for example, by using an exemption or credit method."

These deliberations prove that there is room and even a need for tax treaties, if one wants to achieve the goal of avoidance of double taxation within the EU. One cannot infer from EC law, in its present status, that double taxation must be avoided or that tax treaties have to be concluded. Thus, Member States still have the liberty to decide whether they want to conclude tax treaties with each other. Although the network of tax treaties as far as income taxes are concerned is quite intense, there is room for much improvement in the field of inheritance and gift taxation. However, a different issue is whether a Member State that has already decided to conclude a tax treaty has to take into account requirements in respect of the contents of such a treaty.[17]

Most Favored Nation (MFN) Treatment

One of the possible substantive requirements for tax treaties has been discussed under the heading of "most-favored-nation treatment". The question is whether there is an obligation for a Member State to grant the same benefits it has granted to residents of a second Member State to residents of a third Member State as well. If this were the case, a state that has concluded a tax treaty which is less beneficial for a taxpayer, compared to another tax treaty it has concluded with another state, or a state that has not concluded a tax treaty at all with a certain state, but, however, has done so with other states, infringes EC law.[18] The direct applicability of the fundamental freedoms could lead to the result that this state would be obliged to extend the benefits of its most beneficial tax treaty provisions to taxpayers who are residents of all other Member States. Thus, within the EU the tax treaty network would be harmonized by a big bang, if the Court were to require MFN treatment.[19]

The ECJ has already had the opportunity to take a position on these issues in the *D.* case:[20] The *D.* case is on net wealth taxation and concerns a taxpayer who was a resident of Germany and who had all his taxable property in the Netherlands. If Mr. D. had been a Dutch resident, he would have been entitled to a special allowance, which would have been deducted from his Dutch tax base. Since he was a German resident, he was not entitled to this benefit. However, if he had been a resident of Belgium, he would have been treated in the same way as Dutch residents due to a specific provision in the tax treaty between Belgium and the Netherlands. Mr. D. was of the opinion that he should be treated in the same way as Belgian residents.

The ECJ ultimately did not grant most-favored-nation treatment in the *D.* case: The important part of the Court's reasoning was quite short:[21] "Similar treatment with regard to wealth tax in the Netherlands of a taxable person, such as Mr. D., resident in Germany and a taxable person resident in Belgium presupposes that those two taxable persons are regarded as being in the same situation. [...] It is to be remembered that, in order to avoid the same income and assets being taxed in both the Netherlands and Belgium, Article 24 of the Belgium-Netherlands Convention allocates powers of taxation between those two Member States and Article 25(3) lays down a rule under which natural persons resident in one of those two States is entitled in the other to the personal allowances which are granted by it to its own residents. [...] The fact that those reciprocal rights and obligations apply only to persons resident in one of the two Contracting Member States is an inherent consequence of bilateral double taxation conventions. It follows that a taxable person resident in Belgium is not in the same situation as a taxable person resident outside Belgium so far as concerns wealth tax on real property situated in the Netherlands."

The *D.* case is special. The provision referred to in the tax treaty between the Netherlands and Belgium does not allocate the taxation rights between the two countries. The object and purpose of this provision is to prevent discrimination. Therefore, it has been argued by some authors that this provision is not part of the very sensitive balance of a tax treaty.[22] If the ECJ had granted most-favored-nation treatment in this case, it would not mean that the Court would have to do that in all other cases.

However, the ECJ did not distinguish between tax treaty provisions that are part of this balance, and those that are not. Even the inclusion of non-discrimination clauses might have been more in the interest of one country than of the other. For agreeing to include such a provision this contracting partner may have asked for insertion of another provision more in its interest, and those two provisions do not have to be related at all, but only to the extent that both were part of the same bargaining process. To link non-related issues is often part of the political process. However, to prove that there is a link between two provisions is as difficult as to prove the opposite. In my view, it is impossible to establish such a link between two provisions. Therefore, it is convincing to me to not distinguish between different types of tax treaty provisions. In this respect, I share the ECJ's position.[23]

However, the ECJ's reasoning is less convincing as far as the Court's refusal to compare the situation of different taxpayers is concerned: The situation of a Belgian resident and a German resident in the Netherlands was considered not to be comparable because of the nature of a tax treaty. The Court acknowledged that reciprocity is the inherent consequence of a bilateral treaty. However, this did not prevent it from accepting the different treatment. In addition, the Court had already refused to accept the argument of reciprocity as a justification for different treatment in other cases. As a consequence of the ECJ's decision in the *D.* case, the legal status of a rule seems to make a difference: If a provision providing for a different treatment between non-residents is part of domestic law, it probably has to be justified. If the same provision is packaged in a bilateral treaty, there is no need for further justification. This result is surprising. However, it is not at all certain whether Member States are free to distinguish between non-residents in whatever way they want to: Under ECJ case law, the principle of proportionality also plays a role. Thus, Member States could be prevented from agreeing on completely different provisions in their tax treaties with different Member States.[24]

However, the ECJ seems to assume that EC law does not impose any limits on the Member States when they conclude a treaty. In its recent decision in the *ACT*

Group Litigation case the Court referred to the decision in the *D.* case and stated:[25] "In order to avoid distributed profits being taxed both by the Member State in which the distributing company is resident and by that of the company receiving them, each of the DTCs concluded by the United Kingdom provides for an allocation of taxing powers between that Member State and the other Contracting State. While some of those DTCs do not provide for dividends received by a non-resident company from a company resident in the United Kingdom to be subject to tax in that Member State, other DTCs do provide for such a liability to tax. It is in the latter case that the DTCs provide, each according to its separate conditions, for the grant of a tax credit to a non-resident company to which dividends are paid. As the United Kingdom Government, supported in that regard by most of the other Governments which submitted observations to the Court, observes, the terms under which the DTCs provide for a tax credit for non-resident companies which receive dividends from a resident company vary depending not only on the particular characteristics of the national tax regimes concerned, but also on when the DTCs were negotiated and the extent of the issues on which the Member States concerned managed to reach agreement. [...] Thus, the grant of a tax credit to a non-resident company receiving dividends from a resident company, as provided for under a number of DTCs concluded by the United Kingdom, cannot be regarded as a benefit separable from the remainder of those DTCs, but is an integral part of them and contributes to their overall balance (see, to that effect, D., paragraph 62). The same applies to the provisions of the DTCs which make the grant of such a tax credit subject to the condition that the non-resident company is not owned, directly or indirectly, by a company resident in a Member State or a non-member country with which the United Kingdom has concluded a DTC which does not provide for such a tax credit. Even where such provisions extend to the situation of a company which is not resident in one of the contracting Member States, they apply only to persons resident in one of those Member States and, by contributing to the overall balance of the DTCs in question, are an integral part of them. The fact that those reciprocal rights and obligations apply only to persons resident in one of the two contracting Member States is an inherent consequence of bilateral double taxation conventions. It follows, as regards the taxation of dividends paid by a company resident in the United Kingdom, that a company resident in a Member State which has concluded a DTC with the United Kingdom which does not provide for such a tax credit is not in the same situation as a company resident in a Member State which has concluded a DTC which does provide for one (see, to that effect, D., paragraph 61)."

Personal Scope of Tax Treaties

Another question is whether the personal scope of a tax treaty is broad enough to comply with EC law requirements. The landmark decision was the *Saint-Gobain* case.[26] Saint-Gobain was a French corporation that had – inter alia – a permanent establishment in Germany. Part of the business property of this permanent establishment was shares and bonds. Thus, Saint-Gobain received interest and dividend income from U.S., Swiss, Italian and Austrian sources through this German permanent establishment. According to general tax treaty principles, Saint-Gobain was not entitled to the benefits of the tax treaties Germany had concluded with these countries. The French corporation argued that it was discriminated against vis-à-vis a German corporation, which would benefit from the German tax treaty network.

The ECJ shared Saint-Gobain's position:[27] "In those circumstances, the refusal to grant the tax concessions in question to the permanent establishments in Germany of non-resident companies makes it less attractive for those companies to have intercorporate holdings through German branches, since under German law and double-taxation treaties the tax concessions in question can only be granted to German subsidiaries which, as legal persons, are subject to unlimited tax liability, which thus restricts the freedom to choose the most appropriate legal form for the pursuit of activities in another Member State, which the second sentence of the first paragraph of Article 52 of the Treaty [now Art 43 EC] expressly confers on economic operators. The difference in treatment to which branches of non-resident companies are subject in comparison with resident companies as well as the restriction of the freedom to choose the form of secondary establishment must be regarded as constituting a single composite infringement of Articles 52 and 58 of the Treaty [now Art. 43 and 48 EC].

The question which must be examined therefore is whether that difference in treatment may be justified in view of the provisions of the Treaty on freedom of establishment.

The German Government maintains that, as far as direct taxation is concerned, the situations of resident companies and of non-resident companies are not, as a general rule, comparable.

It argues that the permanent establishments of non-resident companies in Germany are in a situation which is objectively different from that of companies resident in Germany. Because of the income received through their branches in Germany and the assets held in those branches, non-resident companies are subject in Germany to limited tax liability whereas resident companies are subject in Germany to unlimited tax liability.

In response to that argument it must be stated that, as regards liability to tax on dividend receipts in Germany from shares in foreign subsidiaries and sub-subsidiaries and on the holding of those shares, companies not resident in Germany having a permanent establishment there and companies resident in Germany are in objectively comparable situations. First, the receipt of dividends in Germany is liable to tax there irrespective of whether the recipient is a resident company or a non-resident company, since the latter receives them through a permanent establishment located in Germany. Second, shareholdings in foreign subsidiaries and sub-subsidiaries in Germany are liable to tax there irrespective of whether they are held by a resident company or by a non-resident company, since the latter holds such shares in a permanent establishment located in Germany.

The situations of resident companies and of non-resident companies are made even more comparable by the fact that the difference in treatment applies only as regards the grant of the tax concessions in question, which allow resident companies either to deduct from corporation tax the amount of foreign tax levied on dividends from shareholdings in foreign companies or to exclude those dividends or holdings from their income and from their global assets which are taxable in

Germany. The refusal to grant those advantages to non-resident companies having a permanent establishment in Germany produces the result that their tax liability, theoretically limited to 'national' income and assets, comprises in actual fact dividends from foreign sources and shareholdings in foreign companies limited by shares. For the matters in question, the difference between limited tax liability and unlimited tax liability is certainly not relevant in so far as the global income and assets do not include dividends received from foreign companies or shareholdings in foreign companies, owing to the grant of the tax concessions in question, for which taxpayers subject to limited tax liability cannot qualify."

The ECJ also dealt with the question whether the specific nature of the tax treaties justified the different treatment:[28] "Finally, as justification for not allowing the tax concessions in question, the German Government maintains that the conclusion of bilateral treaties with a non-member country does not come within the sphere of Community competence. Taxation of income and profits falls within the competence of the Member States, which are therefore at liberty to conclude bilateral double-taxation treaties with non-member countries. In the absence of Community harmonisation in this area, the question whether, in the case of dividends, the tax exemption for international groups should be granted to permanent establishments under a tax treaty concluded with a non-member country is not governed by Community law. To extend to other situations the tax advantages provided for by treaties concluded with non-member countries would not be compatible with the division of competences under Community law.

The Swedish Government observes that double-taxation treaties are based on the principle of reciprocity and that the balance inherent in such treaties would be disturbed if the benefit of their provisions was extended to companies established in Member States which were not parties to them.

In this regard, it must be observed first of all that, in the absence of unifying or harmonising measures adopted in the Community, in particular under the second indent of Article 220 of the EC Treaty (now the second indent of Article 293 EC), the Member States remain competent to determine the criteria for taxation of income and wealth with a view to eliminating double taxation by means, inter alia, of international agreements. In this context, the Member States are at liberty, in the framework of bilateral agreements concluded in order to prevent double taxation, to determine the connecting factors for the purposes of allocating powers of taxation as between themselves (see, to this effect, Case C-336/96 Gilly [1998] ECR I-2793, paragraphs 24 and 30).

As far as the exercise of the power of taxation so allocated is concerned, the Member States nevertheless may not disregard Community rules. According to the settled case-law of the Court, although direct taxation is a matter for the Member States, they must nevertheless exercise their taxation powers consistently with Community law (see ICI, cited above, paragraph 19, and the case-law cited there).

In the case of a double-taxation treaty concluded between a Member State and a non-member country, the national treatment principle requires the Member State which is party to the treaty to grant to permanent establishments of non-resident companies the advantages provided for by that treaty on the same conditions as those which apply to resident companies.

As the Advocate General points out in point 81 of his opinion, the obligations which Community law imposes on the Federal Republic of Germany do not affect in any way those resulting from its agreements with the United States of America and the Swiss Confederation. The balance and the reciprocity of the treaties concluded by the Federal Republic of Germany with those two countries would not be called into question by a unilateral extension, on the part of the Federal Republic of Germany, of the category of recipients in Germany of the tax advantage provided for by those treaties, in this case corporation tax relief for international groups, since such an extension would not in any way affect the rights of the non-member countries which are parties to the treaties and would not impose any new obligation on them."

Thus, the ECJ did attack a fundamental principle of tax treaty law, namely the requirement of being a resident of at least one of the two Contracting States in order to be entitled to the tax treaty benefits. On the other hand, one could also argue that EC law is not even necessary to arrive at this result. If the tax authorities had properly applied the permanent establishment non-discrimination clause enshrined in the tax treaty between France and Germany (which was drafted along the lines of Art. 24 para. 3 OECD Model Convention), Germany would have had to grant the benefits deriving from a tax treaty with other countries to Saint-Gobain as well through its German permanent establishment. In fact, some EU Member States have implemented the *Saint-Gobain* decision by changing their view on their tax treaties' non-discrimination clauses and, thereafter inferring from these provisions that tax treaty benefits provided by the tax treaty between the permanent establishment state and third countries have to be granted.

It is worth mentioning that the decision of the ECJ did not necessarily have the consequence that the tax treaty as such was not compatible with EC law.[29] Germany, the Member State where the permanent establishment was located, had to grant the same benefits to EU corporations with German permanent establishments for income attributed to such a p.e., as Germany does under a tax treaty. The ECJ decision therefore neither changed the contents of the tax treaties between Germany and those countries nor did it declare the tax treaty itself to be in conflict with EC law.

Therefore, it seems to be clear that EC law does not require the U.S. or Switzerland to grant benefits to French corporations with German p.e. income under the tax treaties the U.S. and Switzerland have concluded with Germany. ECJ decisions cannot be binding on third countries. However, on the lines of the ECJ's decision in *Open Skies*[30] one could argue that Member States are prohibited from concluding such a treaty that "acknowledges" (by not being covered under the treaty) that the Contracting State does not grant tax treaty benefits in such a situation. If they had concluded such a treaty, the legal basis of the infringement is not the domestic law of the Contracting State, which is not under control of the ECJ, but the treaty itself.

Furthermore, it is a different issue whether this is also true for Italy and Austria, both EU Member States. The ECJ was not asked to decide on the treatment by those countries in such a situation, and therefore has not decided yet. One could argue that Italy and Austria also have to treat German corporations and French corporations with German permanent establishments alike.[31] However, this only becomes practical if the tax treaties Italy and Austria have concluded with France and Germany provide for different withholding tax rates (to be precise: lower rates in the treaties with Germany), since it is beyond doubt that in any case Austria and Italy have to grant the benefits under their tax treaties with France.

Source Taxation

The ECJ has already had the opportunity to decide whether the allocation rules of a tax treaty were in accordance with the freedoms.[32] Mr. and Mrs. Gilly resided in France, near the German border. Mr. Gilly, a French national, taught in a State school in France. Mrs. Gilly, who was a German national having also acquired French nationality by marriage, taught in a State primary school in Germany, in the frontier area. The public-service remuneration received by Mrs. Gilly in Germany was taxed in Germany in accordance with Art. 14(1) of the Tax Treaty concluded between France and Germany, because she was a German national. That remuneration was also taxed in France under Art. 20(2)(a) of the Convention. However, under Art. 20(2)(a)(cc), the fact that it was taxed in Germany entitled her to a tax credit equal to the amount of the French tax on the relevant income. Mrs. Gilly felt she was discriminated against because her income, due to her German citizenship, was taxed in Germany and since the tax rates in Germany were higher than in France the tax credit she received in France did not match her complete tax burden in Germany. Therefore, her overall tax burden was as high as the tax burden in Germany. If she had not been a national of Germany, her income would have been taxed in France and not in Germany. The tax burden would have been lower. Due to her German nationality she had to pay more taxes. Therefore, she argued that she was discriminated against on grounds of nationality.

The ECJ decided otherwise:[33] "Although the criterion of nationality appears as such in the second sentence of Article 14(1) for the purpose of allocation of fiscal jurisdiction, such differentiation cannot be regarded as constituting discrimination prohibited under Article 48 of the Treaty. It flows, in the absence of any unifying or harmonising measures adopted in the Community context under, in particular, the second indent of Article 220 of the Treaty, from the contracting parties' competence to define the criteria for allocating their powers of taxation as between themselves, with a view to eliminating double taxation.

Nor, in the allocation of fiscal jurisdiction, is it unreasonable for the Member States to base their agreements on international practice and the model convention drawn up by the OECD, Article 19(1)(a) of the 1994 version of which in particular provides for recourse to the paying State principle. According to the commentary on that article, that principle is justified by 'the rules of international courtesy and mutual respect between sovereign States' and 'is contained in so many of the existing conventions between OECD member countries that it can be said to be already internationally accepted'.

In the present case, the first sentence of Article 14(1) of the Convention reproduces the tenor of Article 19(1)(a) of the OECD model convention. It is true that under the second sentence the paying State principle is abandoned where the taxpayer has the nationality of the other Contracting State without being at the same time a national of the first State, but the same type of exception, based at least in part on the criterion of nationality, is found in Article 19(1)(b) of the model convention in cases where the services are rendered in the other Contracting State and the taxpayer is a resident of that State who '(i) is a national of that State; or (ii) did not become a resident of that State solely for the purpose of rendering the services'. [...]

Nor is it established in the present case that the choice of the paying State as the State competent to tax income earned in the public sector can of itself be to the disadvantage of the taxpayers concerned. As has been pointed out by the governments of the Member States which have submitted observations and by the Commission, whether the tax treatment of the taxpayers concerned is favorable or unfavorable is determined not, strictly speaking, by the choice of the connecting factor but by the level of taxation in the competent State, in the absence of any Community harmonisation of scales of direct taxation." Therefore "Article 48 of the Treaty does not preclude the application of provisions such as those in Articles 13(5)(a), 14(1) and 16 of the Convention, under which the tax regime applicable to frontier workers differs depending on whether they work in the private sector or the public sector and, where they work in the public sector, on whether or not they have only the nationality of the State of the authority employing them, and the regime applicable to teachers differs depending on whether their residence in the State in which they are teaching is for a short period or not".

The ECJ emphasizes that the tax treaty between Germany and France is drafted along the lines of the OECD Model Convention. Although it merely cites the OECD Commentary in which it is stated that the paying-state principle is internationally accepted, one gets the impression that the ECJ shares this view. However, the Court goes on to hold that it is up to the Contracting States to decide what the "connecting factors" are to allocate the taxation rights between them. Obviously, even if the "connecting factor" in a bilateral tax treaty were to deviate from the OECD Model Convention, this would not constitute discrimination. The ECJ allows the Contracting States to allocate the taxation rights in which ever way they want.[34]

The *Gilly* judgment has been viewed as very disappointing by many authors. Some scholars had hoped that the ECJ would take the opportunity to develop some guidelines on how tax treaties should be construed within a Common Market. In my view, it is not only the connecting factors that cause a problem. Even more questionable is the way the tax treaties distinguish between different allocation rules that are based on different "connecting factors". For example, sometimes it is difficult to draw a borderline between artistic activities and other independent activities. However, the connecting factors are very different. In other cases it may not be difficult to identify the borderline, but it is very difficult to justify why there are different connecting factors for quite comparable situations. The taxation of public servants was the issue in the *Gilly* case: Is it really justified to allocate taxation rights for teachers in public schools differently than for teachers in private schools? Is it justified to allocate the taxation rights for their pensions to different countries?[35] Doubts can be raised whether it is in accordance with EC law to allocate taxation rights on the income of taxpayers who are in a rather comparable situation so differently.

Tax treaties quite often provide for taxation rights for Source States on a gross basis. Under the OECD Model this is the case with regard to dividends and interest; many tax treaties allow the Source Country to levy a withholding tax for royalties on a gross basis as well. However, taxing non-residents on a gross basis may constitute an infringement of the freedoms. Under the *Gerritse* and *Scorpio* case law the tax base of non-residents may not be less favorable compared to residents. However, if the tax base is calculated on a gross amount, expenses are not deducted. Furthermore, if taxes are levied on a gross basis, a flat tax rate, instead of a progressive tax rate, is provided for as well. Each of these factors could lead to disadvantages for non-residents in certain situations.[36] This does not, maybe with the possible exception of third-country relations,[37] necessarily mean that a tax treaty allowing the levy of a withholding tax that is calculated on a gross basis constitutes an infringement of EC law. However, a Member State would not be able to exercise the taxation right provided for in the tax treaty. Therefore, it would not make sense to agree on such a provision in a tax treaty.

Residence Taxation

The discussion on most-favored-nation treatment focuses on the tax rules for the Source State. However, there is no reason not to raise the same issue in the State of residence.[38] The State of residence usually takes care of the avoidance of double taxation and there are two different ways to do this, either by granting a tax credit or by exempting the foreign income. Some countries prefer, for historic or economic reasons, the credit method; others, the exemption method. Many countries combine both methods in their tax treaty system by applying the credit method for some types of income and the exemption method for other types.

The Court has never explicitly been asked to decide on the conformity of these two methods with European law, but seems to be quite relaxed about both of them. The Court has already decided a lot of cases where one of the two or both of them had to be applied and has never indicated that it sees a problem. However, some authors have argued that the credit method has compensatory effects and hinders equal access to national markets of other EU Member States:[39] If the tax burden in the State of residence is higher, the overall tax burden of such a taxpayer is higher, compared to the tax burden of a resident of that country where the economic activity takes place. On the other hand, the exemption method could also be seen as a restriction for residents of other EU Member States in getting access to the domestic market of another EU Member State: If the tax burden in the Source State is higher than in the Residence State, the overall tax burden of such a taxpayer is higher compared to the tax burden of a resident of the same Member State who is engaged in purely domestic activities.[40] Furthermore, the exemption method could also be attacked on grounds of state aid rules, since this method accepts double non-taxation where the Source Country does not levy any tax.

However, if we assume that there are good reasons to believe that both methods are in principle in accordance with European law, there are still doubts as to how to evaluate the tax treaty of a country that for the same type of income has agreed on the exemption method with one Member State, and on the credit method with another Member State. In my view, these situations are rather comparable and I cannot see any reason why resident taxpayers that run a business through a permanent establishment in Member State A could be treated differently by their own residence state vis-à-vis resident taxpayers with a permanent establishment in Member State B. Even if one takes the view that tax treaty provisions that are part of a coherent balance of a certain tax treaty should not be viewed under most-favored-nation treatment aspects,[41] the problem cannot be ignored in such a situation: According to many tax treaties, the methods differ within the treaty, depending on which Contracting State is the State of residence in the individual situation. They provide e.g. for the credit method for State A's residents and for the exemption method for State B's residents. Although the methods to avoid double taxation are usually governed by the tax treaty, during tax treaty negotiations states seem to leave it up to themselves to decide which method each state wants to apply for its own residents. Thus, there are good reasons to believe that EU Member States have to be consistent in the way they avoid double taxation for their residents.

Third-Country Relations

So far we have exclusively dealt with intra-Community relations. In general, the application of the freedoms requires the existence of an intra-Community cross-border situation. However, this is only true for the freedom of establishment, the freedom to provide services and the free movement of workers and for the non-discrimination clauses of Arts. 12 and 18 EC. As far as the free movement of capital and payments is concerned, the situation is different. The wording of the provision does not give any indication that its application is restricted to intra-Community situations. According to prevailing opinion, the free movement of capital and payments has also to be applied in relation to non-Member States. There are examples in ECJ case law, although not yet in the field of tax law, that the Court does not hesitate to apply the free movement of capital and payments provision in relation to third countries in the same way it applies these provisions to Member States, and does not even find it necessary to give a special reason for this.[42] However, there are more and more tax cases pending before the ECJ in which the free movement of capital and payments was invoked and where third-country relations are at stake.[43] Therefore, scholars and practitioners all around Europe are interested in seeing whether the Court will apply the same standards it has developed for intra-Community situations.

Uncertainties in the application of the free movement of capital and payments in relation to third countries arise because it is not at all clear what the objective behind the liberalization of capital movements towards third countries is. Scholars suggest that the purpose cannot be as far-reaching as that which lies behind the provisions on the free movement of capital within the EU.[44] Within the EU the freedoms serve the purpose of establishing an internal market and an economic and monetary union. In relation to third countries it is different. It has been pointed out that the liberalization of the free movement of capital towards third countries is unilateral. There is no guarantee at all that the countries outside the EU will carry out a corresponding liberalization of capital movements to and from the EU countries.

The ECJ may find different ways to develop a different standard in relation to third countries.[45] The Court could examine whether taxpayers who are in a domestic situation or in a cross-border intra-Community situation and taxpayers who are in a cross-border situation with a third country are really in a comparable situation as far as direct taxation is concerned.[46] Even if the ECJ agreed that this is the case, it is not at all clear whether the Court will reject possible justifications for different treatment in the same way as it does when it decides on an intra-Community cross-border situation.[47] It could be the case that the Court puts more weight on the danger of tax avoidance, the lack of fiscal supervision or the loss of revenues in such situations. Quite often the Court has rejected in particular the lack of fiscal supervision as a justification due to the existence of the Mutual Assistance Directive. However, this Directive is only applicable within EU Member States. In relation to third countries the tax authorities may, if at all, only apply the exchange of information provisions of their tax treaty network. In many cases they do not provide for the same standard of cooperation as the Mutual Assistance Directive does, or at least, should. Furthermore, the legal quality of exchange of information provisions, on the one hand, and the Mutual Assistance Directive, on the other hand, are different, since the application of the exchange of information provision is usually not under the control of the Court.[48]

However, it would not be wise to completely rule out the application of the freedom of capital and payments to third-country relations altogether. There is no doubt that this freedom is applicable in third-country relations. The question is whether the Court will apply the same standards it has developed for intra-Community relations. However, even if the Court does apply different standards, it will not exclude third-country relations altogether. The principle of proportionality will be relevant.[49] Therefore, Member States should be prepared to have to provide a justification when they deviate in their treaty relations towards third countries from the treaty policy they have adopted for intra-Community relations.

Although the scope of the other freedoms does not directly cover third-country relations, treaties with third countries could be taken into account when assessing whether tax treaties between Member States fulfill all the requirements imposed by ECJ case law.[50] In case a Member State applies a rule towards a third country that is a very beneficial one and is not prepared to grant the same benefits to residents of other EU Member States or to apply it on income sourced in other EU Member States, this Member State may have difficulties when it tries to invoke justifications for this treatment within the EU. One could argue that such a Member State has waived the cohesion of its own tax law or its tax treaty policy by granting those benefits in third-country relations.

The example of withholding taxes could serve as an illustration. If a Member State levies, in accordance with a bilateral treaty, higher withholding taxes in relation to EU Member States than to non-Member States, this might be considered as not giving access to the market to citizens of other Member States. In case the Member State tries to defend the levy of the higher withholding tax and presents a justification for doing so, it will at the same time be necessary to give reasons why the situation is different in relation to third countries.

8.3 Room for Domestic Tax Policy under Tax Treaty Law

OECD Model Convention as Soft Law

Tax treaties are both part of international law and of domestic law. Since they are part of domestic law as well, one could raise the question whether it makes sense to distinguish between domestic tax policy, on the one hand, and tax treaty policy, on the other hand. If tax treaties are part of domestic law, tax treaty policy is part of domestic tax policy as well. No EU Member State is obliged to conclude a tax treaty that is not in line with its tax policy.

However, although Member States are free to conclude a tax treaty or not, the conclusion of a tax treaty requires the consent of the other Contracting State. Therefore, it is difficult for a State to implement all its policy goals in a tax treaty. If a State takes the position that it will not conclude a tax treaty with another State unless all of its policy goals are implemented, this State has to have adequate negotiation power or it will not conclude many tax treaties.

In international practice the OECD Model Convention has a lot of relevance. Although many countries have developed their own tax treaty model as a starting point for tax treaty negotiations, these models do not deviate a lot from the OECD Model Convention, especially as far as EU Member States are concerned. States that want to insert provisions in a tax treaty that deviate from the OECD Model Convention usually have to give a reason for this when explaining their position to the tax treaty partner. In contrast, there is usually no need to give an explanation if a State tries to agree on tax treaty provisions that are in line with the OECD Model Convention. Therefore, States usually consider very carefully whether they want to deviate from the OECD Model Convention. They have to expect that their negotiation partner will demand the inclusion of other provisions as a "price" for allowing a certain deviation from the OECD Model Convention.

For that reason the substance of the OECD Model Convention determines the tax treaty policy of EU Member States to a great extent. It would be unrealistic to take a formal approach by exclusively referring to the requirement that domestic legislation has to approve every tax treaty and a Member State is therefore free to determine completely the content of a tax treaty. On the contrary, States have to pay a rather high "price" if they want to deviate from the OECD Model Convention.

Taxation of Residents

As far as a State is in the position of a Residence State, however, tax treaties have relatively little impact on domestic tax policy. A State that levies residence taxation on a worldwide basis may protect its taxation rights by applying the credit method in its tax treaties. There are disadvantages to this method, especially for businesses that want to compete in the other Contracting State with corporations that are residents of that State on an equal footing., but, nevertheless, a State is relatively free to decide on the method to avoid double taxation in a tax treaty: The OECD Model Convention offers both, the credit and the exemption method, and the other Contracting State usually accepts that its tax treaty partner has a preference for a certain method it wants to apply for its own residents, as long as this State accepts that the Contracting State has a certain policy as far as methods are concerned as well.

However, a State that prefers to insert the exemption method in its tax treaties, limits its domestic tax policy to a higher extent: If their resident taxpayers want to escape residence taxation, they can transfer many of their sources of income to the other Contracting State by, e.g. creating a permanent establishment there, as far as business income is concerned. This might cause problems for a Residence State that wants to increase the tax burden of its resident taxpayers. It is a very time-consuming effort to revise tax treaties since such an exercise usually requires the consent of the tax treaty partner unless this State terminates a tax treaty. Termination is unrealistic as well, since there will be a "price" for this consent to be paid to the other Contracting State. The alternative would be to ignore tax treaty obligations by creating a "treaty override". However, this would not only constitute a breach of international law, but undermine the international credibility of this State both in the eyes of other States and of potential investors.

Taxation of Non-Residents

However, the taxation of non-residents is much more influenced by tax treaty provisions. This can be illustrated by the example of business income. Under the OECD Model Convention Source States may only levy taxes if there is a permanent establishment. Therefore, countries that provide for source taxation on advisory or consulting activities usually have no possibility to apply these provisions in relation to a Contracting State. However, in tax treaties with less developed countries the extension of taxation rights to these type of activities is sometimes accepted, but this does not happen in relation to other EU Member States or economically powerful third countries.

A current problem in many countries concerns Art. 18 OECD Model Convention.[51] Under this provision the State of residence has the exclusive taxation rights for pensions. For countries that tax pensions at the time when the money is paid to the recipient, this provision causes problems if the State where the activity is performed and the Residence State are different States: Contributions to pension schemes are very often deductible. The consequence is that the contribution to the pension scheme reduces the tax base in the State where the activity is performed, while the other Contracting State may levy the tax once the pension is paid. More and more often countries try to insert provisions in their tax treaty network that provide for source taxation for pensions, but, however, it is difficult for them to persuade the Contracting State to accept this. Thus, if States do not want to waive their taxation right, they have no choice but to levy taxes on pensions at an earlier stage, by not allowing the deduction of the contribution to the pension scheme.

Another example is withholding taxes. Under tax treaty law, there is room for withholding taxes as far as the artistes and athletes are concerned, since the Source State may tax their income according to Art. 17 OECD Model Convention. However, in the case of business income without a permanent establishment in the

Source State, withholding taxes would not be very effective, since they have to be reimbursed to the taxpayer.

As far as dividends and interest, and very often royalties as well, are concerned, tax treaties allow the Source State to levy a withholding tax. Although the rate of the withholding tax often differs from treaty to treaty and deviates from the OECD Model Convention, it is only the exception that the rate is higher than 15%. Therefore, higher withholding taxes cannot be levied in relation to Contracting States.

Avoiding Double Non-Taxation

However, sometimes States may be interested in providing for taxation despite the fact they cannot levy the tax due to a tax treaty. The reason for that is that these Source States want to prevent a situation from arising where no tax might be levied in one State due to the tax treaty, and no tax is levied in the other State due to the fact that the income is not declared by the taxpayer. If the first-mentioned State wants to encourage the taxpayer to declare the income in the other State, this State could do so by establishing a tax obligation under its domestic law and providing for relief only if the taxpayer presents a certificate of residence, issued by the tax authority of the other State. If the taxpayer asks his Residence State to issue such a certificate, the tax authorities of the Residence State will suspect that the taxpayer is receiving income from the other State. Thus, the taxpayer will be motivated to declare his income there.

However, the avoidance of double non-taxation is only prevented in such a situation if the Residence State exercises the taxation right that is allocated to this State under the tax treaty. If the Residence State does not levy taxes on this income under its domestic law, double non-taxation will be the result. If this result is not in line with the policy goals of the two States, they have to include a subject-to-tax-clause in the treaty.[52]

"Built-in" Sacrifices to Get a Treaty

There is another situation as well where there is a temptation for, at least, the Source State to establish tax obligation under its domestic law that cannot be exercised in relation to tax treaty partners: If one State is interested in negotiating a tax treaty, but, however, fears that the conclusion of a tax treaty is not in the interest of the other Contracting State, such a policy would make it attractive for the first-mentioned State to conclude a tax treaty. If the Source State creates tax liability under its domestic law only for situations where this State is not prevented from levying the tax under the scope of a tax treaty, the other State might feel that there is no advantage for it if a tax treaty becomes applicable.

Thus, the existence of tax treaties might lead to a domestic tax policy under which a State might even create a tax liability in order to get a tax treaty that it would not have created otherwise. This is a kind of paradox: Tax treaties could lead both to a domestic tax policy where tax liability is reduced and where it is enlarged as well.

8.4 Concluding Remarks on the Tax Treaty Policy

There is interaction both, between European law and tax treaty policy, on the one hand, and tax treaty policy and domestic tax policy, on the other hand. ECJ case law has started to have a lot of impact on the tax treaty policy of the Member States. Still, the OECD Model Convention plays an important role. Thus, many tax treaties follow the OECD Model Convention and in reality it is difficult for the States to deviate from the OECD Model Convention. Tax treaties can both lead to the result that countries do not establish tax liability for situations where they do not have taxation rights under a treaty, or that they establish an extended tax liability merely to ensure that the taxpayer has to declare his income in his State of residence or that one State creates an incentive for the other State to start treaty negotiations.

Endnotes

1. ECJ 12 May 1998, C-336/96, *Gilly*, [1998] ECR I-2793, paras. 15 and 16.
2. See e.g. ECJ 12 December 2006, C-374/04, *Test Claimants in Class IV of the ACT Group Litigation*, paras. 51 et seq. with references to further case law of the ECJ.
3. See, in detail, Hofstätter, in: Lang/Schuch/Staringer, eds., *Tax Treaty Law and EC Law*, Vienna 2007, 29 et seq.
4. In this sense e.g. ECJ 12 May 1998, C-336/96, *Gilly*, paras. 23 et seq. and 30; ECJ 21 September 1999, C-307/97, *Saint-Gobain*, [1999] ECR I-6161, para. 56; ECJ 7 September 2006, C-470/04, *N*, para. 44; ECJ 12 December 2006, C-374/04, *Test Claimants in Class IV of the ACT Group Litigation*, paras. 51 and 52.
5. ECJ 14 February 1995, C- 279/93, *Schumacker,* [1995] ECR I-225.
6. ECJ 14 February 1995, C- 279/93, *Schumacker*, [1995] ECR I-225, para. 38.
7. Advocate General Léger, 22 November 1994, C-279/93, *Schumacker*, point 67.
8. ECJ 14 February 1995, C-279/93, *Schumacker*, para. 38; ECJ 11 August 1995, C-80/94, *Wielockx*, [1995] ECR I-2493, para. 21; ECJ 12 December 2002, C-385/00, *de Groot*, [2002] ECR I-11819, paras. 99 et seq.; ECJ 1 July 2004, C-169/03, *Wallentin*, [2004] ECR I-6443, para. 17; Advocate General Léger, 1 March 2005, C-152/03, *Ritter-Coulais*, point 84.
9. ECJ 14 February 1995, C-279/93, *Schumacker*, para. 38; ECJ 11 August 1995, C-80/94, *Wielockx*, [1995] ECR I-2493, para. 21; ECJ 12 December 2002, C-385/00, *de Groot*, [2002] ECR I-11819, paras. 99 et seq.; ECJ 1 July 2004, C-169/03, *Wallentin*, [2004] ECR I-6443, para. 17; Advocate General Léger, 1 March 2005, C-152/03, *Ritter-Coulais*, point 84.
10. See particularly ECJ 14 November 2006, C-513/04, *Kerckhaert and Morres*, paras. 20 et seq.
11. See e.g. Cordewener, *Europäische Grundfreiheiten und nationales Steuerrecht* (2002), 888 et seq.; Lüdicke, in: Schön, ed., *GS Knobbe-Keuk,* Cologne 1997, 651 et seq.; Wattel, *European Taxation* 2000, 210 et seq.; Lang, *Recht der Internationalen Wirtschaft* 2005, 336 et seq.
12. ECJ 14 February 1995, C-279/93, *Schumacker*, para. 32.
13. ECJ 14 February 1995, C-279/93, *Schumacker*, para. 32; explicitly referring to Art. 24 para. 3 OECD Model Convention, Advocate General Léger, 22 November 1994, C-279/93, *Schumacker*, paras. 59 et seq.

14. See in more detail, Lang, *Recht der Internationalen Wirtschaft* 2005, 336 et seq.
15. Advocate General Léger, 30 June 2005, C-513/03, *van Hilten-van der Heijden*; ECJ 23 February 2006, C-513/03 *van Hilten-van der Heijden*, [2006] ECR I-1957; see e.g. Hohenwarter/Plansky, *Steuer & Wirtschaft International* 2005, 417 et seq.
16. Advocate General Geelhoed, 6 April 2006, C-513/04, *Kerckhaert and Morres*, point 33; affirmative ECJ 14 November 2006, C-513/04, *Kerckhaert and Morres*, paras. 19 et seq.
17. See e.g. Lang, in: Gassner/Lang/Lechner, eds., *Tax Treaties and EC Law*, London 1997, 20 et seq.
18. See e.g. Cordewener, in: Cordewener/Enchelmaier/Schindler, eds, *Meistbegünstigung im Steuerrecht der EU-Staaten,* München 2006, 123 et seq.; Kofler, *Houston Business and Tax Law Journal* 2005, 31 et seq.
19. See e.g. Schuch, in: Gassner/Lang/Lechner, eds., *Tax Treaties and EC Law*, London 1997, 119 et seq.
20. ECJ 5 July 2005, C-376/03, *D.*, [2005] ECR I-5821.
21. ECJ 5 July 2005, C-376/03, *D.*, [2005] ECR I-5821, paras. 59-61.
22. See Van der Linde, *EC Tax Review* 2004, 16; Van Thiel, *Intertax* 2005, 456; Kofler, *Österreichische Steuerzeitung* 2005, 436 et seq.; in this direction also Advocate General Colomer, 26 October 2004, C-376/03, *D.*, point 82.
23. See Lang, *Steuer & Wirtschaft International* 2005, 370.
24. See Lang, *Steuer & Wirtschaft International* 2005, 370 et seq.; Lang/Dommes, in: Lang/Schuch/Staringer, eds., *Tax Treaty Law and EC Law*, Vienna 2007, 73 et seq. with further references.
25. ECJ 12 December 2006, C-374/04, *Test Claimants in Class IV of the ACT Group Litigation*, paras. 85 et seq.
26. ECJ 21 September 1999, C-307/97, *Saint-Gobain.*
27. ECJ 21 September 1999, C-307/97, *Saint-Gobain*, paras. 42 to 48.
28. ECJ 21 September 1999, C-307/97, *Saint-Gobain*, paras. 54 to 59.
29. Other opinion: Pistone, *EC Tax Review* 2005, 9.
30. ECJ 5 November 2002, C-466/98, *Commission/United Kingdom*, [2002] ECR I-9427; ECJ 5 November 2002, C-467/98, *Commission/Denmark,* [2002] ECR I-9519; ECJ 5 November 2002, C-468/98, *Commission/Sweden*, [2002] ECR I-9575; ECJ 5 November 2002, C-469/98, *Commission/Finland*, [2002] ECR I-9627; ECJ 5 November 2002, C-471/98, *Commission/Belgium*, [2002] ECR I-9681; ECJ 5 November 2002, C-472/98, *Commission/Luxembourg*, [2002] ECR I-9741; ECJ 5 November 2002, C-475/98, *Commission/Austria*, [2002] ECR I-9797; ECJ 5 November 2002, C-476/98, *Commission/Germany*, [2002] ECR I-9855; better known as the "*Open Skies*" cases.
31. See e.g. Langoth, in: Sutter/Zehetner, eds., *Triangular Tax Cases*, Vienna 2004, 39 et seq.
32. ECJ 12 May 1998, C-336/96, *Gilly.*
33. ECJ 12 May 1998, C-336/96, *Gilly,* paras. 30 to 35.
34. See Hohenwarter, in: Lang/Schuch/Staringer, eds., *Tax Treaty Law and EC Law*, Vienna 2007, 102 et seq.
35. See, in more detail, Lang, in: Gutmann, ed., *Regards Critiques et Perspectives sur le Droit et la Fiscalité – Liber Amicorum Cyrille David,* Paris 2005, 230 et seq.
36. ECJ 12 June 2003, C-234/01, *Gerritse*, [2003] ECR I-5933; ECJ 3 October 2006, C-290/04, *FKP Scorpio Konzertproduktionen GmbH*; see e.g. Lang, *Steuer & Wirtschaft International* 2006, 22 et seq.; also Hohenwarter, *Recht der Wirtschaft* 2006, 783 et seq.
37. Fur further details see Lang, in: Simonart/Remiche/de Cordt, eds., *Liber Amicorum Jacques Malherbe,* Brussels 2006, 696 et seq.

38. See e.g. Cordewener, in: Cordewener/Enchelmaier/Schindler, eds., *Meistbegünstigung im Steuerrecht der EU Staaten*, Munich 2006, 140 et seq.
39. Pistone, *EC Tax Review* 2005, 5.
40. See e.g. Hey, *Steuer und Wirtschaft* 2004, 201.
41. See Van der Linde, *EC Tax Review* 2004, 16.
42. See in detail Ståhl, *EC Tax Review* 2004, 51 with further references.
43. See e.g Hohenwarter, *Steuer & Wirtschaft International* 2005, 226 et seq.; in: Lang/Schuch/Staringer, eds., *Tax Treaty Law and EC Law*, Vienna 2007, 302 et seq. with further references.
44. See Ståhl, *EC Tax Review* 2004, 51.
45. Pointing in this direction ECJ 12 December 2006, C-446/04, *Test Claimants in the FII Group Litigation*, para. 171.
46. See e.g. Schön, in: Gocke/Gosch/Lang, eds., *Körperschaftsteuer – Internationales Steuerrecht – Doppelbesteuerung, FS Wassermeyer*, Munich 2005, 511 et seq.; Lang, *Internationales Steuerrecht* 2005, 295 et seq.
47. In detail also Plansky, in: Lang/Schuch/Staringer, eds., *Tax Treaty Law and EC Law*, Vienna 2007, 312 et seq.
48. See Lang, *Internationales Steuerrecht* 2005, 296.
49. See e.g. Lang, *Internationales Steuerrecht* 2005, 295 et seq.
50. See Lang, *Internationales Steuerrecht* 2005, 296.
51. See Lang, in: Gutmann, ed., *Liber Amicorum in honor of Cyrille David*, Paris 2005, 227 et seq.
52. See in detail Schilcher, *Subject-to-tax-Klauseln in der österreichischen Abkommenspraxis*, Vienna 2004.

References

Cordewener, A. (2002) Europäische Grundfreiheiten und nationales Steuerrecht, Cologne: O. Schmidt.

Cordewener, A. (2006) EG-rechliche Meistbegünstigungspflicht im Steuerrecht: Aktuelle und potentielle Fallgestaltungen, in: Cordewener/Enchelmaier/Schindler (eds.), Meistbegünstigung im Steuerrecht der EU-Staaten, Munich: Beck.

Hey, J. (2004) Perspektiven der Unternehmensbesteuerung in Europa, Steuer und Wirtschaft, 193-211.

Hofstätter, M. (2007) Member States or Community Competence - Who is Competent to Issue Measures for the Elimination of Double Taxation within the Community?, in: Lang/Schuch/Staringer (eds.), Tax Treaty Law and EC Law, Vienna, in press.

Hohenwarter, D. and Plansky, P. (2005) Besteuerung von Erbschaften nach Wegzug in einen Drittstaat im Gemeinschaftsrecht – Schlussanträge des GA Léger in der Rs. van Hilten – van der Heijden, Steuer und Wirtschaft International, 417-425.

Hohenwarter, D. (2005) Vorlagebeschluss des VwGH zur Kapitalverkehrsfreiheit im Verhältnis zu Drittstaaten, Steuer und Wirtschaft International, 225-232.

Hohenwarter, D. (2006) Ende der Abzugssteuer bei beschränkter Steuerpflicht?, Recht der Wirtschaft, 783-787.

Hohenwarter, D. (2007) The Allocation of Taxing Rights in the light of the Fundamental Freedoms of EC Law, in: Lang/Schuch/Staringer (eds.), Tax Treaty Law and EC Law, Vienna, in press.

Kofler, G. (2005) Most-Favoured-Nation Treatment in Direct Taxation: Does EC Law Provide for Community MFN in Bilateral Double Taxation Treaties?, Houston Business and Tax Law Journal, 1-89.

Kofler, G. (2005) Das Ende vom Anfang der gemeinschaftsrechtlichen Meistbegünstigung, Österreichische Steuerzeitung, 432-438.

Lang, M. (1997) Double Taxation Treaties and EC Law, in: Gassner/Lang/Lechner (eds.), Tax Treaties and EC Law, London: Kluwer.

Lang, M. (2005) Ist die Schumacker-Rechtsprechung am Ende?, Recht der internationalen Wirtschaft, 336-344.

Lang, M. (2005) Public Sector Pensions and Tax Treaty Law, in: Gutmann (ed.), Regards Critiques et Perspectives sur le Droit et la Fiscalité- Liber amicorum in honour of Cyrille David, Paris: LGDJ.

Lang, M. (2005) Das EuGH-Urteil in der Rechtssache D. – Gerät der Motor der Steuerharmonisierung ins Stottern?, Steuer und Wirtschaft International, 365-375.

Lang, M. (2005) Wohin geht das Internationale Steuerrecht?, Internationales Steuerrecht, 289-297.

Lang, M. (2006) Triangular Situations: Tax Treaty Entitlement in the Source State under EC Law, in: Simonart/ Remiche/ de Cordt (eds.), Liber Amicorum Jacques Malherbe, Bruxelles: Bruylant.

Lang, M. and Dommes, S. (2007) Reciprocity and the Balance of a Tax Treaty, in: Lang/ Schuch/Staringer (eds.), Tax Treaty Law and EC Law, Vienna, in press.

Langoth, B. (2004) *Treaty Entitlement of Permanent Establishments*, in: Sutter/Zehetner (eds.), Triangular Tax Cases, Vienna: Linde.

Lüdicke, J. (1997) Die Besteuerung Nichtansässiger im Spannungsverhältnis zwischen Gemeinschaftsrecht und Doppelbesteuerungsabkommen, in: Schön (ed.), GS Knobbe-Keuk, Cologne: O. Schmidt.

Pistone, P. (2005) Towards European international tax law, *EC Tax Review,* 4-9.

Plansky, P. (2007) The impact of the fundamental freedoms on the tax treaties with third countries, in Lang/Schuch/Staringer (eds.), Tax Treaties and EC Law, Vienna, in press.

Schilcher, M. (2004) Subject-to-tax-Klauseln in der österreichischen Abkommenspraxis, Vienna: Linde.

Schön, W. (2005) Der Kapitalverkehr mit Drittstaaten und das internationale Steuerrecht, in: Gocke/Gosch/Lang (eds.), Körperschaftssteuer-Internationales Steuerrecht-Doppelbesteuerung, FS Wassermeyer, Munich: Beck.

Schuch, J. (1997) Will EC Law Transform Tax Treaties in Most-favoured-Nation Clauses?, in: Gassner/M. Lang/Lechner (eds.), Tax Treaties and EC Law, London: Kluwer.

Stahl, K. (2004) Free movement of capital between Member States and third countries, *EC Tax Review,* 47-56.

Van der Linde, R. (2004) Some thoughts on most-favoured-nation treatment within the European Community legal order in pursuance of the *D* case, *EC Tax Review,* 10-17.

Van Thiel, S. (2005) A Slip of the European Court in the D case (C-376/03): Denial of the Most-Favoured-Nation Treatment because of Absence of Similarity?, Intertax, 454-457.

Wattel, P. (2000) Progressive Taxation of Non-Residents and Intra-EC Allocation of Personal Tax Allowances: Why Schumacker, Asscher, Gilly and Gschwind Do Not Suffice, European Taxation, 210-223.

Chapter 9
National Tax Policy, the Directives and Hybrid Finance

Eva Eberhartinger and Martin Six

9.1 Introduction

The right of legislation in the area of taxation is part of the sovereign right of each Member State, providing that State with autonomy of decision-making as regards its tax policy measures. This autonomy, however, is restricted by EU law in three ways:

1. Member States are bound by the Four Freedoms,[1] and in the determination of those freedoms by the jurisdiction of the ECJ.[2]
2. Member States are subject to secondary EU Law in the form of regulations, directives and decisions.[3]
3. Member States are bound by the code of conduct for business taxation.[4]

The focus of this article rests on the effect of secondary EU Law, in the form of directives, on the autonomy of national tax policy in the Member States in the area of direct taxation. Up to now, directives have been a major tool used by the Council in bringing the national law of the Member States into line with the requirements of a common domestic market within the European Community.[5] Most of these directives contain very detailed provisions in order to achieve their intended goals.[6] Directives in the area of direct taxation, although few in number, are rather detailed and, thus, effectively constrain the Member States' autonomy in implementing tax policy. Nevertheless, apart from a wilful decision not to implement a directive, either in full or in part, some leeway remains for tax policy in the Member States in the course of the implementation of the directives.

It is the aim of this chapter to show that there is indeed room for tax policy in the Member States, taking the treatment of hybrid cross-border finance between associated companies as an example. We look at this in the context of the Parent-Subsidiary Directive (90/435/ECC) and the Interest and Royalties Directive (2003/49/EC). These directives have been chosen, because they are interrelated, very detailed and have been implemented by the majority of the Member States.[7]

From the standpoint of the taxation of hybrid financial instruments, these are the most relevant directives, as hybrid financial instruments combine elements of debt and equity, by definition.[8] This means that the Member States' classification of the relevant instrument as equity or as debt, respectively, for domestic tax purposes, defines the yield as a dividend or as an interest payment. This, in turn, may or may not fall within the scope of application of the Parent-Subsidiary Directive or of the Interest and Royalties Directive. Since these classification issues have immediate consequences for the total amount of income taxes levied by the Member States concerned, we regard them as a good example in showing what can still be done by the Member States despite the EU directives. We will, therefore, concentrate on the options remaining for policy makers in the Member States in the following analysis, and examine the application of the terms dividend, interest and holding in capital on hybrid instruments in the course of the implementation of the aforementioned directives.

The chapter is organized in the following way. Section 9.2 focuses on hybrid finance and the research question. Section 9.3 addresses the implementation of the directives into national law. In Sect. 9.4 the aim and scope of the Parent-subsidiary directive is discussed, whereas in Sect. 9.5 the focus is on the aim and scope of the Interest and royalty directive. Section 9.6 analyzes the role of hybrid finance in these two directives. Finally, concluding remarks are provided in Sect. 9.7.

9.2 Hybrid Finance - The Problem

The compartmentalisation of company finance into equity and debt does not truly capture the enormous diversity of financial securities available. A wide variety of financial instruments incorporate elements of both equity and liability.[9] Usually, these financial instruments cannot be clearly attributed to either equity or debt and are, therefore, referred to as "hybrid"-instruments or mezzanine finance. The spectrum of hybrid instruments ranges from corporate shares with features typical of loans (such as certain preference shares) to loans with features usually associated with equity investments (such as participation in profit and loss). Such equity-type loans would include *inter alia* jouissance rights, silent partnerships, participation bonds, convertible bonds, warrant bonds, profit participation loans and preference shares.

The classification of such instruments as equity or debt may or may not be of particular interest from an investor's point of view, as hybrid instruments may be issued for a variety of non-tax reasons.[10] From a fiscal point of view, however, the classification as equity or debt is crucial for two reasons. First of all, the issuer can treat interest on the latter as tax-deductible in most cases, and secondly, for the investor the classification determines whether the payments received from the respective instrument is treated as a dividend or as interest.[11]

This classification for tax purposes is the source of important opportunities and risks in the area of international tax management, especially in international groups, where hybrid instruments can be used efficiently as flexible, tailor-made forms of finance. As long as no anti-avoidance rules, such as "Subject-To-Tax" Clauses are applicable, the qualification of the hybrid instrument as debt in the source state and as equity in the state of residence of the parent company could lead to double non-taxation of the profits. In such cases, the payment would then be deductible as interest in the source state and exempt as a dividend in the state of residence of the parent company. The opposite case, where the hybrid instrument is treated as equity in the source state and as debt in the state of residence of the parent company, might lead to double taxation, when the payment is subject to withholding tax in the source state and to income tax in the state of residence of the parent company.

EC law does not affect the Member State's decision as to how to classify hybrid instruments for tax purposes, as long as the domestic law treatment does not constitute a forbidden discrimination or restriction under the EC Treaty.[12] EC law, however, may affect the tax treatment of the payments on such instruments *via* the directives.[13]

For associated companies within the European Union using hybrid instruments, the definition of the payments received from, or paid on, hybrid instruments as dividends or interest, respectively, is therefore of particular relevance

- in respect of the differential treatment of dividends and interest payments in most national tax laws and double tax treaties, but also
- in respect of the decision whether or not those payments fall under the scope of the Parent-Subsidiary Directive, or the Interest and Royalties Directive, or neither.

Since the focus or our discussion rests on this second point, we will disregard the existence of double tax treaties between Member States for the purpose of this article, in order not to overcomplicate the analysis unduly. This limitation is in line with our aim to show options for tax policy despite these directives, since these are not influenced by double tax treaties. It is, therefore, possible to analyse separately the treatment of hybrid finance in the directives and in double tax treaties from a tax policy perspective.[14]

Furthermore, we chose to limit the analysis on the treatment of hybrid finance in the directives to cases where their use does not constitute fraud and abuse in domestic tax law. Therefore, we will not to go into detail on the implications of the general fraud and abuse provisions in Art 1 (2) of the Parent-Subsidiary Directive and Art 5 of the Interest and Royalties Directive for tax policy options in the context of hybrid finance.

9.3 The Implementation of the Directives into National Law

General Issues in the Implementation of EC Directives into National Law

The Member States[15] are obliged to implement EC directives into national law in compliance with the fundamental provisions of the EC treaty,[16] but have freedom of choice as regards the form and the methods to be used in realising the aims of the directive.[17] In this two-stage legislation process, the content of the final norm is defined by the institutions of the European Union, whereas the decision about the actual form lies in the competence of each Member State.[18] The provisions of a directive therefore do not replace existing national law, but oblige the Member States to adapt their laws to the provisions of the directive. The measures to be taken are at the discretion of the Member State and depend on the national legal system. According to *Prechal,*[19] the Member States have a choice between *verbatim* transposition on the one hand, and translation of the directive into legal concepts and terminology on the other (plus all possible combinations of the two). As mentioned above, many directives are very detailed, thus leaving little room for the implementing authorities in respect of either the substance of the measure or its mode of implementation.[20]

All Member States are obliged to adapt their national law within the time limit in the directive.[21] These adaptations need to be conducted by a legal act of the same quality as the legal acts which are generally used on a national level in the area of the directive. The Member State must refer to the directive in these legal acts or in the official publication of those legal acts.[22]

Nevertheless, many countries do not implement the directives within the given time limits. On the contrary, in many cases Member States lag years behind those limits.[23] For this reason the question arises if citizens of the EU can appeal to the content of directives that have not been implemented in national law within the given time limits. In prevailing legal practise the European Court of Justice (ECJ) decided[24] that under certain circumstances the individual may rely on the provisions of the directive against the State (direct effect). Those circumstances are:[25]

- The provisions appear, as far as their subject is concerned, to be unconditional[26] and sufficiently precise.
- The State failed to implement the directive in national law by the end of the period prescribed or failed to implement the directive correctly.

The Status of Implementation of the Parent-Subsidiary Directive and the Interest and Royalties Directive

Table 9.1. shows the status of implementation of the original Parent-Subsidiary Directive, the 2003 Directive Amending the Parent-Subsidiary Directive and the Interest and Royalties Directive. The data on the Parent-Subsidiary Directive is based on entries in the EUR-Lex Database before 4 July, 2006.[27] The data on the Interest and Royalties Directive is based on the Survey on the Implementation of the EC Interest and Royalty Directive carried out by the International Bureau of Fiscal Documentation (IBFD) published on the homepage of the Commission by 2 June, 2006.[28]

Table 9.1. Status of implementation of the directives

Member State / Directive	90/435/EEC	2003/123/EC	2003/49/EC
Belgium	✓	✓	✓
Czech Republic	✓	✓	✓
Denmark	✓	✓	✓
Germany	✓	✓	✓
Estonia	✓	✓	✓
Greece	✓	*	✓
Spain	✓	*	✓
France	✓	✓	✓
Ireland	✓*	✓*	✓*
Italy	✓*	*	✓
Cyprus	✓	✓	✓
Latvia	✓	✓	✓
Lithuania	✓	✓	✓
Luxembourg	✓*	*	✓
Hungary	✓	✓	✓
Malta	✓	✓	✓
Netherlands	✓*	*	✓
Austria	✓	✓	✓
Poland	✓	✓	✓
Portugal	✓	✓	✓
Slovenia	✓	✓	✓
Slovak Republic	✓	✓	✓
Finland	✓	✓	✓
Sweden	✓*	✓*	✓
United Kingdom	✓**	✓**	✓

* No reference available in the EUR-Lex database. In these cases the information given is based on the online editions of IBFD, Europe – Company Taxation 2005 and IBFD, EC Corporate Tax Law, 2005.

** Since UK tax law largely satisfies the Parent-Subsidiary Directive the only implementation legislation was to remove the charge to UK tax on paying agents which potentially conflicts with Art 6 of the directive. See *Tomsett*, County Chapter United Kingdom, recital 82 et. seq. in: *IBFD*, EC Corporate Tax Law, 2005.

9.4 The Parent-Subsidiary Directive

The Aims of the Parent-Subsidiary Directive

The Council Directive 90/435/ECC on the common system of taxation applicable to parent companies and subsidiaries of different Member States (the Parent-Subsidiary Directive) was adopted on 23 June 1990 and was to be implemented by the Member States by 1 January 1992.

The Parent-Subsidiary Directive is part of the general process of approximating the conditions within the EU to those of a single domestic market, to ensure the effective functioning of the common market.[29] The right of the Council to issue directives for the approximation of such laws, regulations or administrative provisions of the Member States as directly affect the establishment or functioning of the common market derives from Art 94 ECT.[30] In such a market it is considered necessary by the Council of the European Communities to allow enterprises to adapt to the requirements of the common market, to increase their productivity and to improve their competitive strength on an international level by grouping together companies of different Member States, without any restrictions, distortions or disadvantages arising from the tax provisions of the Member States.[31]

The establishment of a subsidiary in another Member State usually results in a corporate tax liability of the subsidiary in this Member State. It may result in additional corporation tax on dividends received by the parent company in its state of residence, once the subsidiary's profit is distributed. Thus, the profit would be taxed twice if no measures were taken. While the corporation tax levied on a subsidiary within the same state is frequently accounted for in the calculation of the corporation tax of the parent, this is often impossible or at least not possible to the same extent, when the subsidiary is situated in another state. This leads to double taxation of the distributed income of the subsidiary in all those cases where no double-taxation treaties exist. Furthermore, the source state generally levies a withholding tax on the profits. This leads, in the absence of a double-taxation treaty, to an additional double taxation of the profits since the parent company effectively has to pay company tax to its state of residence and withholding tax to the state of residence of the subsidiary.[32] If these combined effects appear, they represent an infringement of the principle of non-discrimination and the freedom of establishment.[33]

Against this background the original Parent-Subsidiary Directive was designed to eliminate those tax obstacles in the process of the distribution of profits (dividends) from subsidiary to parent within the EU by

- abolishing withholding taxes on distributed profits between associated companies[34] of different Member States in the source state, and
- preventing double taxation of parent companies on the profits of their subsidiaries.

On 22 December 2003, the Council adopted Directive 2003/123/EC[35] to broaden the scope and improve the operation of the Parent-Subsidiary Directive, by updating the list of companies that the directive covers, relaxing the conditions for exempting profits from withholding tax (reduction of the participation threshold) and eliminating double taxation for subsidiaries of subsidiary companies.[36]

The Effect of the Parent-Subsidiary Directive

In implementing the Parent-Subsidiary Directive the Member States could choose between exempting from tax the profits received by the parent company, or giving credit for tax already paid.[37] Every Member State except for Malta,[38] Poland,[39] and the UK,[40] opted for the exemption system for profits within the scope of the directive.[41] For this reason the focus lies on the exemption method to show the tax effect of the Parent-Subsidiary Directive.

Table 9.2. shows the effect of the Parent-Subsidiary Directive on the total tax burden borne by dividends received by the parent company, compared to the tax burden without the directive under the (imaginary worst case) assumption of no double-taxation treaty between the two States involved. It is also assumed that the State of the parent company does not provide any unilateral double-taxation relief measures. Corporation tax rates and withholding tax rates in both countries are assumed to be 25%.

Table 9.2. Tax effect of the Parent-Subsidiary Directive

	Before Parent-Subsidiary Directive	After Parent-Subsidiary Directive
Source State:		
EBIT	100,000	100,000
Deductible Interest	0	0
EBT	100,000	100,000
Corporate Tax (25%)	–25,000	–25,000
Distributable Profit after Corporate Tax	75,000	75,000
Withholding Tax (25 %)	–18,750	0
Dividends paid	56,250	75,000
Parent State:		
Dividends received	56,250	75,000
Tax Base for Corporate Tax	75,000	75,000
Corporate Tax (25%)	–18,750	0
Income after Tax	37,500	75,000
Total Tax Burden	62,500	25,000

The Scope of the Parent Subsidiary Directive

The following analysis of the scope of the directive shall be limited to those provisions and definitions which are of relevance to the discussion of the treatment of payments on hybrid instruments. Since it makes no difference to our discussion whether the distributed profits flow to, or from, a permanent establishment provided the requirements of the directive are met, the analysis will concentrate on the case of payments between associated companies.[42]

Company of a Member State

The Parent-Subsidiary Directive applies to Companies which

- take one of the forms listed in the Annex of the directive
- are resident in a Member State for tax purposes according to the tax laws of this State and are not, under the terms of a double taxation agreement concluded with a third State, considered to be resident for tax purposes outside the Community, and
- are subject to one of the taxes (all of them corporate taxes) listed in Article 2(c) of the directive, without the possibility of an option, or of being exempt.

As a result of this last provision, partnerships are generally exempt from the benefits of the directive, even if they are entitled to opt for a corporation-tax liability. Companies which are liable for corporation tax in principal, but do not actually pay such a tax due to certain tax exemptions, are nevertheless subject to the directive.[43]

Parent Company

According to Art 3 (1) of the original Parent-Subsidiary Directive a parent company is a company which fulfils the conditions set out in Art 2 and has a minimum holding of at least 25% in the capital of a company in another Member State fulfilling the same conditions. This minimum requirement has been changed through the last amendment of the Parent-Subsidiary Directive in December 2003. The limit is now 15% and will be lowered to 10% by 1 January 2009.

The term "holding in the capital" itself is not defined in the directive. This gives Member States an opportunity to include or exclude other forms of participation, apart from classic shares in equity, in the determination of the holding level required in the national implementation of the directive (as for example indirect participation via an intermediary).

According to Art 3 (2) Member States have the option to replace the criterion of a holding in capital by that of a holding of voting rights, by means of bilateral agreements. They also have the option of not applying the directive to companies, (a) which do not maintain holdings qualifying them as parent companies for an uninterrupted period of at least two years, or (b) to those of their companies in which another Member State does not maintain such a holding for an uninterrupted period of at least two years.

Profits

The Parent-Subsidiary Directive itself contains no definition of the term profits, but merely states that the Member State shall apply this directive to distributions of profits (Art 1 (1), 90/435/ECC). Moreover, the state of residence of the parent company (and the state of its permanent establishment) shall refrain from taxing such distributed profits (Art 4 (1), 90/435/ECC) and that profits, which a subsidiary distributes to its parent company, shall be exempt from withholding tax (Art 5 (1), 90/435/ECC).

Unquestionably the term distributed profits includes dividends which, in turn, is a term that is difficult to define[44]. Although the terms dividends and distributed profits are often used synonymously, the latter has a broader scope including other profit distributions as well. In the introduction to directive 2003/123/EC the Council of the European Communities itself states that the objective of the Parent-Subsidiary Directive is to exempt "*dividends and other profit distributions*". The term profit distribution therefore can be interpreted to cover any payment based on the shareholder-company relationship or the association between companies.[45] The directive leaves it to the Member states and their national definitions to decide which profits to include within the scope of the national application of the directive.

From the wording of the directive it is unclear whether profits on liquidation, and disguised profits, fall within the scope of the term profit distributions in the Parent-Subsidiary Directive as well. Profits on the liquidation of a subsidiary are specifically exempt from the scope of application of the directive, which seeks to prevent the double taxation of parent companies on the profits of their subsidiaries (Art 4). However, these liquidation profits are not exempt from the directive with regard to the abolition of withholding taxes on payments of profits in the source state. Consequently, profits on the liquidation of the subsidiary would have to be exempt from the withholding tax as well.[46] On the treatment of disguised profits, the directive contains no rules, thus leaving it to the Member States whether or not to include disguised profits.[47]

9.5 The Interest and Royalties Directive

The Aims of the Interest and Royalties Directive

The Council Directive 2003/49/EC on a common system of taxation applicable to interest and royalty payments between associated companies in different Member States (the Interest and Royalties Directive) was adopted on 3 June 2003 and was to be implemented by the Member States by 1 January 2004.

The primary aim of this directive is to ensure that associated companies in different Member States are not discriminated against relative to associated companies in the same Member State through less favourable tax conditions than those applicable to parent/subsidiary structures within a Member State. It therefore serves as an instrument to harmonise income taxes within the EU domestic market.[48] The Interest and Royalties Directive was considered necessary by the Council of the European Communities, because national tax laws and bilateral agreements, in the form of double-taxation treaties, are not always sufficient to eliminate the double taxation of those payments, and often entail burdensome administrative formalities, cash flow problems and a loss of interest for the companies involved.[49]

For example, should a Member State, in which the Company which pays interest and royalties is based (source state[50]), impose a withholding tax on interest payments that exceeds the amount of income tax the receiving company has to pay in the other Member State and (according to the double tax treaty or national tax law) this Member State grants a tax credit for the withholding tax, the receiving company (beneficial owner[51]) can only utilise part of the total amount of the tax withheld in the sources state as tax credit (or none, if the taxable income is zero). Additionally the receiving company will have a loss of interest for the time between receiving the net payments (less the withholding tax) and the credit of the withholding tax.[52]

To achieve equal treatment of interest and royalty payments between associated companies[53] in the EU the directive ensures that such payments are subject to tax only in the Member State of the beneficial owner. The source state has to exempt those payments from tax, including withholding tax.

The Effect of the Interest and Royalties Directive

Table 9.3. shows the effect of the Interest and Royalties Directive on interest received by the parent company, compared to the tax burden in the absence of the directive, on the (imaginary worst case) assumption that there was no double-taxation treaty between the two Member States involved, and that the Member State of the parent company did not provide any unilateral double-taxation relief measures. Corporation tax rates and withholding tax rates in both countries are assumed to be 25%.

The Scope of the Interest and Royalties Directive

As with the Parent-Subsidiary Directive the following analysis of the scope of the directive is limited to those provisions and definitions which are of relevance to the discussion of the treatment of hybrid finance in the directives. Again, the discussion does not include payments to/from permanent establishments, due to lack of relevance to our analysis. We focus on payments between associated companies.[54]

Table 9.3. Tax effect of the Interest and Royalties Directive

	Before Interest and Royalties Directive	After Interest and Royalties Directive
Source State:		
EBIT	100,000	100,000
Deductible Interest	–100,000	–100,000
EBT	0	0
Corporate Tax (25 %)	0	0
Distributable Profit after Corporate Tax	100,000	100,000
Withholding Tax (25%)	-25,000	
Interest Paid	75,000	100,000
Parent State:		
Interest Received	75,000	100,000
Tax Base for Corporate Tax	100,000	100,000
Corporate Tax (25%)	–25,000	–25,000
Income after Tax	50,000	75,000
Total Tax Burden	50,000	25,000

Associated Companies

As under the Parent-Subsidiary Directive, the benefits of the Interest and Royalties Directive are only granted to companies which are

- of a type listed in the annex to the directive,
- tax resident in an EU Member State and
- subject to corporation tax in the EU

if, at least

- the first company has a direct minimum holding of 20% in the capital of the second company, or
- the second company has a direct minimum holding of 20% in the capital of the first company, or
- a third company has a direct minimum holding of 20% both in the capital of the first company and in the capital of the second company.[55]

Holdings must involve only companies resident in Community territory.

The annex to the directive originally included the types of companies which existed in the 15 Member States that were already members of the EU before 1 May 2004. The types of companies in the new Member States within the scope of the directive have been added by Council Directive 2004/66/EC of 26 April 2004.[56] Furthermore, the Commission proposed an amendment to Directive 2003/49/EC on 30 December 2003[57] to provide for an update of the list of companies in the annex to the directive. This new list would also include;

- the European Company (*Societas Europaea*)[58]
- the European Co-operative Society[59]

Beneficial Owner

According to Art 1 (4) of the directive, a Company of a Member State[60] is treated as the beneficial owner of interest and royalties only if it receives those payments for its own benefit and not as an intermediary, such as an agent, trustee or authorised signatory, for some other person.[61]

The term "for its own benefit" is not defined in the directive, which only states that intermediaries, agents, trustees or authorised signatories do not receive payments for their own benefit. *Distaso/Russo*[62] assume that providing the recipient has been remunerated at arm's length, it should be entitled to the benefits of the directive. Therefore, a company in a Member State which receives a loan from a company outside the EU and then, in turn, lends this money to one of its subsidiaries in another Member State, will be entitled (provided all other requirements are met) to the benefits from the Interest and Royalties Directive for the interest received from this subsidiary, as long as both deals are conducted at arm's length. Although it could be argued that the company in that example only acts as an intermediary in terms of Art 1 (4) and, therefore, does not qualify as beneficial owner in terms of the directive, *Distaso/Russo* seem to be correct in assuming that the definition of the term beneficial owner in the directive covers such cases as well.[63]

Interest and Royalties

Art 2 of the directive provides the definition of the terms interest and royalties.[64] It reads as follows:

The term "interest" means income from debt-claims of every kind, whether or not secured by mortgage and whether or not carrying a right to participate in the debtor's profits. In particular, it covers all income from securities, bonds or debentures, including premiums and prizes attaching to such securities, bonds or debentures. Penalty charges for late payment are not regarded as interest.[65]

This definition is the same as in Art 11 of the 2005 OECD Model Tax Convention.[66] The directive in Art 4, however, allows Member States to exempt certain payments from the benefits of the directive. Those benefits are:

- Payments which are treated as a distribution of profits or as a repayment of capital under the law of the source country.
- Payments from debt-claims which carry a right to participate in the debtor's profits.
- Payments from debt-claims which entitle the creditor to exchange his rights to interest for a right to participate in the debtor's profits.

- Payments from debt-claims which contain no provision for repayment of the principal amount or where the repayment is due more than 50 years after the date of issue.

It is up to each Member State to decide, which of these four cases will be excluded from the scope of the directive. The aim of this option seems to be to provide Member States with a tool to counteract the abuses of the directive, through disguising distributions of profit or returns on the provision of equity as interest within the definition of the directive and to avoid major distortions of the national tax system.

9.6 Hybrid Finance in the Directives

Hybrid Finance Under the Terms of the Parent-Subsidiary Directive

As explained above, the Parent-Subsidiary Directive applies to profit distributions to a parent company in one Member State by its (associated) subsidiary in another Member State. In the context of hybrid finance two questions arise:

- Do payments on hybrid instruments qualify as distributed profits in terms of Art 1 of the Parent-Subsidiary Directive at all, and if so, which instruments would have to be included?
- Does participation via hybrid instruments attribute to the holding level required by the Parent-Subsidiary Directive in Art 3 at all and if so, which instruments would have to be included?

In answering these questions one will find out about the discretionary leeway of Member States when implementing the directive.

To answer these questions, it is necessary once again to have a look at the aims of the Parent-Subsidiary Directive, which is essentially the elimination of double taxation in the relations between parent companies and subsidiaries in context with hybrid finance.

Should the state of residence of the subsidiary (source state) classify a hybrid instrument as equity and, thus, deny a (tax) deduction on the payments on the instrument and levy a withholding tax, double taxation would be the result whenever the state of residence of the parent company (residence state) qualifies the hybrid instrument as equity as well. In this case, the payments would be subject to corporation tax in both countries and to withholding tax in the source state.[67] Since the purpose of the directive is precisely to eliminate such cases of double taxation,[68] the directive has to be applied in these situations.[69] This means, that payments on hybrid instruments, which are deemed returns on equity investment and, therefore, as dividends by the source state, would always have to be subject to the benefits of the Parent-Subsidiary Directive. Member States could, therefore, determine which hybrid instruments would benefit from the Parent-Subsidiary Directive *via* their treatment in national tax law.

In this regard, it is interesting to have a look at the origins of the Interest and Royalties directive:[70]

The last section of Art 4 of the *Proposal* for the Interest and Royalties Directive,[71] which contains an option for Member States to exempt certain payments from the benefits of the directive, indicates that this interpretation corresponds to an (at least originally) intended interrelation between the two directives. It reads as follows:

Interest that has been re-characterised as a distribution of profits shall accordingly be subject instead to the provisions of Council Directive 90/435/EEC (The Parent-Subsidiary Directive), where it is paid between companies to which the present Directive applies.

The commentary on the Proposal for the Interest and Royalties Directive stated that such a switch in the applicable directive could arise, if for example the re-characterisation as a distribution of profits follows from a tax treaty between two Member States or is based on the domestic tax law of the source state.[72]

The proposed text seems to refer primarily to thin capitalisation and disguised dividends. As *Helminen*[73] correctly states, one could deduce from these text passages that the Commission was of the opinion that income from hybrid instruments should usually qualify as a profit distribution under the Parent-Subsidiary Directive, if treated as a dividend in the source state or if treated as a dividend for tax treaty purposes. The logical consequence of this opinion is that payments on hybrid instruments between companies which fulfil the requirements of both directives[74] are either subject to the Parent-Subsidiary Directive or to the Interest and Royalties Directive, depending on the treatment in the tax law of the source state or in the tax treaties between those countries.[75]

Interestingly though, the reference to the Parent-Subsidiary Directive is not included in the final legal version of the Interest and Royalties Directive. This raises the question whether, in the opinion of the Commission, payments on hybrid instruments that have been excluded from the benefits of the Interest and Royalties Directive on the basis of Art 4(a) as profit distributions, necessarily qualify as profit distributions in the terms of the Parent-Subsidiary Directive; otherwise, they need not fall within the scope of either of these directives.[76]

From our point of view it seems reasonable to assume that the benefits of the Parent-Subsidiary Directive should always be applicable to payments on hybrid instruments in the national implementation of a Member State, if this Member State treats such payments as dividends under national tax law. In any case the Member State would be hard put to argue why these payments, representing dividends in national tax law, should be exempt from the benefits of the directive.[77] Consequently profit distributions on hybrid instruments, which are qualified as interest in the Member State, should not benefit from the Parents-Subsidiary Directive.

Assuming that payments on such hybrid instruments should be treated as profits under the terms of the Parent-Subsidiary Directive, the question arises whether these hybrid instruments should then be included in the determination of the holding level required for the status of a parent company in the terms of the directive. Again the directive itself contains no definition of the term "holding in capital",[78] which gives Member States the freedom to define the term in the national implementation of the directive and, therefore, the option to include or exclude certain hybrid instrument. This option however can only go so far, because the payments on the relevant hybrid instrument are treated as profit distributions under the terms of the directive. Therefore, the problem can be narrowed to the question whether hybrid instruments, whose payments qualify as profit distributions under the directive, have to be included in the determination of the minimum holding requirement for the implementation of the directive, or whether the Member States enjoy some discretion in the matter. *Helminen*[79] reasonably argues that, if hybrid debt is treated as equity, it would also have to be taken into account in calculating the fulfilment of the holding requirement between two countries for the purpose of the directive.

If the source state must grant the benefits of the Parent-Subsidiary in cases where hybrid instruments qualify as equity in national tax law, the question arises whether the state of residence of the parent company has to grant these benefits symmetrically, thereby accepting the classification of the source state. If it does not, but treats the hybrid instrument as debt instead, the profits distributed by the subsidiary would be subject to income tax in the state of the recipient. In this case, it would be possible for the residence state to levy income tax on the profits distributed by the subsidiary, even though the source state applies the Parent-Subsidiary Directive. It clearly cannot be required of the parent state to accept the qualification of the source state in any case, but *Helminen*[80] seems to be correct in arguing that it should at least do so in the following two cases:

- If, in the opposite situation, the recipient's state of residence itself would have qualified the hybrid instrument as equity.
- If it the recipient's state of residence has to accept a treatment as equity for tax treaty purposes.

Hybrid Finance in the Scope of the Interest and Royalties Directive

As explained in Chapter D, the Interest and Royalties Directive contains on the one hand a very wide definition of the term interest ("Income from debt claims of any kind"), and on the other allows Member States to deny the application of the directive in the four cases listed in Art 4, thus enabling them to narrow the definition of interest for the purpose of the directive considerably. From the perspective of hybrid finance these four specific cases are of special relevance, since they mainly apply to hybrid instruments. They shall therefore be analysed separately:

Art 4(a) allows the source state to exempt payments which are treated as a distribution of profits or as a repayment of capital under its domestic law from the benefits of the directive. From the perspective of hybrid finance (e.g. jouissance rights which are treated as equity in the source state) this provision is especially interesting, since the author's share the view that these payments, if the option is executed and provided the other requirements are met, should fall under the scope of application of the Parent-Subsidiary Directive.[81] As mentioned above, this connection was explicitly stated in the Proposal for the Interest and Royalties Directive in 1998[82] and it is not apparent why this statement was not included in the final version of the directive.

Presuming that any payments which qualify as profit distributions under the tax law of the source state fall under the scope of the Parent-Subsidiary Directive, the question arises as to what happens if the source state does not execute the option in Art 4(a) of the Interest and Royalties Directive and if these payments fall under the scope of both directives.[83] Since both directives prescribe an exemption from any withholding tax on the payments, the effect on the tax burden would be the same, but it nevertheless seems interesting that under these circumstances the same payment might qualify as interest and as profit distribution.

Apart from these considerations, it seems to be the case that, although the provision of Art 4(a) (in the context of the sovereignty to qualify a given instrument as equity or debt) allows the Member States to deprive certain hybrid instruments from the benefits of the Interest and Royalties Directive, the effect on tax revenue would be nil, because these instruments would subsequently fall under the application of the Parent-Subsidiary Directive. In our opinion it can be assumed that this was indeed the intention of the Commission, as the requirements of a common single market are then fulfilled.[84] The question remains, why Art 4(a) of the directive gives the Member States an option instead of generally exempting such payments from the scope of the directive.

Art 4 (b) allows the exemption of debt-claims which carry a right to participate in the debtor's profits.[85] These include participation bonds and profit participation loans as well as forms of jouissance rights and silent partnerships which are qualified as debt. The source state, therefore, has the option to exclude jouissance rights and silent partnerships from the scope of application of the Interest and Royalties Directive as well as the Parent-Subsidiary Directive by first qualifying them as debt on a national level, thus exempting them from the benefits of the Parent-Subsidiary Directive, and then using the option in Art 4 (b) to exempt them from the benefits of the Interest and Royalties Directive.

Art 4 (c) refers to convertible debt instruments, which "entitle the creditor to exchange his right to interest for a right to participate in the debtor's profits". Literally interpreted this wording does not include hybrid instruments, such as convertible bonds and warrant bonds which grant the right of conversion into share capital of the creditor. The question is, if Art 4 (c) is indeed meant to include only interest bearing loans with an option to exchange the entitlement to interest against the entitlement to profit participation, or if the term "a right to participate in the debtor's profits" is used as an equivalent for the term "a right to participate in the debtor's equity" which would include hybrid instruments like convertible bonds or warrant bonds.[86]

Art 4 (d) finally allows the exemption of debt-claims which from an economic point of view serve as equity, because they contain no provision of repayment of the principal amount or a provision where the repayment is due more than 50 years after the date of issue.

Art 4 (b), (c) and (d) all apply to cases where the treatment under the domestic tax law of the source state corresponds to the general definition of interest in Art 2 (1) of the directive. This means that Member States can decide to exempt payments on certain (hybrid) financial instruments from the benefits of the directive, while still qualifying the same payments as interest in domestic tax law. The reason behind these provisions is hard to see, since it seems to foil the general aim of the Interest and Royalties Directive, which is to eliminate double taxation on interest payments.[87]

Distaso/Russo[88] argue that the intention behind these provisions might be to give Member States a tool to eliminate cases of double non-taxation, by excluding instruments that create a tax deduction in the source state, while giving rise to an exemption from taxation of the corresponding income received, because the residence state of the recipient treats the income as profit distributions. If this were indeed the case, the provisions in Art 4 seem to be a rather inadequate instrument since the directive affects not only payments between one pair of Member States, but all payments within its scope. Apart from that, Art 4 includes no reference to the treatment of the payments in the residence state of the recipient. It is therefore possible for the source state to exempt payments from the scope of the directive which are treated symmetrically as interest in both states, thereby creating double taxation instead of avoiding double non-taxation, specifically.

The bottom line, nevertheless, is that the directive leaves room for national tax policy measures in the Member States to exempt hybrid instruments from the scope of application of the directive altogether, without having to include them in the scope of the Parent Subsidiary Directive.

9.7 Concluding Remarks on Hybrid Finance and National Tax Policy

EC-Law restricts fiscal sovereignty and, therefore, the possibilities for tax policy on the part of the Member States. The goal is to ensure the establishment and effective functioning of the common market, by approximating the conditions within the European Union to those of a domestic market.

The directive is a major tool of the Council in bringing the national law of the Member States into line with the conditions of such a domestic market. It stands to reason to assume that the more detailed a certain directive is, the less discretionary freedom remains for tax policy in the Member States.

This assumption has been tested for the Parent-Subsidiary Directive and the Interest and Royalties Directive as applied to the tax treatment of hybrid finance. These directives were chosen because they are interrelated, very detailed and have been implemented by most Member States. Furthermore, they are of particular importance for national tax policy in direct taxation as they influence attempts to encourage equity finance, and collide with the ambition to safeguard national tax revenue. It is therefore of great interest for the Member States to know what can still be done in terms of tax policy in spite of these directives.

The leeway for tax policy in the context of the Parent-Subsidiary Directive seems rather limited. Assuming that payments on hybrid instruments are treated as returns on equity by the source state, and therefore as dividends in terms of the directive, such payments have always to be subject to the benefits of the Parent-Subsidiary Directive. The only way for a Member States to circumvent the directive then is *via* a general, national classification of a certain hybrid instrument as debt. But then, however, the hybrid instrument would come under the terms of the

Interest and Royalties Directive. This means that no withholding tax could be levied on the payments to those hybrid instruments as long as the source state did not execute any of the options in Art 4 of the Interest and Royalties Directive. For the parent state on the other hand, a classification as debt in terms of the Interest and Royalties Directive, instead of equity in terms of the Parent-Subsidiary Directive, would mean that it was still possible to levy corporation tax on the payments received.

The Interest and Royalties Directive provides considerably more leeway for tax policy. Art 4 of the directive allows Member States to deny the application of the directive in four specific cases, which encompass several forms of hybrid finance. This enables the Member State to levy withholding tax on certain hybrid instruments despite the directive. While this seems clear cut in the case of Art 4 (b-c), there is some doubt in the case of Art 4 (a) where payments, which the source state chooses to exempt because they are treated as a distribution of profits or as a repayment of capital under its domestic law, should subsequently fall under the scope of application of the Parent-Subsidiary Directive. This would be the case in the circumstances mentioned above, i.e. where payments on hybrid instruments which are treated as equity in the source state, have always to come under the sway of the Parent-Subsidiary Directive. The source state would not then be allowed to levy withholding taxes, irrespective of the national qualification of the hybrid instrument, provided Art 4 (b-c) is not applicable. If, on the other hand, payments on such instruments did not qualify as dividends in terms of the Parent-Subsidiary Directive, Art 4 (a) as well as Art 4 (b-c) provide the source state with an option of levying withholding tax in certain cases of hybrid finance in spite of the directives.

Should the aim of its tax policy in a Member State be in opposition to the directives, i.e. if national tax policy were aimed at safeguarding national tax revenue in the area of hybrid finance (rather than simplifying its tax procedures for domestic companies or to create incentives for foreign investment), it seems that a Member State to a certain extent could adhere to

- its right to levy withholding tax (as a source state) and
- its right to levy corporation tax (as a parent state),

in spite of the directives. This could be achieved by treating, or classifying, hybrid financial instruments, in general, as debt under national tax law.

Whether this would be a good strategy for Member States to pursue is another matter, but it certainly shows, that the main objective of the two directives – the elimination of double taxation in the area of dividend and interest payments – has not been achieved to a hundred percent so far. Thus it seems that the use of directives, even very detailed ones, as a tool for harmonisation in the area of direct taxation limits options for national tax policy considerably, but does not eliminate them altogether.

Endnotes

1. The free movement of goods (Art 23 et seq., ECT), the free movement of capital (Art 56 et seq., ECT), the free movement of services (Art 49 et seq., ECT), and the freedom of establishment (Art 39 et seq., ECT) within the internal market of the EU.
2. Art. 228, ECT; Cf. *Craig/De Búrca* (2003), p. 402 et seq.; *Callies/Ruffer* (2007), p. 1252 et seq.
3. Art. 249, ECT; Cf. *Craig/De Búrca* (2003), p. 112 et seq.; *Callies/Ruffert* (2007), p. 2171 et seq.
4. Resolution of the Council and the Representatives of the Governments of the Member States, meeting within the Council of 1 December 1997 on a code of conduct for business taxation, OJ C 002 , 6 January 1998.
5. Art. 94 of the EC Treaty gives the Commission the right to propose to the Council directives for the approximation of such laws, regulations or administrative provisions of the Member States as directly affect the establishment or functioning of the common market. Cf. *Callies/Ruffert* (2007), p. 1252 et seq.; Cf. *Craig/De Búrca* (2003), p. 202, 1170, 1184; *Bieber/Epiney/Haag*, (2005), p. 193 & p. 305 et seq.
6. Cf. *Prechal* (2005), p. 14 & 74; *Bieber/Epiney/Haag* (2005), p. 193 et seq.
7. The Savings Directive (Council Directive on taxation of savings income in the form of interest payments, 2003/48/EC)) has not been included in the analysis, as its aim and scope of application are considerably different from those of the Parent-Subsidiary Directive and the Interest and Royalties Directive. Nevertheless, the Savings Directive will have an effect on the tax policy options of Member States as regards hybrid finance, where the yield of certain hybrid instruments received by individuals may qualify as interest in terms of the Directive. On the effect and the scope of application of the Savings Directive see e.g. *Bell* (2003), p. 201 et seq.; *Gläser* (2006).
8. Cf. *Larking* (2005), p. 212; *Duncan* (2000), p. 22 et seq.; *Eberhartinger* (2005), p. 121.
9. Cf. the list of features of hybrid instruments that can blur the differentiation between equity and debt in *Duncan* (2000), p. 24 et seq. and the various hybrid instruments analysed in the National Reports in the same Volume.
10. For examples for such reasons see *Duncan* (2000), p. 23.
11. *Eberhartinger* (2005), p. 122 with further references; *Duncan* (2000), p. 27; *Helminen* (2004), p. 56; *Wittendorff/Banner-Voigt* (2000), p. 3.
12. E.g. *Helminen* (1999), p. 266; Cf. the following examples of ECJ case-law on discrimination cases in connection with dividend or interest payments: ECJ, 7 September 2004, *Case C-319/02, Petri Manninen*; ECJ, 15 July 2004, Case C-315/02, *Anneliese Lenz v Finanzlandesdirektion für Tirol*, ECJ, 4 March 2004, Case C-334/02, *Commission of the European Communities v. French Republic*; ECJ, 24 September 2003, Case C-168/01, *Bosal Holding BV v Staatssecretaris van Financiën*, ECJ, 12 December 2002, Case C-321/00, *Lankhorst-Hohorst GmbH v. Finanzamt Steinfurt.*
13. Since this article only examines the treatment of hybrid finance between associated companies in EC Law, the Council Directive 2003/48/EC of 3 June 2003 on taxation of savings income in the form of interest payments will not be taken into account in the analysis, since it only affects interest payments to individuals (Cf. Art. 2 (1), 2003/48/EC). For a comprehensive survey on the Savings Directive see e.g. *Bell* (2003), p. 201 et seq.; *Gläser* (2005).
14. For a comprehensive survey on the treatment of hybrid instruments in double tax treaties, see *Lang* (1991).

15. Although directives, as opposed to regulations, do not have to be addressed to all Member States, most of them are addressed to all of them. Cf. *Craig/De Búrca* (2003), p. 114; *Prechal*, (2005), p. 55 with further evidence.
16. See e.g. ECJ, 24 September 2003, Case C-168/01, *Bosal Holding BV v Staatssecretaris van Financiën*, in connexion with the implementation of the Parent Subsidiary Directive; Cf. with further references *Zanotti*, (2004), p. 502.
17. Art. 249, III ECT.
18. Cf. *Haslach* (2001), p. 40, with further evidence.
19. *Prechal* (2005), p. 76.
20. Cf. *Prechal* (2005), p. 74.
21. This follows from Art. 10, I ECT. Before the time limit is reached, the directives already have legal effect insofar as the Member States "must refrain during that period from taking any measures liable seriously to compromise the result prescribed", ECJ, 18 December 1997, Case C-129/96, *Inter-Environnement Wallonie ASBL v Région wallonne*; Cf. *Prechal* (2005), p. 20; *Bieber/Epiney/Haag* (2005), p. 194.
22. See e.g. ECJ, 4 April 1974, Case C-167/73, *Commission of the European Communities v French Republic*; ECJ, 25 May 1982, Case C-96/81, *Commission of the European Communities v Kingdom of the Netherlands*; Cf. *Craig/De Búrca* (2003), p. 420. Bieber/Epiney/Haag (2005), p. 194.
23. Cf. *European Commission*, International Market Scoreboard 14, July 2005, 9 et seq.; *European Commission*, International Market Scoreboard 13, July 2004, p. 9 et seq.
24. Cf. e.g. ECJ, 5 April 1979, Case C-148/78, Pubblico Ministero v Tullio Ratti; ECJ, 26 January 1984, Case C-301/82, *SA Clin-Midy and others v Belgian State*; ECJ, 26 February 1986, Case C-152/84, *M. H. Marshall v Southampton and South-West Hampshire Area Health Authority (Teaching)*; ECJ, 23 February 1994, Case C-236/92, Comitatio di Coordinamento per la Difesa della Cava and others v. Regione Lombardia and others; ECJ, 11 August 1995, Case C-431/92, *Commission of the European Communities v Federal Republic of Germany* ("Großkrotzenburg"), Cf. also *Craig/De Búrca* (2003), p. 202 et seq.; on the supremacy of EC law see e.g. ECJ, 15 July 1964, C-6/64, *Flaminio Costa v E.N.E.L.*; *Craig/De Búrca* (2003), p. 186 et seq. & 275 et seq.
25. Cf. *Prechal* (2005), p. 20.
26. A provision is unconditional where it is not subject, in its implementation or effects, to the taking of any measure either by the institutions of the Community or by the Member State. See ECJ, 23 February 1994, Case C-236/92, *Comitatio di Coordinamento per la Difesa della Cava and others v. Regione Lombardia and others.*
27. Note that the fact that there is a reference in the EUR-Lex to measures of national implementation does not necessarily mean that these measures are either comprehensive, or in conformity with the directive.
28. http://ec.europa.eu/taxation_customs/resources/documents/common/publications/studies/survey_IR_dir.pdf
29. On the general issues of the completion of the single market within the EU in a legal context and the scope of application of Art. 94 ECT cf. *Craig/De Búrca* (2003), p. 1170 et seq., especially p. 1186; Cf. *Meerpohl* (1998), p. 26 et seq. on the legal basis for the approximation of company taxes in the EU.
30. Cf. *Callies/Ruffert* (2007), p. 1252 et seq.; Cf. *Craig/De Búrca* (2003), p. 202, 1170, 1184; *Bieber/Epiney/Haag* (2005), p. 193 & p. 305 et seq.
31. Cf. 90/435/ECC, 22.09.1990, OJ L 225, p. 6.
32. See Chap. C, Sect. 2.

33. Art. 12 & Art. 43 ECT, Cf. *Meerpohl* (1998), p. 33; on the principle of non-discrimination see at length *Craig/De Búrca* (2003), p. 387 et seq. with further references.
34. The Directive also applies to profits paid to or received by a permanent establishment of a company of a Member State in another Member State. A permanent establishment is defined in Art. 2(2) of the Directive as a fixed place of business situated in a Member State through which the business of a company or another member state is wholly or partly carried on in so far as the profits of that place of business are subject to tax in the Member State in which it is situated by virtue of the relevant tax treaty or, in the absence of such a treaty, by virtue of national law. See *Distaso/Russo* (2004), p. 145, for a detailed discussion of the term permanent establishment.
35. Council Directive 2003/123/EC, 22.12.2003, OJ L 7.
36. Cf. *Brokelind* (2003), 451 et seq.
37. Cf. Art. 4 (1) of the Directive; *Terra/Wattel* (2005), p. 504 et seq.
38. Cf. Manduca/Torregiani (2007).
39. Cf. *Krempa* (2007).
40. Cf. *Tomsett* (2007), recital 77 et seq.
41. Note that in the Estonian tax system incoming dividends are never subject to corporation tax. Instead they are taxed when redistributed by the parent company. To avoid double taxation on the incoming dividends in these cases, credit relief is given for the foreign tax paid. Cf. *Riikjärv/Tulvig* (2007),recital 786 et seq.
42. For a comprehensive survey on the definition and the scope of application of the term permanent establishment in EC Law, see *Eicker*, (2007). For a detailed analysis of the cases covered by the Parent-Subsidiary Directive in the presence of a permanent establishment before and after the amendment through Council Directive 2003/123/EC see *Zanotti*, (2004), p. 503, with further evidence.
43. For a detailed analysis of Art. 2(c) see *Meerpohl* (1998), p. 58.
44. Cf. the preliminary remarks to the OECD Commentary on article 10 of the OECD Model Convention concerning the taxation of dividends according to which by "dividends" is generally meant the distributions of profits to the shareholder by companies limited by shares, limited partnerships with share capital, limited liability companies or other joint stock companies, but which also states (Sect. 23) that "in view of the great differences between the laws of OECD Member countries, it is impossible to define dividends fully and exhaustively".
45. Cf. *Helminen* (2004), p. 60; Since the Parent-Subsidiary Directive does not employ the term dividend as in Art. 10, Sect. 3 of the OECD Model Convention, the definition of the term dividend in the OECD Commentary on Article 10 can only be applied conditionally to the term profit distributions in the Parent-Subsidiary Directive.
46. Cf. *Meerpohl* (1998), p. 50; *Terra/Wattel* (2005), p. 514.
47. According to *Terra/Wattel* (2005) the term distributed profits encompasses disguised profits, which would therefore have to be subject to the benefits of the Directive as well. Note that the commentary on Art 10 of the OECD Model Tax Convention states that the term dividends may include disguised distributions of profits. See commentary on OECD Model Tax Convention, recital 28.
48. Cf. fn 4.
49. See Para. 2 of the preamble to Council Directive 2003/49/EC, OJ L 157, 26.6.2003, p. 49. *Tumpel* (1998), p. 211; *Terra/Wattel* (2005), p. 625 et seq.
50. Art. 1 (2), Council Directive 2003/49/EC.
51. Art. 1 (4), Council Directive 2003/49/EC, Cf. Chap. D, Sect. 3.1.

52. For the same reasons the credit method itself is often considered to violate the fundamental freedoms. See e.g. *Vogel* (2002), p. 4; *Schönfeld* (2005), p. 160; *Cordewener/Schnitger* (2006), p. 56.
53. The Directive also applies to interest or royalties paid to, or received by, a permanent establishment of a company of a Member State in another Member State. See Chap. D, Sect. 3.4.
54. See *Distaso/Russo* (2004) p. 145 for a detailed discussion of the term permanent establishment used in the Interest and Royalties Directive. For a comprehensive survey on the definition and the scope of application of the term permanent establishment in EC Law, see *Eicker* 2007.
55. The Directive does not apply to interest paid by a company located in a Member State to its grandparent company located in another Member State. See *Distaso/Russo* (2004), p. 145 who also discuss the problem of interest paid via fiscally transparent partnerships.
56. OJ L168, 1.5.2004, p. 67; In addition, the Council, on 29 April, adopted Directive 2004/76/EC (Official Journal L 157, p. 106) on the basis of the Commission's proposal of 1 April 2004 (see COM(2004) 243 final), granting some of the new Member States transitional periods resulting in their not applying the provisions of the Directive immediately from the date of their accession.
57. COM(2003) 841 final - see also press release at IP/04/105.
58. Council Regulation (EC) 2157/2000; Council Directive 2001/86/EC, see also press release IP/01/1376.
59. Council Regulation (EC) 1435/2003; Council Directive 2003/72/EC, see also press release IP/03/1071.
60. For a critical examination of the differing definition of the term beneficial owner in the case of a permanent establishment see *Distaso/Russo* (2004), p. 148.
61. For a comprehensive discussion of the meaning of the term beneficial owner, also in respect to the relation of the OECD Model Tax Convention and the EC Directives see e.g. *Oliver* et al., Beneficial Ownership, 54 Bulletin for International Fiscal Documentation 7/2000, p. 310.
62. *Distaso/Russo* (2004), p. 148.
63. *Distaso/Russo* (2004), p. 148 further state, that only purely artificial transactions should be excluded from the application of the Directive by this definition, although they do not define the term *purely artificial transactions*. Reversing their example, a purely artificial transaction would be one where one of the deals is *not* conducted at arm's length.
64. Since it is of no importance for hybrid cross border finance the definition of the term royalties shall not be discussed in this article.
65. Art. 2, Council Directive 2003/49/EC.
66. *OECD*, Model Tax Convention on Income and Capital, 15 July 2005.
67. See Chapter C, Section 3 for the effect on the total tax burden on payments.
68. Cf. the preamble to 2003/123/EC and the preamble to 90/435/EEC; *Helminen* (1999), p. 266.
69. See *Terra/Wattel* (2005), p. 514 et seq.; *Helminen* (2004), p. 60; *Helminen* (1999), p. 266. Also see chapter B on the Member States obligation to implement the directive according to the objectives specified by the Council.
70. Cf the procedure files of the European Parliament on the Parent-Subsidiary Directive (CNS/1993/1205 and CNS/2003/0179).
71. COM (1998) 67 final, OJ C 123/9. Cf. *Helminen* (2004), p. 60.
72. Commentary on Art. 4 of the Proposal for the Interest and Royalties Directive, COM (1998) 67 final. 8

73. *Helminen* (2004), p. 60.
74. For example the minimum requirements for the holding in capital under both directives would have to be fulfilled, which would be the case anyway, if the parent company held more than 25% in the capital of the subsidiary. Cf. Chapters C and D for the scope of the directives.
75. This opinion seems to be confirmed by Para. 19 of the Commentary on Art. 11 of the OECD Model Tax Convention 2005 which in the context of thin capitalization cases states that, "it should be noted that the term "interest" as used in Art. 11 does not include items of income which are dealt with under Art. 10".
76. See Chap. E, Sect. 3 for tax policy issues in this context.
77. Cf. *Helminen* (2004), p. 60.
78. See Chap. C, Sect. 3.1.
79. *Helminen* (1999), p. 267.
80. *Helminen* (1999), p. 269.
81. See Chap. E, Sect. 3.1.; Cf. *Distaso/Russo* (2004), p. 150; *Helminen* (2004), p. 60;
82. COM (1998) 67 final, OJ C123/9.
83. Again provided all other requirements are met.
84. Cf. Para. (1) of the Preamble to the Interest and Royalties Directive and Para. (1) of the Preamble to the Parent-Subsidiary Directive.
85. Since Art. 4 (b) refers only to participation in the debtor's profits a literal interpretation would mean that interest payments connected to another entity, e.g. a subsidiary of the debtor, would not be included in the option. Cf. *Distaso/Russo* (2004), p. 150.
86. *Distaso/Russo* (2004), p. 150 plead for a literal interpretation of Art. 4 (b) on the grounds that the provisions in Art. 4 are meant to be exceptions from the general rule of application in Art. 2 (1) and that a broader interpretation of the exceptions in Art. 4 therefore would run the risk of frustrating the Directive.
87. See Chap. D, Sect. 1.
88. *Distaso/Russo* (2004), p. 150.

References

Bell S. (2003) EU Directive on the Taxation of Savings Income, *IBFD DFI* 2003, 201-211.

Bieber R. and Epiney A. and Haag M. (2005) *Die Europäische Union*[6], Baden-Baden: Nomos.

Brokelind, C. (2003) The Proposed Amendments to the Parent-Subsidiary Directive: Some Progress? *IBFD European Taxation*, 451-456.

Callies, Ch. and Ruffert, M. eds. (2007) *Kommentar zu EU-Vertrag und EG-Vertrag*[3], Munich: Beck.

Cordewener, A. and Schnitger, A. (2006) Europarecht und Vermeidung der internationalen Doppelbesteuerung im Wege der Anrechnungsmethode, *Steuer und Wirtschaft*, 50-78

Craig P. and De Búrca, G. (2003) *EU Law*[3], Oxford: Oxford Univ. Press.

Distaso, M. and Russo, R. (2004) The EC Interest and Royalties Directive – A Comment, *IBFD European Taxation*, 143-154.

Duncan, J. (2000) General Report, in IFA *Cahiers de droit fiscal international, Volume LXXXVa, Tax Treatment of hybrid financial instruments in cross-border transactions*, The Hague: IBFD, 21-85.

Eberhartinger, E. (2005) Hybride Finanzierungsinstrumente, in Bischof, M. and Eberhartinger E. eds., *Hybride Finanzierungsinstrumente*, Wien: Linde, 119-141.

Eicker, K. (2007) EC Law aspects of permanent establishments, in IBFD, *Permanent Establishments*, Amsterdam: IBFD.
Gläser, L. (2006) *Handbuch der EU-Quellensteuer*, Wien: Linde.
Haslach, Ch. (2001) *Die Umsetzung von EG-Richtlinien durch die Länder*, Frankfurt: Lang.
Helminen, M. (2004) Classification of Cross-Border Payments on Hybrid Instruments, *IBFD Bulletin*, 56-61;
Helminen, M. (1999) *The Dividend Concept in international Tax Law*, The Hague: Kluwer.
Krempa, S. (2007) Country Chapter Poland, in IBFD, *EC Corporate Tax Law*, Amsterdam: IBFD
Lang, M. (1991), *Hybride Finanzierungen im Internationalen Steuerrecht*, Wien: Orac.
Larking, B. (2005) *IBFD International Tax Glossary*[5], Amsterdam: IBFD.
Meerpohl, J. (1998) *Die Mutter-/Tochter-Richtlinie der Europäischen Gemeinschaft und ihre Umsetzung in das Recht der Mitgliedstaaten*, Frankfurt: Lang.
Manduca, A. and Torregiani, S. (2007), Country Chapter Malta, in: IBFD, EC Corporate Tax Law, Amsterdam: IBFD
Prechal, S. (2005), *Directives in EC Law*[2], Oxford: Oxford Univ. Press
Riikjärv, M. and Tulvig E. (2007), Country Chapter Estonia, in: IBFD, *EC Corporate Tax Law*, Amsterdam: IBFD.
Schönfeld, J. (2005) Hinzurechnungsbesteuerung zwischen Steuerwettbewerb und Europäischen Grundfreiheiten, *Steuer und Wirtschaft*, 158-170..
Terra, B. and Wattel, P. (2005) *European Tax Law*[4], The Hague:Kluwer.
Tomsett E. (2007) Country Chapter United Kingdom, in IBFD, *EC Corporate Tax Law*, Amsterdam:IBFD.
Tumpel, M. (1998) Neuer Vorschlag der Kommission für eine Richtlinie über die Besteuerung von Zahlungen für Zinsen und Lizenzgebühren, *SWI*, 211-215.
Vogel, K. (2002) Which Method Should the European Community Adopt for the Avoidance of Double Taxation, *IBFD Bulletin*, 4-10.
Wittendorff, J. and Banner-Voigt, E. (2000), Taxation of Hybrid Instruments, *IBFD DFI*, 3-8.
Zanotti, E. (2004), Taxation of Inter-Company Dividends in the Presence of a PE: The Impact of the EC Fundamental Freedoms, *IBFD European Taxation*, 493-505 & 535-546.

Chapter 10
The Room for National Tax Policy in the Future Europe

Krister Andersson, Eva Eberhartinger and Lars Oxelheim

10.1 Introduction

The research question we address in this book concerns the potential scope for national tax policies within the European Union in the years to come. As demonstrated in the book the question can be tackled from many angles and be analyzed in several ways. The tax systems of the 27 Member States of the enlarged European Union vary widely and are very complex. However, the comprehensive and harmonized framework of the European system of national and regional accounts (ESA95), which is now adopted throughout Europe, has improved the possibilities for comparisons of individual countries' tax revenues at different levels of aggregation.

A first search for trends will provide us with indications about the direction in which the tax situation is heading. However, there is a considerable lag with which data are published. The most recent year for which data is available is 2004 (European Commission, 2006). Below we show the trends for the variables that are most important for the understanding of the magnitude of the potential scope for national tax policy.

We start with the total tax ratio (inclusive of social security contributions) and find as shown in Fig. 10.1 that this ratio in 2004 amounts to 39.3% for the EU-25 (GDP-weighted average). During the five-year period prior to that year, the ratio trend-wise declined by about 0.3 percentage points. The EU-25 weighted average is fairly unchanged as compared to the situation 10 years earlier. The total tax ratio is high in an international comparison and about 14 percentage points higher than those ratios recorded in the US and Japan. The gap to these countries has remained fairly unchanged following from the fact that they as well have reduced their tax ratios during the period. The overall impression is therefore that the EU remains one of the highest taxed areas in the world.

However, the total tax ratio differs substantially between the individual EU-member countries as shown in Table 10.1. A few trends can be observed. For instance, new member states (NMS-10) have on average lower tax ratios (see Fig. 10.1). Moreover, some of the biggest declines from 1995 are found in these member states. Malta and Cyprus are two exceptions with substantial increases (more than 7%) in the period.

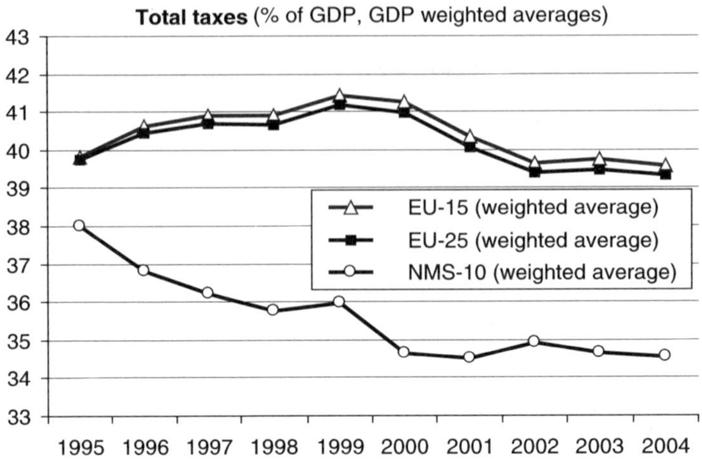

Fig. 10.1. Total taxes in the EU

Table 10.1. Total taxes in the EU – individual countries

Tax/GDP (%)	2004	%-pt ch. since -95
Belgium	45.2	1.4
Czech rep	36.6	0.4
Denmark	48.8	0.0
Germany	38.7	–1.1
Estonia	32.6	–5.3
Greece	35.1	2.4
Spain	34.6	1.9
France	43.4	0.7
Ireland	30.2	–2.8
Italy	40.6	0.6
Cyprus	34.1	7.2
Latvia	28.6	–5.0
Lithuania	28.4	–0.2
Luxembourg	40.1	–2.3
Hungary	39.1	–2.6
Malta	35.1	7.6
Netherlands	37.8	–2.7
Austria	42.6	1.3
Poland	32.9	–5.6
Portugal	34.5	2.6
Slovenia	39.7	–0.6
Slovakia	30.3	–10.1
Finland	44.3	–1.3
Sweden	50.5	1.5
United kingdom	36.0	0.7

The tax mix, or distribution of revenue sources by type of tax has traditionally been an important policy variable. It is a structural variable that generally evolves only slowly, but with the accession of a group of low-tax countries it has received renewed policy attention. In this setting, increased capital mobility will make governments more inclined to turn to taxation of immobile factors.

Labour taxes provide the largest contribution to the overall tax revenue in government budgets. There is a widespread consensus on the desirability of lower taxes on labour. In recent years in most Member States policymakers have started to argue in favor of a reduction of the tax burden on labour. The aim of reducing labour costs and increasing work incentives to stimulate higher employment is conducive to reaching the Lisbon objectives. However, the reduction of the tax burden on labour in order to increase employment has been achieved only to a marginal extent. Figure 10.2 shows a more or less unchanged implicit tax rate (ITR) in recent years.

In this tax base, high income earners are traditionally seen as more mobile than low income earners. It is worth notice in the figure that there are indications that Member States have succeeded in the more circumscribed objective of reducing the tax burden on low-income earners: the tax wedge indicator for a single worker at 2/3 of average earnings shows a much steeper decline than the ITR, which refers to the entire working population. Contrary to general beliefs the more mobile high income earners have experienced rather limited decreases in labour taxes.

Consumption is the second most important tax revenue. Figure 10.3 shows an upward trend in the area in recent years. The increase is strongest among new Member States, although still on a lower level of taxation. The rise among new Member States partly owes the effect of increases in VAT upon EU accession. An increase in consumption taxation can be seen as a move away from distorting taxation on mobile capital income.

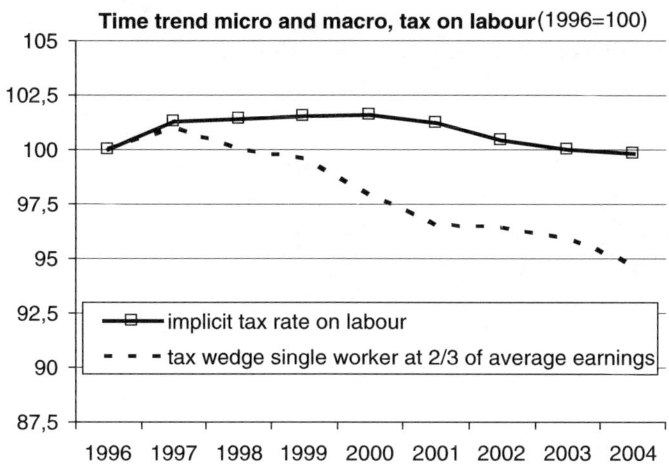

Fig. 10.2. Labour taxes

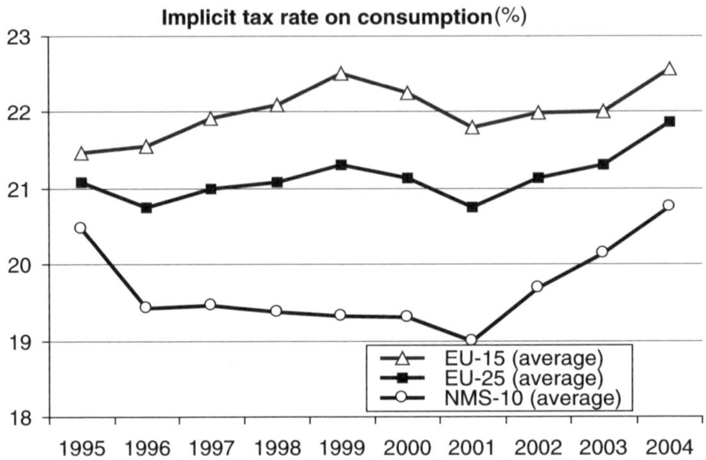

Fig. 10.3. Tax rate on consumption

Can we see a race to the bottom for taxes? In this context the development in the corporate taxation area is especially interesting. The downward trend in the statutory corporate income tax rate, uninterrupted since 1995 as shown in Fig. 10.4, has meant a decline by close to 10 percentage points since 1995 – an yearly average of .9 percentage point. Starting from a lower level, the continuous descent in statutory rate is steepest among new Member States.

The revenues from the corporate income tax do not exhibit a corresponding trend. Despite the large cuts in corporate income tax rates, tax revenues in the EU 25 are in 2004 – after a decline in the early 2000s – back to their 1996-level (see Fig. 10.5).

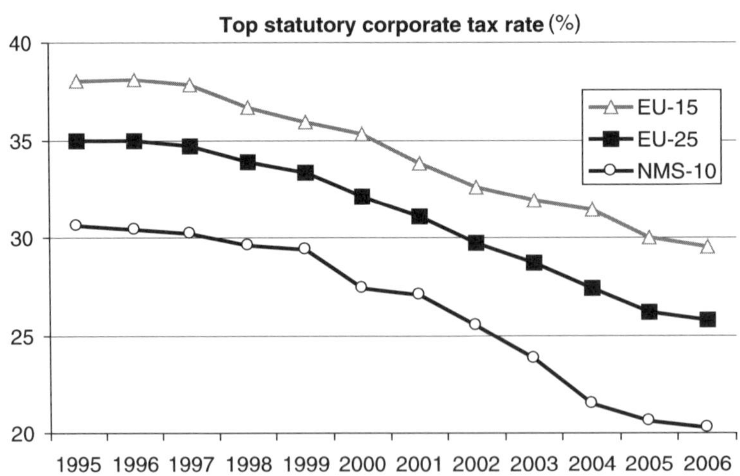

Fig. 10.4. Statutory corporate income tax rate

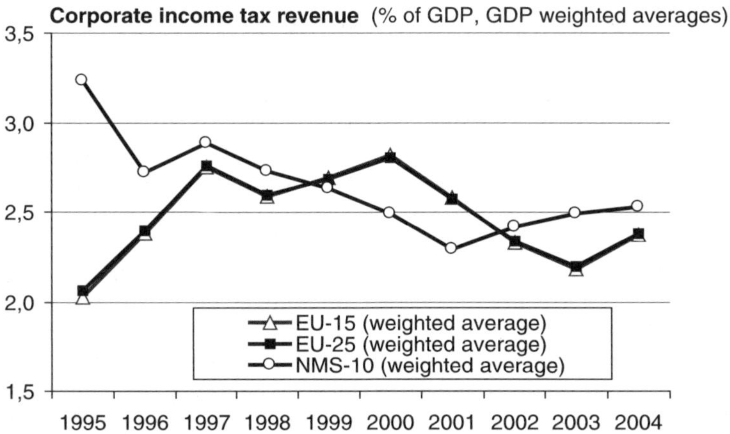

Fig. 10.5. Corporate income tax revenues

Among new Member States there is even a small increasing trend since 2001. Hence, based on the development of the statutory tax rates there might be a race to lower taxes. Considering the development of tax revenues this race might reflect the insight that due to dynamic effects lower tax rates might be compatible with stable or higher tax revenues. Maybe this phenomenon should be labeled something else than a race to the bottom.

The trend towards increasing consumption taxes in the EU-25 in particular can be interpreted as a policy trend towards shifting the tax burden from capital income to consumption. It is also motivated by the European requirement of a minimum VAT rate. To conclude, we have not in the figures above found any overwhelmingly clear evidence of a race to the bottom.

We find indications that the Member States have been able to pursue national tax policies keeping tax revenues in relation to the size of the economy almost unchanged. However, maybe the focus should be on the effects on long term economic growth rather than on immediate response in the tax revenues to GDP? The high level of taxation in combination with increased competition from other economic areas may have reduced employment opportunities and growth. Member States have vigorously defended their right to pursue national tax policies and they have been reluctant to remove cross-border tax obstacles or to implement decisions made by the European Court of Justice to create a level playing field. It is likely that the effect of these policies is more pronounced on the growth rate of the economy than on the ratio of taxes to GDP.

Limitations on national tax policies may therefore not be easily detected from a simple analysis of revenue statistics. It is only when tax policy is also seen in the context of the Lisbon objectives, growth rate requirements and the overall size of the labour market, that the limitations become apparent. The limitations may take the form of legal or economic constraints that prevent the Member State from freely adopting national taxation to political needs.

10.2 Trends and Tendencies for National Tax Policy

As noted above, the research question formulated and addressed in this book calls for an interdisciplinary approach. The question has to be discussed from an economic as well as a legal standpoint with focus on tax as well as welfare aspects. Triggered by recent cuts of corporate income taxes in Central- and East European Countries, Christian Bellak and Marcus Leibrecht analyzed the nexus between the overall theme of the book, namely the scope for national tax policy and tax competition in an enlarged Europe. They examined whether corporate income tax competition for mobile capital – Foreign Direct Investment in particular – is a likely scenario in the enlarged Europe. Four preconditions for the existence of corporate income tax competition were presented and analyzed. They find that corporate income tax competition is indeed a likely scenario in the enlarged Europe. Given this result they discuss whether attempts to coordinate corporate income taxation in Europe should and will restrain the scope for national tax policy. Thereby they discuss the normative implications of theories of tax competition and of simulation studies for the scope of national tax policy and discuss the actual position of the European Commission in the tax competition versus tax coordination debate.

They conclude that from an economic point of view there is no need for full harmonization, but national tax policies should be complemented by a certain degree of tax coordination, which could combine positive effects of tax harmonization and competition. Furthermore, upon studying official documents of the European Commission no arguments can be derived for a position against tax competition, with the exception of "harmful" tax competition. Hence, in the foreseeable future tax policy in the European Union should, and will be, determined mainly by national tax policy.

Even if there is no empirical evidence that integration has lead to shrinking welfare states, thus far, there can according to Åsa Hansson be little doubt that increased factor mobility, not only within the European Union but globally, will impose an increasing challenge to generous welfare states that redistribute from richer to poorer and from one generation to another. In order to guarantee an acceptable living standard for society's most vulnerable, coordination of tax and transfer policies will become increasingly necessary. This will be a great challenge as the benefits and costs of coordination are unevenly distributed across the Member States and, even if coordination is politically successful, the economic gains from regional coordination may still be limited because of global competition.

In a global perspective European welfare states are characterized by high levels of state expenditure and redistributive activity. However, respective indicators also vary largely across Europe. Differences in the scale and scope of social protection imply differences in funding levels and schemes. In increasingly integrated market economies this poses serious challenges to mostly national social policy regimes. Ulrike Schneider and August Österle discuss the relationship between social policies and tax policies and address political options to cope with fiscal competition in the EU. Rather than discussing passive integration of social policy brought about by fiscal competition, they focus on active integration as a response to potential negative implications of tax competition on social policy objectives. Following the concepts of harmonisation and coordination, Schneider and Österle conclude that an extended EU social policy dimension ("getting the horse back in front of the cart") could provide the instruments for preventing an intense pressure on welfare states to minimize corrective intervention. However, given the difficulties of harmonizing social policies, these instruments will only be implemented more extensively by the European Union members or subgroups of members when increases in inequality strengthen the idea of coherent European social rights.

There is a need to increase investment and growth in the European Union. Major obstacles are the very complex tax structure and the tax uncertainty an investor faces. To make more investments economically viable Member States have reduced tax rates. At the same time preferential tax regimes have been reduced or eliminated since they distort investment decisions. Furthermore, many countries in East and Central Europe have streamlined their tax systems and several have introduced flat taxes. Member States have also embarked on a process of developing an optional Common Consolidated Corporate Tax Base (CCCTB). Krister Andersson argues that such a tax system would make consolidation possible but would call for some mechanism for the allocation of tax revenues across countries. With an optional CCCTB, tax transparency will increase while Member States set the tax rate, ensuring national attractiveness and macro-economic stability. Tax competition in the corporate area is therefore likely to continue between countries introducing the possibility for corporations to be taxed according to the CCCTB, as well as with countries not adopting the CCCTB and with non-EU-countries.

Aims of national welfare can not only be pursued by spending the tax money collected, but also by shaping the national tax law in a way that supports the development of crucial and sensitive areas of the national economy. Due to the extensive application of the European State Aid Prohibition in tax matters Member States have been confronted with a narrowing room of tax sovereignty in recent years rendering national business tax policy by far more complex. The European efforts to gather more control over national business tax incentives and privileges have however according to Franz Sutter also created several new legal uncertainties, as there are still huge inconsistencies in the relationship of national tax sovereignty and the strict application of the EC State aid rules and their directly applicable standstill-clause. It is important to consider both the legal and political dimensions of the current influence of the European State aid rules on national tax law. Considering the emerging recapture threats it should not be forgotten that the European State aid rules ought to serve the European business development and not create new, incalculable risks for business operators making them solely bear the current shortfalls of a clear State aid doctrine, a transparent procedural concept and a sober notification discipline by the Member States.

The fundamental freedoms of the EC Treaty have a major impact on the shaping of national tax laws in the Member States. In an increasing number of cases, the European Court of Justice has found national tax law to be in breach of fundamental freedoms. Consequently, national tax law cannot be enacted without having been tested against the freedoms. It has been said that European Court of Justice takes "political" decisions when it decides tax cases. Moreover, it has been argued that the Court in recent years has decided cases more favourably towards Member States than it did in its early case law. Matthias Dahlberg finds no evidence for such a shift in actual case law. It is true that the decision in the Marks & Spencer case (C-446/03) means that Member States only in limited circumstances shall grant cross-border loss-relief. However, that hardly marks any shift in the case law, since the Marks & Spencer situation was new in relation to previous case law. The fundamental freedoms of the EC treaty are strong freedoms with huge political impact, but as such they express the will of the Member States and not of the European Court of Justice.

Tax treaty policy is part of a State's domestic tax policy. However, States are not free to determine the contents of their tax treaties. First, they need the consent of the other Contracting State. Second, if they are EU Member States, they are bound by EC Law. Third, in reality the OECD Model Convention plays an important role and it is difficult for States to deviate from the OECD Model Convention. According to Michael Lang, for these reasons, most States do not have too much room to develop their own tax treaty policy. On the other hand, tax treaties concluded by a State determine to a certain extent the rest of its domestic tax policy. As far as a State is in the position of a Residence State, tax treaties have relatively little impact on domestic tax policy. However, the taxation of non-residents is much more influenced by tax treaty provisions.

Michael Lang also points out that it would not be wise to completely rule out the application of the freedom of capital and payments to third-country relations altogether. There is no doubt that this freedom is applicable in third-country relations. The question is whether the Court will apply the same standards it has developed for intra-Community relations. However, even if the Court does apply different standards, it will not exclude third-country relations. The principle of proportionality will be relevant. Therefore, Member States should be prepared to have to provide a justification when they deviate in their treaty relations towards third countries from the treaty policy they have adopted for intra-Community relations.

What is the limiting effect of secondary EU Law, in the form of directives, on the autonomy of national tax policy in the Member States in the area of direct taxation? Eva Eberhartinger and Martin Six address this issue by taking the treatment of hybrid cross-border finance in the Parent-Subsidiary Directive and the Interest and Royalties Directive as an example. They show that there is indeed still room for national tax policy despite the directives. At least in the area of hybrid finance a Member State can still adhere to its right to levy withholding tax (as a source state) and its right to levy corporation tax (as a parent state) to a certain extent in spite of the directives. Thus the main objective of these two directives, the elimination of double taxation in the area of dividend and interest payments, has not been achieved to a hundred percent so far. It seems that the use of directives, even very detailed ones, as a tool for harmonization in the area of direct taxation limits options for national tax policy considerably, but so far does not eliminate them altogether.

To conclude, the existing limitations on national tax policy, such as the need to finance social security and the welfare state, as well as legal restrictions in the field of EU law in particular, do certainly not prevent Member States from pursuing tax policy. In other words, tax competition between Member States will continue, albeit in slightly modified forms to comply with EU Law.

10.3 Features of a Sustainable Room for National Tax Policy – the Steady State

We have found a policy trend towards shifting the tax burden from capital income to consumption. In the area of corporate taxation the downward trend in the statutory corporate income tax rate has continued. Given this tendency as well as the relative stability of tax revenues, there does not seem to be any clear evidence of a race to the bottom so far. A possible decrease in (income) tax rates seems to be compensated by an increase in the tax base.

It is then an open question whether Member States have found a temporary steady state or not. If it is a steady state, it is not characterised by full employment and buoyant growth. The Lisbon objectives are not likely to be fulfilled, despite the fact that more than half of the time since they were announced has passed.

National tax policies are a key element of decision-making in the European Union. So is compliance with the Treaty of Rome (as Chaps. 6, 7 and 8 illustrate). Member States are affected also by decisions made by the ECJ. By enforcing the Treaty, Member States are obliged to change their national laws to make them EU compliant. However, the Court can not suggest how Member States should change their national laws. It can only rule on whether the national law is EU compliant or not. It is up to parliaments to legislate. There is a considerable reluctance to change national laws and make them EU compliant. Often, there are no penalties for postponing or ignoring to undertake proper changes.

In this respect, there is a huge difference between the developments experienced in the monetary and fiscal area. In the run-up to introducing the common currency, Member States agreed to form a Stability Pact. Insufficient compliance with the convergence criteria would mean exclusion from the right to introduce the Euro. After the introduction of the Euro, violations could lead to economic penalties.

In the tax policy area, there are no discussions about a proper speed of adjustment to comply with the Treaty, not to mention any penalties. The EU Commission has to approach tax coordination in a very different way. By forming working groups (e.g. for a Common Consolidated Corporate Tax Base) or processes to reduce harmful tax competition and promote best practice (e.g. Joint Transfer Pricing Forum), the Commission tries to enhance the effectiveness of the internal market and the achievement of the Lisbon objectives.

One way to speed up compliance of national laws with the Treaty could be for countries after each ECJ ruling always to try to identify similar rules that need to be changed in other Member States. Ideally, such a Forum should include not only Member States but academics and representatives of the Business community, and it should carry such a weight that Member States can be held accountable for Treaty violations. Such a system would speed up a process towards EU compliant national tax laws, without infringing on national sovereignty. However, it would still be up to Member States to change the national laws in such a way that the freedoms and non-discrimination clauses of the Treaty are fulfilled.

Member States can make those changes in basically two different ways. They can either take away targeted benefits or extend provisions to universal rules.

Unfortunately, many decisions in Member States have focused on short-term revenue measures, leaving taxpayers worse off and with even greater obstacles for economic activities. Only when the tax changes are made in such a way that achieving the Lisbon objective is part of the decision, the overall coherence of tax and growth policies will be at hand. At present, we see no or little development in this direction.

An alternative scenario is one of slower growth and only gradual movement away from mobile tax bases. This seems to be the path Member States have taken so far. The issue of public expenditure and availability of social protections for residents in the EU union then naturally follows (see Chap. 4). Should a resident be eligible for social services in another Member State? We have no definite answer to questions of this kind but we note a shift away from taxes on mobile bases to immobile bases and consumption rather than capital income. This development can certainly continue but will eventually raise issues about regressive taxation and not enough publicly financed social goods.

There is an interesting policy discussion going on in Member States in the corporate tax area (see Chap. 5). The EU Commission is expected to present a legislative proposal for an optional common consolidated tax base. It remains to be seen how many countries will be willing to allow for the introduction of a completely new corporate tax system which will compete with the national system. Tax competition will then become transparent, both between countries since the tax base is identical and between the national system and the common system – perhaps too transparent for some Member States. The extent to which countries are willing to introduce this type of tax competition, even if tax rates are strictly national, is an open question. It may be perceived as a threat to national tax policies. However, it should be seen as a complement to national tax policies. It will allow Member States to achieve the tax coordination which is necessary to remove cross-border tax obstacles in the corporate area without abandoning national tax policies and priorities.

The chapters of this book all highlight various aspects of the scope for national tax policies in the EU. There is a broad agreement on the forces of tax competition but it is harder to assess whether the present situation is stable or not. Tax revenues in relations to GDP are rather stable but at the same time it is obvious that Member States do not manage to fulfil the Lisbon objectives. Member States have agreed to these objectives in order to have a well functioning economy conducive to facing an ageing population and increasing social needs. Tax obstacles need to be reduced or eliminated at the same time as social objectives and short term revenue constraints are met. Tax competition is likely to play a major role in this process.

Reference

European Commission (2006) Structures of the Taxation Systems in the European Union, TAXUD E4/2006/DOC/3201.

Index

Printing: Krips bv, Meppel
Binding: Stürtz, Würzburg